Strategies for Helping Severely and Multiply Handicapped Citizens

Strategies for Helping Severely and Multiply Handicapped Citizens

Edited by
John G. Greer, Ph.D.
Associate Professor
Special Education and Rehabilitation
Memphis State University
Memphis, Tennessee
Robert M. Anderson, Ed.D.
Professor
Special Education and Rehabilitation
Memphis State University
Memphis, Tennessee
Sara J. Odle, Ed.D.
Assistant Professor
Special Education and Rehabilitation
Memphis State University
Memphis, Tennessee

University Park Press
Baltimore

UNIVERSITY PARK PRESS
International Publishers in Science, Medicine, and Education
300 North Charles Street
Baltimore, Maryland 21201

Copyright © 1982 by University Park Press

Typeset by Britton Composition
Manufactured in the United States of America by The Maple Press Company

Library of Congress Cataloging in Publication Data
Main entry under title:

Strategies for helping severely and multiply handicapped citizens.

Includes bibliographies and index.
1. Rehabilitation-Addresses, essays, lectures.
I. Greer, John G.   II. Anderson, Robert Meredith.   III. Odle, Sara J.
[DNLM: 1. Handicapped.   2. Education, special.   3. Rehabilitation.
LC   4015   S898]   RM930.S77   362.4'0483   81-11499
ISBN 0-8391-1692-6   AACR2

Contents

Contributors

Robert M. Anderson, Ed.D.
Professor
Special Education and Rehabilitation
Memphis State University
Memphis, Tennessee 38152

Wendy Ashcroft, M.Ed.
Teacher
Farmington Elementary School
Germantown, Tennessee 38138

Barbara H. Connolly, Ed.D.
Chief of Physical Therapy
Child Development Center
Center for the Health Sciences
University of Tennessee
Memphis, Tennessee 38105

Bonnie B. Greer, Ph.D.
Associate Professor
Special Education and Rehabilitation
Memphis State University
Memphis, Tennessee 38152

John G. Greer, Ph.D.
Associate Professor
Special Education and Rehabilitation
Memphis State University
Memphis, Tennessee

Virginia K. Laycock, Ed.D.
Assistant Professor
Child Study Special Education
   Department
Old Dominion University
Norfolk, Virginia 23508

Sheldon S. Maron, Ph.D.
Associate Professor
Special Education
Portland State University
Portland, Oregon 97207

Wellington L. Mock, Ed.D.
Assistant Superintendent for
   Community Services
Arlington Developmental Center
Arlington, Tennessee 38002

Sara J. Odle, Ed.D.
Assistant Professor
Special Education and Rehabilitation
Memphis State University
Memphis, Tennessee 38152

H. Lyndall Rich, Ph.D.
Professor
Special Education and Rehabilitation
Memphis State University
Memphis, Tennessee 38152

Janice Schultz, B.S.
Occupational Therapist
Jefferson County Schools
Lakewood, Colorado

Suzanne Selph, M.Ed.
Doctoral Student
Special Education and Rehabilitation
Memphis State University
Memphis, Tennessee 38152

Anne C. Troutman, Ph.D.
Assistant Professor
Special Education and Rehabilitation
Memphis State University
Memphis, Tennessee 38152

Chris E. Wethered, Ed.S.
Doctoral Student
Special Education and Rehabilitation
Memphis State University
Memphis, Tennessee 38152

Nancy P. Wilder
Special Education and Rehabilitation
Memphis State University
Memphis, Tennessee 38152

Preface

Until very recently, indeed within the last decade, severely and multiply handicapped citizens have been largely forgotten by society. Suffering from profound and complicated disabilities, they were typically "warehoused" in dismal and often inhumane institutional settings. Those charged with the responsibility of caring for them commonly shared the conviction that, beyond physical shelter and sustenance, little could be done. Not only were their disabilities incurable, but their behaviors were believed by most to be unmodifiable.

Fortunately, there have been dramatic changes in both the attitudes toward this group and the services now provided for them. After a long series of court cases, which ultimately climaxed in the passage of the Education for all Handicapped Children Act of 1975, all children, regardless of the severity of handicap, were guaranteed the right to a free and appropriate education. Subsequently, the educational establishment has moved rapidly toward a more humane system of instructional alternatives for this population. Public schools and other community-based programs are playing an ever-growing role in this process.

The continuation and further development of these services will of course depend upon the public willingness to fund them. Human services of every kind are being heavily affected by inflation, tax rates, and cuts in government appropriations. Austerity budgets at local, state, and federal levels could limit programs to only those functions and personnel considered indispensable. Nevertheless, we believe that there is an awareness of the plight of severely and multiply handicapped persons that did not previously exist and that will be manifest by a widespread unwillingness to return to the terrible neglect of this population that prevailed in the past.

As is characteristic of any abrupt change in social patterns, the sudden call for appropriate education and training for severely and multiply handicapped citizens has left many professionals frightened, confused, and woefully unprepared. They are faced with a very heterogeneous population, which varies tremendously in physical stigmata and behavioral handicaps. In addition to being mentally retarded, most severely and multiply handicapped persons manifest some type of gross physical abnormality or neurological involvement. Among other complications, sensorimotor deficits, minimally controlled seizures, and lowered resistence to disease are common. To adequately serve such a population, it is abundantly clear that profound changes must be made very quickly. Above all, new personnel must be trained to successfully cope with the instructional and managerial problems associated with teaching seriously handicapped youngsters.

Although this challenge is undoubtedly a very serious one, there is every reason to be optimistic about the future. Progress has been made in virtually every area of behavior with this population. Positive results stemming from the application of systematic instructional methods and programs with multiply handicapped individuals have been documented repeatedly in recent literature. Although it is likely that most of these individuals will remain dependent throughout their lifetime, the prognosis is continually improving with advances in educational sophistication. This book carries that message. It is replete with theoretically sound yet practical strategies for helping severely and multiply handicapped citizens.

The book is divided into 10 chapters. The first describes severely and multiply handicapped persons and provides an historical overview of the treatment afforded them by society. Chapters 2, 3, and 4 present the basic educational and management strategies fundamental to current programming. Diagnostic and prescriptive teaching techniques, behavior modification procedures, and response-contingent materials are covered, with emphasis on their practical application with severely and multiply handicapped citizens. Chapters 5, 6, 7, and 8 present the four content areas on which most educational efforts for this group are focused: motor development, self-care, communication, and social skills. Each includes detailed descriptions and illustrations of approaches commonly and successfully used. Chapter 9 looks at the unique needs of the sensorially impaired. Since many severely and multiply handicapped persons manifest some type of auditory or visual problem, it is important that teachers of this population be aware of the various techniques and devices that can be used to facilitate learning. Finally, Chapter 10 considers placement issues, looking at traditional institutional practices and the growing array of community-oriented options now available.

Acknowledgments

We would like to acknowledge with special gratitude the tolerant and dependable effort that Tina Ervin and Barbara Horrice provided in helping to process the manuscript.

Strategies for Helping Severely and Multiply Handicapped Citizens

Chapter 1

An Introduction to Severely and Multiply Handicapped Persons

Robert M. Anderson, John G. Greer, and H. Lyndall Rich

INTRODUCTION

This book is about children and adults whose intellectual, psychological, sensory and physical characteristics are so atypical that they function on the lowest levels of adaptive behavior. Classified as severely and profoundly handicapped, these individuals until recently had a bleak outlook on the hope of reasonable service, humane treatment, or social adjustment. Usually housed in the impersonal, isolated back wards of institutions, these outcasts of humanity have historically existed in unbelievably dehumanizing circumstances. "The truth is that...our ancestral lawgivers, physicians, and philosophers seem to have been indifferent toward the afflicted among many categories of the young and, for that matter, of the grown-ups as well" (Kanner, 1962, p. 92). Even today, this indifference is reflected in the life-support conditions of many severely and multiply handicapped. In 1973, the following observation was made of a state institution for the severely and profoundly handicapped:

Part of this chapter was adapted from material published in: Anderson, R. M., and Greer, J. G. *Educating the Severely and Profoundly Retarded.* Baltimore: University Park Press, 1976.

Large numbers of retarded persons have been herded together to live as animals in a barn, complete with stench. Many are forced into slave labor conditions; deprived of privacy, affection, morality; suffering the indignities of nakedness, beatings, sexual assaults and exposure. Some are doped out of reality with chemical restraints while others are physically deformed by the mechanical ones. Many are sitting aimlessly without motivations, incentives, hope or programs. (Lippman & Goldberg, 1973, p. 17)

Although such dehumanizing services continue to exist in facilities for severely and profoundly handicapped throughout the country, an escalation in public awareness and social conscientiousness has caused the pendulum to swing toward the improvement of services for the severely and multiply handicapped.

Who are these individuals who have been so neglected? What has recently awakened society to their plight? In what direction must we go to find solutions that will correct the injustices of the past and adequately provide for a more normal existence for them? Although comprehensive answers are obviously beyond the scope of this chapter, the discussions included are designed to provide the general frame of reference necessary for an understanding of the challenge that the severely and multiply handicapped now present to special educators.

A Proposed Definition

Despite increased interest in and commitment to severely and multiply handicapped people, no single, inclusive definition can adequately describe this population. Baker (1979) has reviewed the recent literature and analyzed the problems of defining the severely handicapped. Acknowledging the constraints inherent in attempting to adequately identify these individuals, she proposed the following definition:

The severely handicapped individual is one whose ability to provide for his or her own basic life-sustaining and safety needs is so limited, relative to the proficiency expected on the basis of chronological age, that it could pose a serious threat to his or her survival. (Baker, 1979, p. 60)

This noncategorical definition of the *severely handicapped* serves as a point of departure for the population under study in this book. As used here, the definition incorporates the characteristics typically included to describe severely and profoundly and multiply handicapped persons.

Common Characteristics

The severely and multiply handicapped represent a heterogeneous population. These handicapped individuals vary tremendously in terms of the physical stigmata, intellectual limitations, psychological conditions, sensory impairment, and behavioral handicaps they manifest. This wide range of handicapping conditions is reflected in the numerous categorical labels that have been used to describe these children and adults. Over the years a variety of labels has been used to describe or identify individuals with theoretically specific handicapping conditions. These labels not only tended to stigmatize individuals by reflecting public attitudes, but were also ineffective functional descriptors for planning appropriate services. Prior to the twentieth century, individuals with severe multiple handicapping conditions were given such labels as *idiot, lunatic, incurable,* and *deaf-and-dumb.* During the early 1900s the influence of the scientific revolution spawned new labels that were reported to be descriptive, such as *retardation, dementia praecox, paraplegia,* and *mutism.* Today, categorical labels have evolved into a new series of terms, including *custodial, autistic, nonambulatory,* and *sensory impaired,* that have come to be associated with the severely and multiply handicapped. The changes in labels per se have not produced greater understanding nor better service. They do, however, reflect changing attitudes of both professionals and the general public regarding the handicapped population; the attitudes tend to be more descriptive, more humanitarian, and more service oriented.

Despite the ambiguity of these labels, and the variation in the population they purportedly describe, there are four generalizations that can be made of the severely handicapped. The first generalization is that most severely and multiply handicapped children manifest some type of gross physical abnormality or neurological involvement. In addition to the primary handicapping condition, other complications such as sensorimotor deficits, minimally controlled seizures, and lowered resistance to disease are frequently evident.

The second generalization concerns the typical level of functioning attained by this population. At present there are divergent viewpoints regarding the prognosis and perceived limitations of severely and multiply handicapped individuals. These points of view were recently debated in a series of articles in *Exceptional Children* (Burton & Hirshoren, 1979a, 1979b; Sontag, Certo, & Button, 1979). Although the prognosis is continually improving with advances in educational sophistication, there are nevertheless competencies that this population normally does not achieve. Severely and profoundly handicapped persons must often be dressed, fed, and toileted by others, even as adults. Meaningful communication, if any, is frequently restricted to nonverbal gesturing and physical contact. Although the issues related to prognosis are still being debated, it is likely that many severely handicapped individuals will remain relatively dependent throughout their lifetimes. Alternative ways of defining this population, however, may provide a much more optimistic perspective of functional prognosis as well as more appropriate educational programming.

Third, a large proportion of severely and multiply handicapped individuals, as the term implies, do indeed have multiple disabilities with associated handicaps. There are almost unlimited combinations of multiple disabilities: hearing impairment and mental retardation; visual impairment and cerebral palsy, and deafness, blindness, and physically crippling conditions. As Wolf and Anderson (1969) have suggested, the number and complexity of such conditions proliferate endlessly. The more severe or profound the handicap, the greater the likelihood that there are accompanying handicapping conditions. Dunn (1973) stated that "it would appear that only half of the handicapped children have one educationally significant disability; another quarter have two; and the other quarter have three or more" (p. 12). Obviously this fact will have a very pervasive effect on all aspects of working with this population (i.e., assessment, treatment, and training).

The fourth generalization forecasts that the prevalence of these individuals in education will rise due to increased litigation and legislation, as well as changes in the field of medicine. Court cases concerning rights to education and treatment, with consequent laws enacted to protect other rights of these individuals, have forced society's recognition of them. Many individuals, who formerly spent lifetimes in basements, attics, and back wards of institutions, have suddenly been thrust into society for habilitation and education. As a result of the increased use of drugs, new strains of viruses, and environmental pollution, the potential for prenatal damage (resulting in severe and multiple handicaps) is greater than before. Furthermore, postnatal poisonings, accidents, and diseases continue to cause severe or profound consequences. Finally, technological advances in medicine are keeping many of these individuals alive much longer than in the past.

Currently, it is impossible to estimate precisely the prevalence of individuals falling under the classification of severely and multiply handicapped. Since the inception of services for the handicapped in the United States, the countless surveys that have attempted to establish prevalence estimates have resulted in widely different findings. Problems related to definition, geographic region, inadequacy of assessment instruments, sampling techniques, and divergent populations have complicated attempts to obtain accurate prevalence figures.

The following section of this chapter provides an overview of severe and profound intellectual, psychological, physical, and sensorial handicapping conditions. The handicapping conditions are typified by the four generalizations discussed in the previous paragraphs. In effect, many severely handicapped individuals may be considered multiply handicapped. The problems associated with one handicapping condition are compounded by the fact that characteristics of other handicapping conditions may coexist within a single individual. The fact that each identified handicapping condition may include characteristics of other handicapping conditions is illustrative of the problems encountered by children and adults variously labeled and categorized according to standard disability groupings. Because of the complexity and ambiguity often involved in differentiating the severely and profoundly handicapped from the mildly and moderately handicapped, the range of severity for each condition is discussed. This discussion, however, is limited to a brief overview, and the emphasis is on the lowest functional levels. In addition, an overview of the range of severity is included because many severely and profoundly handicapped individuals have multiple conditions that are considered mild or moderate. For example, a severely intellectually handicapped child may have additional moderate handicaps including a psychological, sensorial, and physical handicap. Thus, a knowledge of the range of severity is a prerequisite to describing the severely and profoundly handicapped and the multiply handicapped.

SEVERELY AND MULTIPLY HANDICAPPED PERSONS

Intellectually Handicapped

Intelligence has been defined as "the ability to understand, comprehend and adapt rapidly to new situations and learn from experience" (Kelly & Vergason, 1978, p. 76). Although a large number of individuals with severe and multiple handicapping conditions may exhibit intellectual limitations, the categorical term *mental retardation* has been used to describe individuals whose primary handicapping condition is intellectual in nature.

Definition and Classification   Professional personnel representing a wide spectrum of disciplines have traditionally defined mental retardation relative to their own professional frames of reference; hence, no single definition of mental retardation has been satisfactory or suitable to all who work with the mentally retarded. Because numerous textbooks have dealt in detail with this and related issues, the various points of view relative to defining mental retardation are mentioned only briefly in this chapter.

Robinson and Robinson (1965, 1976) presented an excellent review of traditional definitions of mental retardation. In general, past definitions have focused on capacity to learn, knowledge possessed, social adaptation, and personal adjustment. Although the controversies that center on the definition are significant to the education of mildly handicapped children, severely and profoundly retarded children, most of whom have substantial organic involvement, are generally defined as retarded no matter what criteria are used. Therefore, in defining this population, it is of small consequence to debate the criteria of classification. Of more significance is the understanding that the ultimate level at which a handicapped person functions is the product of the interaction of many hereditary and environmental factors and that this level can be modified by appropriate intervention (Begab, 1973). The concept of potential for behavioral change in even the most severely disabled has gained widespread acceptance in recent years and is reflected in the definition of mental retardation as stated by the American Association on Mental Deficiency (AAMD). This definition, briefly examined in this section, serves as a point of departure for defining the severely and profoundly retarded.

The AAMD has published a series of six manuals on terminology and classification. The most recent manual (Grossman, 1973) presents a comprehensive review of the revised definition of mental retardation. Although the dual requirement of impairment in both measured intelligence and adaptive behavior has been retained, this definition reflects a number of significant changes. As revised, the definition reads:

> Mental retardation refers to significantly subaverage general intellectual functioning existing concurrently with deficits in adaptive behavior, and manifested during the developmental period. (Grossman, 1973, p. 5)

Intellectual functioning is separated into four levels of mental retardation. Translated into intelligence quotient (IQ) values, the corresponding levels of mental retardation and IQ ranges for three frequently used intelligence tests are illustrated in the manual (Grossman, 1973, p. 18) and in Table 1.

As can be seen in Table 1, the term *significantly subaverage* refers to performance that is two or more standard deviations below the mean of the tests. The previously used borderline category has been deleted.

The upper age limit of the *developmental period*, another important concept in the AAMD definition, is set at 18 years and serves to distinguish mental retardation from other disorders of human behavior.

The third significant term *adaptive behavior* is defined as the effectiveness or degree to which the individual meets the standards of personal independence expected of his or her age and cultural group (Grossman,

Table 1.   AAMD classification of mental retardation by obtained intelligence quotient

Levels	Stanford-Binet and Cattell (s.d. 16)	Wechsler scales (s.d. 15)
Mild	68–52	69–55
Moderate	51–36	54–40
Severe	35–20	39–25 (extrapolated)
Profound	19 and below	24 and below (extrapolated)

Reprinted by permission from: Grossman, H. J. (Ed.). *Manual on terminology and classification in mental retardation.* Washington: American Association on Mental Deficiency, 1973, p. 18.

1973, p. 11). Because these expectations vary for different age groups, deficits in adaptive behavior vary at different ages. For example, deficits in adaptive behavior during infancy and early childhood might be manifested by lags in sensorimotor skill development and delays in speech. For an adolescent, on the other hand, self-help and socialization skills may provide a more accurate estimate of the general ability to adapt.

The AAMD manual presents a series of tables that illustrate patterns of adaptive behavior ranging from infancy and early childhood through adulthood. Space in this volume does not permit the inclusion of all the AAMD tables; however, Table 2 illustrates the highest level of adaptive behavior functioning generally expected at the ages and levels of retardation indicated in the left margin (Grossman, 1973, p. 29).

An extensive medical classification system designed to classify groups according to etiology is also included in the AAMD manual. This system, which provides descriptive symptoms of clinical conditions, views mental retardation as a manifestation of some underlying disease process or medical condition (Grossman, 1973). The biomedical system is used primarily by physicians for diagnostic purposes and it encompasses 1) infec-

Table 2.   Illustrations of highest level of adaptive behavior functioning

Age and level indicated	
6 years (mild) 9 years (moderate) 12 years and above (severe) 15 years and above (profound)	Independent functioning: Feeds self with spoon or fork, may spill some; puts on clothing but needs help with small buttons and jacket zippers; tries to bathe self but needs help; can wash and dry hands but not very efficiently; partially toilet trained but may have accidents. Physical: May hop or skip; may climb steps with alternating feet; rides tricycle (or bicycle over 8 years); may climb trees or jungle gym; plays dance games; may throw ball and hit target. Communication: May have speaking vocabulary of over 300 words and use grammatically correct sentences; if nonverbal, may use many gestures to communicate needs; understands simple verbal communications including directions and questions ("Put it on the shelf." "Where do you live?"); some speech may be indistinct sometimes; may recognize advertising words and signs (ice cream, STOP, EXIT, MEN, LADIES); relates experiences in simple language. Social: Participates in group activities and simple group games; interacts with others in simple play (store, house) and expressive activities (art and dance).

Reprinted by permission from: Grossman, H. J. (Ed.). *Manual on terminology and classification in mental retardation*. Washington: American Association on Mental Deficiency, 1973, p. 29.

tions and intoxications, 2) trauma or physical agents, 3) metabolism and nutrition, 4) gross brain dysfunction, 5) unknown prenatal influence, 6) chromosomal abnormalities, 7) gestational disorders, 8) psychiatric disorder, 9) environmental influences, and 10) other conditions.

Although the severely and profoundly retarded suffer from many of these medical problems, a classification system based on such factors has very limited usefulness in education. Therefore, the AAMD definition focuses on behavioral performance without reference to etiology. Mental retardation describes current behavior and does not imply prognosis. As defined and interpreted by this definition, an individual may meet the criteria of mental retardation at one time and not at another. The manual states that prognosis is related more to factors such as associated conditions, motivation, treatment, and training opportunities than to mental retardation itself. It must be recognized, however, that even under the most optimal circumstances severely and profoundly retarded individuals cannot be habilitated to nonretarded status.

An Alternative Definition   Mark Gold (1980), expressing dissatisfaction with the current AAMD definition and manual, proposed a revolutionary way of defining mental retardation. His definition, a much more optimistic perspective of mental retardation, views the adaptive behavior of community, parents, and professionals in the fields dealing with the retarded as at least as critical as that of the retarded themselves:

> Mental retardation refers to a level of functioning which requires from society significantly above average training procedures and superior assets in adaptive behavior on the part of society, manifested throughout the life of both society and the individual. (Gold, 1980, p. 148.)

This definition suggests that it is not difficult to get the retarded to adapt — the real problem lies in the inability to get society to adapt, move, and change. This unique definition of mental retardation represents an important concept in Gold's "try another way" philosophy, a systematic approach to providing effective services to people who find it difficult to learn. In this system, the severely retarded person would be characterized by the level of power in the training process required for the person to learn, and not by limitations in what he or she can learn. Power refers to the amount of intervention, assistance, or direction required by the trainer in order for the learner to reach criterion. This philosophical approach obviously places the burden of responsibility squarely on the shoulders of society and its willingness to allocate resources to education and training rather than on significant limitations in biological potential.

This point of view regarding the mentally retarded is supported in this chapter and it is believed that Gold's tenets, applied generically, can lead to more effective programs for the psychologically handicapped, the sensorially handicapped, and the physically handicapped, as defined and described in the following sections.

Psychologically Handicapped

Psychology is a term that is broadly used to describe "the science of mental life" (Harrison, 1965, p. 154). Although the intellectually handicapping conditions discussed in the preceding section are technically included within this definition, the focus of psychological handicaps is on extreme behavioral deviations that are attributable to mental disorders.

Definition and Classification   There is a great deal of myth, bias, and misinformation that surrounds the concept of psychologically handicapping conditions. Consequently, the available literature does not present a clear or consistent body of knowledge regarding either definitions or classifications. This situation has been created by the fact that there are few, if any, scientifically accountable procedures for determining the existence of specific mental disorders. Aside from the fact that an individual's behavior does not conform to social expectations, there is relatively little empirical data to substantiate one diagnostic classification over another (Zubin, 1967). For example, individual children have been diagnosed as autistic, brain damaged, psychotic, and even mentally retarded.

Of all the definitions and classification systems currently in use, the *Diagnostic and Statistical Manual of Mental Disorders* (American Psychiatric Association, 1968, 1980) is probably the most comprehensive and widely accepted resource. The 1968 edition of the manual (DSM-II) lists 10 major categories with numerous subclassifications of mental disorders. DSM-II does not classify psychological handicaps according to the degree of severity; the following typically constitute severe and profound conditions evidenced by children, according to the manual.

Organic Brain Syndrome (OBS) — OBS is "a basic mental condition characteristically resulting from diffuse impairment of brain tissue function for whatever cause" (p. 22). Disorders in this category are characterized by impairment of orientation, memory, intellectual functions, judgment, and affect. Within the OBS category are several subcategories listed as "psychosis" referring to individuals "sufficiently impaired to interfere grossly with their capacity to meet the ordinary demands of life" (p. 23). OBS psychosis is reported to be caused by a variety of physiological factors including intracranial infection (e.g., encephalitis), other cerebral conditions (e.g., epilepsy), brain trauma (e.g., head injury) and other physical conditions (e.g., infection).

Psychosis (other than OBS) — Psychosis constitutes a large category of psychological conditions that is composed of schizophrenia, affective disorders, and paranoid states. Schizophrenia "includes a group of disorders manifested by characteristic disturbances of thinking, mood and behavior. Disturbances in thinking are marked by alterations of concept formation which may lead to misinterpretation of reality and sometimes to delusions and hallucinations, which frequently appear psychologically self-protective.... Behavior may be withdrawn, regressive and bizarre. The schizophrenias, in which the mental status is attributable primarily to a thought disorder, are to be distinguished from the major affective illnesses which are dominated by a mood disorder. The paranoid states are distinguished from schizophrenia by the narrowness of their distortions of reality and by the absence of other psychotic symptoms" (p. 33).

Neurosis — Neurosis is characterized by high levels of subjective stress. Although this psychological classification rarely constitutes a severe or profound condition, there are circumstances under which neurosis is associated with gross distortions of reality and could be considered a severe or profound condition (e.g., hysterical neurosis).

DSM-II presents other psychologically handicapping definitions and classifications (e.g., personality disorders and transient situational disturbances), but they are inappropriate for discussion in this chapter since they are not typically considered to be psychological conditions of a severe or profound nature.

Because DSM-II placed the greatest emphasis on the classification of adult mental disorders, there was increasing dissatisfaction among childhood and adolescence professionals for a new classification system. Consequently, the American Psychiatric Association developed a revision of the *Diagnostic and Statistical Manual* (DSM-III, 1980). Among the numerous changes that affect children and adolescents are a deemphasis of the term *psychosis*, the accentuation of the term *developmental disorders*, and the introduction of *autism*.

Among the childhood and adolescence mental disorders DSM-III includes the diagnostic category "pervasive developmental disorder" that represents the primary severe and profound psychologically handicapping condition.

Pervasive Developmental Disorders   The disorders in this subclass are characterized by distortions in the development of multiple basic psychological functions that are involved in the development of social skills and language, such as attention, perception, reality testing, and motor movement (p. 86).

Infantile Autism (Diagnostic Criteria)
  A. Onset before 30 months of age.
  B. Pervasive lack of responsiveness to other people (autism).
  C. Gross deficits in language development.

D. If speech is present, peculiar speech patterns, e.g., immediate and delayed echolalia, metaphorical language, and pronominal reversal.

E. Bizarre responses to various aspects of the environment, e.g., resistance to change and peculiar interest in or attachment to animate or inanimate objects (pp. 89–90).

Childhood Onset [of] Pervasive Developmental Disorder
(Diagnostic Criteria)

A. Gross and sustained impairment in social relationships, e.g., lack of appropriate affective response, inappropriate clinging, asociality, and lack of empathy.

B. At least three of the following:

(1) sudden excessive anxiety manifested by such symptoms as free-floating anxiety, catastrophic reactions to everyday occurrences, inability to be consoled when upset, and unexplained panic attacks.

(2) constricted or inappropriate affect, including lack of appropriate fear reactions, unexplained rage reactions, and extreme mood liability.

(3) resistance to change in the environment (e.g., upset if the dinner time is changed) or insistence on doing things in the same manner every time (e.g., always putting on clothes in the same order).

(4) oddities of motor movement, such as peculiar posturing, peculiar hand or finger movements, or walking on tiptoes.

(5) abnormalities of speech, such as questionlike melody and monotonous voice.

(6) hyper- or hypo-sensivity to sensory stimuli, e.g., hyperacusis [increased hearing acuteness].

(7) self-mutilation, e.g., biting or hitting self and head banging.

C. Onset of the full syndrome after 30 months of age and before 12 years of age.

D. Absence of delusions, hallucinations, incoherence, or marked loosening of associations (p. 91).

The use of the term autism has rapidly escalated over the past decade. Increasingly, more children with severe and profound psychologically handicapping conditions have been diagnosed as autistic, and terms like *psychosis, schizophrenia,* and *brain damaged* have begun to fade as preferred classifications. The reasons for this changing emphasis in classification are numerous, but some of the more critical causes seem to be:

1. Autism is suspected of having a biological cause or, at least, a predisposition, and so is a more palatable explanation, particularly for parents.

2. Even though the prognosis for normality is minimal, and the condition is viewed as a lifelong developmental disability, autism does not convey the notion of permanence often associated with mental retardation and brain damage.
3. The characteristics of children diagnosed as autistic are substantively different than those of children diagnosed as having other severe and profound handicapping conditions.
4. Autism, as opposed to a purely psychiatric classification, is a condition that is responsive to educational procedures and not limited to medical and therapeutic approaches.

Together, autism, childhood psychosis, and pervasive developmental disorders form a group of psychological classifications that are considered severe and profound conditions. Although the term *seriously emotionally disturbed* has been used to describe this population (e.g., P.L. 94-142), this global classification is inadequate for defining or classifying children and youth with severe psychological problems.

Sensorially Handicapped

Sensorially handicapping conditions refer to limitations in one or both of the primary sensory functions — hearing (auditory) and seeing (visual). Among a great many severely and profoundly handicapped persons, particularly those with intellectual or physical conditions or both, sensory handicaps are also evident. In many instances, however, sensorial handicaps may exist in the absence of other handicapping conditions. Because sensorial handicaps present unique life-sustaining and safety needs, they are discussed apart from other handicapping conditions. Furthermore, visual and auditory limitations, even though they are both sensory handicaps, are distinctively different.

Visually Handicapped*

Visually handicapped children represent a relatively small and heterogeneous group of exceptional individuals. Under the label *blind*, their ability to see varies markedly, from absence of sight to high levels of functional visual ability. Hatfield's (1975) study of visually handicapped school children indicated that: 1) more than three-fourths became blind before age 1, 2) the vast majority had some degree of usable vision, and 3) males outnumbered females 54% to 46%. Hatfield's study of blind preschoolers (1972) resulted in similar findings, as well as the fact that prenatal factors

---

*Part of this discussion was adapted from material published in: S. S. Maron and D. H. Martinez, "Environmental Alternatives for the Visually Handicapped," in J. W. Schifani, R. M. Anderson, & S. J. Odle (Eds.), *Implementing Learning in the Least Restrictive Environment*. Baltimore: University Park Press, 1980.

were the most common cause of blindness, especially in those cases that were genetic in origin.

Visual loss can be classified in many ways and, because of this, it is often difficult to determine or agree on how well a person can see. Measuring sharpness of distance vision (acuity) or visual fields (overall area seen by the fixed eye) often conflicts with functional visual ability, that is, how well vision is used for the purposes of everyday life. Furthermore, the younger the child the less accurate the visual determination and the greater the probability of visual score fluctuations. Other classification categories include binocular vision (simultaneous use of both eyes with production of a single image), near vision (e.g., for reading), color vision, and night vision. Thus, vision is a highly complex sense; its physical measurement in a doctor's office may differ from its functioning ability in the classroom, at home, or in the community. It can vary with factors such as motivation, presence of additional disabilities, use of educational aids, lighting conditions, and stability of the eye problem.

The Social Security Act of 1935, which coined the term *legal blindness*, established a level of vision below which an individual could receive financial, educational, and social services. This assistance included textbooks and other educational aids, special income tax benefits, talking book machines and discs (specially modified phonographs for recorded material), and financial aid of various kinds (Kirk, 1972). Blindness, thus defined, was a distance visual acuity of 20/200 or less in the better eye after best correction, or an acuity better than 20/200 where the visual fields were constricted to 20 degrees or less (National Society for the Prevention of Blindness, 1966). An acuity of 20/200 means that at a test distance of 20 feet, a person can see what a normally sighted individual sees at a distance of 200 feet. Best correction refers to the use of eyeglasses or contact lenses, medicine or surgery, or both. Although written as a fraction, this visual designation should not be interpreted as such. For example, 20/40 does not indicate 50 percent of normal vision, but 85 percent of visual efficiency. Partial sight, on the other hand, refers to a range of visual acuity better than 20/200, up to and including 20/70 after best correction.

Both legal blindness and partial vision are based on medical information, namely, distance vision and visual fields. Teachers, however, have long noted a consistent discrepancy between medical measurement and classroom functioning. For example, two children with the same visual acuity may function quite differently in school — one can be a print reader and the other a braille reader.

For that reason, two more educationally descriptive terms are introduced, *visual impairment* and *blindness*. The visually impaired child is capable of reading a printed work, and the blind child is a tactual reader. In this chapter, blindness refers to the absence of usable vision. Visual impairment is used to indicate the presence of functional residual vision. The terms *visual handicap* or *visual limitation* are broader labels, encompassing both visual impairment and blindness.

Today, print readers far outnumber braille readers. An earlier study by Jones (1961) indicated that more than four-fifths of the legally blind children sampled were print readers. There was a much greater probability of print readers attending day school programs than residential school programs (92% vs. 51%). Nolan's studies (1965) showed a consistent trend toward greater use of print in both types of educational settings (Maron & Martinez, 1980, pp. 149–151).

Auditorially Handicapped**

The numerous educational definitions and classifications that deal with hearing impairment testify to the inability of administrators and teachers alike to reach a consensus on terminology. Ambiguity in dialogue, even between professionals, is attributable to the fact that the same terms are often used to refer both to the auditory deficit and to its effects. A common example arises with the use of the term *hearing loss*. Many professionals still refer to a child's hearing loss in decibels. This is not correct. It comes about because the ASA standards of 1951 and 1952 required the intensity dial on the audiometer to be labeled "hearing loss." The newer revision of standards (American National Standards Institute, 1969) recommended the term *hearing threshold level* (HTL), however, so that hearing loss could correctly be reserved for the general condition of hearing impairment or the process that causes it. Further confusions also arise when dealing with children, because the deficits and their effects must often be interpreted predictively in a developmental context.

Hearing impairment means not only loss of auditory sensitivity but also what Davis and Silverman (1978) called *dysacusis*. Loss of sensitivity is readily measured and covers a continuum from a mild intermittent loss of auditory acuity to an irreversible and almost total, if not complete, loss of hearing. Dysacusis covers other important dimensions of hearing, which may range from malfunction of the sense organ (e.g., poor discrimination for amplified speech) to abnormal function of the brain (e.g., auditory agnosia).

There is no hard-and-fast distinction between a disability and a handicap, and in the past the term hearing impaired has unfortunately been used as a synonym for both of these concepts. The handicap of

---

**Part of this discussion was adapted from material published in: B. Clarke and P. Leslie, Environmental Alternatives for the Hearing Impaired, in J. W. Schifani, R. M. Anderson, & S. J. Odle (Eds.), *Implementing Learning in the Least Restrictive Environment.* Baltimore: University Park Press, 1980.

deafness is the degree to which a person's overall function is limited by the disability or the extent to which a disadvantage renders success more difficult. Whether the disability constitutes a handicap for an individual child and to what extent depends on a variety of factors. The effects of the disability stem primarily from organic correlates which include the physiological impairment (structural deficits or damage), abnormalities in auditory function (loss of sensitivity and dysacusis), and other structural conditions (handicaps to the brain, central nervous system, vision, etc.) and are evidenced in the behavioral and developmental areas of language acquisition and communication. When the dynamic interaction of sociocultural factors, including value systems, expectations, and prejudices, are added, the final effects are encapsulated in cognition, social development, and academic achievement. Thus the distinction between disability and handicap is very difficult to disentangle. What is not hard to conceptualize is that under one set of circumstances a particular child with a hearing impairment may be handicapped, whereas under different conditions the same child may not be as handicapped. When seen in this light, it is clear that the concept of handicap must not be used as an explanation but rather as a means to formulate and to implement procedures to change environmental conditions.

The report of the committee to redefine the terms *deaf* and *hard-of-hearing* for educational purposes (Frisina, 1975) recommended that the term deaf be used only as a modifier and not as a noun and that deafness be the preferred term in reference to hearing disability. They also suggested use of the generic term *hearing impaired* to include both deaf and hard-of-hearing persons. It is important to bear in mind that neither of these terms is, in any significant measure, indicative of the handicap involved. To describe someone as hearing impaired conveys nothing of the educational help or provision that is required.

The committee's report, adopted by the Conference of Executives of American Schools for the Deaf, differentiates between a deaf and a hard-of-hearing person as follows:

> A deaf person is one whose disability precludes successful processing of linguistic information through audition, with or without a hearing aid.
> A hard-of-hearing person is one who, generally with the use of a hearing aid, has residual hearing sufficient to enable successful processing of linguistic information through audition.
> Prelingual deafness is deafness present at birth or occurring early in life at an age prior to the development of speech and language.
> Postlingual deafness is deafness occurring at an age following the development of speech and language.

In addition, the committee specified the following hearing threshold levels of classification, based on the average pure-tone threshold for 500, 1,000 and 2,000 Hz in the better ear.

Mild (26–54 dB)—Students in this category generally do not require special class placement but usually require special speech and hearing assistance.

Moderate (55–69 dB)—These students occasionally require special class placement and generally require special speech, hearing, and language assistance.

Severe (70–89 dB)—Those in this category generally require special class or special school placement; they usually require speech, hearing, language, and educational assistance.

Profound (90 dB and above)—These students generally require special school placement for speech, hearing, language, and educational assistance.

Although the new definitions reflect a greater educational orientation than previously and contain a warning that the classifications are not directly related to hearing sensitivity, the necessary distinction between sensitivity and auditory function is not made. The emphasis on prediction of educational placement from hearing threshold level is not sound. The parameters of any classification system for educational services must be based on needs of individual children. Accepting hearing-threshold levels as criteria is as futile as using IQ measures to categorize educable mentally retarded and trainable mentally retarded children (Clarke & Leslie, 1980, pp. 201–203).

Sensorially handicapped persons have visual or auditory limitations or both. The most severe and profound conditions of this type are blindness and deafness. Although partially sighted and hard-of-hearing conditions constitute handicaps, they are considered mild or moderate when compared with the limitations imposed by blindness and deafness. This book does not discuss the problems associated with visual or auditory limitations when either condition exists without the complications of a concurrent handicapping condition.

Physically Handicapped

Children with crippling conditions and chronic health problems represent an extremely heterogeneous population. They are afflicted with a large variety of problems, including such things as cerebral palsy, spina bifida, muscular dystrophy, spinal cord injury, arthritis, cardiac conditions, and epilepsy. Some of these handicaps are congenital problems, and others occur after birth through accidents or disease. Some can be controlled effectively and are relatively limited in their effect on the child, and others get progressively worse and can even result in death.

The effects on the children involved, whether academic, social or personal, are just as varied as the physical handicaps and health problems with which they are afflicted. Because intelligence is sometimes unaffected, some children may overcome tremendous disadvantages to reach very high standards in the classroom. Motivation and a limited number of special devices or adaptive aids may be all that are required.

The thrust of this book, however, is toward those individuals for whom this level of accomplishment is impossible. For them, the physical handicap is accompanied by intellectual, psychological, or sensorial deficits. Sometimes individuals manifest problems in all of these areas.

Cerebral palsy is one of the most frequent conditions found among the multiply handicapped population. It is most commonly caused by anoxia and physical trauma that damage the areas of the brain controlling body movement and coordination. Although cerebral hemorrhaging, poisonings, and congenital malformations of the brain can also result in cerebral palsy, cases of genetic determinants are quite uncommon. Approximately 1.5% of 1,000 live births are cerebral-palsied children (Cruickshank, 1976).

In describing the characteristics of a cerebral-palsied child, a diagnostic team would usually classify the condition in two ways: 1) the limbs that are involved and 2) the type of neuromotor involvement. The first method of classification (by number of extremities) is used to describe all types of motor dysfunction, paralysis, or both. Denhoff (1976) estimated the approximate percentage of cerebral-palsied children that fall into each of these following classes:

Hemiplegia—one half of the body, right or left side (50%)

Quadriplegia—all four limbs involved (15%-20%)

Paraplegia—only legs involved (10%-20%)

Diplegia—all limbs affected but with greater involvement in legs (10%-20%)

Monoplegia—one limb affected (rare)

Triplegia—three limbs affected (rare)

Double Hemiplegia—all four limbs affected but with greater involvement in one side of the body (rare)

The second classification, according to the type of neuromotor involvement, encompasses the areas of 1) spasticity, 2) athetosis, 3) ataxia, 4) rigidity, and 5) tremor. The first two, spasticity and athetosis, comprise approximately 75% to 80% of cerebral-palsied persons (Kirk & Gallagher, 1979).

Spasticity—This condition refers to involuntary contractions of the muscles resulting in short, jerky movements that are uncontrolled. Approximately 40% to 60% of cerebral-palsied persons show characteristics of spasticity.

Athetosis—The involuntary writhing, twisting, and fluctuations of movement in the athetoid child create difficulties when any purposeful movement is attempted. Athetoid children often have involvement in the fingers and wrists that makes writing extremely difficult. About 20%-25% of the cerebral-palsied children have some athetoid movements.

Ataxia — Balance and coordination are affected, which makes the ataxic child unsteady and causes him or her to fall easily. Approximately 20% of the children with cerebral palsy exhibit ataxic symptoms.

Rigidity — This type of cerebral palsy causes continuous muscle tension, thereby inhibiting movement because of the extreme stiffness in the involved limbs. This type of cerebral palsy is rare.

Tremor — The affected limb(s) or entire body moves rhythmically or vibrates uncontrollably. This type is also rare.

A child with any type of cerebral palsy may exhibit very mild involvement or may be so severely involved that extraordinary adaptations must be made to accommodate him or her in the school environment. Stress, noise, and movement can have a pronounced effect even on a mildly involved child, and the teacher should be prepared for fluctuations in the child's motor ability related to these factors.

Epilepsy is a convulsive disorder that is also commonly found among the multiply handicapped. Sometimes its cause can be traced to a brain lesion or tumor, but often the cause is unknown. An electroencephalogram (EEG) is used to record the brain's electrical output in an attempt to ascertain a cause for the seizures. The seizure occurs because there is a sudden abnormal discharge of electrical activity in the brain that consequently affects the motor and sensory capabilities of the body for the duration of the seizure.

The four major types of seizures are 1) grand mal, 2) petit mal, 3) Jacksonian, and 4) psychomotor. Grand mal and petit mal seizures, alone or in combination, are the most common.

Grand mal — This type of major motor seizure usually develops in stages — *auric, tonic, clonic,* and *sleep* — and lasts from 2 to 6 minutes. The person often senses a particular feeling or odor that warns him or her of an impending seizure. The aura can occur immediately before the tonic stage of the seizure or may precede the convulsion by an hour or even a day. Following the aura, the person stiffens (tonic state) and often falls or slumps unconscious to the floor. During the convulsive clonic stage, the muscles of the body contract and relax involuntarily while the person may thrash around, lose bladder or bowel control, vomit, and breathe heavily. It is important to remove any objects nearby that might cause injury and to refrain from sticking anything in the person's mouth. As the clonic stage lessens, the person will awaken, exhausted, and should be allowed to rest or sleep as long as needed. In some unusual instances, the person may continue in seizure without a return to consciousness (*status epilepticus*). This should signal immediate medical attention.

Petit mal — This very mild seizure occurs more frequently than a grand mal. It is characterized by a momentary loss of consciousness that may go unnoticed by the person but is viewed by another as rapid blinking, a vacant stare, dropping an object, or any other brief loss of contact in the environment. The entire seizure lasts no more than a few seconds.

Jacksonian—This is a type of focal seizure that begins with involuntary twitching in one part of the body. It often progresses throughout that side of the body and may encompass the entire body in a grand mal type of seizure. Adults are more apt to have this form than children.

Psychomotor—One who is experiencing a psychomotor seizure acts automatically in a trancelike motion while engaging in curious behaviors. He or she may have facial grimaces, mumble, become violent or move in a robotlike fashion. The duration can be several hours or even a day. After returning to normal, the person has no recollection of the events that occurred. This type is also very uncommon in children.

Medication can greatly reduce the number and severity of seizures in an epileptic. With proper dosage and monitoring of activities the epileptic child may function quite well in the regular classroom.

Spina bifida is a congenital defect characterized by an incomplete closure of the bony spinal column. When no neurological impairment is evident and there is no protrusion of the spinal cord, it is technically-called *spina bifida occulta*. When there is an opening in the back along the spine, however, and a sac containing cerebrospinal fluid without nerve tissue protrudes through the opening, the spina bifida is termed a *meningocele*. A *myelomeningocele* condition is more debilitating because by definition there is neurological involvement and often paralysis of the legs, bowel, and bladder muscles. This occurs when parts of the spinal cord are contained in the sac that protrudes through the opening in the spine and back.

Soon after birth, a large percentage of children born with spina bifida develop hydrocephalus (an increase of the cerebrospinal fluid causing extreme pressure and consequent enlargement of the head). This condition is also associated with increased incidence of mental retardation. Although spina bifida itself does not cause a deviation in normal intellectual functioning, if it is accompanied by hydrocephalus, meningitis, or some other congenital abnormality there is a significantly increased chance of lowered intellectual ability.

HISTORICAL PERSPECTIVE

Historically, the treatment of handicapped persons can generally be characterized as a deplorable tragedy by today's standards. Throughout the centuries many, if not most, of the individuals who today are considered severely and profoundly handicapped once died or were put to death at a very early age, were kept isolated from society, or were simply ignored. Social attitudes and, consequently, the treatment of handicapped persons, however, have evolved toward more humanitarian concerns through the centuries. According to Hewett (1974), four distinct treatment determinants can be traced through the history of civilization: survival, superstition, science, and service.

From primitive and ancient societies until the Middle Ages (approximately 3000 B.C. to A.D. 1300), physical strength and agility were the primary prerequisites to survival. Because a physically sound and efficient body was held in high regard, the physically handicapped particularly were often killed or subjected to conditions that resulted in death (e.g., abandonment). Under such a climate of physical importance, the killing of infants with physical anomalies was a commonly accepted practice.

Toward the latter part of this 4,300-year period, superstition began to replace survival as the primary determinant for viewing the handicapped. Although the concept of the "survival of the fittest" did not disappear, the rise of religious doctrines gave birth to pseudo-religious explanations and treatment of handicapping conditions. Individuals without obvious physical handicaps but who were, for example, epileptic, blind, or mentally ill, were thought to be "possessed." Those considered to be possessed by "good" spirits were held in high regard and often placed in positions of importance; those thought to be possessed by "bad" spirits were killed, abandoned, or alienated from society.

The increased importance of science, particularly during the Renaissance period, caused it to become the predominant mode of viewing the handicapped. Commensurate with the development of scientific inquiry, individuals with a variety of severe and profound handicapping conditions were subjected to more objective study and categorization. Although the earliest studies of handicapping conditions focused on the physical dimension, scientific inquiry led ultimately to the development of techniques for classifying and analyzing behavior and psychological conditions, including intelligence and mental disorders.

The final determining factor, service, represents the current attitude toward severely and profoundly handicapped individuals. Although far from ideal, the pattern today is characterized by more humanitarian care, including education and social acceptance. This service orientation is an outgrowth of increased knowledge about the characteristics and treatment of the handicapped that most notably began less than 200 years ago. The history of service to the handicapped, however, had only a meager beginning and followed a cyclic, but fortunately an ascending, pattern. It should be noted that most of the historical literature dealt with the intellectually handicapped—the mentally retarded. Consequently, much of the service pattern described in the following paragraphs can be generalized to other handicapped populations because differential diagnosis was so unsophisticated that many children labeled as retarded were, in fact, suffering from other handicapping conditions associated with reduced intellectual functioning. Thus, many children who were by today's classifications autistic, sensorily impaired, or multiply handicapped were labeled retarded—and were treated accordingly.

In the early 19th century, two physicians were especially notable for their work with the handicapped, particularly the mentally retarded. Jean Itard's work with Victor (*The Wild Boy of Aveyron*) and Edward Seguin's methodology of training the retarded represent two initial attempts in what is now called "special education." Their work created a worldwide hope that the "idiocy" problem had been solved. Because they expected to cure the retarded through training, Itard, Seguin, and many others felt they had failed when this was not accomplished. From an educational viewpoint, however, both men were incredibly successful, and their work is still a valuable resource for special educators.

Prior to 1850, very little was done for the severely and multiply handicapped in the United States. In 1650, Maryland became the first colony to pass a law that allowed for the appointment of guardians for feebleminded children. In some cases the feebleminded, along with other deviants, were auctioned to the highest bidder, who could use them for manual labor in return for caring for them. In 1793, Kentucky was the first state to pass a "pauper idiot" law that allowed remuneration to families with feebleminded individuals. Residential arrangements before 1850 did not include remediation or rehabilitation. The feebleminded were merely placed in almshouses, jails, or insane asylums (Baumeister & Butterfield, 1970).

The period from 1850 to 1880 was one of considerable progress, largely through the efforts of Edward Seguin, Samuel Howe, and others. Seguin's contributions to the establishment of training schools for the feebleminded extended beyond his actual participation in the founding of schools in Massachusetts, New York, Ohio, Connecticut, and Pennsylvania; his writing provided the inspiration and philosophy upon which these training institutions were founded. He stated, "the mental defective, regardless of the reasons for his backwardness, is entitled to be treated with dignity, warmth, and kindness and with the best skills and resources available" (Baumeister & Butterfield, 1970). Dr. Samuel Howe was chosen to head a commission to look into the condition of the "idiots" in Massachusetts. Upon Howe's recommendation, the Massachusetts legislature authorized the first training school for idiots in 1848. In addition to state-authorized schools, many private schools were established and those who pioneered these schools felt that through education and training, the mental "defective" could be made to live a more normal life. Wolfensberger (1976) labels the era from 1850 to 1880 a period when an attempt was made to "make the deviant less deviant" (p. 48).

The institutions of this period were quite successful in achieving many of their goals and did return many handicapped persons to the community. Although these successes may not have been deliberately contrived, some of the reports of their successes can be considered somewhat exaggerated; attempts were being made to win over a skeptical public and an often recalcitrant state legislature. These claims, however, eventually undermined their intended purpose and contributed to a feeling of hopelessness during the last 2 decades of the 19th century. It seems that many of the early founders' peers, as well as some who reflect back on this era, "had misunderstood the objectives of the pioneers in expecting complete and rapid cures in large numbers, and interpreted any lesser accomplishments as tantamount to failure" (Wolfensberger, 1976, p. 51). With this perceived failure, ideologies changed between 1870 and 1880. Developmental attitudes were replaced by pity.

Toward the end of the 19th century, there was a general aversion to deviancy of all forms. This, coupled with the accumulation of nonrehabilitated residents, gradually changed the training "school" to an "asylum." The idea now was to offer the severely and multiply handicapped person "benevolent shelter."

By 1875 several states had begun to plan and build the large, diversified institutions that we see today. The utilization of these large institutions led to three dangerous (and ultimately disastrous) trends: 1) isolation, 2) enlargement, and 3) economization (Wolfensberger, 1976). The trend toward isolation dictated that institutions should be far away from population centers, and this led to suspicion and fear of the handicapped on the part of the normal population. In order to group the similar handicaps together "so [the handicapped] could associate with his own kind," the institution had to be enlarged from small, homelike facilities to large, dormitorylike arrangements. The trend toward labor and economization is characterized by Pennsylvania, which in 1887 passed an act that increased the number of state-supported residents and reduced the per capita expenditure from $200 to $175 per year. The higher grade "imbecile" was utilized to help the institution run more economically by farming and taking care of lower-grade defectives.

This transition period (1870–1890) gave way to one of the worst periods for the intellectually and psychologically handicapped. The prevalent idea was to "protect society from the deviant," and so the mentally deficient became a "menace" to society. Wolfensberger, in quoting Fernald (1915), identified four causal factors associated with this period. The first was the widespread use of mental tests that pointed out the extent of feeblemindedness. Second, studies of family histories of the feebleminded confirmed the fear that feeblemindedness was hereditary. Third, extensive surveys, studies, and inquiries purported that feeblemindedness was an important factor in all sorts of social evil and disease (e.g., delinquency, vagrancy, venereal disease, crime, and immorality). Finally, because of the aforementioned factors, the estimates of the extent and prevalence of feeblemindedness were greatly increased. As these factors were comprehended by society, the treatment of the mentally retarded became inhumane and dehumanizing; one author stated that it was very similar to the Nazi's treatment of the Jews in World War II (Nirje, 1969b). During this period (1880–1895), the retarded woman was regarded as the most dangerous: "It is certain that the feebleminded girl or woman in the city rarely escapes the sexual experiences that too often result in the birth of more defectives and degenerates" (Fernald, 1912, in Wolfensberger, 1976, p. 56). Furthermore, "their children are apt to be mentally defective, with more or less pronounced animal instincts, diseased and depraved, a curse and menace to the community (Bullard, 1910, in Wolfensberger, 1969, p. 103). Around 1895, Connecticut passed House Bill 681, the first of the preventive marriage laws. These laws were enacted because "the feebleminded woman who marries is twice as prolific as the normal woman" (Fernald, 1912, in Wolfensberger, 1976, p. 56).

The ineffectiveness of these marriage laws spawned preventive sterilization laws. It was stated, "greater liberty, therefore greater happiness to the individual [will accrue by]...invoking the aid of surgical interference" (Barr, 1902, in Wolfensberger, 1969, p. 111). The absurdity to which this line of thinking was carried is ably noted by Wolfensberger (1969).

> An apparently widely held view was stated by Taylor (1898), who reasoned that if procreation was rendered impossible by surgery, there would be no further value in preserving the sexual instinct of the retardate. Since much harm was seen to result in the cultivation or even retention of this instinct, Taylor recommended that it would be just as well '...to remove the organs which the sufferers are unfit to exercise normally, and for which they are the worse in the unnatural cultivation and use' (p. 81). Thus, for males, castration was widely preferred over vasectomy (Cave, 1911; Van Wagenen, 1914). In one stroke, it not only accomplished sterilization; it also eliminated 'sexual debaucheries' (Cave) and masturbation (Van Wagenen), and perhaps even improved 'the singing voice' (Barr, 1905) and diminished epileptic seizures (Barr, 1904). Sometimes, castration was performed '...after every other means...' as a '...cure for masturbation,' even without the perceived need for sterilization (Reports from States, 1895, p. 348). By 1914, sterilization was used not only for eugenic but also for penal reasons, sometimes in addition to a prison sentence. The courts upheld this measure as constituting neither cruel nor unusual punishment for certain crimes (Van Wagenen). In cases where vasectomy was performed, retardates did 'not require an anesthetic since all that is required is to cut the *vas deferens*' (Risley, 1905, p. 97). (p. 111)

When mating and sterilization laws failed to alleviate the perceived menace, only segregation, or "strict sexual quarantine" as Fernald called it in 1915, prevailed as the answer. Not only were the feebleminded to be removed from society, but the sexes from each other. In fact, Barr suggested that the federal government could create one or more reservations to encompass all the feebleminded on the same basis as another group of deviants, the Indians: "The national government has provided for the mute, the Negro, and the Indian—then, why not for this branch of the population increasing as rapidly as they, and becoming yearly more inimical to national prosperity" (1897, in Wolfensberger, 1976, p. 61).

By now it is quite evident that society not only had placed the mentally retarded in the status of seriously deviant, but also, because retardation was considered incurable, they were not to be rehabilitated. Therefore, the retarded were merely stored until death and this is what Wolfensberger refers to as "inexpensive warehousing." Beds were lined up side by side and head to foot, so close in many cases that one had to walk from bed to bed to move about the room. In addition, during this period the retarded were exploited to the limit of their capacities and sometimes beyond:

> They should be under such conditions that many of them shall not cost the taxpayer anything...the state must...say to them, 'We will take care of you: you shall be happy and well cared for and clean and useful; but you shall labor and earn your bread in the sweat of your face according to the divine command.' That is what should be done with the whole class of degenerates, just so far as it is possible to do it. (Johnson, 1901, in Wolfensberger, 1976, p. 64)

Between 1908 and 1920 the rationales had run out. Studies on community adjustment during this period began to dispute the fact that the retarded were a menace to the community and the idea that segregation would stem the tide of the retarded was proven false. Follow-up studies of retardates released from institutions prompted Fernald to say "We have begun to recognize that there are good morons and bad morons" (1919, in Wolfensberger, 1976, p. 68). The depressing aspect of this whole mess is that even though scientific evidence and common sense have proven how wrong the institutional policies of 1925 had been, the momentum gained over a 30-year period (approximately 1885–1915) has left us with a situation that is almost impossible to reverse. As Wolfensberger (1976) states:

> We cannot understand this institution, as we know it, with all its objectionable features, unless we realize whence it came. I propose that essentially, many of our institutions, to this very day, operate in the spirit of 1925 when inexpensive segregation of a scarcely human retardate was seen as the only feasible alternative to combat a social menace. I am not proposing that this view is still held; I am proposing that most institutions function as if this view were still held. (p. 69)

In actuality, historical references to the mentally retarded probably included the psychologically handicapped. Because of the lack of diagnostic skills, behavioral differences in the handicapped and lack of motivation to understand individual differences, handicapping conditions were generally not differentiated. It was not until the 20th century "that consistent attempts were made to study children with severe emotional disturbances from the point of view of diagnosis, etiology, therapy, and prognosis" (Kanner, 1962, p. 99). Before this time, infrequent and general references were published about "little homicidal maniacs," children with "evil habits," and those "possessed by the devil."

By the 1940s the psychiatric profession had established a number of psychological classifications, such as "atypical," "dementia praecox," and "childhood schizophrenia." Once diagnosed, these children were typically placed in institutions for the "mentally ill" under the direction of a psychiatrist. The conditions within these institutions were remarkably similar to those for the retarded, that is, generally dehumanizing. Psychologically handicapped children, however, did often receive "treatment" in the form of therapy (e.g., Freudian therapy), medication and drugs, and, in some cases, psychosurgery and electroconvulsive therapy (i.e., "shock treatment").

Because psychological handicaps were the creation of the psychiatric profession, education played a minimal and often nonexistent role in the treatment of these children. This remained the case for the severely and profoundly psychologically handicapped until the 1970s when parental pressure, public awareness, and legislation began shifting the responsibility to educational systems. Disappointed with the results, inconvenience, and expense of residential psychiatric treatment, emphasis was shifted to schools as the primary education and treatment service. Today, it is generally believed that most children are best served in special education programs with supportive services (National Society for Autistic Children (1977).

Although the situations in institutions across the United States have improved to a great extent through the impetus of litigation and legislation, there is still a long way to go before we will be rid of dehumanizing conditions in institutions. To illustrate, one should consider the Forest Haven (Brockett, 1978) and Pineland (Gettings, 1978) institutions and their current problems. Jack Anderson, in his syndicated column, wrote of today's institutions:

> These are often nothing more than human warehouses; a few can be classified as snake pits. They have pleasant names like Applecreek, Forest Haven, Rosewood, Sonoma. But they are more like concentration camps, where society quietly hides away its mental misfits until they die. (June 6, 1978)

In all fairness, not all institutions are bad today nor were all of them ever as bad as those singled out above. The problems of institutions have been, and still are in some instances, a matter of degree; some institutions are much worse than others. Unfortunately, there are still many institutions with grave problems that even today almost defy solution. The following example illustrates Blatt and Kaplan's (1966) initial impressions during a series of tours of four institutions for the mentally retarded:

> Several things strike the visitor to most institutions for the mentally retarded upon his arrival. Often there are fences. Sometimes with barbed wire. Frequently the buildings impress him with their massiveness and impenetrability. We have observed bars on windows and locks — many locks — on inside as well as outside doors. As we entered the dormitories and other buildings, we were impressed with the contrast of the functional superiority of the new buildings and the gross neglect of the older buildings. We have observed gaping holes in ceilings of the main kitchen. In toilets, one sees urinals ripped out, sinks broken, and toilets backed up. In every institution discussed in this section, we found incredible overcrowding. Beds are so arranged — side by side and head to head — that *it is impossible, in some dormitories, to cross parts of the rooms without actually walking over beds.* Often the beds are without pillows. We have seen mattresses so sagged by the weight of bodies that they were scraping the floor. In summary, we were amazed by the over-crowdedness, by the disrepair of older buildings, by the excessive use of locks and heavy doors, and by the enormity of buildings and number of patients assigned to dormitories. (pp. 1, 2)

In describing the dormitories for the severely retarded, Blatt talks about "therapeutic isolation," which is, more realistically speaking, solitary confinement in its most punitive and inhumane form:

> These cells are generally tiny rooms, approximately seven feet by seven feet, shielded from the outside with a very heavy metal door having either a fine strong screen or metal bars for observation of the "prisoner." Some cells have mattresses, others blankets, still others bare floors. None that we had seen (and we found these cells in each institution visited) had either a bed, a washstand, or a toilet. What we did find in one cell was a thirteen or fourteen year old boy, nude, in a corner of a starkly bare room, lying on his own urine and feces. The boy had been in solitary confinement for several days for committing a minor institutional infraction. . . . In another institution, we had a good opportunity to interview the attendant in charge. We asked him what he needed most in order to better supervise the residents and provide them with a more adequate program. The attendant's major request was for the addition of two more solitary confinement cells, to be built adjacent to the existing two cells that, we were told, were always occupied, around the clock, day in and day out. We saw children with hands tied and legs bound. (1966, p. 13)

Blatt further discussed the typical "day room" in such dormitories:

> The odor in each of these rooms is over-powering. After a visit to a day room we had to send our clothes to the dry cleaners to have the stench removed. The facilities often contributed to the horror. Floors are sometimes wooden and excretions are rubbed into the cracks, leaving permanent stench. Most day rooms have a series of bleacher benches, on which sit unclad residents, jammed together, without purposeful activity, communica-

tion, or any interaction. In each day room is an attendant or two, whose main function seems to be to "stand around" and, on occasion hose down the floor "driving" excretions into a sewer conveniently located in the center of the room. We were invited into female as well as male day rooms, in spite of the supervisor's knowledge that we, male visitors, would be observing naked females. In one such dormitory, with an overwhelming odor, we noticed feces on the wooden ceilings, and on the patients as well as the floors. (1966, p. 22)

Even more depressing were the infant dormitories where cribs were placed — as in the other dormitories — side by side and head to head:

Very young children, one and two years of age, were lying in cribs, without interaction with any adult, without playthings, without any apparent stimulation. In one dormitory, that had over 100 infants and was connected to 9 other dormitories that totalled 1,000 infants, we experienced a heartbreaking encounter. As we entered, we heard a muffled sound emanating from the "blind" side of a doorway. A young child seemed to be calling. "Come. Come play with me. Touch me." We walked to the door. On the other side were forty or more unkempt infants crawling around a bare floor in a bare room. One of the children had managed to squeeze his hand under the doorway and push his face through the side of the latched door. His moan was the clearest representation we have ever heard of the lonely, hopeless man. In other day rooms, we saw groups of 20 and 30 very young children lying, rocking, sleeping, sitting-alone. Each of these rooms was without toys or adult human contact, although each had desperate looking adult attendants "standing by." In another dormitory, we were taken on a tour by the chief physician who was anxious to show us a child who had a very rare medical condition. The doctor explained to us that, aside from the child's dwarfism and misshapen body, one of the primary methods for diagnosing this condition is the deep guttural voice. In order to demonstrate this, he pinched the child. The child did not make any sound. He pinched her again, and again harder and still harder. Finally, as if in desperation, he insured her response with a pinch that turned into a gouge and caused the child to scream in obvious pain. (1966, p. 34)

Nirje, a highly respected Scandinavian and prominent spokesman for the principle of "normalization" (see next section), summarizing his impressions of a visit to institutions in the United States, stated:

Foreign visitors to the United States are likely to be impressed by the inexhaustible resources and wealth of America. Thus, a visitor who works in the field of mental retardation in another country would be inclined to expect that public institutions for the retarded are planned, constructed, and operated with the same thoroughness and lavish disregard for cost that appear evident in the planning, construction and operation of other facilities such as expressways, motels, skyscrapers. A visitor with such expectations is in for a rude shock.

In the last 2 years, I have visited a number of public institutions in several states, and on each occasion, I have reacted with disbelief and bewilderment to what I saw. I found it difficult to understand how a society which is built on such noble principles, and which has the resources to make these principles a reality, can tolerate the dehumanization of a large number of its citizens in a fashion somewhat remindful of Nazi concentration camps. (1969a, p. 53)

Anderson provided additional testimony in his comments about conditions at Forest Haven, an institution for the mentally retarded in Laurel, Maryland when he quoted the mother of a resident who eventually died:

"Joy resided in Dogwood Cottage....Dogwood was a veritable snake pit. I once witnessed a nurse open the cottage door only to find 80 half-clad screaming women come running to the door; the nurse quickly shut it. On one occasion, we found Joy's entire back raw. When we took Joy to a private doctor...we were informed that her back injury was caused by urine burns from being restrained on a rubber sheet." (June 6, 1978)

Anderson further stated:

Another Forest Haven resident, Bertha Brown, also died recently. She suffocated from eating her own feces. The woman suffered from a disease which caused her to eat almost anything in sight. Yet she was tied to a toilet and left unattended. She bit through the restraining garments, ate her feces and choked to death. (June 6, 1978)

From the above it is quite obvious that what these writers had seen and written about was pervasive dehumanization of retarded individuals who were unfortunate enough to be severely and profoundly retarded and forced to live on a back ward of a public institution. One would think that these conditions, as the public, politicians, and professionals become aware of them, would be eradicated. Although dramatic changes have occurred in many instances, some institutions are still characterized by intolerable conditions.

A number of recent court cases involving institutionalized plaintiffs who are considered either mentally retarded, mentally ill, or emotionally disturbed provide some hope for the future. Decisions stemming from complaints at Pineland Center, Willowbrook, and Forest Haven, to cite a few, seem to be among the most promising. In the Forest Haven decision (*Evans v. Washington*, 1978), the court entered a consent judgment, which held that "mentally retarded residents have a federal constitutional right to habilitation in the least restrictive environment and a right to be free from harm" (Lilly, 1980). As such, the court ordered the defendants to devise a plan for more suitable habilitation, which in effect requires eventual deinstitutionalization of all class members.

On the surface, this decision should have eliminated the dehumanizing conditions at Forest Haven as summarized above by Anderson. A status report (Lilly, 1980) reveals, however, that serious instances of noncompliance continue to occur in all areas covered by the decree. Implementation has also been hindered by budgetary problems that have drastically reduced the number of persons placed in the community and that have undermined the development of support services for those persons who are deinstitutionalized.

Despite such problems in implementation, there is increasing evidence that institutions are getting better because of public awareness, changed attitudes, successful training programs, litigation and consequent legislation, and the ideology of normalization. It is because of the still-too-frequent negative conditions that the principle of normalization has become the possible answer to these intolerable situations.

NORMALIZATION

Providing the best possible services for the severely and multiply handicapped must begin with the contemporary principle of normalization, which dictates that society provide services and facilities that allow the individual to live in as normal a manner as possible. Based on a philosophical position that had its inception in the Scandinavian countries (Nirje, 1969b; Wolfensberger, 1972; Baroff, 1974), the concept of normalization emphasizes the right of the retarded citizen to live in a family environment or, at least, in his or her home community. Even in cases in which the severity of the handicap dictates institutionalization, the living conditions are expected to approximate the patterns of mainstream society.

The definition of normalization is so simple that it borders on the naive: to provide the severely and profoundly handicapped with an existence as close to normal as possible (N. E. Bank Millelsen, in Nirje, 1970). Situations that are normal are certainly not found in most large institutions for the handicapped. Therefore, normalization infers doing away with large, diversified institutions that euphemistically have been called "schools," "farms," "colonies," "hospitals," and "homes."

Normalization extends beyond architectural or structural considerations; it is actually a philosophy or principle that provides "patterns and conditions of everyday life which are as close as possible to the norms and patterns of the mainstream of society...consequently it should serve as a guide for medical, educational, psychological, social and political work in this field" (Nirje, 1970). Normalization also means that a handicapped person should have the opportunity to experience the normal rhythm of the day, the week, the seasons, and the years. It allows for a self-identity, bisexual contacts, the problems of everyday living, and normal living facilities—all these within the context of the individual's specific handicap (Nirje, 1970). Also, as Gunzburg (1970) suggested, "subnormal people who are given 'normal' opportunities for living, for experiencing, for choosing, for shouldering responsibilities, for working, will be encouraged and stimulated to function on a higher level of competence than if they are deprived of these opportunities" (p. 56).

The refreshing aspect of normalization is that it refocuses services to the person. Whereas in the past, services or patterns of dealing with the mentally subnormal have been for the entertainment of others (the court jester or fool), the convenience of society (isolated asylums), or the convenience of staff (the medical model of treatment and architectural considerations), society is today beginning to recognize the severely and multiply handicapped as human beings. Positive results do not accrue from a particular method as much as from the quality of the human relationship. Although normalization is very much person centered, the principle and its advocates are not so naive as to think that it can be a cure-all for those labeled subnormal. Obviously, the prognosis for each person depends on a variety of factors including the degree of handicap, competence and maturity, and the need for training activities and availability of services.

Gearheart and Litton (1975, p. 12), recognizing that serious attempts at normalization will involve some degree of calculated risk, suggested that the following proposals provide a starting point for more thought and consideration of the implications of this concept:

1. Almost all services for the handicapped provided at the community level.
2. Educational and training programs integrated to a much greater extent with programs for "normal" individuals.
3. Residential facilities in small units resembling homes.
4. Adult handicapped in much more daily contact with normal adults.
5. More involvement with bisexuality.
6. Work stations alongside those for nonhandicapped individuals.

Clearly, the degree of normalization that can ultimately be realized will depend on a number of factors. First of all, efforts to implement this principle must be based on a sound estimate of the capabilities and characteristics of each handicapped individual. Second, the attitudes and misconceptions that typify the public's understanding of the severely and multiply handicapped must be replaced by more enlightened conceptions. Finally, a continuum of services and programs must be made available to accommodate all the divergent habilitative and placement needs of the severely and multiply handicapped.

This latter factor, a continuum of services for the retarded, implies an array of services that has both vertical and horizontal dimensions. As described by Baroff (1974), the horizontal level refers to the need of services from more than one community agency at any given time, for example, "the preschool-age child might be living in a foster home, attending a child development center, receiving medical care for a retardation-related physical disability, and participating in a community-sponsored summer day camp program" (p. 122).

The vertical dimension of the continuum includes the need for services at each stage of development from infancy to adulthood. Nursery and day-care centers for severely handicapped preschoolers are a necessity. For school-age children, a substantial array of community services, staffed by practitioners representing a variety of habilitative disciplines, must be provided to satisfy their educational, medical, and recreational needs. At the adult level, opportunities for employment and meaningful social interaction are required. The provision of these basic programs, as well as supportive services like crisis centers, respite facilities, and counseling services, will enable many parents and relatives to avoid the desperate decision to institutionalize.

LITIGATION

The precedent established by several recent court cases and the impetus supplied by other litigation focused on the denial of civil rights for handicapped children is now being reflected in the mandate to develop programs for the severely, profoundly, and multiply handicapped. Although these developments on behalf of the handicapped are generally associated with the 1970s, their roots stem from decades of neglect and inadequate services. In addition, compulsory school attendance laws, the movement from a rural to an urban society, the public disenchantment with special classes and labels for categorizing handicapped children, and the inadequacy of techniques and evaluative instruments used as a basis for special class placement have all contributed to the changes now taking place.

Of paramount importance was the landmark legal case in Pennsylvania, described in detail by Lippman and Goldberg (1973). Perhaps Gallagher's recent review of Lippman and Goldberg's book most aptly summarizes the major implications of what has come to be known as the Pennsylvania "Right to Education" case. Gallagher pointed out that the implementation of full service to retarded children would not be without problems and that the task was not completed with the rendering of judicial action. He stated:

> The cries of agonized school administrators that they had neither the funds, nor the personnel, nor the facilities to provide the kinds of services that the court was requiring are old stories to those who have struggled to get better programs for handicapped children. (Gallagher, 1973, p. 218)

Following the judgment and a subsequent needs assessment, 11,000 children in Pennsylvania were identified as having no educational services. Nevertheless, according to Lippman and Goldberg, the court rejected arguments related to lack of funds, personnel, and facilities and referred to the philosophy as stated by a spokesman for the Council for Exceptional Children:

> If, in fact, the state does not have sufficient funds to educate all of its children, the handicapped youngster must take his share of the cut with the others. . . but do not expect the exceptional child to bear the whole burden of the state's financial difficulty, Mr. Governor and Mr. Legislator. He will suffer his share of the burden—but, by order of the federal courts, he will no longer carry the whole burden. (Lippman & Goldberg, 1973, pp. 64–65)

Sontag, Burke, and York (1973) discussed the implications of another court decision that they consider to be of even greater significance to the severely handicapped. The *Mills* v. *Board of Education of the District of Columbia* (1972) case expanded the implications of the Pennsylvania case to all handicapped children, not just those labeled mentally retarded.

Finally, Public Law 94-142 has *mandated* the nationwide provision of special education and related services to all handicapped children, regardless of the severity of their handicap.

These events reflect a strong movement in American education to hold the public schools of the nation accountable for providing quality education for all children, regardless of educational problems. Consequently, for many handicapped children, the responsibility is being interpreted as education within the regular classroom (Davis, 1973). This interpretation is undoubtedly valid for many children with educational problems, however, it is not generalizable to all. It is self-evident that the severity of the handicapping conditions of some children will preclude placement in regular classes. There is no doubt, however, that the country must respond to the mandate to provide an appropriate free education to all children, including the severely, profoundly, and multiply handicapped. All children in the nation, regardless of level of functioning, will have access to an education in the least restrictive environment and, consequently, the issue now centers on how to provide the best possible developmental services to the lowest functioning individuals in society.

PROBLEMS AND TRENDS IN PROGRAM DEVELOPMENT

This section summarizes the problems and needs of those professionals now faced with the challenge of providing quality educational programs for handicapped children. Caught between court-ordered deadlines and financial restrictions, responsible persons still must quickly find acceptable solutions to a wide range of problems, including not only instructional matters but also complicating factors such as transportation, medical services, cooperation with nonschool agencies, and community resistance and misunderstanding. Although the professional literature in this area has previously been limited, a growing body of information is now available. A number of issues and problems have been identified. Summarized as follows, these issues delineate the task that lies ahead for professionals and laymen committed to adequate and effective programs for the severely and profoundly handicapped.

Meaningful Assessment

Severely and multiply handicapped children differ tremendously in terms of intellectual functioning and adaptive behavior. Their educational needs are likewise very different. Diagnostic labels and traditional approaches to training therefore provide little or no help in developing a strong, effective instructional program. Alternative strategies for assessment must be identified and employed if the goal of normalization is ever to be realized.

Because there is little instructional validity in using labels and IQ scores, educators must focus on skills or competencies that each child does or does not have. Starting with this direct measurement of relevant behavioral dimensions, they must subsequently determine, on a frequent basis, whether the child is getting the desired skills and progressing in the program. The feedback to the teacher is necessary for responsive programs in which modifications can quickly be made to encourage and facilitate learning.

Sound Instructional Programs

Severely and multiply handicapped children frequently differ from those with milder handicaps in a number of important instructional dimensions. Such factors as imitation, generalization, and retention must therefore be carefully considered in the design of instructional materials, as well as in the planning of lesson sequences and in the selection of learning activities. The current dearth of commercially produced materials or programs places a premium on competencies that will allow individual teachers to task analyze instructional objectives and develop homemade materials with which to accomplish them.

The following important principles underlie the development of sound educational programs:

1. Severely and multiply handicapped children need intensive training to develop *sensorimotor skills*. A variety of methods have been used in this area. Such supportive personnel as physical and occupational therapists play a significant role in implementing sensorimotor training programs.
2. Although *self-care skills* are learned by most children during early childhood, severely and multiply handicapped individuals must be given these skills through systematic instruction and training. In

some cases the time and effort required to accomplish these self-care objectives is extensive. Attempts are being made, however, to develop procedures that can be used to teach skills to groups of severely handicapped children. In any case, every effort must be made to provide these children with the skills necessary for a more independent existence.

3. If the severely and multiply handicapped are now to be served by public school systems, the development of their *functional language skills* must be given great emphasis. This is true for several reasons. First, any approximation of normalization is largely dependent on the presence of language. Second, the development of this ability will facilitate the attainment of many other educational objectives. Finally, if and when verbal control replaces overt physical prompting by teachers or attendants, staff time can be more efficiently used to encourage higher levels of functioning.

4. Severely and multiply handicapped children and adults often engage in behavior that is annoying, disturbing, and even frightening to other persons. There are an abundance of descriptions of *maladaptive behaviors* exhibited in the seclusion of institutional settings, ranging from masturbation and smearing of feces to a variety of aggressive and possibly self-destructive behaviors.

Although current evidence of the effect of the various intervention attempts used to reduce such maladaptive behaviors is inconclusive, a number of behavior modification programs have had very good results. It is imperative that such programs be utilized.

In line with these principles, Luckey and Addison (1974) presented a table outlining suggested areas of program emphasis (Table 3). In the past, these skill areas have not been considered to be within the domain of the public schools. Considering the serious learning, behavioral, and medical problems that characterize this population, it is clear that a wide range of administrative alternatives and instructional settings must be developed to accommodate the various needs of such children.

DEVELOPMENT OF SUPPORTIVE SERVICES

Parent Training Programs

The presence of a severely or multiply handicapped child within the family constellation usually has an alarming impact upon parents and siblings who are responsible for care and management. Conversely, catastrophic reactions of family members will have adverse effects on the child. Acceptance by the family contributes immeasurably to the normalization of a severely or multiply handicapped individual. Nevertheless, the tremendous emotional and financial burden that accompanies caring for such persons often precludes this possibility. Although many parents are willing to keep their children in the home, the lack of services and community support frequently makes this an insurmountable task. Programs must be developed to help parents better cope with their emotions, to provide the skills necessary to play a more active role in training their children, and to keep them aware of any available assistance.

Without question, parents need help in learning how to cope with the problems of their handicapped children as well as their own emotional problems generated by the handicapped children's presence.

Trained Personnel

Considering the multiple learning and behavior deficiencies that characterize the severely handicapped, it is evident that low student-to-teacher ratios are a prerequisite to success. Preservice and inservice training programs are therefore critically necessary in order to provide the personnel required. Such programs must identify the competencies needed to work with the severely handicapped and prepare teachers accordingly. At the same time, every effort must be made to utilize more effectively ancillary personnel, paraprofessionals, and volunteers to assist the teachers and allow for increased flexibility and individualization in pursuing their educational objectives.

Vocational Rehabilitation Programs

Until recently, occupational opportunities for the severely and multiply handicapped have been virtually nonexistent. As a result of the legislation and litigation, increasing numbers of severely involved adults are requesting habilitative services and a few are now being served in organized programs.

Community Programs

Since President Kennedy's challenge to Congress in 1963 regarding the deinstitutionalization of the retarded, numerous programs and approaches have been attempted. Although many of the programs have failed, a few have been successful and can serve as prototypes in the development of community services for the severely and profoundly retarded.

Research Programs

The field of special education has experienced a period of rapid transition. As the focus continues to shift to the plight of the more severely handicapped youngsters, the gaps in current knowledge and expertise become painfully obvious. To develop more adequate facilities, better methods and techniques, and more appropriate instructional materials, a

Table 3.   Suggested areas of program emphasis for profoundly retarded persons ·

Pre-school aged	School aged	Adults
Sensori-Motor Stimulation	Sensori-Motor Development	Sensori-Motor Integration
a. stimulating sight, hearing, touch, smell, and muscular response	a. identifying shapes, colors, sizes, locations, and distances	a. sorting, transferring, inserting, pulling, folding
b. enriching environment and encouraging exploration of interesting and attractive surroundings	b. identifying sound patterns, locations, tonal qualities, rhythms	b. responding to music activities, signals, warnings
	c. identifying textures, weights, shapes, sizes, temperatures	c. making personal choices and selections
	d. identifying familiar, aversive and pleasant odors	d. discriminating sizes, weights, colors, distances, locations, odors, temperatures, etc.
Physical Development	Physical Mobility and Coordination	Physical Dexterity and Recreation
a. body positioning	a. practicing ambulation	a. riding vehicles; participating in gymnastic-like activities and track and field events
b. passive exercising	b. overcoming obstacles; walking on ramps and stairs; running, skipping, jumping, balancing, climbing	b. marking with pencil; cutting with scissors; stringing beads; pasting and assembling
c. rolling, creeping and crawling	c. using playground equipment	c. swimming and water play
d. balancing head and trunk	d. participating in track and field events	d. using community parks, playgrounds, and other recreational resources
e. using hands purposefully		
f. standing practice		
g. training for mobility		
Pre-Self Care	Self-Care Development	Self-Care
a. taking nourishment from bottle and spoon; drinking from cup and finger feeding	a. self-feeding with spoon and cup; eating varied diet; behaving appropriately while dining	a. eating varied diet in family dining situation; using eating utensils; selecting foods

b. passive dressing; accommodating body to dressing; partially removing clothing
c. passive bathing; handling soap and washcloth; participating in drying
d. passive placement on toilet; toilet regulating

Language Stimulation
a. increasing attention to sounds
b. encouraging vocalization
c. responding to verbal and non-verbal requests
d. identifying objects

Interpersonal Response
a. recognizing familiar persons
b. requesting attention from others
c. occupying self for brief periods
d. manipulating toys or other objects

b. removing garments; dressing and undressing with supervision; buttoning, zipping, and snapping
c. drying hands and face; partially bathing
d. toilet scheduling; indicating need to eliminate; using toilet with supervision

Language Development
a. recognizing name, names of familiar objects, and body parts
b. responding to simple commands
c. imitating speech and gestures
d. using gestures, words or phrases

Social Behavior
a. requesting personal attention
b. playing individually alongside other residents
c. using basic self-protective skills
d. playing cooperatively with other residents

b. dressing with partial assistance or supervision
c. bathing with partial assistance or supervision
d. using toilet independently with occasional supervision

Language and Speech Development
a. listening to speaker
b. using gestures, words, or phrases
c. following uncomplicated directions

Self-Direction and Work
a. using protective skills
b. sharing, taking turns; waiting for instructions
c. traveling with supervision
d. completing assigned tasks
e. participating in work activity center program

Reprinted by permission from: Luckey, R. E., and Addison, M. R. The profoundly retarded: A new challenge for public education. *Education and Training of the Mentally Retarded*, 1974, *9*, 125.

comprehensive research and development program must be initiated. With an emphasis on empirical validity, researchers can objectively identify those procedures that optimize the chances for severely retarded children to learn and develop.

Accountability

The financial commitment required to implement the various educational, occupational, and social programs needed by the severely and multiply handicapped is extensive. To promote its continuance, those responsible for the education and care of these individuals must conduct their programs in a manner that is clearly accountable to the public. Meaningful objectives must be specified for each handicapped individual, and desired changes in behavior must be demonstrated.

These trends and problems in program development reflect the dimensions of the task that now faces not only special educators but also the numerous other professionals who necessarily will be concerned with the challenge of normalization for the severely and multiply handicapped. Although there is a very long way to go, the traditional fatalistic attitude toward this handicapped population is now being replaced by frequent reports of success and a growing optimism. It is now clear that the severely and multiply handicapped can, with the assistance of an increasingly sophisticated educational technology, function at levels far above those commonly expected of them today.

Cooperation Among Professions and Services

The various professions and organizations concerned with the well-being of the severely handicapped must join together in planning an effective community-wide program for them. Because the majority of these individuals will remain totally dependent throughout their lifetimes, services and programs must be made available to them in all phases of their development. To ensure the effectiveness of these efforts, open communication between professionals in education, rehabilitation, occupational therapy, physical therapy, speech pathology and audiology, recreation, and health care must prevail.

CONCLUSION

Despite the optimism and the promise of future successes, in all likelihood many severely and multiply handicapped individuals will remain at least partially dependent on society. Although this might discourage some people, the endeavor itself may be one of our most important. A society's effort to help and care for those who can contribute very little in return pays dividends that far outweigh the required financial investment. Undertaking programs of the scope discussed throughout this book exemplifies a belief in the equality of opportunity for every human being. The cost required to actually enact this principle seems a small price to pay if it will help avoid the mistakes of past societies in which it has been disregarded. In the preceding section was summarized Blatt's (1966) dramatic documentation of the horrors of the institutional setting in his pictorial presentation, *Christmas in Purgatory*. In his introduction to this poignant collection of photographs, Blatt stated that:

> Our "Christmas in Purgatory" brought us to the depths of despair. We now have a deep sorrow, one that will not abate until the American people are aware of — and do something about — the treatment of the severely mentally retarded in our state institutions. (Blatt & Kaplan, 1966, p. 6)

Indeed, this exposé and other events have forced society as a whole, and special educators in particular, out of the complacency that permitted such conditions to exist.

Fortunately, Blatt's concluding prophecy has come to pass:

> It is our belief that now that our most undefensible practices have been laid bare for public scrutiny, men of good will from all walks of life and all professions will sit down at the planning table and seek solutions to the plight of our brethren. (Blatt & Kaplan, 1966, p. 121)

The proof is in the content of this book.

REFERENCES

American National Standards Institute. *American national standard specifications for audiometers* (ANSI-S3,6-1969). American National Standards Institute, New York.

American Psychiatric Association. *Diagnostic and statistical manual of mental disorders* (2nd ed.). Washington, D.C.: American Psychiatric Association, 1968.

American Psychiatric Association. *Diagnostic and statistical manual of mental disorders* (3rd ed.). Washington, D.C.: American Psychiatric Association, 1980.

Anderson, J. Warehousing the retarded. *Herald Statesman,* Yonkers, N.Y., June 6, 1978.

Baker, D. B. Severely handicapped: Toward an inclusive definition. *AAESPH Review*, 1979, *4*(1), 52–65.

Baroff, G. S. *Mental retardation: Nature, cause, and management.* Washington, D.C.: Hemisphere Publishing, 1974.

Barr, M. W. President's annual address. *Journal of Psycho-Asthenics*, 1897, *2*, 1–13.

Barr, M. W. The imperative call of our present to our future. *Journal of Psycho-Asthenics*, 1902, *7*, 5–14.

Baumeister, A. A., & Butterfield, E. C. (Eds.). *Residential facilities for the mentally retarded.* Chicago: Aldine Publishing, 1970.

Begab, M. J. Preface In J. Grossman (Ed.). *Manual on terminology and classification in mental retardation.* Washington, D.C.: American Association on Mental Deficiency, 1973.

Blatt, B., & Kaplan, F. *Christmas in purgatory: A photographic essay on mental retardation.* Boston: Allyn & Bacon, 1966.

Brockett, D. Court decree finally dooms Forest Haven. *Washington Star,* Washington, D.C., June 15, 1978.

Bullard, W. N. State care of high-grade imbecile girls. *Proceedings, national conference on charities and correction,* 1910.

Burton, T. A., & Hirshoren, A. The education of severely and profoundly retarded children: Are we sacrificing the child to the concept? *Exceptional Children,* 1979a, *45*(8), 598–602.

Burton, T. A., & Hirshoren, A. Some further thoughts and clarifications on the education of severely and profoundly retarded children. *Exceptional Children,* 1979b, *45*(8), 618–625.

Clarke, B., & Leslie, P. Environmental alternatives for the hearing handicapped. In J. W. Schifani, R. M. Anderson, & S. J. Odle (Eds.), *Implementing learning in the least restrictive environment.* Baltimore: University Park Press, 1980.

Cruickshank, W. M. The problem and its scope. In W. M. Cruickshank (Ed.), *Cerebral palsy: A developmental disability* (3rd rev. ed.). Syracuse, N.Y.: Syracuse University Press, 1976.

Davis, H., & Silverman, S. R. *Hearing and deafness.* New York: Holt, Rinehart & Winston, 1978.

Davis, M. D. Foreword In E. Deno (Ed.), *Instructional alternatives for exceptional children.* Arlington, Va.: The Council for Exceptional Children, 1973.

Denhoff, E. Medical aspects. In W. M. Cruickshank (Ed.), *Cerebral palsy: A developmental disability* (3rd rev. ed.). Syracuse, N.Y.: Syracuse University Press, 1976.

Dunn, L. M. *Exceptional children in the schools: Special education in transition.* New York: Holt, Rinehart & Winston, 1973.

Evans v. Washington (Forest Haven), D.D.C., June 14, 1978 (459 F. Supp. 483).

Fernald, W. E. What is practical in the way of prevention of mental defect? *Proceedings, national conference on charities and correction,* 1915.

Fernald, W. E. State programs for the care of the mentally defective. *Journal of Psycho-Asthenics,* 1919, *24*, 114–125.

Frisina, R. Summary of Report of the ad hoc committee to define deaf and hard of hearing for educational purposes. *American Annals of the Deaf,* 1975, *120*, 509–512.

Gallagher, J. Media reviews. *Exceptional Children,* 1973, *40*, 217–219.

Gearheart, B. R., & Litton, F. W. *The trainable mentally retarded: A foundations approach.* St. Louis: C. V. Mosby, 1975.

Gettings, R. M. Community standards developed in Maine. *New Directions,* 1978, *8*(7), 1.

Gold, M. W. *Marc Gold: "Did I say that?"* Champaign, Ill.: Research Press, 1980.

Grossman, H. J. (Ed.). *Manual on terminology and classification in mental retardation.* Washington, D.C.: American Association on Mental Deficiency, 1973.

Gunzburg, H. G. Editorial. *Journal of Mental Subnormality,* 1970, *16*, 55–56.

Harrison, P. L. *Handbook of psychological terms.* Totowa, N.J.: Littlefield, Adams & Co., 1965.

Hatfield, E. Blindness in infants and young children. *Sight-Saving Review,* 1972, *42*(2), 69–89.

Hatfield, E. Why are they blind? *Sight-Saving Review,* 1975, *45*(1), 3–22.

Hewett, F. M. *Education of exceptional learners.* Boston: Allyn & Bacon, 1974.

Hewett, F. M., & Forness, S. R. *Education of exceptional learners* (2nd ed.). Boston: Allyn & Bacon, 1977.

Johnson, A. Discussion on care of feebleminded and epileptic. *Proceedings, national conference on charities and correction*, 1901, 410–411.

Jones, J. *Blind children, degree of vision, mode of reading* (Bull. 24). Washington, D.C.: U.S. Office of Education, 1961.

Kanner, L. Emotionally disturbed children: A historical review. *Child Development*, 1962, *33*, 92–102.

Kelly, L. J., & Vergason, G. A. *Dictionary of special education and rehabilitation*. Denver: Love Publishing, 1978.

Kirk, S. A. *Educating exceptional children* (2nd ed.). Boston: Houghton Mifflin, 1972.

Kirk, S. A., & Gallagher, J. J. *Educating exceptional children* (3rd ed.). Boston: Houghton Mifflin, 1979.

Lilly, K. Deinstitutionalization: Right to treatment litigation. *Amicus*, 1980, *5*, 90–97.

Lippman, L., & Goldberg, I. *Right to education: Anatomy of Pennsylvania case and its implications for exceptional children*. New York: Columbia University Teacher's College Press, 1973.

Luckey, R., & Addison, M. R. The profoundly retarded: A new challenge for public education. *Education and Training of the Mentally Retarded*, 1974, *9*, 123–130.

Maron, S. S., & Martinez, D. H. Environmental alternatives for the visually handicapped. In J. W. Schifani, R. M. Anderson, & S. J. Odle (Eds.), *Implementing learning in the least restrictive environment*. Baltimore: University Park Press, 1980.

Mills v. Board of Education of the District of Columbia, 348 F. Supp. 866 (D.D.C., 1972).

National Society for Autistic Children. Working definition of the syndrome of autism. Mimeograph, 1977.

National Society for the Prevention of Blindness. *NSPB fact book: Estimated statistics on blindness and visual problems*. New York: National Society for the Prevention of Blindness, 1966.

Nirje, B. A Scandinavian visitor looks at U.S. institutions. In R. B. Kugel & W. Wolfensberger (Eds.), *Changing patterns in residential services for the mentally retarded*. Washington, D.C.: President's Committee on Mental Retardation, 1969a.

Nirje, B. The normalization principle and its human management implications. In R. B. Kugel & W. Wolfensberger (Eds.), *Changing patterns in residential services for the mentally retarded*. Washington, D.C.: President's Committee on Mental Retardation, 1969b.

Nirje, B. The normalization principle: Implications and comments. *Journal of Mental Subnormality*, 1970, *16*, 62–70.

Nolan, C. Blind children: Degree of vision, mode of reading: A 1963 replication. *New Outlook for the Blind*, 1965, *59*, 233–238.

Robinson, N. M., & Robinson, H. B. *The mentally retarded child: A psychological approach*. New York: McGraw-Hill, 1965.

Robinson, N. M., & Robinson, H. B. *The mentally retarded child: A psychological approach* (2nd ed.). New York: McGraw-Hill, 1976.

Sontag, E., Burke, P. J., & York, R. Considerations for serving the severely handicapped in the public schools. *Education and Training of the Mentally Retarded*, 1973, *8*, 20–26.

Sontag, E., Certo, N., & Button, J. E. On a distinction between the education of the severely and profoundly handicapped and a doctrine of limitations. *Exceptional Children*, 1979, *45*(8), 604–616.

Wolf, J., & Anderson, R. *The multiply handicapped child.* Springfield, Ill.: Charles C Thomas, 1969.

Wolfensberger, W. The origin and nature of our institutional models. In R. B. Kugel & W. Wolfensberger (Eds.), *Changing patterns in residential services for the mentally retarded.* Washington, D.C.: President's Committee on Mental Retardation, 1969.

Wolfensberger, W. *The principle of normalization in human services.* Toronto: National Institute on Mental Retardation, 1972.

Wolfensberger, W. The origin and nature of our institutional models. In R. B. Kugel & A. Shearer (Eds.), *Changing patterns in residential services for the mentally retarded* (rev. ed.). Washington, D.C.: President's Committee on Mental Retardation, 1976.

Zubin, J. Classification of behavior disorders. In P. R. Farnsworth (Ed.), *Annual review of psychology*, 1967, *18*, 373–406.

Chapter 2

Basic
Educational Practices

Virginia K. Laycock

Until recently, severely and multiply handicapped children were basically thought to be uneducable. In line with this belief, they were provided with only custodial care. As educators now begin to recognize the rights, needs, and actual potential of this population, there is an urgent demand for appropriate instructional technology.

It is doubtful that what will emerge from this search will be different in essence from the models and approaches that have evolved for teaching the mildly and moderately handicapped. What may prove critically different is the precision with which these teaching techniques must be applied because the handicaps involved are more severe and pervasive.

Whereas normal children acquire many skills through their independent experiences in nonstructured settings, the handicapped are often notoriously poor incidental learners. Most skills have to be taught through formal instruction. Furthermore, considering the degree of developmental delay and the accompanying learning difficulties, there is simply no place for instruction that is inadequately conceived or presented. The severely handicapped have such limited cognitive flexibility that only the most carefully directed programs are likely to be effective. To work with these children, teachers need to develop highly sophisticated skills for program design and implementation.

Descriptors chosen to characterize various teaching models currently advocated for the handicapped convey the emphasis on more high-powered instructional technology. Systematic (McCormack et al., 1976;

Snell, 1978), directive (Haring & Schiefelbusch, 1976; Stephens, 1977), programmed (Tawney et al., 1979), clinical (Smith, 1974; Lerner, 1976), prescriptive (Peter, 1965; Moran, 1975; Charles, 1976; Mercer, 1979), and precision (Bijou, Lindsley, & Haughton, 1972) teaching are all titles of special education models with basically similar goals and philosophies.

All these approaches are student centered. A thorough assessment of learner attributes serves as the basis for the selection of instructional objectives, strategies, and materials. Teaching activities are always goal directed, chosen specifically to advance the learner through a sequence of behavioral skills toward a designated target. Continuous measurement of student performance is an integral part of each model, providing the primary means of evaluating program effectiveness.

Although these models represent very structured organizational systems, they are sufficiently flexible to be appropriate for programming in all three domains of learning—the cognitive, affective, and psychomotor. They are not bound to any one particular method of teaching but can accommodate a variety of instructional strategies and materials. Such characteristics make these models not only effective, but also highly practical in application.

A final important asset of the systematic teaching models is that they are clearly consistent with current regulations of the Education of All Handicapped Children Act of 1975 (P.L. 94-142). Federal guidelines specify that an individualized education program (IEP) be developed for each handicapped student prior to the provision of any special services. Although no reference is made to any particular teaching model, the required components of the IEP necessitate an approach that is student centered, goal directed, and accountable. As set forth in P.L. 94-142, the written IEP must contain:

a) A statement of the child's present levels of educational performance, including academic achievement, social adaptation, prevocational and vocational skills, psychomotor skills, and self-help skills.
b) A statement of annual goals that describes the educational performance to be achieved by the end of the school year under the child's IEP.
c) A statement of short-term instructional objectives, which must be measurable intermediate steps between the present level of educational performance and the annual goals.
d) A statement of specific educational services needed by the child (determined without regard to the availability of those services) including a description of:
    (1) all special education and related services needed to meet the unique needs of the child, including the type of physical education program in which the child will participate, and
    (2) any special instructional media and materials needed.

e) The date when those services will begin and length of time the services will be given.
f) A description of the extent to which the child will participate in the regular educational programs.
g) A justification for the type of educational placement the child will have.
h) A list of the individuals responsible for implementation of the IEP.
i) Objective criteria, evaluation procedures, and schedules for determining, on at least an annual basis, whether the short-term instructional objectives are being achieved (Section 121a, 225).

Educators who are not accustomed to using a systematic approach to instructional programming are likely to find it difficult to comply fully with IEP regulations. Within the framework of a comprehensive model, however, IEP development is far more than simply a mandated requirement. It is an essential step toward delivering appropriate educational experiences to each handicapped student.

Although the various teaching models identified have many benefits in common, they differ in other respects of orientation and implementation. The remainder of this chapter focuses, therefore, on one particular model for diagnostic prescriptive teaching readily applicable to the severely and multiply disabled.

THE DIAGNOSTIC PRESCRIPTIVE APPROACH

Figure 1 presents a model for individualized educational programming that incorporates all the critical features discussed above. There are seven basic steps that comprise each programming cycle. The first four tasks in each cycle involve planning and decision making. The student's needs are carefully identified (step 1) to permit the selection of appropriate objectives, strategies, and materials (steps 2, 3 and 4). In step 5, the program is implemented as planned. The remaining steps in each cycle call for evaluation of program effectiveness (step 6) and revision of the program as necessary (step 7).

As the diagram illustrates, the same basic sequence of tasks is repeated on different levels. The large oval at the top represents the long-range planning cycle corresponding to the development and implementation of the annual IEP. According to regulations of P.L. 94-142, the complete IEP committee is to be involved in decision making at this level. Because the program addresses major educational concerns, for an entire year in most cases, elements of the program are somewhat more broad based and general in scope. The annual program sets forth an educational blueprint, or master plan, giving direction to the more specific instructional programming that must then take place.

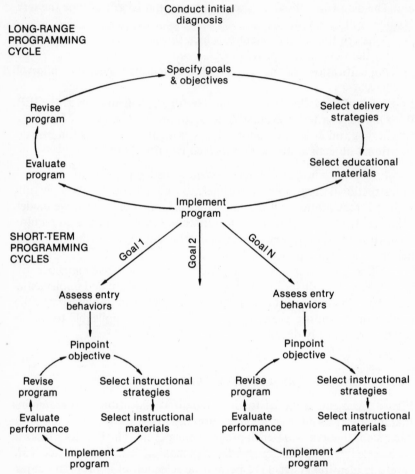

Figure 1.   The diagnostic prescriptive teaching model showing both long-range and short-term programming cycles.

The second tier of the diagram shows a series of short-term programming cycles occurring during the implementation phase of the IEP. As illustrated, each long-range, more general educational goal is approached through its own carefully designed instructional program. The same sequence of seven tasks is replicated to accomplish a more specific purpose within a shorter time frame. These minicycles are roughly analogous to the familiar notion of instructional units. Each is tightly organized to advance the student through a sequence of objectives toward the attainment of the target goal. Collectively, these short-term programs constitute the heart of the instructional experience and determine the ultimate effectiveness of the entire educational program.

The number of goals and hence the number of short-term instructional cycles will vary with the perceived complexity of student needs. In all cases, the short-term programs should flow logically from the long-term plan to function as an integrated, cohesive system. Each step of the long- and short-term programming sequence is described below in greater detail.

CONDUCTING THE INITIAL DIAGNOSIS

Diagnosis or evaluation is necessarily the first step in educational programming. An individualized approach depends on thorough, accurate, and up-to-date information on student performance. The results of meaningful evaluation enable the IEP committee to develop a program suited to the learner's unique needs.

Diagnosis is never an easy process. The degree and complexity of handicaps within the severe and multiply handicapped population make it even more difficult. A team approach is essential because no one professional has sufficient expertise in all areas involved. The terms *multidisciplinary* and *interdisciplinary* have been used to describe the composition and functioning of these evaluative teams. A typical team might include several or all of the following: physician, nurse, psychologist, speech therapist, audiologist, physical therapist, occupational therapist, social worker, teacher. Each member of the team assumes responsibility for evaluating certain aspects of a child's development. Each specialist also interprets his or her results to the group and contributes professional recommendations.

The effectiveness of a team evaluation depends greatly upon the ability of the group to integrate diverse bits of information in a form directly relevant to educational programming. The danger of fragmentation exists whenever a single child is viewed from many different perspectives. To offset this, a new version of the team approach has recently been suggested, the *transdisciplinary model* (Hart, 1977). Although the composition of the team may not differ from the multidisciplinary and interdisciplinary approaches, the responsibilities of team members are more encompassing. Specialists continue to be involved beyond the initial planning and decision making. In most instances, only one of the team members is actually charged with implementing the program, but all others participate in a supportive capacity. Specialized information and techniques are shared, so that the entire team remains accountable for the child's program.

Interdisciplinary Evaluation

The information to be gathered during the diagnostic phase will vary depending on each individual child's problems. The purpose and orientation of evaluations conducted by the specialists most frequently serving the severe and profound are now briefly described as follows.

Role of the Physician   The basic medical examination usually includes a complete physical along with tests of visual and auditory acuity. If further, more extensive diagnostic measures seem indicated, the child may be referred to an appropriate specialist in, for example, in pediatric neurology, cardiology, orthopedics, or ophthalmology. Current data is interpreted in light of the child's medical and developmental histories. Particular attention is directed toward health conditions having implications for educational performance.

Physicians should carefully explain any restrictions pertaining to diet or participation in certain activities. If the student experiences seizures, teachers need to know what to expect and how to react appropriately. Whenever medication is prescribed, special instructions should be provided regarding dosage, administration, and monitoring. The physician may request that the teacher collect specific types of data on student behavior having particular medical significance. This data is often invaluable in making reliable diagnoses and in judging the effectiveness of prescribed interventions.

Role of the Physical or Occupational Therapist   One or both of these specialists may evaluate a student's motor functioning. Present gross and fine motor skills are assessed with particular emphasis on the child's posture, mobility, and manual dexterity in daily living tasks. The occupational therapist typically determines proper positioning, physical limitations, and current levels of self-help and vocational development. The student's unique difficulties are appraised so that appropriate adaptive devices may be provided as necessary.

Role of the Audiologist   The audiological examination attempts to measure the extent of a child's auditory sensitivity. Tones of varying intensity and frequency are presented to determine responsiveness to environmental sounds and potential for development of speech and language. Special physiological measures may be used if the child is uncooperative or unable to comprehend directions. When there is evidence of a hearing loss, the audiologist assesses possible benefit of amplification.

Role of the Communication Disorders Specialist   This individual evaluates the student's receptive and expressive language abilities. The clinician may test the child's skills in discriminating and producing specific sounds, and in comprehending and using vocabulary and sentence structures. With nonverbal children, the evaluation may focus on the ability to use gestures, manual signs, or both effectively.

Role of the Psychologist   The psychologist's evaluation typically involves the formal measurement of functional levels. This task is particularly difficult with severely and multiply handicapped youngsters, because of their limited receptive and expressive capabilities and the probable presence of many interfering behaviors. Furthermore, it is generally recognized that few standardized instruments are appropriate for use with this population (Dubose, Langley, & Stagg, 1977; Sailor & Horner, 1976). In an attempt to adequately tap the abilities of a particular child, the psychologist often selects several different measures. In presenting the results of the testing battery, the psychologist should explain the nature of the items and testing limitations, as well as the normative scores obtained. This information should be interpreted in terms of the child's abilities and needs, with specific attention to the implications for instructional programming.

Role of the Social Worker   The social worker often serves as the liaison between the child's family, the school, and other agencies. By interviewing parents and observing family interactions, the social worker is able to assess the family's adjustment to the child's handicap. Significant incidents in the student's developmental and educational backgrounds are reported. Information is also provided on parenting practices, sibling relations, and other conditions of home life that might either support or interfere with the student's progress.

Role of the Educator   The educational portion of the interdisciplinary assessment is likely to be the most extensive. Information is gathered through both formal and informal means in order to describe student characteristics in terms of levels of performance, specific strengths and weaknesses, and learning style.

In attempting to pinpoint a student's critical needs, educators typically begin by determining how far the child has progressed through normal developmental sequences. The terms *developmental level, performance level*, and *functional level* are often used interchangeably to refer to an individual's current standing in an ongoing progression of skills. The major developmental areas of concern with the severely and multiply handicapped include gross and fine motor, communication, self-help, and socialization skills. With older students, preacademic and vocational development may also be assessed. Levels of performance in these areas are generally reported in terms of age equivalents. Thus, a student who earns an age equivalent of 2-4 on a certain assessment device demonstrates skills comparable to children in the normative sample who were 2 years, 4 months of age.

With higher functioning students, formal standardized tests are the primary tools for gathering norm-referenced data; however, developmental checklists and rating scales are generally preferred for use with the severely and multiply handicapped. Rather than having the examiner attempt to elicit a desired behavior under controlled testing conditions, checklists and rating scales credit the student for behaviors performed in natural settings over the recent past. Parents, teachers, and other significant adults serve as major sources of information when these devices are used. The evaluator may also observe the child and interact with him or her to sample particular skills in question.

Developmental checklists are usually completed by simply indicating whether the student demonstrates each skill in a given sequence. An age equivalent is calculated based on the number of skills currently mastered. With rating scales, respondents must specify either the degree of proficiency or the frequency with which a certain behavior is performed. Ratings are then converted into normative results.

Table 1 presents a listing of selected checklists and rating scales for use with the severely and multiply handicapped. Specific developmental areas assessed and the publishing source are identified for each entry. All of the devices cited in this table survey several different aspects of functioning. More specialized instruments for assessing skills within specific developmental areas are discussed in subsequent chapters.

Teachers should select instrument(s) most appropriate for a given child and the assessment situation based on the following considerations:

1. It should adequately address specific skill areas of concern
2. It should be suited to the student's age and handicapping condition
3. It should have acceptable reliability and validity
4. It should be relatively easy to administer, score, and interpret

Determination of performance levels in major areas of development is but one important use of the assessment devices under consideration. Of even greater significance for educational programming is the precise identification of the student's strengths and weaknesses. It is essential to pinpoint exactly which skills have already been mastered and which have not yet been attained. Most of the instruments cited in Table 1 yield this criterion-referenced information in addition to norm-referenced scores. It is this knowledge of specific skills that can be translated directly into appropriate goals and objectives for the student's educational program.

Another major focus of the educational assessment involves an analysis of the student's characteristic approach to testing and learning situations. This aspect of performance is generally referred to as *learning style*. An alert evaluator is gathering information about learning style throughout the sessions devoted to determination of performance levels and specific skills by carefully attending to the student's methods of handling different tasks. Additional questions about learning style can be answered by interacting further on a one-to-one basis.

Dubose et al. (1977) stressed the assessment of five different parameters of learning style relevant to the severely and multiply handicapped — rapport, comprehension, response patterns, skill acquisition, and learning efficiency.

Table 1. Selected educational assessment devices for use with the severely and multiply handicapped

Assessment device	Source	Areas assessed
AAMD Adaptive Behavior Scale	American Association on Mental Deficiency 5201 Connecticut Ave., NW Washington, D.C. 20015	Developmental independence—independent functioning, physical development, economic activity, language development, numbers and time, domestic activity, vocational activity, self-direction, responsibility, socialization; and maladaptive behavior—violent and destructive behavior, antisocial behavior, rebellious behavior, untrustworthy behavior, withdrawal, stereotyped behavior, inappropriate mannerisms, unacceptable vocal habits, eccentric habits, self-abusive behavior, hyperactive tendencies, sexually aberrant behavior, psychological disturbance, and use of medications
Assessing Perceptual Motor Functioning: Checklist	Alleghany Intermediate Unit No. 3 Suite 1300, Two Alleghany Center Pittsburgh, PA 15212	Body image—body parts, directionality, dominance; gross motor experiences (movement, integration, proficiency); and specific coordination skills—eye, oral, hand, and finger coordination
Basic Skills Screening Test	Mid-Nebraska Mental Retardation Services, Region III 518 Eastside Blvd. Hastings, NE 68901	Sensorimotor functioning, visual processing, auditory processing, language, symbolic operations, social-emotional development, and work skills
Balthazar Scales of Adaptive Behavior	Consulting Psychologists Press, Inc. 577 College Ave. Palo Alto, CA 94302	Functional independence—eating, dressing, undressing, toileting; social adaptation—unadaptive interpersonal behaviors, adaptive self-directed behaviors, adaptive interpersonal

continued

Table 1. *(continued)*

Assessment device	Source	Areas assessed
		behaviors, verbal communication, play activities, response to instructions, and personal care
Callier-Azusa Scale	Callier Center for Communication Disorders 1966 Inwood Rd. Dallas, TX 75235	Motor development, perceptual abilities, daily living skills, language development, and socialization
Camelot Behavioral Checklist	Camelot Behavioral Systems P.O. Box 607 Parsons, KS 67357	Self-help, physical development, vocational development, home duties, economic behavior, independent travel, numerical skills, communication skills, social behavior, and responsibility
Developmental Pinpoints	Cohen, M. A., Gross, P. J., & Haring, N. G., Developmental pinpoints. In N. G. Haring and L. J. Brown (Eds.), *Teaching the severely handicapped*, Vol. 1. New York: Grune & Stratton, 1976.	Fine motor, gross motor, receptive language, expressive language, self-help, social interaction, leisure time activities, prereading, prewriting, premath, and reinforcement activities
Down's Syndrome Assessment Inventory Forms	Experimental Education Unit Child Development and Mental Retardation Center University of Washington Seattle, WA 98195	Six assessment forms for different levels — infant, early preschool, intermediate preschool, advanced preschool, kindergarten, Primary A. Each examines 5 to 10 relevant skills such as gross motor, fine motor, language, self-help, play, self-image, and preacademics.

Learning Accomplishment Profile (LAP)	Chapel Hill Training Outreach Project University of North Carolina Chapel Hill, NC 27514	Gross motor, fine motor, social, self-help, cognitive, and language
Pennsylvania Training Model Individual Assessment Guide	Pennsylvania Training Model 123 Foster St. Harrisburg, PA 17102	Sensory development, gross motor, fine motor, self-help, communication, perceptual-cognitive, and social interaction
Portage Project Checklist	Cooperative Educational Service Agency No. 12 Portage, WI 53901	Cognitive, self-help, motor, language, and socialization
Programmatic Guide to Assessing Severely/Profoundly Handicapped Children	Experimental Education Unit Child Development and Mental Retardation Center University of Washington Seattle, WA 98195	Self-help, communication, gross motor, fine motor, sensory discrimination, and pre-academics
Programmed Environments Curriculum: Class Observation Record Form	Tawney, J. W., Knapp, D. S., O'Reilly, C. D., Pratt, S. C. *Programmed environments curriculum.* Columbus: Oh.: Charles E. Merrill, 1979.	Receptive language, expressive language, cognitive, fine motor, gross motor, eating, dressing, and grooming skills
Project Memphis Developmental Scale for Severely and Profoundly Handicapped	Fearon-Pitman Publishers, Inc. 6 Davis Drive Belmont, CA 94002	Personal-social skills, gross and fine motor skills, language and perceptual-cognitive development.
Special Education Objective Checklist Developmental Program	Pupil Personnel Services Tacoma Public Schools Tacoma, WA 98401	Self-help, social, language development, academic, motor, and leisure time skills

continued

Table 1. *(continued)*

Assessment device	Source	Areas assessed
Student Progress Record	MR/DD Program Office Mental Health Division 2575 Bittern St., NE Salem, OR 97310	Social, receptive language, expressive language, reading, writing, number concepts, money, time, eating, dressing, personal hygiene, motor skills, and physical fitness
TARC Assessment Inventory	H&H Enterprises, Inc. Box 3342 Lawrence, KS 66044	Self-help, motor, communication, and social skills
TMR Performance Profile for Severely and Moderately Retarded	Educational Performance Associates 563 Westview Ave. Ridgefield, NJ 07657	Social behavior, self-care, communication, basic knowledge, practical skills, and body usage
Uniform Performance Assessment System (UPAS)	Experimental Education Unit Child Development and Mental Retardation Center University of Washington Seattle, WA 98195	Gross motor, preacademic, communication, and social/self-help skills

The author wishes to acknowledge the contribution of Dr. Bonnie Greer, Associate Professor, Memphis State University, in compiling this list of assessment devices.

Assessment of rapport is an investigation of the child's ability to form a working relationship with an adult in a structured setting. The evaluator attempts to find out how quickly the student adapts to demands of a new situation. By experimenting with different contingencies and reinforcers, the examiner can identify behavior management techniques to which the learner responds most favorably.

The child's ability to comprehend expectations is evaluated by altering task demands and noting effects on performance. It is then possible to identify the types of presentations and cues that lead to more successful learning.

The child's characteristic response patterns can be detected through careful observation of performance and analysis of errors. Many severely and multiply disabled youngsters have developed maladaptive habits for coping with difficult demands. Some will use task materials to self-stimulate; others echo instructions; and still others perseverate on a particular response set. These are but a few examples of behavior patterns commonly encountered. Student performance may also reveal the use of productive strategies, such as imitation or trial-and-error. By studying both successes and failures, the evaluator can often uncover the student's preferred style of processing information.

Assessment of skill acquisition requires another type of error analysis. When a child fails a task, the evaluator may back up to slightly easier versions of the skill in an effort to pinpoint just how far the child's concepts have developed. Through successive adaptations of tasks, the evaluator can locate the learner's level in any given hierarchy of skills.

To assess learning efficiency, a test-teach-test paradigm is often employed. By teaching the child a brand-new skill, the evaluator can observe the number of trials necessary for acquisition. He or she can also assess the learner's ability to retain and to generalize from one situation to another.

The inclusion of these parameters of learning style in the assessment process, as recommended by Dubose et al. (1977), provides information critical for judging an individual's educational needs. After the educational evaluator shares the findings concerning the student's present performance levels, specific strengths and weaknesses, and learning style, the team is in a position to decide appropriate goals, strategies, and resources.

SPECIFYING EDUCATIONAL GOALS AND OBJECTIVES

The selection of individualized goals for a particular pupil must always be guided by consideration of the ultimate goal for education of the severely handicapped — to maximize independence in personal, social, and occupational functioning within the least restrictive environment possible. All instructional targets should be justifiable in these terms. Given the magnitude of developmental delay and the very slow rate of learning acquisition by the severely handicapped, there is no time to waste in teaching skills not essential for more independent living.

Setting priorities can be a difficult task when a student's needs are so extensive. For this reason, no one individual but the entire IEP committee is charged with responsibility for decision making. Several important factors ought to be taken into account in the attempt to select long-range goals that are both meaningful and realistic for the student.

Nature and Severity of the Learner's Needs   The results of the interdisciplinary evaluation should clearly indicate performance levels in self-help, communication, motor, socialization, vocational, and preacademic areas. By examining the student's unique pattern of development, the committee should be able to determine in which areas his or her needs are more pronounced.

Age of the Learner   Although more attention is generally directed toward developmental ages, chronological age must also be considered in program planning. The committee must not overlook certain age-appropriate concerns. For the 5-year-old just entering school, separation anxiety may be a concern. For the adolescent, sex education may be in order. Different ages present their own problems. Another critical determinant is the number of years of formal education remaining. As students approach adulthood, their classroom time is running out, and goals must be chosen with even greater care.

Critical Needs in the Present Environment   It is important for parents and teachers on the assessment team to clarify expectations for the student in his or her current situation. Many times, parents can identify skills for the student that would greatly improve the family's home life. Other skills, such as riding the school bus or carrying a lunch tray, may be deemed necessary in the child's educational setting.

Critical Needs in the Next Least Restrictive Environment   Not only should demands of the present environment be considered, but also behavioral expectations for future placements. The student who is residing in an institution, for example, should be gaining skills that will eventually enable him or her to function in a community setting. The educational program for an adolescent should focus on developing skills for living and working as independently as possible.

Logical Sequencing within Each Developmental Area   Considerations thus far have dealt with the process of narrowing down critical needs in order to specify meaningful educational priorities. The goals that are chosen must also be realistic. Unless a student demonstrates the necessary prerequisites or entry behaviors, a goal is likely to be unattainable. In order to make informed decisions, the committee must be familiar with assessment results and the logical progression of skills within each area of concern. Setting goals then becomes a matter of specifying what important skills should come next to advance a particular student through the developmental sequence.

In certain instances, skills that have seemingly little value in themselves will have to be taught as prerequisites simply to permit further instruction. Such on-task behaviors as sitting in a chair, looking at the teacher or materials, imitating, and following basic commands fall in this category. In and of themselves, they may be difficult to justify as relevant goals; they are often included in an educational program, however, because these behaviors must be mastered before other target skills can be addressed. The committee should be wary of including "general readiness skills" in a program simply because a sequence has traditionally been approached in a certain way. Only those skills that directly link the student's present performance to identified needs should be cited as goals.

Learning History   Because long-range goals typically specify what is to be accomplished in the coming school year, it is often difficult for the team to decide how much progress should be expected. In addition to noting the degree of overall developmental delay, as suggested above, it may also be helpful to consider the learner's past history. The scope of the goals undertaken during previous school years and the number of goals actually attained should provide reasonable guidelines. The IEP can always be amended at a later time should the team discover that its projections were clearly inappropriate.

The above factors are to be considered in determining the focus or content of educational goals, a highly individualized process. The mechanics of goal writing are far easier to master, because a standard format is involved. Generally, each long-range goal is written in the form of a verb phrase, specifying clearly what the student will be expected to do upon completion of the educational program. The choice of the verb itself is critical. Only verbs that denote observable, measurable actions should be used. Verbs such as *"improve"* and *"develop"* should be avoided because they indicate a process rather than an end product. Improvement and development can go on indefinitely, and it is, therefore, impossible to note when a goal has actually been met.

Examples of goals for the severely handicapped written in standard form are the following: to communicate basic needs, to dress, to use the toilet independently, and to cooperate in group activities. Goals that are written in such specific and concise terms serve effectively to direct the educational program toward desired outcomes.

Short-term objectives are also to be developed as part of each student's IEP. These may be thought of as instructional milestones closing the gap between present performance and the long-range goal. Objectives included in the IEP need not be as fine-grained and detailed as the objectives that are used in daily lesson planning. As a general rule of thumb, each long-range goal should be broken down into two to five subobjectives. In terms of the time frame covered, the short-term objectives should indicate progress expected on at least a quarterly or semester basis.

All short-term objectives must be written in complete behavioral form. Each should clearly specify the target skill, the conditions under which it is to be performed, and the criterion for mastery. An example of a long-range goal with accompanying short-term objectives is provided below. The long-range goal in this example is: to state identifying information upon request. The short term objectives are:

1. When asked "What is your name?" by five different adults in five different settings, Connie will state her first and last name correctly four out of five times.
2. When asked "Where do you live?" by five different adults in five different settings, Connie will tell her home address by giving the correct house number and street four out of five times.
3. When asked "How old are you?" by five different adults in five different settings, Connie will state her age correctly four out of five times.

Each short-term objective will later be broken down into very fine pinpoints for actual instruction to begin.

SELECTING DELIVERY STRATEGIES

After individualized goals and objectives have been set, the committee must then develop a plan of action for attaining them. In long-range programming, the selection of delivery strategies consists mainly of determining the kinds of special services necessary to assist the student in mastering each designated skill. The IEP regulations cited above require the specification of all types of services needed, the extent and duration of these services, and the individuals responsible for providing the services as indicated. Other chapters in this volume describe delivery options in home, school, community, and residential settings. It is beyond the scope of this chapter to discuss placement considerations and criteria. Several points, however, are stressed in reference to this decision making.

First, the intent of the law is clear in indicating that services chosen are to be based on the child's unique needs and not on the availability of such services. Even the order in which IEP components are listed is significant. Data on present performance is to be translated into goals and objectives, which in turn dictate the types and terms of services required.

This is far different from the traditional practice of assigning children to placements by category or label. The responsibility of the team, therefore, is to examine each goal and objective and to select the appropriate setting for training or intervention. At the same time, the committee must decide which member is best suited to assume responsibility for this aspect of the student's program.

A second critical consideration in selecting delivery strategies concerns the concept of least restrictive environment. To the greatest extent possible, handicapped students are to be educated with their nonhandicapped peers. Although it is very doubtful that the severely and multiply impaired are capable of learning in the same classroom as nonhandicapped students, special classes and related services can be provided within regular schools to permit at least some degree of interaction. Each student should be removed from the mainstream no further than is absolutely necessary to meet his or her special needs.

It is often difficult for the team to reconcile the two considerations that seem to be at odds — maximum individualization with maximum integration. Appropriate decisions can only be made by carefully weighing the options in light of defined goals. The nature, level, and scope of these IEP goals should be the major determinants of delivery strategies.

SELECTING EDUCATIONAL MATERIALS

Once the interdisciplinary team has analyzed the learner's needs and determined goals and delivery strategies for his or her educational program, appropriate curricula and materials can be located to facilitate implementation. Although instruction of the severely and multiply handicapped is a relatively new field, there are already numerous instructional systems on the market. If there is an educational program available that covers skills designated in the student's IEP in a manner consistent with his or her learning style, then such a program can be a valuable resource for the teacher. It is senseless to design curricula and materials from scratch when there may be suitable programs in existence. In addition to saving the teacher countless hours of work, the adoption of existing programs offers benefits to the learner as well. Packaged instructional systems typically represent input from more than one professional. Many hold the added advantage of having been field tested and refined before dissemination. Certainly there is much to be gained by utilizing available educational systems whenever appropriate.

The appropriateness of a particular instructional program for use with a given student is determined by the degree of correspondence of material characteristics with identified needs. The ideal available program would be one that most closely approximates specifications in a student's own IEP. A rating scale has been developed by the author to

MATCHING MATERIALS TO INSTRUCTIONAL NEEDS: A RATING SCALE

Learner: _____

Title of Instructional Material: _____

Publisher: _____

For each of the following factors, indicate to what degree material characteristics correspond to identified instructional needs by circling the appropriate number. If certain variables are not applicable, write NA in the right-hand column. Where low correspondence is observed, comment briefly on the potential for adaptation or modification in that area.

INSTRUCTIONAL SPECIFICATIONS

| | Degree of correspondence | | | |
	High	Adequate	Low	Notes
Objectives				
Scope	3	2	1	
Sequence	3	2	1	
Target population				
Chronological age	3	2	1	
Mental age	3	2	1	
Grade equivalent	3	2	1	
Other descriptors	3	2	1	
Prerequisite skills	3	2	1	
Learning modalities				
Input	3	2	1	
Output	3	2	1	
Format				
Medium	3	2	1	
Quality	3	2	1	
Safety features	3	2	1	
Pacing				
Rate	3	2	1	
Flexibility	3	2	1	
Feedback mechanisms				
Type of reinforcement	3	2	1	
Schedule	3	2	1	
Motivating factors				
Aesthetic appeal	3	2	1	
Thematic appeal	3	2	1	

Total
Number of factors rated ___
Mean rating ___

TEACHING CONCERNS

| | Degree of correspondence | | | |
	High	Adequate	Low	Notes
Teacher competencies				
Training	3	2	1	
Specialized skills	3	2	1	
Teaching environment				
Classroom organization	3	2	1	
Physical requirements	3	2	1	
Teaching aids				
Teachers' guide	3	2	1	
Supplementary resources	3	2	1	
Evaluative criteria				
Test items	3	2	1	
Scheduling	3	2	1	
Teacher time				
Preparation	3	2	1	
Supervision	3	2	1	
Evaluation	3	2		

COST EFFECTIVENESS

	High	Adequate	Low	Notes
Cost				
Total price	3	2	1	
Component prices	3	2	1	
Replacement parts	3	2	1	
Durability	3	2	1	
Number served	3	2	1	
Research data	3	2	1	
Nondiscriminatory representation	3	2	1	

Total
Number of factors rated ___
Mean rating ___

Figure 2.   A checklist for selecting appropriate materials.

guide teachers in the process of selecting suitable educational programs and materials (Laycock, 1978). A copy of this scale is provided in Figure 2. The use of such a rating scale helps teachers to focus on critical dimensions of instructional programs in order to identify those that are most likely to be effective with a given learner in the designated educational setting.

The 18 different factors to be evaluated are clustered into three areas entitled Instructional Specifications, Teaching Concerns, and Cost Effectiveness. Factors included in the first set assess the essential instructional attributes of the program. The teacher analyzes program suitability in terms of what it purports to teach, for whom it is intended, and how it attempts to accomplish its purposes. For a program to be judged as appropriate, these first eight characteristics should closely match student skill needs and learning style.

The second set of factors deals with teaching concerns, those features of a program that make it attractive to a particular teacher for use in a given instructional setting. In this case, suitability to teaching style is being assessed. The teacher considers the feasibility of actually utilizing a program as prescribed within his or her own situation.

The final set of factors to be evaluated pertains to cost effectiveness. Here the teacher weighs investment in an instructional program against the benefits likely to be derived from its use. Matters of cost, durability, and versatility are considered, along with other evidence of worthiness such as research data and avoidance of discriminatory representation.

Examination and comparison of mean scores obtained on the rating scale indicate which instructional programs might be used most effectively with the student in question. If none of the programs rated seem to be appropriate, the teacher may attempt to locate others that are more promising, or he or she may decide to adapt a program that initially fell short of expectations in certain respects. Although this selection process may seem time consuming at first, it does direct the teacher to educational resources that can greatly enhance efficiency in the long run.

IMPLEMENTING THE EDUCATIONAL PROGRAM

Although the planning steps thus far described are both thorough and time consuming, they are typically accomplished by a team within a week or two. Such systematic efforts continue to pay off throughout the longest phase of the diagnostic prescriptive cycle, program implementation. In part, implementation consists simply of carrying out the terms stipulated in the student's written IEP. That is, the designated services are to be rendered by the individuals indicated according to the agreed-upon specifications. There is far more to the implementation stage, however, that makes the IEP truly operable on a daily basis.

Because the long-range IEP deals with the learner's total program, it is necessarily broad in scope. Each specialist who has been delegated responsibility for particular goals or objectives must then develop more detailed instructional programs suited precisely to these targets. As the diagnostic prescriptive model introduced in Figure 1 suggests, several different short-term programs will be in progress at the same time. The exact number of cycles and the length of time consumed by each will vary depending on the complexity of individual student needs. The steps used in short-term instructional programming parallel those used in long-range educational programming. Each step is just more focused and fine grained when carried out for the more narrowly defined purpose of meeting one specific goal. Although any professional involved in service delivery may employ this model, discussion will deal with its particular application by the special educator.

Assessing Entry Behaviors

The initial educational diagnosis was concerned primarily with the identification of functional levels and specific skills attained in major developmental areas. This information led to the selection of appropriate individualized goals and objectives for the IEP. As the teacher is faced with actually developing the desired skills, it becomes essential to pinpoint the student's present behaviors even more precisely in order to determine exactly what must be taught. Task analysis and informal assessment are the procedures generally used for this purpose.

The process of task analysis involves breaking down a target skill into component steps that are sequenced in logical, developmental order. Thorough task analysis is essential not only for assessing a student's entry performance but also for organizing subsequent instructional presentations. The importance of adequate sequencing in teaching the handicapped cannot be overemphasized (Engelmann, 1977; Knapczyk, 1975; Williams & Gotts, 1977). Curriculum guides currently available for the severely and multiply handicapped generally reflect a strong task-analytic orientation (Anderson et al., 1975; Bender & Valletutti, 1976; McCormack et al., 1976; Somerton & Myers, 1976; McCormack & Chalmers, 1978; Tawney et al., 1979). Such resources can be of great help to the teacher for both assessment and instructional purposes. These guides can save the teacher valuable time because they cover most of the commonly needed skills. There is no sense in creating teacher-made task analyses when adequate ones have already been published.

When appropriate sequences cannot be located, the teacher must be able to adapt those available or to generate original ones. There are many different versions of task analysis that vary in complexity from simple vertical sequences to elaborate branching lattices. Teachers can perform their own basic task analyses by completing the following steps:

1. Define the target skill in precise behavioral terms
2. Specify prerequisite or readiness skills for learning the target behavior
3. Identify the steps involved in advancing a learner from the prerequisite level to performance of the target behavior
4. Sequence all steps in developmental order
5. Check for gaps in the sequence, ensuring that all steps are of comparable magnitude
6. Eliminate any nonessential steps

It should be recognized that no task analysis is ever a completed product. All are subject to continuous refinement and revision in use. Figure 3 shows a sample task analysis for the dressing skill of putting on a T-shirt that has been constructed according to the above guidelines. Notice that this one has been written with the target skill at the top and the prerequisites at the bottom. The en route behaviors indicate a smooth progression from the prerequisites to the final skill.

A task analysis lists only the behaviors that must be performed to demonstrate the desired skill. It makes no reference to the specific learner or situation. In order to utilize a task analysis for informal assessment, a teacher should proceed as follows:

1. Locate or develop an appropriate task analysis
2. Ensure that each step is described as an observable, measurable behavior
3. Specify the conditions for performance of each skill in terms of materials and mode of presentation
4. Establish criteria for mastery of each skill in terms of number correct, rate, percentage, or other standard
5. Prepare stimulus materials and scoring sheets
6. Present designated tasks to the learner
7. Record responses
8. Evaluate performance in reference to criteria (Laycock, 1980)

Target Behavior	Putting on a T-shirt without assistance
Enroute Behaviors	Pulling down tails of shirt to fit Adjusting shirt over shoulders Inserting head through neck opening Raising arms to position shirt over head Inserting other arm into other sleeve Inserting one arm into sleeve on same side of shirt Spreading shirt face down on flat surface Picking up T-shirt
Prerequisites	Taking off T-shirt without assistance Cooperating with dressing by an adult

Figure 3.   A sample task analysis for putting on a T-shirt.

In scoring during informal assessment, it is helpful not only to record customary pluses and minuses but also to note the student's actual response whenever errors are made. In this way, the teacher is able to analyze the learner's difficulties, which usually have direct implication for instruction. During assessment, no differential feedback is provided. The purpose of evaluation is not to change behavior but to describe it accurately as it presently occurs; therefore, no measures are taken to correct errors or to shape more efficient responses. The teacher has to find out just what skills the learner already possesses before meaningful instruction can begin. This type of pretesting is an indispensable part of individualized instruction because it allows the teacher to gear the program to the student's exact level of skill development.

Pinpointing Instructional Objectives

As a result of task-analytic assessment, the teacher has targeted the skill to be taught. Only conditions and criteria remain to be determined in order to formulate a complete behavioral objective. Both conditions and criteria should be selected in such a way that performance of the objective effectively represents mastery of the skill in question. These considerations become especially significant in light of the characteristic learning difficulties of the severely and multiply impaired related to generalization, proficiency, and retention.

Williams, Brown, and Certo (1975) stress the importance of having students perform skills across different environmental configurations to ensure adequate generalization or carryover. They recommended that instructional objectives include as performance conditions at least three different language cues given by at least three different control figures in at least three different settings using at least three different functional tasks. In this way, a degree of generalization would be demonstrated across commands, persons, places, and instructional materials.

A criterion for mastery is often specified in terms of the number or percentage of correct responses. Although this may be adequate in many cases, other skills are more meaningfully evaluated in terms of rate data, a proficiency measure. In advocating for the inclusion of rate criteria as components of skill mastery, Williams, Brown, and Certo (1975) emphasized the fact that students will have to perform skills at acceptable rates if they are truly to compete with and be tolerated by individuals in the community. They also pointed out that a slow rate of response is likely to interfere with the performance of later components in a task sequence by decreasing the probability of recalling the complete response chain. For these reasons, it is often advisable to set a rate criterion requiring a certain number of correct responses within a given time period.

Behavioral objectives written for short-term instructional programs are necessarily highly specific. With severely and multiply handicapped students, such objectives are likely to govern teaching efforts for anywhere from one week to several months, depending on the nature of the objective and the characteristics of the learner involved.

Selecting Instructional Strategies

The instructional objective that has been prepared stipulates exactly how the student is to perform to demonstrate mastery of the target skill. It is now necessary for the teacher to decide exactly what he or she must do to guide the student to perform in the manner desired. Knowledge of a child's learning style gained during the initial educational diagnosis and expanded during later interactions should serve as the basis for the selection of teaching strategies. Any task might be presented in a number of different ways. A teacher seeks to find an instructional approach that is particularly compatible with a student's learning preferences, because this offers the greatest promise of success. The major aspects of instructional strategy to be determined involve presentation cues, reinforcement, grouping arrangement, physical setting, and timing.

Presentation Cues   Presentation cues refer to the stimulus pattern used to elicit response from the student. Typically, these cues take the form of verbal commands. They may or may not be accompanied by signaling gestures, such as pointing. With the deaf and certain other nonverbal students, signing may substitute as the primary cue to respond. The teacher must decide the exact cue to be used consistently in the initial training sessions. The same wording and sequence of signals should be repeated for each trial until the desired response is acquired.

The teacher must also formulate several other, very similar, presentation cues to be used for generalization training. For example, in a spoon recognition task, it may be decided that the initial cue to respond will be the verbal command "Point to the spoon." After the learner has demonstrated mastery of the response to this command, a slightly different cue, such as "Show me the spoon," will be introduced. After mastery, a new cue, such as "Pick up the spoon," will be used. Although the patterns are intentionally similar, the learner is having to generalize the response across language cues.

When selecting the specific commands to be applied in a given situation, the teacher must consider both vocabulary and sentence structure. Cues should always be simple and straightforward to avoid interference with the concept to be learned.

Reinforcement   A second aspect of instructional strategy that must be tailored to individual needs is reinforcement. The teacher must select a form of positive feedback for consequating correct responses. Verbal praise, hugs and pats, and preferred toys or activities are frequently used reinforcers. In many instances, severely and multiply handicapped children may respond only to primary reinforcers at first. Bits of fruit, cereal, and crackers are often used because they are healthier than other sweet treats and are also easy to administer. Primary reinforcers should only be used when a student is not reinforced by higher-level, less artificial forms of feedback. Throughout acquisition training, positive reinforcement should be provided immediately following each correct response by the learner. Specific considerations regarding the selection and use of reinforcers are more fully discussed in Chapters 3 and 8, in conjunction with behavior modification techniques.

Desired behaviors are shaped through the contingent application of positive reinforcement. Teachers also need to have strategies ready for dealing with errors as they occur. Because error correction procedures are usually similar for different learners and should be automatic in the teaching interaction, such procedures are not considered here as individualized strategies. A general error correction procedure is described in a later section of this chapter as part of instructional implementation. Any time that interventions deviating from the customary pattern are deemed necessary for handling errors or off-task behavior, however, they should be included in the individualized plan at this point.

Grouping Arrangement   A third component to be considered in the instructional approach deals with grouping configurations. The teacher must decide whether the program in question necessitates one-to-one instruction or whether the same objective might be accomplished in a small group. One factor of obvious significance concerns the overlap of learning needs. Unless other students in the class are working toward the same objective, a group lesson is clearly inappropriate. When students do share common needs, the teacher must weigh the possible advantages against disadvantages in terms of learning efficiency. Until students are able to follow basic directions and wait their turn, it is doubtful that much intensive instruction can take place in a group setting. Later, when basic compliance responses have been established and when students are able to benefit from modeling and imitation, it is possible for the teacher to instruct several students effectively at once.

Physical Setting   A fourth consideration in planning strategy concerns the physical setting for training. A desirable setting is one in which the response would naturally occur. Teaching a student to unfasten his or her clothing, for example, ought to take place in the bathroom or bedroom. The teacher who works on this response within the classroom not only runs the risk of having the behavior exhibited inappropriately but also must later teach generalization to the desired settings. Such difficulties can be avoided by developing responses in the natural settings whenever possible.

Another major consideration, however, is control. Many natural settings are inappropriate for initial instruction because they simply do not afford the teacher adequate control of critical variables. The severely and multiply handicapped stand little chance of learning as desired when a setting presents many distractions, complex stimulus cues, and nonsystematic reinforcement. When natural settings cannot be used for instruction, the teacher should attempt to approximate important conditions as closely as possible. After the student has acquired the target response in the controlled training setting, the teacher should carefully extend the behavior to the setting where it is actually needed.

Timing   A fifth decision to be made in planning instructional strategy regards the use of time. The teacher should be concerned with the placement and the duration of lessons. Severely and multiply handicapped students often demonstrate activity-level disturbances. A child's behavior may be persistent or it may fluctuate from periods of hyperactivity to extreme lethargy as a function of physical condition or prescribed medication. The child who is overstimulated on arrival, hungry before lunch, or tired at midmorning is less likely to profit from intensive instruction, and it is usually better to avoid placing excessive demands on him or her at such times. Once a teacher recognizes a student's unique pattern, more difficult lessons can be planned for the more productive periods of the day. It may also be helpful to take advantage of the Premack Principle (see Chapters 3 and 8) by planning more pleasurable activities to follow work sessions.

Students also differ in the length of time they are able to work constructively. Initial training sessions may have to be as brief as 2 or 3 minutes. Later on, as the student has acquired better on-task behaviors, training sessions may last up to 15 minutes at a time. It is seldom advisable for the severely and profoundly impaired to spend longer at a single activity. Brief training sessions can be interspersed throughout the day to maximize instructional time.

Selecting Instructional Materials

Materials serve as the vehicles of instruction, bringing the learner in direct contact with the chosen task. They must always be selected to suit learner characteristics, planned objectives, and strategies. A rating scale to assist teachers in the search for appropriate instructional programs and materials was introduced earlier in relation to long-range planning. Although the same considerations apply to the selection of separate materials on a day-to-day basis, a teacher seldom needs to use the entire scale for this purpose. Usually, objectives and strategies for the severely and multiply handicapped are so highly specific that the choice of materials is fairly obvious. In addition to the instructional specifications, teaching concerns, and cost effectiveness factors emphasized on the rating scale, only a few special considerations deserve mention here.

First, teachers should attempt to use real rather than contrived items for instruction whenever possible. If students initially learn to use materials as they occur in the natural environment, time is not sacrificed in generalization training. For example, it is wiser to use a child's own sweater or other article of clothing with large buttons for teaching buttoning and unbuttoning skills. Dressing frames may be attractive and readily available, but having the learner fasten buttons on the frame may simply be adding another nonessential step to the training program. Functional usefulness should always be kept in mind in materials selection.

Another important factor concerns purity of the concept under instruction. Learners form concepts by noting likenesses and differences among items; therefore, it is imperative that materials initially presented differ only on the critical dimension. If one is teaching the concept "red," for instance, an assortment of red and non-red items is needed. It would be highly confusing for the learner, however, to use a set of blocks with red cubes and blue cylinders. The student may easily be learning to associate the label "red" with shape instead of color. To avoid confounding concepts, items presented initially should be of the same shape, size, and texture, and the order or position of the items should be varied. In this way, the child is taught to focus on color as the critical difference. Furthermore, materials chosen to represent instances of the concept should be grossly dissimilar to non-instances at first. For the color discrimination task, it is advisable to begin by having the student distinguish red from blue, green, or yellow rather than pink or orange. These cautions pertain to the selection of materials for initial training only. Later, as the student demonstrates mastery of the concept under these controlled stimulus conditions, more complex materials can be progressively introduced.

A third serious concern in materials selection for everyday use involves safety precautions. Severely and multiply handicapped learners need to actively handle materials. No matter what the intended purpose of a material, it may well end up being eaten, torn, or thrown. Materials with sharp points, rough edges, or parts that might be easily swallowed should be avoided. Teachers must be continually alert to possible hazards. Even certain necessary materials may have to be used only under close supervision.

Implementing Instruction

The systematic planning preceding instruction greatly facilitates its actual delivery. Major components of the lesson have been chosen with care. The teacher is able to begin instruction with knowledge of the student's behavior and with a clear sense of direction regarding his or her own performance. it is impossible, however, for the written plan to cover all the variables that come into play during an actual lesson. It is here that the richly human, interactive nature of instruction is most apparent. Each teacher possesses a unique style in relating to children. Furthermore, different situations elicit different behaviors from a teacher's repertoire.

Although some teaching skills may seem highly personalized and difficult to cultivate, there are many others that can be consciously acquired to enhance teacher effectiveness. These skills should be developed and practiced to the point that they become second nature in the instructional setting. Such methods need not be written into specific plans because they pertain to all lessons presented. Basic behavior modification techniques, as described in Chapter 3, fall into this category. Teachers of the severely and multiply impaired need to be so well versed in principles of learning theory that the application of these principles becomes automatic. Several other practices are considered essential and warrant mention at this time.

Stainback and Stainback (1976) suggested four basic considerations to be kept in mind when implementing instruction with severely or profoundly handicapped learners.

1. *Get the handicapped child physically relaxed before beginning a training sequence.* Because many severely handicapped students become very tense, sometimes even physically rigid, when faced with new situations, it is essential to begin each lesson with an adequate warm-up. Many children respond well to soothing talk, gentle rocking, or soft massaging of contracted muscles. It is often helpful to have a familiar toy available or to allow the student to explore new materials until he or she seems relaxed and comfortable.

2. *The handicapped child should be properly positioned for good body alignment and optimal visual range and movement.* Before beginning any instructional activity, the learner should be positioned in such a way that the desired response is likely to occur. This usually means facing the child away from background distractions and removing all nonessential materials from reach. When learners have severe physical handicaps, proper positioning becomes even more crucial. Individuals lacking mobility should never be allowed to lie or to sit for long, uninterrupted periods of time. Frequent repositioning is necessary to prevent deformities, to provide additional visual and kinesthetic stimulation, and to aid respiration, circulation, and digestion. Many adaptive devices, such as special chairs, wedges, supports, stabilizers, and footrests, are available to assist in positioning the learner for varied activities. Physical or occupational therapists should always be consulted concerning a particular student's needs and appropriate treatment. (Chapter 5 in this volume provides suggestions for therapeutic handling of the severely physically handicapped child.)

3. *Get the handicapped child actively involved.* Teachers of the severely and multiply handicapped must be continually concerned with overcoming passivity and dependence. Nothing should be done for the student that he or she is capable of doing. In every activity, the learner should participate to the utmost extent possible. Careful instructional programming and the use of prosthetic aids, when necessary, should contribute to more active and independent functioning.

4. *Continue to talk to the handicapped child.* Because many of the severely and multiply handicapped are nonverbal, there is often a tendency for teachers to use limited oral language in their presence, even though these students desperately need language stimulation. During all training and daily care activities, the teacher should verbalize with the student, using simple sentences with concrete vocabulary. It is often helpful to use parallel, repetitious structures. For example, while assisting a child with dressing, the teacher might say, "Let's put on Joey's shirt," "Let's put on Joey's shoes," and so on. With continual exposure to language, the child begins to realize its essential role in communication. As receptive and expressive skills develop, the teacher's speech can be expanded into actual verbal interactions with the child.

The above practices emphasized by Stainback and Stainback (1976) are applicable in all instructional sessions with the severely and multiply handicapped. When utilized, they set the stage for more comfortable and effective teaching and learning. In addition to these general facilitative procedures, teachers working at this level should have internalized a basic teaching sequence. A structured format for each trial can be easily mastered and then applied without deliberation at each step. In this way, lessons proceed more efficiently, permitting the student maximal opportunities to respond.

The basic teaching sequence recommended by Tawney and his associates in *Programmed Environments Curriculum* (1979) provides a useful model format (see Figure 4). Attention focusing is the initial step, to be followed by the presentation of selected materials and commands. After the child responds, the teacher provides feedback. Each trial concludes with the recording of response data. Tawney's model is uncomplicated, yet complete and systematic. Within this framework, the sequence of

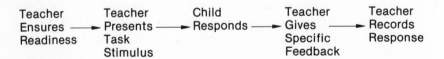

Figure 4.   The basic teaching sequence utilized in *Programmed Environments Curriculum* (Tawney et al., 1979).

teacher behaviors is automatic. This frees teachers to concentrate more on the quality and precision of their instructional presentations.

It is also helpful for teachers to have a definite pattern to follow when dealing with error responses because the severely and multiply handicapped have such difficulty in acquiring new skills. Unless a teacher is proficient in correcting errors, the learner may be just practicing mistakes. Furthermore, the teacher who is unsure of how to remedy an incorrect response is likely to encounter repeated roadblocks to learning.

Alberto and Schofield (1979) suggested an interaction pattern to guide teachers in error correction. The model contains five steps to be used sequentially as needed, until the learner produces the desired response.

In the Alberto and Schofield model, the teacher begins each trial by presenting a predetermined *verbal cue*. This should be a simple, straightforward request for the target behavior. Anytime that the learner produces the desired response on cue, the teacher immediately reinforces that response and continues the instructional sequence. Whenever the student fails to respond correctly, the teacher proceeds to the next step of the interaction pattern. Step 2 involves *priming*. The teacher presents a signal or gesture in conjunction with the verbal cue. The prime may consist of tapping, pointing, or other appropriate visual cue. If the prime does not elicit the desired response, the next step of the pattern calls for *modeling*. The teacher demonstrates the target response following the same verbal cue. If the learner does not imitate the response correctly, the teacher moves immediately to Step 4, *physical prompting*. As the verbal cue is again presented, the teacher assists the student in initiating the response. If the learner does not take over and complete the response after the initial prompt, then the teacher resorts to the final step in the pattern, *guiding*. After repeating the verbal cue, the teacher physically assists the student through the entire target behavior. It is important to note that when this interaction pattern is applied every trial must culminate with the child's performance of the target response.

The teaching techniques discussed in this section are but a few of the factors that may influence the success of a given lesson. Each teacher develops additional, personalized methods suited to him or her and to the situation. Although a written lesson plan has been tailored as closely as possible to individual learner needs, it is often the performance of the teacher in the actual instructional setting that ultimately determines the impact of the program.

Evaluating Learner Performance

With severely and multiply handicapped learners, even the most effective instructional programs are likely to produce changes in performance in very small increments. Continuous, objective monitoring is perhaps more critical with this population than with any other group of students. Only through careful measurement can a teacher determine whether a particular instructional program is of benefit to the learner, and only this type of data enables the teacher to decide when and how the program should be modified.

Data collection for evaluative purposes should be recognized as an integral part of individualized teaching. The diagnostic and prescriptive cycle always begins with evaluation of present performance. Even in early planning, as objectives are initially formulated, one is forced to consider criteria for evaluating mastery. The teaching sequence outlined in the previous section on instructional implementation includes the recording of response data as the final step of each trial. Evaluation of learner performance thus threads through the entire diagnostic and prescriptive process as the major basis for decision making.

Performance data can be collected in many different forms. According to Gentry and Haring (1976), desirable classroom measurement procedures should fulfill the following requirements:

1. The measures should be taken directly on the task or objective being taught.
2. The measures taken should provide information about intended or critical outcome of the learning task or phase.
3. The measurement scale and the behavior unit should be sensitive enough to readily reflect change in the learning task or behavior being measured.
4. Measurements should be taken frequently. Usually, behavioral measurements should be taken daily.
5. Measurement results should be reliable.
6. Measurement procedures should be practical.
7. Data procedures should be efficient and economical. (pp. 212–213)

Generally, the nature of the target behavior and the ultimate aim of training dictate the type of data-collection procedure to be utilized. If the major concern is accuracy of performance, a straight numerical count of correct responses may be sufficient. Percentage data is often preferred because it reveals the proportion of correct responses to the number of overall opportunities. When accuracy and rate of response are both concerns, proficiency data is useful in indicating the number of correct responses per unit of time. In still other instances, the most relevant measure is the length of time a response occurs, and duration recording is in order. Teachers of the severely and multiply handicapped need to be adept at using these basic forms of data collection, as well as other, more specialized, behavior recording techniques.

Data should be summarized in table form, charted on a graph, or both to facilitate interpretation. Graphic displays are particularly helpful because they reveal trends in performance more readily. Such charts allow a teacher to review many weeks of data at once and to note the degree of progress over time.

When the data indicates positive learning gains, the teacher has evidence that the instructional program is indeed working as intended. The program should be continued until mastery is achieved, that is, until the learner demonstrates acquisition of the desired response and consistency in its performance according to the terms specified in the original behavioral objective.

It often happens that the data reveal less favorable trends. In many cases, the evidence shows a lack of improvement in performance over time. In other instances, extreme fluctuations are apparent with performance close to criterion level on some days and then dropping to a minimal level on other days. Continuous measurement allows a teacher to detect such performance patterns in early stages, so that adjustments can be made in the instructional program without further delay.

Revising the Instructional Program

Considering the complexity of decisions involved in individualized programming and that student needs are continually changing, it is not surprising that initial plans are not always appropriate. The seventh step in diagnostic prescriptive teaching brings the process full cycle, as the teacher utilizes current evaluative data to update the program as necessary.

The most desirable situation exists when the evaluative data have evidenced mastery of the target objective. The instructional program was therefore successful in helping the learner to achieve criterion level performance. Revision, at this stage, consists of designing a new program for teaching the next, more advanced, skill in the sequence. Generally, the subsequent programs are easier to develop, because the teacher is able to build upon instructional elements proved effective with a particular student.

When performance has not improved as intended, the teacher needs to make certain adjustments in the original program in order to tailor it more closely to learner needs. After working with a student and observing his or her difficulties, the teacher is usually aware of weaker program components. The teacher must systematically review each step in the cycle to locate suspect variables. Initial decisions can be reconsidered and revised as necessary in light of more complete knowledge of student performance.

Summary

At the heart of the student's educational program is the instruction that is actually provided. To closely correlate daily teaching efforts with the IEP, each stated goal or objective must be addressed through its own carefully designed instructional program. The steps involved in planning, implementation, and evaluation at this level parallel the steps in long-range educational programming; the instructional cycles are simply more focused and specific in their orientation. Severely and multiply handicapped learners are likely to be working toward several different objectives at any point in their educational programs. Instructional plans are continually refined until adequate progress is demonstrated. As objectives are mastered, programs are redesigned for more advanced skills.

EVALUATING THE EDUCATIONAL PROGRAM

According to federal regulations, the IEP is to be evaluated on at least an annual basis. Members of the team may request a review after a shorter time period if it is warranted. Evaluation of the overall educational program typically involves a review of two different types of evidence regarding student progress. First, the team considers the number of objectives that have actually been attained within the time frames prescribed. For objectives not yet mastered, the team should note present performance levels and degree of improvement observed. This primary evaluation centering on IEP objectives requires no special testing at all but simply utilizes the performance data already available from the different short-term instructional programs. Thus, one important determinant of the effectiveness of the individualized educational program is the cumulative record of the separate instructional units.

Another source of data for evaluating program effectiveness is posttesting. The same educational assessment devices used for initial diagnosis can be readministered to document changes in performance. This information is often helpful to the team in providing a more comprehensive frame of reference.

There can be no rigid rules for committees to apply in deciding whether an educational program has proved appropriate and effective for a particular student. Each team must exercise its own judgment as to whether satisfactory progress has occurred. Such decisions can only be made in consideration of each student's level of functioning, prior learning history, and established needs.

REVISING THE EDUCATIONAL PROGRAM

Based on the results of evaluation, the IEP committee updates the program to fit changing priorities. The same steps in long-range planning are undertaken once again to formulate a new IEP for the coming year. Goals and objectives, delivery strategies, and curricula are reconsidered from the team's new vantage point.

Goals and objectives often fall into place as the logical extensions of last year's targets. Placements and curricula that proved successful in the past are often continued. Updating should not be handled hastily, however, for new concerns often emerge that can significantly alter priorities or necessitate additional goals. Program revision must be approached with the same care as the initial IEP development. All decisions should represent the team's best efforts to provide for the learner's current needs while always preparing him or her for more independent functioning.

CONCLUSION

Teaching the severely and multiply handicapped presents challenges not encountered with any other group of learners. Because the content to be taught involves the most basic human tasks, many people are of the mistaken opinion that instructional programming must likewise be very simple. Nothing could be further from the truth. As the practices described in this chapter illustrate, educational programming for this population requires a highly thorough, systematic, and precise approach. There are few, if any, hard-and-fast rules. The most useful methods are process-oriented, giving educators a problem-solving model for dealing with whatever specific situations arise. Because every student demonstrates a truly unique array of abilities and disabilities, there must also be great diversity in the educational programs developed. As special education for the severe and multiply handicapped matures as a field of study, strategies for planning, implementation, and evaluation will be continually refined to become even more sensitive and responsive to learner needs.

REFERENCES

Alberto, P. A., & Schofield, P. An interaction pattern for the severely handicapped. *Teaching Exceptional Children*, 1979, *12*(1), 16–19.

Anderson, D. R., et al. *Instructional programming for the handicapped student*. Springfield: Charles C Thomas, 1975.

Bender, M., & Valletutti, P. J. *Teaching the moderately and severely handicapped: Curriculum objectives, strategies, and activities*. Baltimore: University Park Press, 1976.

Bijou, S. W., Lindsley, O. R., & Haughton, E. (Eds.). *Let's try doing something else kind of thing: Behavioral principles and the exceptional child*. Reston, VA: Council for Exceptional Children, 1972.

Charles, C. M. *Individualizing instruction*. St. Louis: C. V. Mosby, 1976.

Dubose, R. F., Langley, M. B., & Stagg, V. Assessing severely handicapped children. *Focus on Exceptional Children*, 1977, *9*(7), 1–13.

Gentry, D. G., & Haring, N. G. Essentials of performance measurement. In N. G. Haring & L. V. Brown (Eds.), *Teaching the severely handicapped, Vol. I*. New York: Grune & Stratton, 1976.

Haring, N. G., & Schiefelbusch, R. L. *Teaching special children*. New York: McGraw-Hill, 1976.

Hart, V. The use of many disciplines with the severely and profoundly handicapped. In E. Sontag, J. Smith, & N. Certo (Eds.), *Educational programming for the severely and profoundly handicapped*. Reston, VA: Council for Exceptional Children, 1977.

Knapczyk, D. R. Task analytic assessment of severe learning problems. In I. Newman & R. Piazza (Eds.), *Readings in severely and profoundly handicapped education*. Guilford, CT: Special Learning, 1978.

Laycock, V. K. Assessment and evaluation in the classroom. In J. W. Schifani, R. M. Anderson, & S. J. Odle (Eds.), *Implementing learning in the least restrictive environment: Handicapped children in the mainstream*. Baltimore: University Park Press, 1980.

Laycock, V. K. Making the match: Rationale for selection. In R. M. Anderson, J. G. Greer, & S. J. Odle (Eds.), *Individualizing educational materials for special children in the mainstream*. Baltimore: University Park Press, 1978.

Lerner, J. L. *Children with learning disabilities* (2nd ed). Boston: Houghton Mifflin, 1976.

McCormack, J. E. *Teaching preacademic skills to severely handicapped students*. Gloucester, MA: Seaside Education Associates, 1977.

McCormack, J. E., & Chalmers, A. J. *Early cognitive instruction for the moderately and severely handicapped: Teaching sequence notebook*. Champaign, Ill.: Research Press, 1978.

McCormack, J. E. et al. *Systematic instruction for the severely handicapped: Teaching sequences*. Medford, Mass: Massachusetts Center for Program Development and Evaluation, 1976.

Mercer, C. D. *Children and adolescents with learning disabilities*. Columbus: Charles E. Merrill, 1979.

Moran, M. R. Nine steps to the diagnostic prescriptive process in the classroom. *Focus on Exceptional Children*, 1975, *6*(9), 1–14.

Peter, J. L. *Prescriptive teaching*. New York: McGraw-Hill, 1965.

Public Law 94-142. *Federal Register*, 1976, *41*(252), 56986, Thursday, December 30.

Sailor, W., & Horner, R. D. Educational assessment strategies for the severely handicapped. In N. G. Haring & L. J. Brown (Eds.), *Teaching the severely handicapped*, Vol. 1. New York: Grune & Stratton, 1976.

Smith, R. M. *Clinical teaching: Methods of instruction for the retarded*. New York: McGraw-Hill, 1974.

Snell, M. E. (Ed.). *Systematic instruction of the moderately and severely handicapped*. Columbus: Charles E. Merrill, 1978.

Somerton, M. E., & Myers, D. G. Educational programming for the severely and profoundly mentally retarded. In N. G. Haring & L. J. Brown (Eds.). *Teaching the severely handicapped*, Vol. 1. New York: Grune & Stratton, 1976.

Stainback, S., & Stainback, W. Teaching the profoundly handicapped in the public school setting: Some considerations. *American Association for the Education of the Severely/Profoundly Handicapped Review*, 1976, *1*, (3), 3–15.

Stephens, T. M. *Teaching skills to children with learning and behavior disorders*. Columbus: Charles E. Merrill, 1977.

Tawney, J. W. et al. *Programmed environments curriculum: A curriculum handbook for teaching basic skills to severely handicapped persons*. Columbus: Charles E. Merrill, 1979.

Williams, W., Brown, L., & Certo, N. Basic components of instructional programs for severely handicapped students. *American Association for the Education of the Severely/Profoundly Handicapped Review*, 1975, *1*(1), 1–39.

Williams, W., & Gotts, E. A. Selected considerations on developing curriculum for severely handicapped students. In E. Sontag, J. Smith, & N. Certo (Eds.), *Educational programming for the severely and profoundly handicapped*. Reston, VA: Council for Exceptional Children, 1977.

Chapter 3

Behavior Modification Techniques

Wendy Ashcroft

INTRODUCTION

The purpose of this chapter is to describe behavior modification techniques, explain the application of these methods to programs for severely and profoundly handicapped persons, and address the ethical issues that arise from the implementation of behavior modification programs. It is the intent of the chapter only to introduce some of the important principles and issues; further information may be gained from the extensive literature on the subject.

Operant conditioning principles provide the basis for the behavior modification techniques to be discussed. These principles focus on the assumption that behavior is a product of environmental events, the premise that behavior operates on the environment to provide desirable consequences, and the theory that the strength or frequency of a behavior can be altered by arranging the events which precede or follow the behavior.

Much of the discussion regarding the application of the techniques will center around their use with severely and profoundly handicapped individuals. These persons have behavior deficits in the areas of language, communication, and other social skills; eating, toileting, and dressing skills; or a combination of deficits. They also have behavior excesses such as aggressive or self-destructive activities; nonfunctional or repetitive movements; and nonsensical or loud verbalizations. However, some of the relevant research deals with subjects who are not severely or profoundly handicapped, but who have many of the same behavior excesses or deficits. Therefore, some of these examples may be included on the basis of potential application with severely and profoundly handicapped individuals because of similarities in behavior.

Because behavior modification is a scientifically validated system of tools for changing behavior, guidelines governing the use of the tools are necessary for ensuring that they are used to improve the quality of life of an individual. These guidelines include meeting prerequisites for the choice of a behavior to be modified, following procedures for the planning and implementation of a program, and setting standards for the evaluation of a program.

Before a program can be implemented, careful study of the situation must be made. First, the trainer must obtain good knowledge of the individual's functioning level and response pattern. This part of the study should yield information about the kinds of behaviors the individual exhibits or lacks, as well as how often, when, and where the behaviors occur or don't occur. Second, scales of normal development should guide the trainer in choosing behaviors to be modified. Using these scales helps the trainer plan a program that will make behavior changes appropriate for the individual's mental age and present functioning level. Understanding of both the individual and of developmental scales helps ensure that the program is built around a reasonable expectation of behavior change.

Planning and implementing a program begins with the choice of one specific behavior to be modified. As the program is designed, consideration must be given to the goals of the program. First, it must be determined that the modification of that behavior will in some way benefit the individual. That is, the goal to change the behavior has to be part of a larger goal such as teaching the individual to do more for him or herself or making the individual more acceptable in his or her environment. Second, it is crucial to consider how the program leads toward the long-range goal óf bringing the behavior under the control of natural consequences. Although the use of artificial teaching situations may be necessary in the beginning, the goal of functioning in as natural an environment as possible must be built into the program. Third, it is extremely important to make the program as positive as possible. Care must be taken to convey to the individual that he or she is acceptable as a human being with feelings, rights, and dignity regardless of the behaviors that are being exhibited. A positive program helps to show that it is the *behavior* of the person that is to be changed. Positive control methods that center around the use of pleasant consequences must be tried and eliminated before any aversive forms of control are considered. When it is decided that an aversive program is the best alternative, the individual must be given love and affection not contingent on behavior.

Evaluating a program begins with the choice of a behavior that is observable and measurable. It is important to count the behaviors before the program is instituted and to periodically collect data to ensure that the program is working. A comprehensive evaluation also includes consideration of such concerns as whether the program is designed around a series of gradual steps, whether the program is as positive as possible, whether the program is a step toward bringing the behavior under the control of natural consequences, and whether the change in behavior benefits the individual. Thus, the decision to employ behavior modification techniques to modify behavior includes consideration of both empirical and moral issues. The position of this paper is that the implementation of well-formulated programs by responsible persons allows for the increase of desirable behaviors, the decrease of undesirable behaviors, and the maintenance of behavioral gains across settings. Furthermore, it is suggested here that successful modification of behavior permits the severely and profoundly handicapped individual to engage in more productive and enjoyable activities and to become more socially acceptable (i.e., more independent and perhaps less frightening, annoying, disturbing, or frustrating to others). Finally, it is proposed that it is not only our responsibility to implement programs with goals for productive behavior change but that it is unethical not to use such procedures in situations where they have been found to be effective.

INCREASING DESIRABLE BEHAVIORS

Reinforcement

Procedures designed to increase the strength or frequency of behaviors center around the principle of reinforcement stating that the immediate consequences of a person's actions or behaviors determine whether those behaviors are repeated. A stimulus is called a reinforcer if it increases the strength or frequency of a behavior. Reinforcement is classified into categories depending on the effects of the reinforcer and on when the reinforcer is presented.

Positive Reinforcement   Operationally defined, a positive reinforcer is a stimulus that increases the probability of the occurrence of a response. Such stimuli are usually pleasant experiences themselves. Common examples include edibles such as candy, potato chips, and juice; attention from others such as smiles, eye contact, and praise; enjoyable activities such as playing with toys and watching television; and money or tokens such as coins or chips to be exchanged for edibles, privileges, activities, or toys (see Appendix A). People tend to repeat those behaviors which have pleasant results.

Using this principle, Whitman, Mercurio, and Caponigri (1970) increased the social interaction (rolling a ball and coloring with crayons together) of two severely retarded children by reinforcing those activities with candy and praise. Self-care skills such as toileting, eating, dressing, and grooming have been developed in severely and profoundly handicapped individuals by Bensberg, Colwell, and Cassel (1965); Treffry, Martin, Samels, and Watson (1970); Azrin and Foxx (1971); Berkowitz, Sherry, and Davis (1971); and Martin, Kehoe, Bird, Jensen, and Darbyshine (1971). Studies by Bricker and Bricker (1970), Barton (1970, 1973), Bricker (1972), and Butz and Hasazi (1973) have demonstrated the effectiveness of positive reinforcement in increasing communication and receptive and expressive language. Sensory-motor skills including perceptual-motor skills, standing without support, and walking have been increased in severely and profoundly handicapped individuals by Hollis (1967a, 1967b); Auxter (1971); Miller, Patton, and Henton (1971); and Haavik and Altman (1977).

Once a target behavior has been chosen, the success of a program involving the use of positive reinforcement depends on finding an effective reinforcer and on presenting it appropriately. Finding a reinforcer with high incentive value consists of consideration of the preferences and condition of an individual. Some stimuli are pleasant experiences for most people most of the time, but preferences for reinforcement do vary among individuals. Giles and Wolf (1966) found that a shower was a positive experience for some and an aversive one for others. Reinforcement preferences vary within individuals, too; for example, going outside may be reinforcing for a child at one time and not at another. The condition of the individual at a particular time influences these preferences. A hot and thirsty person may find ice water very reinforcing; however, as the person becomes satiated, the water loses its reinforcing value. The true effectiveness of a reinforcer can only be known by observing its effect when presented. It is up to the trainer to predict a potentially productive reinforcer, observe the results, and determine whether it is effective enough to modify the target behavior.

Applying the reinforcer appropriately involves presenting it immediately so that another behavior cannot intervene between the target behavior and the delivery of the reinforcer. If this happens, the latter behavior may be reinforced. The target behavior must also be reinforced consistently so that the individual learns the contingency "When I do this [target behavior], this [reinforcement] will happen."

Although the use of positive reinforcement for the development of a variety of specific behaviors has been successful, there are some limitations. First, effective reinforcers that have been of practical use with the severely and profoundly handicapped are limited (Nawas & Braun, 1970). Most programs center around the use of edibles, attention, activities such as playing with toys and watching television, and tokens. Often these reinforcers are not imaginative or effective enough to motivate the individual or the trainer. A wide variety of ideas should be determined for easily implemented, easily obtainable, inexpensive, and undisruptive reinforcers that are highly motivating to the individual and the trainer so that one or more can be adapted for a specific program.

Second, many effective reinforcers have disadvantages as well as advantages. For example, the use of edibles in a program for the development of expressive language can slow down work, as the child must swallow before the next opportunity for performance is given. Continued use of edibles also can cause weight gain problems in some individuals. Frequent use of sweets may cause or complicate dental problems in individuals for whom dental care is not always easy to obtain.

Negative Reinforcement   Reinforcement of a behavior also takes place when the behavior reduces or eliminates an aversive aspect of a situation. An individual can respond and thus either prevent or terminate the occurrence of an unpleasant or painful stimulus. Examples of such stimuli include loud noise, unpleasant temperature, and electric shock (see Appendix B). Because the appropriate response allows the individual to avoid or escape the aversiveness, reinforcement for that response occurs. Consequently, the probability that the individual will repeat that behavior in the future is increased. Even though the employment of a program involving negative reinforcement includes the use of aversive stimuli, the principle of negative reinforcement should not be confused with punishment. Punishment weakens or suppresses behaviors while negative reinforcement strengthens or increases them.

Through the purposeful arrangement of events, the use of negative reinforcement can increase the strength or frequency of a behavior. Lovaas, Schaeffer, and Simmons (1965) increased the social interaction of two 5-year-old autistic twins by wiring the floor with electric grids which ceased conducting electricity if the children approached the examiner within 5 seconds of being asked. Leitenberg (1965) and Sachs (1973) noted that negative reinforcement of appropriate behavior such as sitting or standing quietly occurs when it leads to the termination of time-out (isolation from the teacher or group). Other examples of the development of useful behavior through the use of negative reinforcement are listed in Table 1.

Two abilities of a trainer are essential to a successful program involving the use of negative reinforcement to alter a behavior. First, the trainer must be able to find conditions sufficiently unpleasant for an in-

Table 1. Examples of the use of negative reinforcers

Arrange the environment so that the person:	The objective is for the person to:
is covered by a sheet or wash-cloth	pull off the cover (target behavior might be grasping and pulling or lifting an arm, leg, or head)
is in darkness	turn on the light (target behavior might be pushing a button or flipping a switch)
feels a fan blowing	turn off the fan (target behavior might be pushing a button or flipping a switch)
hears radio static	turn off the static or turn on the music (target behavior might be turning a knob)
feels tape stuck on fingers	pull off the tape (target behavior might be using pincer grasp to pull)
experiences warm temperature	turn on a fan (target behavior might be pushing a button or flipping a switch)

dividual so that the person is motivated to actively reduce the unpleasantness. The conditions must also be mild enough so as not to be harmful or unethical. As stated earlier, preferences among individuals vary, so what is very unpleasant for one person may be only mildly unpleasant or even positively reinforcing for another. Second, the trainer must arrange the conditions so that the unpleasantness of the situation is reduced or eliminated immediately after the appropriate behavior occurs and after each occurrence of that behavior.

There are several limitations involved in the implementation of a program using the principle of negative reinforcement. The greatest limitation is the difficulty in finding an effective stimulus that does not harm an individual or unpleasantly affect others in the area. Once an appropriate stimulus is chosen, some other constraints are necessary. First, the use of negative reinforcement is restricted to behaviors already in an individual's repertoire or which are easily within his or her ability to perform. Otherwise, the individual may be in a situation from which he or she cannot terminate or escape from the unpleasant aspect of a situation. Second, the trainer must ensure that the individual understands the contingency so that he or she knows how to reduce the unpleasantness if desired. Thirdly, the actual implementation of the program requires assurance that the stimuli is terminated immediately following the behavior.

Unconditioned and Conditioned Reinforcement A stimulus such as food or water, which would have reinforcing value even when presented to an individual for the first time, is called an *unconditioned*, or primary, reinforcer. *Conditioned*, or secondary, reinforcers are those which originally had little or no reinforcing value, but which can obtain this value through association with established reinforcers. Because reinforcers are defined only in terms of their effects on behavior, anything (e.g., words, coins, chips, toys, pictures, and sounds) can become a reinforcer. For example, the word "good" can attain reinforcing properties after being paired with a stimulus such as candy that is known to be a reinforcer. At first, it is the candy that will have the value needed to modify the behavior even though the word "good" is said each time the candy is presented. Through association with the candy, "good" itself can acquire the value to increase the rate or strength of the behavior. For the conditioned stimulus to maintain its reinforcing value, it must periodically be paired with an established reinforcer. Thus, a program designed around the use of plastic chips as reinforcers for a behavior must include an opportunity for the person to exchange the token for candy, juice, toys, or privileges.

Programs using conditioned reinforcers with severely and profoundly handicapped individuals have been successful. Girardeau and Spradlin (1964) and Gorton and Hollis (1965) developed self-help skills in severely and profoundly retarded children with the use of tokens as reinforcers. Token systems have also been successfully used to increase various academic skills (Baker, Stanish, & Fraser, 1972; Dalton, Rubino, & Hislop, 1973). Kauffman and Snell (1977) point out that many severely handicapped individuals will not be able to count the tokens or associate specific exchange values with them, although this may be learned later. They hold that these individuals need a token system where they are merely awarded a token contingent on a behavior and are allowed to exchange the token for established reinforcers whenever the trainer deems it necessary. Thus, the individual does not have to initially understand that a specified number of tokens must be accumulated in order to make the exchange.

Advantages of token systems include ease of delivery of tokens, wide variety of back-up reinforcers (and thus little likelihood that the individual becomes satiated), and ease of fading the reinforcement. These seem to outweigh the disadvantages.

The use of conditioned reinforcers in programs for the severely and profoundly handicapped is limited by several factors. At first, an individual may not be able to understand the association between the established reinforcer and a conditioned reinforcer. Prerequisite cognitive abilities and long periods of training may be required to condition a consequence so that it is effective enough to modify an established behavior.

Once the association is made, the trainer must frequently pair the conditioned reinforcer with a more primary reinforcer. Because of the initial difficulty in transferring value from primary to secondary reinforcers, conditioned reinforcers may best be restricted to maintaining behaviors rather than establishing new behaviors.

Artificial and Natural Reinforcement   An *artificial* reinforcer is a stimulus that has reinforcing value but does not ordinarily occur in that particular setting. For example, edibles have reinforcing value when used to teach a dressing skill but they do not ordinarily follow performance of dressing behaviors. A *natural* reinforcer is a reinforcing stimulus that usually occurs in the environment but is contingent on the occurrence of a certain behavior. A morning play period to reinforce bedmaking is an example. A program could be designed so that a child could engage in a regular morning play period only after making his or her bed.

A similar principle involving the use of existing situations as reinforcers is the Premack Principle (Premack, 1959). This principle states that if an individual engages in a particular activity more frequently than in the target behavior, the opportunity to engage in the first activity can be used as an effective reinforcer. That is, the opportunity to engage in a preferred activity may be made contingent upon performance of a target behavior. The strength or frequency of a behavior can be increased by the use of both artificial and natural reinforcers. Artificial reinforcers may best be used to teach a new behavior, while natural reinforcers might best be used to maintain or improve existing behavior. The greatest advantage of natural reinforcers is that they already exist in the individual's environment. They need only be made contingent upon the individual's behavior. Thus, natural reinforcers may be easier to implement, and they may facilitate generalization of learned skills from treatment settings to more normal environments.

Artificial reinforcers are easily associated with target behaviors because they are novel to the environment and therefore more salient in the individual's environment. Thus, artificial reinforcers may have greater potential for motivating an individual to attempt a new behavior. This is particularly important for use with the SPH population because natural reinforcers obviously have not modified the target behavior appropriately. To teach a new behavior then, artificial reinforcers may be instituted.

Artificial reinforcers are important for instituting new behavior but may not be suitable for maintaining behavior over long periods of time. In order to prepare the individual to function in the environments where the behaviors are required, it is best to ensure that the behavior is under the control of the consequences in those environments. Very little "real life" goes on in classrooms and institutions where training typically takes place, so it can be difficult to simulate the natural conditions that occur outside these environments. Nevertheless, natural reinforcers should be identified and phased in slowly so that the behavior can ultimately be maintained at desirable levels in environments where the artificial reinforcers are not present.

Continuous and Intermittent Reinforcement   When reinforcement is delivered after each occurrence of a behavior, the schedule is one of *continuous* reinforcement. *Intermittent* reinforcement refers to fixed schedules in which reinforcement is delivered after a designated number of behaviors or following the first occurrence of a behavior after a designated period of time; it also refers to variable schedules in which reinforcement is delivered after an average number of responses or after varying amounts of time.

Schedules of reinforcement each have particular advantages that determine the best occasions for their use. Continuous reinforcement is best used for establishing new behaviors. Intermittent schedules are more economical and tend to make behavior more resistant to extinction. Consequently, an intermittent schedule is best used when behavior begins to stabilize (level off in rate of occurrence). Depending on the intermittent schedule instituted, behavior can be increased in speed or frequency of response or maintained at a high rate of response.

It is important to use schedules of reinforcement efficiently and economically. This involves beginning with a continuous reinforcement schedule and reinforcing each occurrence of the appropriate behavior until it becomes firmly established. Very short ratio or interval schedules may gradually be introduced. For example, the individual may be reinforced for every second or third occurrence or for the first occurrence of a behavior after a very short period of time. As the behavior stabilizes, the trainer must gradually reduce the amount of reinforcement until the most economical schedule, using the least amount of reinforcement to keep the behavior at a desirable rate, is reached. Once behavior is established, variable schedules tend to maintain it at high rates.

Shaping

Procedures designed to increase the strength or frequency of behaviors also employ *shaping* techniques. These techniques refer to molding simple behavior into more complex behavior. For example, Schiefelbusch (1965) used shaping techniques to develop language. Kerr, Meyerson, and Michael (1965) and Baer, Peterson, and Sherman (1967) used shaping techniques to develop imitative behaviors in mentally retarded people. Shaping techniques are made up of two procedures for molding simple behavior into complex behavior. These two procedures are called *successive approximation* and *chaining*.

Successive Approximation and Chaining   The use of successive approximation involves taking a complex behavior such as pulling up pants, analyzing it into small components, and reinforcing very small approximations of the desired behavior (i.e., first the child is reinforced for touching the pants, later for touching and grasping the waistband, and so on, until he or she can accomplish the behavior).

Chaining is a process that involves connecting all components of a complex behavior into a smooth sequence. This connecting process may involve a forward or backward series. For example, a behavior such as pulling up pants may be divided into components, i.e., touching the pants, grasping the waistband, and pulling the pants up to the waist in successive stages. In forward chaining, the child is reinforced first for touching the pants. Next, reinforcement is delivered only after the child has touched the pants and grasped the waistband. The child is then presented reinforcement for touching, grasping, and pulling the pants up to the knees. The process continues until the child is able to perform the entire sequence. Backward chaining is similar except that the first step reinforced is last to be performed in the sequence. For example, reinforcement is delivered after the pants are pulled from the hips to the waist. The next step to be reinforced is pulling the pants from the thighs to the waist, and so on.

Chaining also refers to a process of linking a series of behaviors into one smooth sequence. For example, dressing may be broken down into putting on underpants, pants, shirt, socks, and shoes. As each step is mastered, the behavior must be linked to the previous, or following, step until the entire behavior is performed in sequence. Although behavior may be chained in forward or backward sequences, the advantage of backward chaining is the association of the trainer's reinforcement of the last step with the natural reinforcement of task completion. The combination of successive approximation with chaining can be combined into a process in which the individual attempts the first step and receives reinforcement; performs the first step, attempts the second step, and receives reinforcement; then performs the first step, performs the second step, and receives reinforcement; etc. In teaching severely and profoundly handicapped individuals, it is crucial to define specific criteria for a successful attempt at a behavior, reinforce that step until it is mastered, and then define a new criteria for a new step. The task must always be small enough to be accomplished, so careful consideration must be made of the individual's functioning level when establishing criteria.

Stimulus Control

Stimulus control refers to a process in which a person learns to perform the target behavior in the presence of a certain cue or stimulus. The stimulus may be visual, tactile, auditory, or kinesthetic. It may be, for example, a word, phrase, visual model, physical prompt, buzzer, or flashing light. The stimulus signals that if the individual performs the desired behavior following the stimulus, reinforcement is likely to take place. Four categories of cues are described here.

Verbal Instructions   Verbal instructions are probably the most common example of stimulus control. After gaining the individual's attention, verbal statements adjusted to the learner's level of comprehension can serve as indicators for the performance of a behavior. When the performance occurs after the verbal cue, the behavior is said to be under the control of that stimulus. For example, if an individual goes to the bathroom when the trainer says, "Go to the bathroom," the behavior is under stimulus control. An individual who does not understand the phrase, or who is not likely to understand the phrase soon, may need to first learn to perform the behavior following the one-word cue "bathroom."

Visual Models   The use of visual models refers to the demonstration of the desired behavior for the learner. After obtaining the attention of the learner, the trainer either performs the behavior or cues a third person to demonstrate the behavior. The model itself (i.e., demonstration of the behavior) may serve as an indicator for the learner to imitate the demonstrator. In some cases, the model can be combined with verbal instructions and physical prompts in order to provide a cue for the behavior. In modeling, the learner performs the behavior and receives reinforcement for the performance. It can also include a component in which the learner watches a third person perform the behavior and sees the reinforcement delivered to the model. Sometimes modeling consists of performances of poor or undesirable behavior so that learners can see instances and consequences of misbehavior. Thus, the learner may learn the boundaries of the desired response.

Physical Prompts   Physical prompts such as hand-on-hand or hand-on-arm guidance can serve as cues for the performance of a behavior. Usually physical prompts accompany or follow the provision of other cues such as verbal instructions or visual models. That is, after gaining an individual's attention, the learner would be told to perform a certain behavior and possibly be shown how to perform that behavior. If the behavior did not occur, a physical prompt would be given. For example, after an individual has been told and shown how to lift a full spoon to his or her mouth, the trainer would lift the individual's hand part of the way to the learner's mouth. An integral part of any program that deals with physical prompts involves fading the cue so that the least amount of physical guidance possible is used. Thus, at first an individual may need hand-on-hand guidance in lifting the spoon all the way up. As the program progresses, the prompt is faded until the learner's hand only needs to be touched to cue the lifting of the spoon.

Artificial Stimuli   Stimuli that do not naturally occur in situations can be used to set the stage for a desired behavior to occur. For example, a flashing light or buzzer may signal the behavior. Thus, if a behavior is established but occurs in situations in which it is not appropriate, an individual can be taught to perform the behavior only in the presence of the cue. The artificial cue can then be paired with the natural cues so that the time for the behavior to occur becomes associated with the natural cue. Then the artificial cues can be faded out.

Instructions, modeling, prompts, and artificial cues set the stage for behavior to occur. The attention of the learner is gained, the cue is given, the behavior is performed, and the reinforcement is delivered. A stimulus helps the learner attend to the relevant aspects of a situation and thus discern when it is appropriate to perform behavior. The use of stimulus control with severely and profoundly handicapped individuals is particularly important because individuals with behavior excesses and deficits have not learned to perform the behavior after cues that occur naturally in the environment. Also, the probability that a behavior is performed correctly is increased with the use of clear cues. That is, good instructions, dynamic models, and physical guidance reduce the potential for error in early performances. The early performance is reinforced and, while the cues are gradually decreased, correct responses are still occurring. Along with this, irrelevant responses which are usually present in the trial and error method of learning are greatly reduced.

DECREASING UNDESIRABLE BEHAVIOR

Programs designed to decrease undesirable behavior should always begin with consideration of the principles of extinction and reinforcement of incompatible behavior. These are the first alternatives to forms of positive control since they are the least oppressive and are the closest approximation of natural forms of control.

Extinction

Extinction refers to the removal of the reinforcing element maintaining the behavior. This causes a decrease in the strength or frequency of the behavior. For example, consistently ignoring a behavior is an employment of the extinction principle if attention is the reinforcer that is maintaining the behavior. If the behavior is being maintained by edibles or activities, then removal of those consequences leads to the extinction of the behavior. If a large number of consecutive performances are not reinforced, the behavior will become extinct.

Understanding the extinction principle can help trainers identify behaviors that in themselves may be reinforcing behavior. That is, if the trainer's attention is given while an individual is crying, the crying behavior may be a device to control the trainer's attention. Once aware of this, the trainer may be able to reverse the contingency, using attention to increase desirable rather than undesirable behavior. The principle of extinction is difficult to employ for a number of reasons. First, it is hard to determine the exact reinforcing element of the situation. It may be impossible to control all the factors that maintain a behavior. Individuals receive reinforcement from other students or residents and from parents, teachers, and staff. Reinforcement can also be obtained from the behavior itself. Examples of this include the pleasure of hearing the sound of a scream and the stimulation of self-injurious behavior. Second, when extinction is first instituted, an increase in behavior typically occurs. It is important to recognize this as a typical phase of extinction and to realize that the program must be continued for extinction to take place. Third, after extinction has taken place a sudden spurt of undesired behaviors may recur, but these behaviors will cease again unless reinforced. Finally, the greatest limitation of the extinction procedure is the length of time required for complete elimination of a behavior to take place. Bucher and Lovaas (1967) studied the behaviors of a 7-year-old severely retarded boy with a high rate of self-injurious behavior. He had been in restraints for 24 hours a day. Released from restraints for 1½ hours per day, he reduced the behavior to near extinction level after eight days. However, during the extinction process, he hit himself in excess of 10,000 times whenever the presumed reinforcer was removed.

Reinforcement of Incompatible Behavior

A decrease in an undesirable behavior takes place when reinforcement increases a behavior that cannot be performed at the same time as the target behavior. For example, increasing the amount of time playing with a toy decreases the amount of time a child engages in hand-waving behavior.

Reinforcement of incompatible behavior with severely and profoundly handicapped individuals is successful in that it produces a desired response simultaneous to decreasing an undesirable behavior. Thus the trainer has a positive goal as well as a negative one. Further, reinforcement of incompatible behavior does not call direct attention to the undesirable behavior. This can be important in cases where misbehavior is an individual's primary method of gaining attention. Reinforcement of incompatible behavior may serve to reduce the attention to the undesirable behavior.

Limitations of the use of reinforcement of incompatible behavior to decrease undesirable behavior include the difficulty in finding an incompatible behavior that is desirable or acceptable. Also, the desirable behavior may be a behavior only appropriate for certain situations. For example, increasing play with a toy in order to decrease hand waving will decrease the waving but playing with the toy may not always be a good substitute. At mealtime, bedtime, or in places such as stores it may not be appropriate. Thus, the use of reinforcement of incompatible behavior in a program may have to include a phase in which the new desirable behavior is brought under stimulus control. That is, once the undesirable behavior is decreased, a special phase may be required to teach the individual the appropriate times to perform the new behavior.

Constant, consistent reinforcement of the incompatible behavior is crucial to the success of a program. Used in conjunction with extinction, it often is one of the most effective ways to eliminate an undesirable behavior.

Punishment

Procedures designed to decrease the strength or frequency of undesirable behaviors often depend on the principle of punishment. Punishment is operationally defined as any consequence to a behavior that decreases the probability of future occurrence of that behavior. Procedural definitions such as Skinner's (1953) and Glasser's (1976) typically involve the use of noxious stimuli (Skinner) or mental or physical pain (Glasser).

After eliminating extinction and reinforcement of incompatible behavior as appropriate behavior modifiers, a trainer may turn to one of several categories of punishment. The categories are presented in increasing levels of negativity and intensity. However, as seen in Figure 1, levels may overlap in degrees of intensity. That is, an extremely aversive overcorrection program may be more forceful than a program involving mildly aversive stimuli.

Verbal Punishment   Exclamations such as "No!," "Don't do that!," "Stop!" and "Stop it!" can serve as effective punishing agents in some situations. Often, these are, and in many cases should be, delivered in a sharp tone of voice and accompanied by looks of disapproval. If disapproval from another person is an aversive enough consequence, the probability of the behavior occurring again is decreased. Verbal reprimands combined with negative attention can serve as a social punisher, causing the individual to feel embarrassed or disappointed. Sometimes the word or phrase will have to be paired with a more salient aversive reinforcer than social disapproval in order to gain punishing properties. Doleys, Wells, Hobbs, Roberts, and Cartelli (1976) compared the effects of social punishment, positive practice, and time-out on the non-compliant behavior of developmentally delayed pre-schoolers. Social punishment consisted of holding the individual's shoulders firmly and loudly scolding the child. The trainer then glared silently at the child for 40 seconds. Doleys, Wells, Hobbs, Roberts, and Carletti (1976) found that this social punishment was more effective than 40-second sessions of positive practice or isolation ("time-out"). Koegel, Firestone, Kramme, and Dunlap (1974) used "No!" to suppress self-stimulatory behavior of autistic chil-

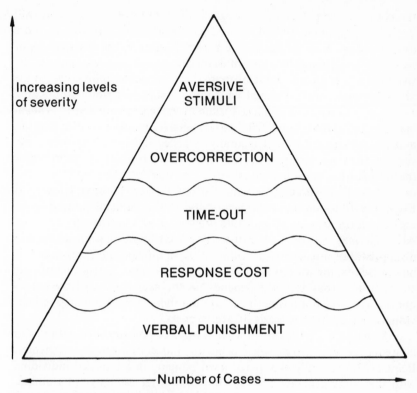

Figure 1.   A hierarchy of methods of punishment.

dren. Lovaas, Freitag, Gold, and Kassorla (1965) and Lovaas and Simmons (1969) paired words with contingent electric shock. In the first study tantrums were suppressed and in the second self-abusive biting was decreased. When the self-abusive biting of an 8-year-old autistic child recurred in a new setting, the use of "No!" alone suppressed the behavior.

There are some advantages to the use of verbal punishment. One advantage is that in different programs a word or phrase can be paired with consequences of different levels of aversiveness. Also, the consequence may be faded so that the word or phrase alone is effective. Thus, an undesired behavior can be brought under the control of natural consequences since verbal reprimands are frequent in society.

There are some obvious limitations in the use of verbal punishers. First of all, a word or phrase itself will not serve as an effective punishing agent unless it has been or is being associated with a stimulus that has some aversive properties. The strength of these conditioned consequences depends on the aversiveness of the primary consequence with which it has been or is being paired. Most of the time, the more aversive the consequence paired with the word, the more aversive the word will become. For example, "No!" paired with a slap will probably be more aversive than "No!" paired with a frown. However, the aversiveness of an event is only partially inherent in the stimulus itself. A stimulus aversive to most people may be reinforcing for a particular individual. In the above example, an individual who finds a slap pleasantly stimulating rather than aversive does not associate aversiveness with "No!" Watson and Sanders (1966) found "No" to be aversive, mildly aversive, neutral, and rewarding to different mentally retarded individuals, possibly because of the relationship of the individual to the trainer. The more status the modifier has in the individual's eyes, the more aversive the "No" is because it is paired with disapproval. Madsen, Becker, Thomas, Koser, and Plager (1970) found that contingent "sit down" commands caused an increase in a trainer's standing, while praise caused a decrease in standing. Also, Thomas, Becker and Armstrong (1968) found that an increase in disapproval of a teacher was followed by significant increases in motor and noise-making aspects of inappropriate behavior. Consequently, the strength of verbal aversives depends on the aversiveness of the consequence with which it has been paired, and there is variation among individuals' perceptions of levels of aversiveness.

A second limitation arises when a word or phrase paired with a mild consequence works to decrease behavior, but does not work efficiently. Peine (1972) virtually eliminated head banging in a retarded individual with the contingent use of "No" but only after 201 days of training. Thus, some methods may involve long periods of time. In many cases this is not advisable (if a child is self-abusive) or possible (when behavior is life threatening, staff is not available, etc.).

Response Cost   Punishment involving removal of a positive reinforcer after the performance of an undesirable behavior will weaken or eliminate the behavior. It must take place in situations where the individual has previously earned or been given rewards and has the opportunity to earn rewards in the future. The individual, then, experiences something like a fine. The trainer takes away such things as tokens, food, or play time (Sulzbacher & Houser, 1968) or colored slips of paper with the person's name on them (Hall, Axelrod, Foundopoulos, Shellman, Campbell, & Cranston, 1971).

Programs involving the use of response cost have been employed by Baer (1962), who reduced thumbsucking with contingent termination of television cartoons (activity response cost), and Hall et al. (1971), who eliminated complaining behavior by taking back colored slips of paper for each complaint. Phillips, Phillips, Fixsen, and Wolf (1971) conducted a study and concluded that point loss was more effective than point gain. Phillips (1968), McNamara (1971), and Burchard and Barrera

(1972) conducted studies that concluded that aggressive behavior, disruptive behavior, and delinquent behavior, respectively, can be reduced with a token program involving response cost.

Effective response cost programs involve the withdrawal of a token or activity established as a reinforcer. The individual must value what is to be taken and must have earned enough of it so that when the target response is emitted, the fine can be imposed. The effectiveness of a program also depends on the individual's ability to understand the relationship between the undesirable behavior and the loss of the reward. Frequently, a good response cost program is combined with an active positive reinforcement program to have the desired effect.

Several studies report a variety of problems encountered with the use of response cost. McLaughlin and Malaby (1972) found that response-cost programs were not universal in their reductive effect. Aggressive responses were noted by Sloane, Young, and Marcusen (1977), and Doty, McInnis, and Paul (1974) noted refusal to pay fines. Meichenbaum, Bower, and Ross (1968) had individuals who rebelled. Iwata and Bailey (1974) found that a response-cost program caused the staff to deliver fewer verbal reinforcers and Kazdin (1977) states that such programs place emphasis on what an individual is not supposed to do rather than what he or she should do.

Time-out   Time-out is the removal of opportunity to obtain reinforcement whenever the specified undesirable behavior occurs. Time-out may take the form of social isolation, including isolation from the trainer. It may also include removal of whatever element is providing reinforcement, for example, removal of the plate during lunch contingent on misbehavior at the meal. Although time-out typically consists of short time periods, it is usually inadvisable to release the individual from time-out until any inappropriate behavior (crying, tantrums, etc.) has passed, which is usually after 1–10 minutes.

Time-out has been used successfully to modify a wide variety of troublesome behaviors in severely and profoundly handicapped individuals (Sachs, 1973). Aggressive and disruptive behavior (Bostow & Bailey, 1969), inappropriate mealtime behavior (Barton, Guess, Garcia, & Baer, 1970), and self-injurious behavior (Lucero, Frieman, Spoering, & Fehrenbacher, 1976) have all been reduced or eliminated by the use of time-out. Risley and Wolf (1967) suggested ignoring distractability and hyperactivity in echolalic children to eliminate those behaviors. Removal of the reinforcing element of the situation has been employed by Barton et al. (1970), who removed food trays for short periods of time to modify the inappropriate table manners of retarded, institutionalized children. Porterfield, Herbert-Jackson, and Risley (1976) removed the offending individual from the group, but allowed him to still see the group's activity.

This reduced disruptive behavior. A time-out booth was used by Blake and Moss (1967) to decrease crying.

McDonough and Forehand (1973) reviewed studies on time-out and made several tentative conclusions regarding the implementation of a time-out program. First, explaining the reason for placement in time-out to the individual did not seem to affect the success of time-out. Second, they found that warnings prior to time-out had an unclear effect on its success. Third, they stated that verbal instruction is preferable to physical force for placing persons in time-out because it does not offer aggression as a model, but that very few of the studies mentioned the technique used. Isolation time-out appeared to be more effective than same-area time-out because reinforcement for maladaptive behavior could be better controlled. McDonough and Forehand also concluded that short-term periods (1–15 minutes) were as effective as long-term periods (30 minutes to 3 hours) if the individual had no prior experience with long-term time-out. This is supported by White, Nielson, and Johnson (1972) who state that short periods (5–10 minutes) are usually as effective as long periods (30–60 minutes) if applied consistently. The McDonough and Forehand study stated that the presence or absence of a signal for the beginning and end of time-out has not been systematically studied. Finally, McDonough and Forehand stated that release from time-out should be contingent upon specified periods of desirable behavior within the time-out situation.

The effective use of time-out requires consistent application of a time-out situation after each occurrence of a misbehavior. The modifier must be able to implement a time-out program with a minimum of anger. This reduces any social reinforcement that an individual may gain from causing stress on the trainer. The modifier must not reinforce the individual during time-out. Reinforcement might include telling the individual to be quiet or to stay in time-out. Although negative, this kind of attention can reinforce inappropriate behavior.

There are several factors that limit the use and success of time-out programs. First, in some instances time-out can serve to increase undesirable behavior instead of decrease it. In some cases, an individual might use time-out to escape from the situation. For example, a person may engage in misbehavior when asked to complete a task in order to be timed-out and thus to escape the work involved in completing the task. In other cases, individuals find isolation itself reinforcing. Time-out may also be a means by which an individual can engage in inappropriate behavior without reprimand. Other limitations of time-out include the difficulty in physically manipulating large subjects, the possibility of forgetting to remove the child from time-out (Neisworth & Madle, 1976), and the fact that long time-outs suppress desirable as well as undesirable behavior

(Zimmerman & Baydan, 1963). Also, Pendergrass (1971) found that response-contingent time-outs that did not include positive reinforcement of an alternative desirable behavior did suppress hitting in a five-year-old brain-damaged child but left the child spending long periods of time lying on the floor. Here, the behavior was suppressed but was not spontaneously replaced by desirable behavior. Baumeister and Rollings (1976) found that time-out was effective for self-injurious behavior, but that it was a slow process that allowed a high incidence of self-abuse before the behavior was eliminated. Neisworth and Madle stated that the staff may be reinforced by prolonging time-out for a disruptive individual. As long as the person is in time-out, the staff does not have to deal with the person's disruptive behavior.

Overcorrection Overcorrection is an "educative punishment" (Foxx, 1976) consisting of two components: restitution and positive practice. Restitutional overcorrection requires the individual to restore the environment that was disturbed by the undesirable behavior and to improve the environment over its original condition. Positive-practice overcorrection requires the individual to perform the desired behaviors that should have occurred instead of the undesirable behavior.

Overcorrection is used to decrease such classes of undesirable behavior as stereotyped and repetitive behavior and destructive and self-abusive behavior. Specific programs have also been designed to eliminate toileting accidents. Azrin, Kaplan, and Foxx (1973) decreased self-stimulating behavior in nine profoundly retarded persons and Foxx and Azrin (1973) reduced similar behavior in autistic and retarded persons. Floor-sprawling behavior was eliminated in a study by Azrin and Wesolowski (1975). Nine profoundly retarded persons were toilet trained by Azrin and Foxx (1971). Azrin, Kaplan and Foxx (1973) and Foxx and Azrin (1972) used an "autism reversal" procedure that required the individual to engage in several different fixed postures that were nonstimulatory. Instructions and manual guidance were used on a contingent basis to direct the fixed postures when self-stimulating behaviors occurred.

Required relaxation was used by Webster and Azrin (1973). An individual who engaged in self-injurious behavior was told that he or she was overexcited and agitated and must relax in bed for two hours.

Azrin and Nunn (1973) gave individuals training in continual awareness of the hand position. This "hand-awareness training" reduced the possibility of self-injurious behavior.

Positive practice successfully reduces an inappropriate behavior while teaching alternative forms of desired behavior. When no environmental disturbances occur, a verbal warning to stop is delivered. The individual is physically stopped, required to practice appropriate behavior, and then returned to the ongoing activity.

According to Foxx and Azrin (1972), restitutive acts must be designed to

1. directly relate to the misbehavior of concern and not to be arbitrary or punitive.
2. be immediately contingent upon the disruptive action.
3. be extended in time to be effective.
4. require active participation and effort (the work or effort serving as an "inhibitory event").

Epstein, Doke, Sajwaj, Sorrel, and Rimmer (1974) state that trainers using overcorrection must tell the person that he or she behaved inappropriately, stop the person from engaging in the inappropriate behavior, provide systematic, verbal instructions for the overcorrection activity, force practice of the desired behavior, and return the person to the ongoing activity.

Overcorrection procedures have some limitations. Axelrod, Brantner and Meddock (1978) concluded that overcorrection procedures changed nontarget behavior in favorable and nonfavorable directions and suggested that precise measurements of the side effects of overcorrection are needed. Also, Murphy (1978) found that overcorrection procedures caused worsening of behaviors in some instances. Axelrod et al. found that generalization and maintenance of behavior have been both good and bad.

Negative consequences of overcorrection were found by Doleys and Arnold (1975), who found that crying and tantrums occurred when it was used. Azrin and Wesolowski (1975), who encountered emotional reaction and physical resistance to overcorrection procedures.

Aside from the possible side effects and negative consequences, there are limitations in practical application as well. Kelly and Drabman (1977a) discontinued overcorrection that rapidly eliminated self-injurious behavior because of the constraints on staff and time and the resistance of the staff to physically manipulate subjects. Overcorrection procedures require individual, close supervision and thus place great demands on the staff involved. The success of overcorrection relies on the absence of client resistance and on the willingness of the staff (Azrin & Foxx, 1971; Webster & Azrin, 1973).

Presentation of Aversive Stimuli

Although an aversive stimulus must be defined operationally as any stimulus that decreases the future rate of undesirable response, this section will deal specifically with stimuli assumed to be painful or annoying. Thus, the presentation of aversive stimuli is differentiated from other methods of punishment. The first part of this section will deal with contingent electric shock (CES) and the second part will describe other aversive stimuli.

Contingent Electric Shock (CES)   Successful employment of a punishment procedure with the use of contingent electric shock has been demonstrated by Tate and Baroff (1966). They report two studies that endeavored to reduce or eliminate the self-injurious behavior of a 9-year-old psychotic boy. Chronic self-injurious behavior was controlled in the first study by contingent withdrawal of human physical contact. Although this procedure produced a dramatic reduction in frequency, it was decided that the risk of further damage to the child's retina precluded long-term use of this method, which only reduced the behavior. In order to reduce the behavior, the second study was implemented with painful electric shock contingent on self-injurious behavior. When the second study was written, CES had followed occurrences of SIB for 167 days at the time of the writing. The last self-injurious behavior was noted on the 147th day. Risley (1968) used punishment with CES to eliminate the disruptive and dangerous climbing behaviors of a deviant child. Time-out procedures, extinction, and reinforcement of incompatible behavior had failed to eliminate the behavior. Bucher and Lovaas (1968) state that the severe self-destructive behavior of one particular subject precluded the use of an extinction procedure, as she could have killed herself. The application of CES was successful in suppressing and virtually eliminating the high rate of self-destructive responses. Corte, Wolf, and Locke (1971) used CES to eliminate the self-injurious behavior of 4 subjects, two of whom had been in an unsuccessful program involving the reinforcement of noninjurious behavior. This program was ineffective when food was not withheld as a reinforcer and effective with one subject on a mild food deprivation program. Elimination of all social consequences as a means of reducing the behavior was not effective with either subject. The effect of the contingent electric shock was successful in eliminating the behavior if it occurred in the setting where it was delivered. Prochaska (1974) used remote-controlled, response-contingent shock to reduce head banging in a 9-year-old profoundly retarded girl. Cunningham and Linschied (1976) instituted the use of mild electric shock to reduce ruminative vomiting in a 9-month-old infant.

The success of programs involving the use of CES seems to depend on producing the shock immediately after the defined response and on making it occur in different settings. Also, the subject cannot be allowed to escape the shock once the specified undesirable behavior has been observed.

There are many limitations in the use of CES in programs. Corte et al. (1971) noted that although the use of CES was successful, the elimination of the self-injurious behavior that occurred was specific to the setting in which the punishment occurred. Regulations and restrictions of agencies often preclude the use of electric shock. Moral and ethical concerns often prevent persons from employing programs using CES. Complications may develop in a CES-treated individual, including fear of the shock device, aggression, emotional upset, aversion to the experimenter, and a tendency to recidivism in the absence of the punishment or the punishing agent. The dangers of electric shock (Butterfield, 1975) as well as the difficulties in obtaining, maintaining, and managing equipment often limit or prevent the use of shock programs in the classroom or home.

Other Aversive Stimuli   Although the use of electric shock seems to dominate the literature on aversive stimuli, a variety of other techniques have been used. Morganstern (1974) used nausea-producing chemicals such as emetine or amorphine. Eight-year-old autistic children were toilet trained with slaps on the buttocks (Marshall, 1966). Tate and Baroff (1966) used a buzzing sound as a conditioned aversive stimuli. More unusual aversive stimuli include Scagliotta's (1975) amplification of a child's own screams, Greene and Hoats' (1969) television distortion, Greene, Hoats, and Hornick's (1970) music distortion, Hewett's (1965) darkness, and Kelly and Drabman's (1976) lemon juice placed on the child's tongue.

The use of such aversive stimuli with severely and profoundly handicapped individuals has at least three distinct advantages. First, the employment of contingent aversive stimuli in an appropriate program can quickly and efficiently decrease dangerous behavior. Tate and Baroff (1966) decreased dangerous self-injurious behavior, Risley (1968) eliminated dangerous climbing behavior, and Lang and Melamed (1969) eliminated life-threatening vomiting. Second, appropriate implementation can decrease socially inappropriate behaviors. Kelly and Drabman (1977b), for example, decreased tongue-thrusting behavior in a 34-month-old female. Third, the use of contingent aversive stimuli can indirectly increase desirable behaviors. Tate and Baroff (1966) noted that increased smiling, listening, attending to the environment, and cooperating with others accompanied the decrease in self-injurious behavior. Although Risley (1968) decreased disruptive and dangerous climbing behavior, he noted no suppression of other behaviors and an increase in the rate of desirable behavior. Cunningham and Linschied (1976) and Kelly and Drabman (1977b) both documented general improvement in social responses. Lang and Melamed (1969) noticed more smiles and interest in toys and games. Employing a program consisting of presentation of aversive stimuli involves two crucial operations: (1) choosing the ideal aversive stimulus and (2) responsibly employing its use. Thomas (1968) concluded that to increase the effectiveness of punishment, the punishment must neither be so mild as to be inconsequential nor so strong as to be devastating, immediately contingent to the undesirable response, matter-of-factly administered, and used for obtaining immediate suppressive effects under the conditions during which the punishment is applied. Thomas also states that alternative responses not compatible with the punished response should be identified and reinforced. Prior to implementation of a punishment program, careful consideration must be given to possible alternative methods and potential side effects. In instances in which aversive stimulation treatment is chosen, a complete plan including permission and cooperation of the parents should be designed. Particularly since the aversive techniques above are easily obtained and implemented, special care must be taken to avoid misuse. Professional design of the program is needed to ensure response-contingent aversive stimulation. Medical consultation may be necessary to escape any harmful effects of the treatment.

Mild but effective techniques such as the use of lemon juice are rare. Aversive stimuli less dramatic than electric shock and nausea-producing chemicals are greatly needed by teachers and parents. Even though the appropriate uses of intensely aversive stimuli are gaining acceptance, most offer little to the teacher or parent. Greene and Hoats (1971) state that "despite the fact that such a variety of punishment techniques are generally accepted in clinically oriented situations, they cannot always be used where legislation, administrative policy, and personal attitudes may preclude their use" (p. 390). This becomes particularly evident in the classroom and home settings where use may also be prohibited by community attitudes, limited funds, and lack of parental consent or permission.

Establishing Aversive Stimuli   The ideal aversive stimulus needs to be easily obtainable, easily implemented, and easily duplicated. Such an aversive stimulus must be consistent, dependable, and effective. It must be relatively inexpensive and cause as little disruption to the classroom or family as possible. Furthermore, the ideal stimulus must offer no escape for the subject and require minimal effort for the teacher or parent. In order to be of use to the teacher or parent, a stimulus must not involve complicated equipment and must be portable enough to apply in many settings. See Appendix B for a discussion of various types of aversive stimuli.

MAINTAINING BEHAVIORAL GAINS

Unless a behavioral program is integral to maintaining a behavioral gain, desirable behaviors will weaken and deviant behaviors will recur when the program is discontinued. Thus, the program must ensure that behavior is under control (1) in different settings and with different cues, (2) with different reinforcement schedules, and (3) with different reinforcing and punishing agents.

Fading

Although fading generally refers to gradually reducing behavior control, there are four specific fading processes. First, fading can decrease the magnitude of the stimulus, as in reducing the amount of an edible, length of time at a pleasant activity, or restraint in time-out. A second form of fading is the substitution of a previously less effective consequence. Examples are arranging for "good!" or gold stars instead of edibles to increase desirable behavior or for "no!" instead of physical restraint to decrease undesirable behavior. Third, fading can gradually reduce the rate of reinforcement or punishment. This requires either more incidents of desirable behavior to occur or a greater length of time to pass before the consequence is presented. Fourth, fading may gradually eliminate physical and verbal prompts or cues.

A previously ineffective reinforcer or punisher gains the magnitude needed to modify behavior when it is presented at the same time as an effective consequence. A new stimulus is presented just before the older, more effective reinforcer or punisher. This allows for the pairing of the consequences and thus the individual associates the two stimuli.

If a child has learned to sit quietly for five minutes consistently when he or she is reinforced every minute with juice, one of several forms of fading may be instituted. The amount of juice for each minute may be reduced, a gold star may be slowly substituted for the juice, or juice may be presented after increasingly longer time periods.

Horner and Keilitz (1975) provide an example of the fourth method of fading. They decreased the amount of assistance from instructions, modeling, and prompting to modeling with instructions, modeling without instructions, and finally without instructions when teaching mentally retarded persons to brush their teeth.

Before fading is instituted, a behavior must be under the control of a stimulus that is either increasing or maintaining the rate of an appropriate behavior or decreasing or maintaining the rate of an undesirable behavior. Data must confirm that the behavior is stable or steadily changing in the desirable direction. All changes in behavioral programs must be made slowly and in small steps.

Increasing the Delay of Consequences

This procedure refers to increasing the latency period preceding the presentation of the stimulus. This can take place through manipulation of reinforcement schedules as well as increasing the delay between the behavior and the presentation of the stimulus. For example, the schedule can be changed so that more incidents of appropriate behavior are required before the stimulus is delivered. Using an interval schedule, reinforcement can be given to the first correct response after a certain period of time and that length of time can be increased.

Although this procedure has value for severely and profoundly handicapped individuals, it is crucial to employ the procedure gradually. Because behavior is tied to its immediate consequences, individuals must not be expected to tolerate long delays in receiving a reinforcement or punishment. Severely and profoundly handicapped individuals may not understand that one consequence applies to the previously emitted behavior.

Shifting to Natural Reinforcers

Kauffman and Snell (1977) state that it is reasonable to expect that responses will have a better chance of being maintained and generalized in new settings if the consequences following those responses are automatic (i.e., food in the mouth following a self-feeding effort) or part of normal social intercourse (i.e., praise and attention). It is often necessary to use artificial reinforcers to establish responses in the severely and profoundly handicapped individual but natural consequences can be phased in slowly.

It is not only expected that responses will be better maintained in the natural environment if natural reinforcers are used; it is the goal of every well-designed behavior program to bring the behavior under the control of consequences that are as natural as possible.

Transferring Behavioral Gains

The long-range goal of any behavior modification program should be to bring the behavior under the control of natural consequences. This includes assuring that the behavior is generalized, that is, that it will occur in all settings in which it is appropriate.

The facilitation of generalization may include:

1. training the behavior until it is firmly established in one setting and then training in each setting necessary.
2. training across settings from the start.
3. training with several trainers, including those from the individual's natural environment.
4. introducing natural consequences by pairing them with the artificial training consequences.
5. introducing an artificial cue for behavior to occur and fading the cue.
6. pairing the artificial cue with cues from the natural environment.
7. reinforcing attempts of the individual to perform the behavior in different settings.

Designing Appropriate Programs

Designing an entire behavioral program includes:

1. choosing and defining a target behavior.
   a. pinpointing a change that will benefit the individual in some way.

   b. breaking down a behavior into components small enough for successful modification.

   c. choosing a behavior that is a prerequisite to the development of a necessary skill.

2. taking data to ensure that the behavior needs modification (i.e. that the behavior is stable and not already improving).

3. considering all possible methods, alternatives, and combination of methods.

4. choosing and implementing the most effective yet least forceful method or combination.

5. taking data to ensure that the program is having the desired effect.

CONCERNS ABOUT THE USE OF BEHAVIOR MODIFICATION

The recent increase in behavioral programs for severely and profoundly retarded individuals has produced a number of ethical concerns. Some of these concerns are discussed here and an attempt is made to justify the use of behavior modification procedures.

Conflict between Behavior Modification and Normalization

There has been controversy over possible conflict between the normalization philosophy now guiding the development of the mentally retarded and the use of behavior-conditioning techniques. Roos (1974), Tennant, Hattersly, and Cullen (1978), and Aanes and Haagenson (1978) are but a few of the persons concerned about this controversy. The normalization principle has been described by Nirje (1972) as "making available to the mentally retarded patterns and conditions of every day life which are as close as possible to the norms and patterns of the mainstream of society." The crux of the conflict between this principle and the conditioning approach is summarized by Tennant, Hattersly and Cullen (1978). They state that although normalization is an "important therapeutic target for the developmentally retarded...many training procedures employ arbitrary relationships...between behavior and its environment which are not typical of similar behavior maintained by society" (p. 44).

     Aanes and Haagenson (1978) endeavor to resolve this conflict by distinguishing between normalization as a goal and as a means to achieve a goal. They argue that nonnormal techniques may be the most effective and efficient means of obtaining normal behavior and that normalization as an end is the important concept.

     Inclusion of a severely handicapped individual in society consists of offering environments approximating the cultural norm and shaping behaviors to the most socially acceptable pattern possible. These two important aspects of normalization become targets for all persons accepted by society, including the most severely and profoundly handicapped individuals. The goals of the behavioral approach are in line with the goals of normalization when conditioning socially acceptable behaviors. Roos (1970) provides an example that contributes to the resolution of the conflict. He asserts that conditioning approaches should maximize a person's interaction with his or her physical and interpersonal environments. Appropriate interaction with the environment and with other persons is socially acceptable behavior and both the behavioral and normalization principles provide the basis for the means to achieve this interaction.

Roos expands on the concurrence of the two approaches, stressing that the conditioning approach, focused on teaching skills to the retarded, aims to increase the opportunity for the staff to meaningfully interact with the retarded by relieving personnel of as much routine custodial activity (e.g., toileting, feeding, and replacing soiled clothing) as possible. This is not only true in institutional settings but is true in families and group homes as well. A more normal interaction may take place when the primary caretaker (e.g., parent, relative, or houseparent) has less menial taskwork.

Roos questions the claim that normalization is the more humane philosophy. He states that advocates of the normalization principle deny the mentally retarded person a choice, whereas advocates of conditioning procedures might elect to abide by the individual's choice. Roos suggests that the mentally retarded might choose "paste" food over "normal" food and noise over music. The advocate of the normalization principle generally supports the more normal pattern for the retarded person. "Which of the alternatives is the most 'humane,' however is a debatable question" (Roos, 1970).

Justification of the Use of Aversive Therapy

Many of the objectives to behavior modification center around procedures and techniques that employ aversive treatment. Some of these criticisms are due to the undesirable side effects that often accompany the frequent use of punishment. Such possible side effects include:

1. identification of the trainer with the aversive event.
2. rebellion against the trainer or toward an irrelevant object.
3. short duration of the suppression of the behavior.
4. suppression of the behavior only in the presence of the punishment agent.
5. increase of undesirable behaviors such as whining and crying.

Other criticisms of punishment point out its focus on negative aspects of behavior, its use of physical aggression as a model, its nonemphasis on acceptable behavior, and its goals of conformity and docility.

There is support for the use of punishment and aversive consequences. Solomon (1964) reviewed the research and concluded that the
scientific premises offered for the rejection of punishment were not ten-
able and that punishment could be a very useful tool for effecting behavior
change. Lovaas et al. (1965) agree with Solomon that objectives of using
pain for therapeutic purposes have a moral rather than a scientific basis.

Part of the controversy over the use of aversive consequences stems
from the fact that it is so often used with individuals who are not voluntarily involved in a behavioral program. Lang and Melamed (1969) state
that their case is of particular interest because the subject was a 9-month-
old infant who could not voluntarily submit to the procedures. Yet their
behavioral treatment was not only effective in eliminating vomiting and
ruminating with contingent electric shock but they increased desirable
behaviors as well. Thus, the effect of the program was so positive that it
seems to justify the use of such treatment even without the consent of the
individual involved. Brandsma and Stein (1973) state that it seems ethical
to use punishment therapy with subjects who do not volunteer if their behavior is physically dangerous to others. In cases where the behavior of
the individual threatens his or her own well-being or that of others, the
use of punishment therapy may be justified.

Many of the objectives to the use of aversive therapy center around
the potential negative side effects. Schriebman (1977) counters these criticisms by stating that "no matter how unpopular, the response-contingent
electric shock is an effective technique and does not have the negative
side-effects that many people feared" (p. 203). Lang and Melamed (1969)
not only decreased the target behaviors of infants and noted the absence
of undesirable side effects, they noted that desirable behaviors emerged.
The infants' responsiveness to adults, smiles, and interest in toys and
games all increased.

In addition to arguments supporting the use of punishment because
of its desirable effects, there is also evidence supporting its use because of
the restricted choice of alternatives. Gardner (1969) defends the consideration of punishment procedures with a convincing argument by showing
the limitations of an extinction procedure (Wolf, Birnbrauer, Williams, &
Lawler, 1965) which would involve a decrease or an eventual elimination
of a behavior by discontinuing the stimulus conditions which reinforce it.
Gardner and Briskin (1969) state that response to extinction procedures
and behavior-shaping procedures is often too little or too slow. Azrin
and Holz (1966) suggest that a reductive method such as punishment is
needed because it is difficult to identify and control the reinforcing
events. Hamilton and Stephens (1967) also state that it is difficult to analyze and control the reinforcing contingencies.

With the increased movement of moderately and severely retarded
and multiply handicapped children into the classroom setting, the quick,

efficient, effective modification of behavior patterns such as aggressiveness, self-destructiveness, and tantrums becomes an immediate necessity. Also, the increasing trends of normalization and deinstitutionalization leave many parents faced with behavior problems in the home. This need to eliminate or reduce in frequency or severity such behavior patterns is problematic for the parent or teacher who may not have the resources to implement therapeutic programs requiring the use of complicated or expensive equipment. Programs that require long periods of training or lengthy or tedious training sessions may also be unsuitable.

Although it is important to recognize negative side effects and potential disadvantages of punishment, its dramatic reductions in the frequency or severity of dangerous behaviors in many cases support further use, including employment in the classroom and home. The speed with which response-contingent aversive stimulation can decrease or eliminate behaviors can be crucial to the safety of mentally retarded persons and those with whom they have contact. It can provide an alternative to long periods of physical restraint, drugs, and continued undesirable or unacceptable behaviors. The use of punishment is also supported by evidence that shows an increase in desirable behaviors (Lang & Melamed, 1969).

Much attention has been given to the use of aversive stimuli with behaviors immediately detrimental to the subject or others (Kelly & Drabman, 1977b). Kelly and Drabman state that there is a class of behaviors that some persons find unpleasant or disquieting and that exert a seriously detrimental influence on the social adjustment of retarded individuals. They advocate the use of aversive stimuli for this class of behaviors. They demonstrated this use with lemon juice for tongue extension with a 34-month-old female. She showed greatly increased social responsiveness when others showed positive reactions to her. Thus it seems justified to use mildly aversive consequences to decrease or eliminate behaviors that are of a less severe nature but nonetheless can be harmful to the individual or interfere with the person's acceptance in society.

Aversive contingencies are criticized because they cause suffering to the client involved in such a program. Although a procedure involving the use of such consequences may cause temporary suffering, it will probably reduce substantial suffering in the long run. In cases of severe self-destructive behavior or life-threatening destructive behavior, the use of aversive consequences seems justified if it can reduce the long-term suffering caused by such behavior. The same argument applies to cases in which the behavior is of a less severe nature; that is, the decrease in unacceptable social behaviors can reduce future suffering caused by rejection or lack of social acceptance.

Justification of the use of aversive techniques can also be argued by viewing such techniques as nonnormal means employed to achieve normative goals. Thus, if a goal is justified and the aversive procedure is the best method of achieving the goal, there is support for the use of these procedures. Aversive techniques may also be viewed as simply applying stricter control of aversive contingencies already present in our environment. That is, aversive consequences are abundant in our society and aversive therapy is only the systematic use of such consequences to modify behavior.

Cooke and Cooke (1974) point out that aversive therapy often relieves a behavior that if left untreated could have consequences far worse than those of the therapy. Cahoon (1968) feels that it would be unethical of behavior modifiers not to apply aversive techniques in situations in which they have been found to be effective. Baer (1970) notes that "Not to rescue a person from an unhappy organization of his behavior is to punish him in that it leaves him in a state of recurrent punishment" (p. 246). It must be noted, though, that despite the usefulness of aversive therapy, it is justifiable only after other methods have been weighed.

Concern for the Rights and Dignity of Individuals

The justification of methods that control behavior raises a deep concern for the rights, dignity, and even safety of those involved in such programs. Repp and Deitz (1978) state that it is not behavior psychology that should be criticized in this regard, but rather the misuse of the procedures through poor training or poor judgement. Because of this concern, statements endorsing and specifying the rights of the retarded have come from both professionals and legal policies (Cook, Altman, & Haavik, 1978).

Guidelines, policies, and statements regarding rights are extremely important to the success of the behavior modification model. Limitations of the model itself must be recognized and acceptable procedures and standards (regarding goals, personnel, etc.) designed to safeguard the inherent shortcomings in the model.

MacMillan and Forness (1970) discuss the fact that learning theory does not guide the teacher in determining educational goals. Although the behavior modification strategy does not claim to determine goals, its inability to do so puts the procedures, powerful tools for behavior change, in the hands of persons who may arbitrarily decide what behaviors are to be changed. Wood (1968) states that like many tools, behavior modification techniques are morally blind. He likens a tool to a stout sword that works equally well in the hands of hero or tyrant. Acknowledging this becomes extremely important in the use of these procedures with the severely and profoundly impaired person who may be completely at the mercy of others.

Given that behavior modification procedures are used by highly trained personnel and that those persons choose appropriate goals and implement appropriate methods, still another issue arises. Behavioral procedures are said to be highly manipulative and to infringe upon the rights of others. Many behavior programs, especially programs for the mentally retarded, involve the therapists choosing goals for behavior modification and designing programs for working toward the goals. Roos (1970) states that although "reinforcement contingencies can indeed be established without the subject's knowledge, this is by no means essential or even desirable" (p. 13). Furthermore, he says that mentally retarded persons can select behaviors to be modified and rewards to be gained. In some instances this may be true; however, even in instances in which this procedure of involving the client is followed, the concern must be the extent to which the therapist is controlling the choices of the client. First, it must be expected that a retarded person, by virtue of his or her retardation, will not be able to fully understand the relationship of his or her behavior to the environment; a client will have a limited viewpoint that will have been greatly influenced by other people. Second, advocates of conditioning procedures generally aim toward goals that will help the person develop behaviors acceptable to society and decrease or eliminate unacceptable behaviors. However valuable a goal, it was predetermined by the behaviorist who, consequently, is controlling and manipulating the client toward that end.

If a therapist determines "humane" goals, he or she is controlling and manipulating. If he or she allows a client to choose between alternatives, the therapist is controlling the choices of that client. If the therapist allows the client to continue as is, he or she may be denying that individual the opportunity to develop the skills a person needs to become accepted in society. Although the behavior modification strategy is one that controls and manipulates, it seems unethical not to use its procedures in situations in which they have been found to be effective.

Skinner (1976) writes that "contingencies designed for explicit purposes can be called manipulative, though it does not follow that they are exploitative; unarranged contingencies must be recognized as having equal power, and also possibly unhappy consequences" (p. 268). It seems, then, that the issue is not one of control or lack of control, but rather what kind of control and toward what ends the control should be used (Cooke and Cooke, 1974).

Roos (1970) states that the conditioning approach aims to maximize a person's control over the environment and to reduce the helplessness that typifies most profoundly retarded persons. Giving a hypothetical example of a bed-ridden, nonverbal, profoundly retarded child who is usually completely helpless in controlling the environment, Roos suggests that if through conditioning procedures the children learn to roll to one side of the crib. If the child is then conditioned to roll to one side to turn lights on, and to the opposite side to turn them off, then the child gains control over one segment of the environment. Roos further suggests that a child might learn to flex each finger and that each finger might be able to activate a circuit turning on a different type of sound of music, offering him an opportunity to select among alternatives. In his conclusion, Roos states that conditioning may offer the nonverbal child a method of communication of needs and preferences. As for the concern as to kind of control and toward what ends, it seems that if techniques offer the severely or profoundly disabled person ways to achieve a behavior or to extend the range of behavior, then those employing the procedures are the most human and humane. They are helping a person to develop a behavior that expands the capacity to choose, to have purposes, and to behave as he or she wishes.

Skinner sums up the supporting arguments:

> Behavior is the achievement of a person, and we seem to deprive the human organism of something which is his natural due when we instead point to the environmental sources of his behavior. We do not dehumanize him; we dehomunculize him. The essential issue is autonomy. Is man in control of his own destiny or is he not? The point is often made by arguing that a scientific analysis changes man from victor to victim. But man remains what he always has been, and his most conspicuous achievement has been the designed construction of a world which has freed him from constraints and vastly extended his range. (p. 263)

There seems to be no controversy over the concern that severely and profoundly retarded persons be treated in a humane manner with dignity and respect (Roos, 1970). In fact, the following quotation from an article on public education for the handicapped signifies the inclusion of the handicapped person in the American ideal of individuality:

> If it is possible to speak of the genius of a culture, the focus or concentration of its energies, of the ends toward which it historically inclines, the genius of American culture might be the ideal of the individual. For us, the worth of the individual is the foundation of value; the well being of the individual is the chief object of social purpose and action. (Schipper, Wilson, & Wolf, 1977, p. 6)

But, as Larsen (1977) points out few people believe that our institutions have provided even humane care, much less effective training and treatment programs. Larsen cites Wolfensberger (1971) as characterizing the average public residential facility as "a deindividualizing residence in which retarded persons are congregated in numbers distinctly larger than might be found in a large family; in which they are highly regimented; in which the physical or social environment aims at a low common denominator; and in which all or most all of the transactions of daily life are carried out under one roof, on one campus, in largely segregated fashion" (p. 17).

The use of conditioning procedures toward a medium between normalizing and individualizing ends implemented by well trained, well intentioned persons seems to be the most humane endeavor to improve the quality of life of the severely or profoundly retarded individual. Conditioning techniques that reduce social processes to the behavior of the individual, that develop behavior that frees persons from constraints and extends their range of behavior, and which makes interaction with other individuals and the environment more meaningful are certainly in line with the American ideal of individuality.

APPENDIX A / Examples of Stimuli to be Used as Positive Reinforcers

ACTIVITIES
Blowing soap bubbles
Climbing a ladder
Drawing on butcher paper
Flipping a switch
Finger painting on a large plastic tray
Hitting suspended balloons
Kicking, catching, or throwing a ball
Listening to tapes of familiar persons, own voice, or music
Listening to the radio, or records
Looking in a mirror
Operating a coke, candy, or gum machine (Toy gum machines are available)
Painting in a plastic swimming pool or large dishpan
Playing in a sandbox, sink, or bathtub
Playing with puppets, clay, cards, Silly Putty, mobiles, macaroni, spaghetti, rice, or beads
Pouring or scooping rice or styrofoam packing material
Riding in a wagon
Rocking in a chair
Scribbling on a chalkboard
Sliding down a slide
Stamping with a stamp pad
Taking a walk or a ride
Using a vibrator or sitting in a vibrating chair or bed
Watching soap bubbles
Watching films, TV, slides, or colored lights
Wearing a smile button, ribbon, feather, or armband
Wearing dress-up clothing
Wearing perfume, lotion, or fingernail polish

ATTENTION STIMULI
Eye contact
Physical contact (hand shake, hug, kiss, pat on the shoulder, tickle, touch, etc.)
Praise ("good!", "good sitting!", "good talking!", etc.)
Sign for "good" or "okay"
Smiles
Verbalizations
Winks

EDIBLES
Apple sauce
Bread
Cake

Candy (M & M's, Lifesavers, Sweet Tarts, Lollipops, Party Mints)
Carrots
Celery
Cereal pieces
Chips (potato chips, corn chips, etc.)
Cookies
Crackers
Croutons
Cucumbers
Fruit cocktail
Fruit pieces
Gum
Ice cream
Icing
Jello
Juice
Koolaid
Mashed potatoes
Marshmallows
Milk
Peanut butter
Peanuts
Raisins
Soft drinks
Water
Whipped cream

MANIPULATABLES

Balloons
Battery-powered toys
Bean bags
Bell (such as those for calling store clerks or hand bells)
Blocks
Books
Buzzers
Catalogs
Clay
Colored pencils
Crayons
Doorbell

Drum
Electronic games that light up or make noise
Fan
Flashlight
Fuzzy material, fuzzy toys
Horns (bike horns, party horns)
Hour glass
Kaleidoscope
Kazoo
Magic markers
Magnifying glass
Music box
Musical instruments
Nerf balls
Pegs
Pencil sharpener
Ping-Pong balls
Puzzles
Radio
Rattles
Ring stands
Rhythm instruments
Rocking chair
Scented cotton
Sunglasses
Swing
Swivel chair
Tambourine
Timer
Tire pump
Top
Toy cars, guns, planes, trains
Typewriter
Unbreakable mirror
Watch
Water pistol
Whistle
Wind up toy
Yo-Yo

TOKENS

Buttons
Checkmarks

Coins
Plastic chips
Plastic flowers
Stars
Stickers

IDEAS FOR
IMPLEMENTATION

Attaching things to persons or to wheelchairs (i.e., bells to shoes or wrists, helium-inflated balloons to wheelchairs)

Connecting sounds or lights to switches

Designing circuits to be completed or broken by specified movement or restraint of movement (i.e., lifting head automatically turns on music)

Hanging things from the ceiling within reach of persons in bed, in chairs, or on the floor.

Putting manipulatables in dishpans, washtubs, sinks, plastic swimming pools, or large plastic finger-painting trays

Restricting a section of the room for activities to take place

APPENDIX B / Potential Aversive Stimuli Easily Obtained and Implemented in Home or School

Stimuli	Easily standardized		Disruptive to others	Documentation	Disadvantages
	in intensity	in duration			
Air Blast Use a balloon or bicycle pump to deliver a short blast of air into or near face of subject. The blast of air is startling and annoying.	yes	yes	no		May be too aversive
Alarm Use a travel or electric alarm clock and set off near subject. The loud noise is startling and annoying.	yes	yes	yes		Difficult to set consistently
Aromatic Ammonia Hold bottle of smelling salts in front of subject's nose. The smell is unpleasant and annoying.	yes	yes	no	Knepler (1974)	Subject can avoid inhalation
Bicycle Horn Squeeze bicycle horn near subject. The sound is startling and annoying.	yes	yes	yes		
Buzzer Press hand-held buzzer on different parts of subject's body. The sound and vibration are startling and annoying.	yes	yes	no		
Radio Static Turn volume up to specified level near subject. The loud noise is startling and annoying.	yes	yes	yes		

Technique				Reference	Comments
Chalkboard Scratches Scrape chalk briefly on board near subject. The sound is startling and and annoying.	yes	yes	yes		Consistency may be difficult at first
Cigarette Smoke Hold lit cigarette in front of subject's nose. The smell is unpleasant and annoying.	yes	yes	no	Morganstern (1974)	Subject can avoid inhalation
Clicker Click a child's clicking toy near ear of subject. The noise is startling and annoying.	yes	yes	no		May be too aversive
Hair Tug Sharply tug lock of subject's hair. The feeling is painful, startling, and annoying.	no	no	no		
Lemon Juice Squirt an eye dropper containing lemon juice into subject's mouth. The taste is unpleasant and annoying.	yes	yes	no	Kelly & Drabman (1977); Sajwaj, Libet, and Agras (1974)	May irritate mouth
Pinch Sharply pinch subject. The feeling is startling, painful, and annoying.	no	no	no		
Rubber Band After stretching a rubber band between index finger and thumb, drawing taut with index finger and thumb of other hand, let the band go in direction of subject. The feeling is painful, startling, and annoying.	yes	yes	no	Mastellone (1974)	

APPENDIX B / Potential Aversive Stimuli Easily Obtained and Implemented in Home or School

Stimuli	Easily standardized		Disruptive to others	Documentation	Disadvantages
	in intensity	in duration			
Soap Squeeze liquid soap into subject's mouth. The taste is unpleasant and annoying.	yes	yes	no	Conway, Bucher and Bradley (1974)	
Tickling Forcefully and aggressively tickle subject. The feeling is annoying.	no	no	no	Green & Hoats (1971)	
Machine or Cap Gun Press trigger of gun near subject. The loud noise is startling and annoying.	yes	no	yes		
Water Pistol Squirt cold water at subject. The cold and wetness are annoying.	yes	no	no		
Whistle or Party Horn Blow whistle or horn near face of subject. The loud noise is startling and annoying.	no	no	yes	Meyer (1975)	

REFERENCES

Aanes, D., & Haagenson, L. Normalization: Attention to a conceptual disaster. *Mental Retardation*, 1978, Vol. 16 (1) 55–56.

Auxter, D. Motor skill development in the profoundly retarded. *Training School Bulletin*, 1971, *68*, 5–9.

Axelrod, S., Brantner, J. P., & Meddock, T. D. Overcorrection: A review and critical analysis. *Journal of Special Education*, 1978, *12*, 367–391.

Azrin, N. H., Gottlieb, L., Mugart, L., Wesolowski, M. D., & Rahn, T. Eliminating self-injurious behavior by educative procedures. *Behavior Research and Therapy*, 1975, *13*, 101–111.

Azrin, N. H., & Foxx, R. M. A rapid method of toilet training the institutionalized retarded. *Journal of Applied Behavior Analysis*, 1971, *4*, 89–99.

Azrin, N. H., Kaplan, S. J., & Foxx, R. M. Autism reversal: Eliminating stereotyped self-stimulation of retarded individuals. *American Journal of Mental Deficiency*, 1973, *78*, 241–248.

Azrin, N. H., & Holz, W. C. Punishment. *Operant behavior: Areas of research and application*. New York: Appleton-Century-Crofts, 1966.

Azrin, N. H., & Nunn, R. G. Habit reversal: A method of eliminating nervous habits and tics. *Behavior Research and Therapy*, 1973, *11*, 619–628.

Azrin, N. H., & Wesolowski, M. D. The use of positive practice to eliminate persistent floor spawling by profoundly retarded persons. *Behavior Therapy*, 1975, *6*, 627–631.

Azrin, N. H., & Wesolowski, M. D. Theft reversal: An overcorrection procedure for eliminating stealing by retarded persons. *Journal of Applied Behavior Analysis*, 1974, *7*, 577–581.

Baer, D. M. Laboratory control of thumb sucking by withdrawal and representation of reinforcement. *Journal of the Experimental Analysis of Behavior*, 1962, *5*, 525–528.

Baer, D. M. A case for the selective reinforcement of punishment. In C. Neuringer & J. Michael (Eds.), *Behavior modification in clinical psychology*. New York: Appleton-Century-Crofts, 1970.

Baer, D. M., Peterson, R. F., & Sherman, J. A. The development of imitation by reinforcing behavioral similarity to a model. *Journal of the Experimental Analysis of Behavior*, 1967, *10*, 5–16.

Baker, J. G., Stanish, B., & Fraser, B. Comparative effects of a token economy in nursery school. *Mental Retardation*, 1972, *10*(4), 16–19.

Barton, E. S. Inappropriate speech in a severely retarded child: A case study in language conditioning and generalization. *Journal of Applied Behavior Analysis*, 1970, *3*, 299–307.

Barton, E. S. Operant conditioning of appropriate and inappropriate speech in the profoundly retarded. *Journal of Mental Deficiency Research*, 1973, *17*, 183.

Barton, E. S., Guess, D., Garcia, E., & Baer, D. M. Improvement of retardates' mealtime behaviors by timeout procedures using multiple baseline techniques. *Journal of Applied Behavior Analysis*, 1970, *3*, 77–84.

Baumeister, A. A., & Rollings, J. P. Self-injurious behavior. In N. R. Ellis (Ed.) *International review in mental retardation*, Vol. 8. New York: Academic Press, 1976.

Bensberg, G. J., Colwell, C. N., & Cassel, R. H. Teaching the profoundly retarded self-help activities by behavior shaping techniques. *American Journal of Mental Deficiency*, 1965, *69*, 674–679.

Berkowitz, S., Sherry, P. T., & Davis, B. A. Teaching self-feeding to profound retardates using reinforcement and fading procedures. *Behavior Therapy*, 1971, *2*, 62–67.

Blake, P., & Moss, T. The development of socialization skills in an electively mute child. *Behavior Research and Therapy*, 1967, *5*, 349–356.

Bostow, D. E., & Bailey, J. B. Modification of severe disruptive and aggressive behavior using brief timeout and reinforcement procedures. *Journal of Applied Behavior Analysis*, 1969, *2*, 31–37.

Brandsma, J. M., & Stein, L. I. The use of punishment as a treatment modality: A case report. *Journal of Nervous and Mental Disease*, 1973, *156*, 30–37.

Bricker, W. A. A systematic approach to language training. In R. L. Schiefelbusch (Ed.). *Language of the mentally retarded*. Baltimore, Maryland: University Park Press, 1972.

Bricker, W. A., & Bricker, D. D. Development of receptive vocabulary in severely retarded children. *American Journal of Mental Deficiency*, 1970, *74*, 599–607.

Bucher, B., & Lovaas, O. I. Use of aversive stimulation in behavior modification. In M. R. Jones (Ed.), *Miami Symposium on the Prediction of Behavior, 1967: Aversive Stimulation*. Coral Gables, Florida: University of Miami Press, 1968.

Burchard, J. D., & Barrera, F. An analysis of timeout and response cost in a programmed environment. *Journal of Applied Behavior Analysis*, 1972, *5*, 271–282.

Butterfield, William H. Electric shock: Safety factors when used for aversive conditioning of humans. *Behavior Therapy*. 1975, *6*(1), 98–110.

Butz, R. A., & Hasazi, J. E. Developing verbal imitative behaviors in a profoundly retarded girl. *Journal of Behavior Therapy and Experimental Psychiatry*, 1973, *4*, 389–393.

Cahoon, D. D. Issues and implication of operant conditioning: Balancing procedures against outcomes. *Hospital and Community Psychiatry*, 1968, *19*, 228–229.

Conway, John B., Bucher, & Bradley, D. "Soap in the mouth" as an aversive consequence. *Behavior Therapy*, 1974, *5*(1), 154–156.

Cook, J. W., Altman, K., & Haavik, S. Consent for aversive treatment: A model form. *Mental Retardation*, 1978, 47–49.

Cooke, T. P., & Cooke, S. Behavior modification: Answers to some ethical issues. *Psychology in the Schools*, 1974, *11*(1), 5–10.

Corte, H. E., Wolf, M. M., & Locke, B. J. A comparison of procedures for eliminating self-injurious behavior of retarded adolescents. *Journal of Applied Behavior Analysis*, 1971, *4*, 201–213.

Cunningham, C. E., & Linschied, T. R. Elimination of chronic infant ruminating by electric shock. *Behavior Therapy*, 1976, *7*, 231–234.

Dalton, A. J., Rubino, C. A., & Hislop, M. W. Some effects of token rewards on school achievement of children with Down's Syndrome. *Journal of Applied Behavior Analysis*, 1973, *6*, 251–259.

Doleys, D. M., & Arnold, S. Treatment of childhood encopresis: Full cleanliness training. *Mental Retardation*, 1975, *13*, 14–16.

Doleys, D. M., Wells, K. C., Hobbs, S. A., Roberts, M. W., & Cartelli, L. M. The effects of social punishment on non-compliance: A comparison with timeout and positive practice. *Journal of Applied Behavior Analysis*, 1976, *9*, 471–482.

Doty, D. W., McInnis, T., & Paul, G. L. Remediation of negative side effects of an ongoing response-cost system with chronic mental patients. *Journal of Applied Behavior Analysis*, 1974, *1*, 191–198.

Epstein, L. H., Doke, L. A., Sajwaj, T. E., Sorrell, S., & Rimmer, B. Generality and side effects of overcorrection. *Journal of Applied Behavior Analysis*, 1974, *7*, 385-390.

Foxx, R. M. The use of overcorrection to eliminate the public disrobing (stripping) in retarded women. *Behavior Research and Therapy*, 1976, *14*, 53-61.

Foxx, R. M., & Azrin, N. H. Restitution: A method of eliminating aggressive-disruptive behaviors of retarded and brain damaged patients. *Behavior Research and Therapy*, 1972, *10*, 15-27.

Foxx, R. M., & Azrin, N. H. The elimination of autistic self-stimulatory behavior by overcorrection. *Journal of Applied Behavior Analysis*, 1973, *6*, 1-14.

Gardner, William. Use of punishment procedures with severely retarded: A review. *American Journal of Mental Deficiency*, 1969, *74*(1), 86-103.

Gardner, William, & Briskin, A. S. Use of punishment procedures in management of behavioral difficulties of the severely retarded. *Journal of Psychiatric Nursing and Mental Health Services*, January-February, 1967.

Giles, D. K., & Wolf, M. M. Toilet training institutionalized, severe retardates: An application of operant behavior modification techniques. *American Journal of Mental Deficiency*, 1966, *70*, 766-780.

Girardeau, F. L., & Spradlin, J. E. Token rewards in a cottage program. *Mental Retardation*, 1964, *2*, 345-351.

Glasser, W. Reality therapy. In V. Binder, A. Binder, & B. Rimland (Eds.), *Modern therapies*. Englewood Cliffs, N.J.: Prentice-Hall, 1976.

Gorton, C. E., & Hollis, J. H. Redesigning a cottage unit for better programming and research for the severely retarded. 1965, *Mental Retardation, 3*(3), 16-21.

Greene, R. J., & Hoats, D. L. Aversive tickling: A simple conditioning technique. *Behavior Therapy*, 1971, *2*(3), 389-393.

Greene, R. J., & Hoats, D. L. Reinforcing capabilities of television distortion. *Journal of Applied Behavior Analysis*, 1969, *2*, 139-141.

Greene, R. J., Hoats, D. L., & Hornick, A. J. Music distortion: A new technique for behavior modification. *Psychological Record*, 1970, *20*, 107-109.

Haavik, S., & Altman, K. Establishing walking by severely retarded children. *Perceptual and Motor Skills*, 1977, *7*(2), 151-163.

Hall, R. V., Axelrod, S., Foundopoulos, M., Shellman, J., Campbell, R., & Cranston, S. The effective use of punishment to modify behavior in the classroom. *Educational Technology*, 1971, *1*, 24-30.

Hamilton, J., & Stephens, L. *Reinstating speech in an emotionally disturbed mentally retarded young woman.* Unpublished paper, Gracewood State School, Georgia, 1967.

Hewett, F. M. Teaching speech to an autistic child through operant conditioning. *American Journal of Orthopsychiatry*, 1965, *35*, 927-936.

Hollis, J. H. Development of perceptual motor skills in a profoundly retarded child: Part I, prostheses. *American Journal of Mental Deficiency*, 1967a, *71*, 941-952(a).

Hollis, J. H. Development of perceptual motor skills in a profoundly retarded child. Part II: consequence, charge, and transfer. *American Journal of Mental Deficiency*, 1967b, *71*, 953-963.

Horner, R. D., & Keilitz, I. Training mentally retarded adolescents to brush their teeth. *Journal of Applied Behavior Analysis*, 1975, *8*, 301-309.

Iwata, B. A., & Bailey, J. S. Reward versus cost token systems: An analysis of the effects on students and teachers. *Journal of Applied Behavior Analysis*, 1974, *7*, 567-576.

Kauffman, J. M., & Snell, M. E. Managing the behavior of severely handicapped persons. In E. Sontag (Ed.), *Educational Programming for the Severely and Profoundly Handicapped.* Boothwyn, Pa.: CEC Division on Mental Retardation, 1977.

Kazdin, A. E. *The token economy:* A review and evaluation. New York: Plenum Press, 1977.

Kelly, J. A., & Drabman, R. S. Overcorrection: An effective procedure that failed. *Journal of Clinical Child Psychology,* 1977a, *6,* 38-40.

Kelly, J. A., & Drabman, R. S. The modification of socially detrimental behavior. *Journal of Behavior Therapy and Experimental Psychiatry,* 1977b, *8*(1), 101-104.

Kerr, N., Meyerson, L., & Michael, J. L. A procedure for shaping vocalizations in a mute child. In L. Krasner & L. P. Ullman (Eds.), *Case studies in behavior modification.* New York: Holt, Rinehart, & Winston, 1965.

Knepler, K., & Sewall, S. Negative practice paired with smelling salts in the treatment of a tic. *Journal of Behavior Therapy and Experimental Psychiatry,* 1974, *5*(2), 189-192.

Koegel, R. L., Firestone, P. B., Kramme, K. W., & Dunlap, G. Increasing spontaneous play by suppressing self-stimulation in autistic children. *Journal of Applied Behavior Analysis,* 1974, *7,* 521-528.

Lang, P. S., & Melamed, B. G. Avoidance conditioning therapy of an infant with chronic ruminative vomiting. *Journal of Abnormal Psychology,* 1969, *74,* 1-8.

Larsen, L. A. Community services necessary to program effectively for the severely and profoundly handicapped. In E. Sontag (Ed.), *Educational programming for the severely and profoundly handicapped.* Boothwyn, Pennsylvania: CEC Division on Mental Retardation, 1977.

Leitenberg, H. Is time-out from positive reinforcement an aversive event? *Psychological Bulletin,* 1965, *64,* 428-441.

Lovaas, O. I., Freitag, G., Gold, V. J., & Kassorla, I. C. Experimental studies in childhood schizophrenia: Analysis of self-destructive behavior. *Journal of Experimental Child Psychology,* 1965, *2,* 67-84.

Lovaas, O. I., Schaeffer, B., & Simmons, J. Q. Building social behavior in autistic children by use of electric shock. *Journal of Experimental Research in Personality,* 1965, *1,* 99-109.

Lovaas, O. I., & Simmons, J. Q. Manipulation of self-destruction in three retarded children. *Journal of Applied Behavior Analysis,* 1969, *2,* 143-157.

Lucero, W. J., Frieman, J., Spoering, K., & Fehrenbacher, J. Comparison of three procedures in reducing self-injurious behavior. *American Journal of Mental Deficiency,* 1976, *80,* 548-554.

MacMillan, D. L., & Forness, S. R. Behavior modification: Limitations and liabilities. *Behavior Therapy,* 1970, *1*(1), 92-107.

MacNamara, Roger. The compleat behavior modifier: Confessions of an overzealous operant conditioner. *Mental Retardation,* 1977, *15*(1), 34-37.

Madsen, C. H., Becker, W. C., Thomas, D. R., Koser, L., & Plager, E. An analysis of the reinforcing function of "sit-down" commands. In R. K. Parker (Ed.), *Readings in Educational Psychology.* Boston: Allyn & Bacon, Inc., 1970.

Marshall, G. R. Toilet training of an autustic eight-year-old through conditioning therapy: A case report. *Behavior Research and Therapy,* 1966, *4,* 242-245.

Martin, G. L., Kehoe, B., Bird, E., Jensen, V., & Darbyshine, M. Operant conditioning in the dressing behavior of severely retarded girls. *Mental Retardation,* 1971, *9,* 27-30.

McDonough, T. S., & Forehand, R. Response-contingent timeout: Important parameters in behavior modification with children. *Journal of Behavior Therapy and Experimental Psychiatry*, 1973, *4*, 231-236.

McLaughlin, T., & Malaby, J. Reducing and measuring inappropriate verbalizations in a token classroom. *Journal of Applied Behavior Analysis*, 1972, *5*, 329-333.

McNamara, J. R. Teacher and students as sources for behavior modification in the classroom. *Behavior Therapy*, 1971, *2*, 205-213.

Mastellone, Max. Aversive therapy: A new use for the old rubber band. *Journal of Behavior Therapy and Experimental Psychiatry*, 1975, *5*(3-4), 311-312.

Meichenbaum, D. H., Bower, K. S., & Ross, R. R. Modification of classroom behavior of institutionalized female adolescent offenders. *Behavior Research and Therapy*, 1968, *6*, 343-353.

Meyer, Robert G. A behavioral treatment of sleepwalking associated with test anxiety. *Journal of Behavior Therapy and Experimental Psychiatry*, 1975, *6*(2), 167-168.

Miller, H. R., Patton, M. E., & Henton, K. R. Behavior modification in a profoundly retarded child: A case report. *Behavior Therapy*, 1971, *2*, 375-384.

Morganstern, K. P. Cigarette smoke as a noxious stimulus in self-managed aversive therapy for compulsive eating: Technique and case illustration. *Behavior Therapy*, 1974, *5*(2), 255-260.

Murphy, G. Overcorrection: A critique. *Journal of Mental Deficiency Research*, 1978, *22*, 161-173.

Nawas, M. M., & Braun, S. M. The use of operant techniques for modifying the behavior of the severely and profoundly retarded. Part II: The techniques. *Mental Retardation*, 1970, *8*, 18-24.

Neisworth, J. T., & Madle, R. A. Time-out with staff accountability: A technical note. *Behavior Therapy, 7*, 261-263, 1976.

Nirje, B. The normalization principle and its human management implications. In R. B. Kugel, and W. P. Wolfensberger (Eds.), *Changing patterns in residential services for the mentally retarded*. Washington, D.C.: United States Government Printing Office, 179-195, 1972.

Peine, H. The elimination of a child's self-injurious behavior at home and school. *School Application of Learning Theory*, 1972, *4*(4), 36-47.

Pendergrass, V. E. Effects of length of time-out from positive reinforcement and schedule of application in suppression of aggressive behavior. *Psychological Record*, 1971, *21*, 75-80.

Phillips, E. L. Achievement place: Token reinforcement procedures in a home-style rehabilitation setting for "pre-delinquent" boys. *Journal of Applied Behavior Analysis*, 1968, *1*, 213-223.

Phillips, E. L., Phillips, E. A., Fixsen, D. L., & Wolf, M. M. Achievement place: Modification of the behaviors of pre-delinquent boys within a token economy. *Journal of Applied Behavior Analysis*, 1971, *4*, 45-59.

Porterfield, J. K., Herbert-Jackson, E., & Risley, T. R. Contingent observation: An effective and acceptable procedure for reducing disruptive behavior of young children in a group setting. *Journal of Applied Behavior Analysis*, 1976, *9*, 55-64.

Premack, D. Toward empirical laws. *Psychological Review*, 1959, *68*, 219-223.

Prochaska, J. Remote control aversive stimulation in the treatment of headbanging in a retarded child. *Journal of Behavior Therapy and Experimental Psychiatry*, 1974, *5*, 285-289.

Repp, A. C. & Deitz, D. E. Ethical issues in reducing responding of institutional-ized mentally retarded persons. *Mental Retardation*, 1978, vol. 16 (1), *45–46*.

Risley, T. The effects and side effects of punishing the autistic behaviors of a deviant child. *Journal of Applied Behavior Analysis*, 1968, *1*, 22–25.

Risley, T., & Wolf, M. M. Establishing functional speech in echolalic children. *Behavior Research and Therapy*, 1967, *5*, 73–88.

Roos, P. Human rights and behavior modification. *Mental Retardation*, 1974, *12*(3), 3–6.

Roos, P. Normalization, dehumanization, and conditioning-conflict or harmony. *Mental Retardation*, 1970, *8*(4), 12–14.

Sachs, D. A. The efficacy of time-out procedures in a variety of behavior problems. *Journal of Behavior Therapy and Experimental Psychiatry*, 1973, *4*, 237–242.

Sajwaj, T., Libet, J., & Agras, S. Lemon juice therapy: The control of life threatening rumination in a six-month-old infant. *Journal of Applied Behavior Analysis*, 1974, *7*(4), 557–663.

Scaggliotta, Edward G. Amplification as aversion therapy for screaming. *Academic Therapy*, 1975, *10*(4), 449–542.

Schiefelbusch, R. L. A discussion of language treatment methods for mentally retarded children. *Mental Retardation*, 1965, *3*(2), 4–7.

Schipper, W. V., Wilson, W. C., & Wolf, J. M. Public education of the handicapped. In E. Sontag (Ed.), *Educational Programming for the Severely and Profoundly Handicapped*. Boothwyn, Pennsylvania: CEC Division on Mental Retardation, 1977.

Schriebman, L. A reply to the comments on "Employing electric shock with autistic children: A review of the side effects." *Journal of Autism and Childhood Schizophrenia*, 1977, *7*(2), 202–204.

Skinner, B.F. *About behaviorism*. New York: Random House, 1976.

Skinner, B.F. *Science and human behavior*. New York: Free Press, 1953.

Sloane, H. N., Young, K. R., & Marcusen, T. Response cost and human aggressive behavior. In E. C. Etzel, J. M. LeBlanc, & D. M. Baer (Eds.), *New developments in behavioral research: Theory, method, and application*. Hillsdale, NJ: LEA Publishers, 1977.

Solomon, R. L. Punishment. *American Psychologist*. 1964, *19*, 239–253.

Sulzbacher, S. I., & Houser, J. E. A tactic to eliminate disruptive behaviors in the classroom: Group contingent consequences. *American Journal of Mental Deficiency*, 1968, *73*, 88–90.

Tate, B. G., & Baroff, G. Aversive control of self-injurious behavior in a psychotic boy. *Behavior Research and Therapy*, 1966, *4*, 281–287.

Tennant, L., Hattersly, J., & Cullen, C. Some comments on the punishment relationship and its relevance to normalization for developmentally retarded people. *Mental Retardation*, 1978, vol. 16 (1), 42–44.

Thomas, E. J. Selected sociobehavioral technique and principles: An approach to interpersonal helping. *Social Work*, 1968, *13*, 12–26.

Thomas, D. R., Becker, W. C., & Armstrong, M. Production and elimination of disruptive classroom behavior by systematically varying teacher's behavior. *Journal of Applied Behavior Analysis*, 1968, *1*, 35–45.

Treffry, D., Martin, G. L., Samels, J. L., & Watson, C. Operant conditioning of grooming behavior of severely retarded girls. *Mental Retardation*, 1970, *8*, 29–33.

Watson, L. S., Jr., & Sanders, C. C. *Stimulus control with severely and profoundly retarded children under varying stimulus conditions in a free operant situation.* Paper read at the 90th annual meeting of the AAMD, Chicago, May 1966.

Webster, D. R., & Azrin, N. H. Required Relaxation: A method of inhibiting agitative disruptive behavior of retardates. *Behavior Research and Therapy*, 1973, *11*, 619–628.

White, G. D., Nielson, G., & Johnson, S. S. Time-out duration and the suppression of deviant behavior in children. *Journal of Applied Behavior Analysis*, 1972, *5*, 111–120.

Whitman, T. L., Mercurio, J. R., & Caponigri, V. Development of social response in two severely retarded children. *Journal of Applied Behavior Analysis*, 1970, *3*, 133–138.

Wolf, M. M., Birnbrauer, J. S., Williams, T., & Lawler, J. A note on apparent extinction of the vomiting behavior of a retarded child. In L. P. Ullman & L. Krasner (Eds.), *Case studies in behavior modification.* New York: Holt, Rinehart, & Winston, 1965.

Wolfensberger, W. Will there always be an institution? The impact of epidemiological trends. *Mental Retardation*, 1971, *9*(5), 14–20.

Wood, F. M. Behavior modification techniques in context. *Newsletter of the Council for children with Behavioral Disorders.* 1968, *5*(4), 12–15.

Zimmerman, J., & Baydan, N. T. Punishment of S responding of humans in conditional matching-to-sample by time-out. *Journal of the Experimental Analysis of Behavior*, 1963, *4*, 589–597.

Chapter 4

Teacher-Made Response-Contingent Materials

Chris E. Wethered

Adaptive training materials provide a valuable link between the disabled student's limited responding abilities and his or her acquisition of desirable sensory stimulation (reinforcement). Merely by placing a hand on a small plastic square, the disabled child can make a mechanical puppy bark; by holding his or her head erect the child can activate a tape player; by pulling on a suspended plastic ring he or she can turn on a radio. Through the performance of a given motor response, the child can activate reinforcing forms of tactile, auditory or visual stimulation. The child is thereby provided with immediate feedback contingent upon correct performance of the selected motor task. Once established, this motoric response can be used to teach a wide range of motor, language, and cognitive skills.

This chapter presents several of these electric devices that can be teacher-made. These units can be connected in a variety of combinations in order to provide appropriately for the student's reinforcement needs, responding abilities, and for the instructor's training objectives. The outstanding benefit of these devices is that they provide continuous training, consistent reinforcement, immediate performance-based feedback, objective performance evaluation, and permit increased training time for the student while making fewer demands on the teacher's time (Arroyo,

1976). Doughty (undated) proposed that through the use of such devices, students were able to learn that their actions had an effect on their environments. In other words, what happens to them can in some part be governed by what is done by them. By teaching these students that they can control their environments, such materials provide access to their untapped potential for motor, cognitive, and language development. For the non-retarded but severely physically disabled child, such materials may eventually lead to a means of gainful employment. Therefore it seems imperative that educators, engineers, and physical and occupational therapists must communicate and collaborate on solutions to the particular problems of the severely/multiply handicapped.

The classroom instructor is the key to this collaboration in the problem-solving process, because of his or her knowledge of the student's abilities, disabilities, skill levels, and skill needs. Through consultation with other relevant professionals, a plan for moving the student from his or her current level of functioning to the successful acquisition of new responses can be devised. The input from the occupational and physical therapists provides information on motor development sequences and on design considerations for the student's neuromotor problems. The speech pathologist will be involved in planning if the unit is to be used for language/communication training. Based on this necessary information, a device will be designed and constructed to meet the student's varied needs. The design team obviously should include a person who is able to perform simple woodworking tasks, solder electrical connections, and so forth. This team member may be an interested janitor, friend, neighbor, spouse, or fellow instructor. The simple battery-powered aids to be described can be easily designed and built to meet the disabled student's unique educational needs, but the instructor should be personally involved in the process of providing the student with access to control over reinforcing environmental events. Such understanding and awareness of the construction and operation of these devices will maximize the student's potential performance.

EXISTING TEACHER-MADE MATERIALS

Many electronic, mechanical, and electromechanical training devices, simple and complex, are discussed in the literature. Driscoll (1975) described several of these training apparatuses that had been designed as toys. The toys were designed by a team of engineering students from the Massachusetts Institute of Technology, in collaboration with Kennedy Memorial Hospital's Occupational Therapy Department, to facilitate learning in a population of developmentally disabled children. The results showed that such devices were highly motivational for teaching eye-hand coordination and other perceptual-motor skills. Doughty (undated) noted that such things as musical toys provided the learner with contingent vibratory stimulation, and that student-operated tape players, modified electronic TV games and other such communication devices could be used as training materials. Hill, Campagna, Long, Munch, and Naecher (1968) discussed a device of their own design, which provided an electromechanical means of communication to a motorically impaired child, and notably also made formal testing possible.

Other devices designed to assist the nonverbal physically handicapped to communicate have been presented by LaVoy (1957), Jones (1961), Miller and Carpenter (1964), and Vanderheiden, Volk, and Geisler (1974). In 1976, Wooldridge and McLaurin published the results of a study that incorporated the use of a device for training control of head position in cerebral palsied children. Aston (1973) and Mavilya and Mignone (1977) noted the existence of toys that were activated by sound and that could therefore be used to reinforce vocalization in deaf or developmentally delayed children. Other investigators have reported devices of greater sophistication, which are used to aid the disabled in both communication and environmental control (Arroyo, 1976; Copeland, 1974). The latter author discussed and illustrated a number of interfaces (off/on switches sensitive to specific controlled responses of the operator) that permitted the disabled person to control output devices through a variety of residual abilities, including eye movement, respiration, and skin contact.

Several electronic and electromechanical forms of recreation were presented by Sheredos (1973). Although these games were designed for disabled veterans, they could be adapted for use by young disabled students. Sheredos' examples included an electronic pong game and a pinball game, operated respectively by interfaces sensitive to chin movement and pneumatic pressure (puff and suck). These interfaces and others noted by various authors (Copeland, 1974; Foulds, Crochetiere, Baletso, & Meyer; Lipskin, 1970; Tawney, 1977; Wethered, 1976) may be prescribed for the individual student, based upon his or her disorder and/or residual abilities. Most severely disabled persons are able to move some body part, if only a fraction of an inch. Therefore, through appropriate interface selection that residual responding ability may be tapped electronically to provide control of any desired device. The student needs only one such controlled response to trigger an interface which in turn will activate and control the device. As a result of the development of such technology, appropriate training materials, avenues of communication and environmental control are available for students having a wide variety of severe and multiply handicapping conditions.

Teacher-Made Devices

Because of the frequent need to adapt, alter, or redesign off/on switches to meet the disabled person's specific needs, there are no standard interfaces, only basic switches from which to build the required interface for the individual. It was the unstandardized nature of these devices that prompted this chapter. The devices presented herein are representative of the technology that is needed by the classroom teacher and that can be made readily available to him or her. The devices can be adapted to the student's particular needs, and can range in cost from free to inexpensive. The purpose of the chapter is to provide the teacher of the disabled student with basic information and techniques for designing, constructing, and otherwise procuring training aids for such students.

The first materials presented are a sampling of adaptive interfaces. These were designed to be activated by simple pressure-producing motor responses such as touch, push, grasp, or pull. A non-pressure responsive interface has also been included. This interface is activated by changes in the student's head position. All of these interfaces are normally off, and are only activated while the student is actually interacting with them in the prescribed manner.

The second set of devices was designed to be activated by any one of the interfaces. Each produces some form of sensory stimulation that might act as a reinforcer to the student. The student may be reinforced by sensory stimulation (light or vibration), by the novelty of the stimulation at his or her command, or just by the fact that he or she has some control over an element of the environment. The reason the child finds the stimulation reinforcing is not as important as the fact that it is reinforcing, and that its use, therefore, results in behavioral change.

The above technology is applied in combination to form a training system. An interface that is responsive to the motor skill targeted for training is selected, and is combined with an output device that the student finds reinforcing. Once a controlled response has been developed it can be used to provide the child with a means of communication or environmental control. This controlled response also opens an avenue to the assessment and development of the student's intellectual, cognitive, and academic skills.

ADAPTIVE OFF/ON SWITCHES

Touch Switch

The touch switch (see Figure 1) is a specialized classroom material for helping physically disabled students to acquire new motor skills, as well as to develop and more fully utilize existing skills. This interface contains an off/on microswitch activated by the application of a small amount of pressure. The microswitch is mounted in a block of wood just below a hinged piece of plexiglass. When pressure is applied to the plexiglass sur-

TOUCH SWITCH

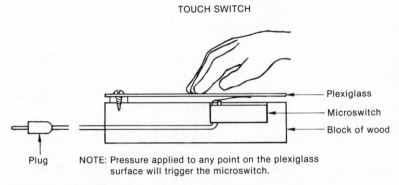

NOTE: Pressure applied to any point on the plexiglass surface will trigger the microswitch.

Figure 1.   A touch switch activated by pressure applied to any point on the plexiglass surface.

face, it causes the microswitch to complete the circuit and activate the selected reinforcing output device. This activation continues only as long as the student continues to apply pressure. Several motor movements or schemes can be used to produce the directional pressure required to activate a reinforcer using the touch switch. This interface can therefore be used with severely to mildly motorically disabled students for reinforcing reaching, pointing, appropriate limb position and limb movement, rolling patterns, and general interaction with elements of the environment. The targeted motor skill should be one that the teacher and physical and occupational therapists would like to strengthen, make more frequent, or use in providing the student with a means of controlling an element of the environment.

The motor response can be quickly developed through the following steps. The touch switch should be placed at some point within the child's current functional range of motion, between the targeted position and his or her typical position. Initially a physical prompt may be used to familiarize the child with the activation of the touch switch and the concept that, through it, he or she can effect a change in the environment. This is something that most severely disabled children have never experienced. As a physical prompt, the teacher could activate the touch switch by putting it in contact with the student's limb. The instructor can thereby allow the student to activate the reinforcer with no initial effort or knowledge of the operation of the touch switch. Following this step, verbal encouragement and demonstration can be used to elicit the desired response necessary for reinforcement. Once the student has learned to make the interface activate the pleasurable or novel sensory stimulation, it should be moved to a slightly different position determined by the teacher and therapist. The new position of the touch switch would require the student to produce a response more like the targeted skill than the previous response in order to activate the reinforcing stimulation. This gradual movement of the switch reinforces each successive approximation of the target skill. The child will therefore be led by the novel reinforcement of these gradually differing responses until he or she produces the desired behavior. The target behavior will thus be shaped from a previously existing skill pattern.

Another strategy calls for the instructor to place the touch switch in such a position that it could be activated only by the use of the targeted skill. The student is then provided with the minimum necessary physical assistance to perform the desired behavior. The student receives sensory stimulation for having performed the complete and correct target response. Using this method, the student is not reinforced for all of the intermediate successive approximations of the response as were delivered in the above instructional method. This second technique, however, is not as effective as the first with children whose muscles are resistive to physical manipulation. With such students, the physical manipulation provides exercise for these muscles, strengthening the muscle tone in opposition to the very response desired. The successive approximation procedure outlined first provides the necessary reinforcement to build skill without physical manipulation. The student would therefore be strengthening the neuromotor patterns in favor of the target response through a desire to receive the stimulation. The two strategies discussed above have general applicability for all of the interfaces that follow (Wethered, 1982).

It should be stressed that with the touch switch the targeted motor response must produce a pressure that will deflect the plexiglass surface toward the microswitch. For this reason, the plexiglass surface of the touch switch should be parallel to the ground for the reaching, pointing, and general interaction applications. When training limb movement, the touch switch should be mounted or held in such a position that the completion of the targeted motion will deflect the plexiglass surface. When applied to the development of a rolling behavior, the touch switch can be placed on the surface where the child is rolling or held parallel to some part of the child as he or she rolls. Body movement will thereby trigger the touch switch upon completion of the rolling response. Additional ideas may be found in Campbell, Green, and Carlson (1977).

Once a pointing or touch response has been developed, the touch switch, as well as the other interfaces to be discussed, can provide continued use in communication, training, and testing applications. In training symbol o/r referent relations for communication board use, for example, the plexiglass surface of the touch switch can be covered with a picture representing the output device that it activates, including a recording on a cassette tape. In this case the pointing response applied to the picture or symbol activates a tape player and thereby the related sounds. In the next step the symbol is removed from the touch switch and presented as in typical communication board training. The teacher directly activates the reinforcer (taped sounds) when the student correctly points to or touches the symbol. The instructor then introduces other symbols for communication of concepts that can not be directly activated by the student. The student is no longer in direct control of the referent sounds, actions, or objects but has to communicate his or her request to the teacher to produce the desired event. In this way, the student first learns that he or she can effect a change in the environment through a pointing response and that his direct control is provided through another person. The controlled response provides the instructor with an avenue through which the student may be tested, assuming that no functional mode of communication has already been established. The touch switch can be used as the teacher's "yes" response to questions and a "no" response can be conveyed by not touching the switch. There can be two touch switches set side by side, one providing the yes response and the other the no response. The two interfaces can also be applied in a two-choice discrimination-type training situation (see Figure 2), wherein only the correct selection produces the reinforcing stimulus. In this situation not only can the instructor determine what the student knows, but he or she can also start to train the student in the concept. The touch switch can be connected to the rotary dial communicator (see discussion on output devices), which puts a rotary dial under the student's control and thus can be used to point to various pictures or words for standardized testing in place of the pointing response typically used.

The touch switch can continue to be useful in the event that the student's physical disability is such that he or she will eventually need some form of automated communication board because of his or her limited range of motion. The interface can be used to train the child to use the similar touch switch provided by Prentke Romich Co. and ZYGO Industries, Inc. for control of their respective electronic scanning communication and environmental control devices.

The touch switch can also be used with intellectually, emotionally, or behaviorally disabled students who experience no physical limitations. With these students, the touch switch can be used without assistance to provide the student with reinforcement while not providing him with the opportunity to handle or damage the reinforcement device. For example, contingent upon good classroom behavior the student can listen to music; the tape player is placed out of reach, and the touch switch alone is accessible to the student.

Squeeze Switch

This interface actuates a form of reinforcing stimulation for disabled students when they produce a palming and grasping response similar to that which children use in spoon holding. It can also be used to reinforce the thumb-forefinger opposition response used in picking up small objects, buttoning and manipulating educational materials such as pegs and

TOUCH SWITCHES
FOR
TWO CHOICE DISCRIMINATION
TRAINING

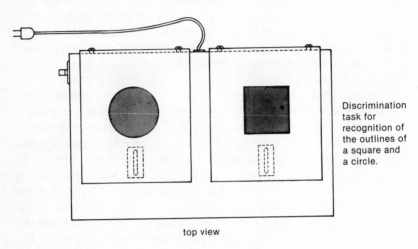

Discrimination task for recognition of the outlines of a square and a circle.

top view

(pressure may be applied at any point on the plexiglass surfaces)

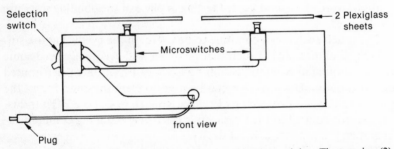

Figure 2.   Touch switches for two-choice discrimination training. The top view (2) illustrates a discrimination task for recognition of the outlines of a square and a circle.

beads. It also has application with students having little more control than the voluntary opening and closing of their fists. In this case, the squeeze switch provides an initial response to work from in developing other responses. As discussed before, this interface could provide access to a means of testing, training and communication.

The squeeze switch consists of a microswitch sewn into a tube of gauze or built into a dowel (see Figure 3). The attached reinforcing output device is activated only as long as the child applies a grasp or squeeze response to the squeeze switch. The interface is placed in the palm of the child's hand and he or she is prompted to squeeze it. A simple program for developing this skill may be found in Utley, Holvoet, and Barnes (1977). The gripping action depresses the lever of the microswitch and

SQUEEZE SWITCH

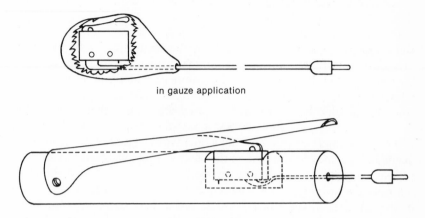

in gauze application

in dowel application

Figure 3.   A squeeze switch in a gauze application (a) and in a dowel application (b).

thereby activates the output device. The squeeze or grasp response can be developed into a pointing response by positioning the squeeze switch in the student's palm so that several fingers will trigger it upon hand closure. One finger can then be physically prompted into an extended position. The student is therefore reinforced for the prompted finger extension, paired with the palm-directed movement of his or her remaining fingers. The squeeze switch can eventually be replaced by the touch switch, which is responsive to the desired pointing response. This is valuable only if the student has potential for increasing his or her range of motion to provide an indicating response across a surface. In the event that the child's range of motion shows no indication of greater development, a gross-pointing, refined pointing, or squeeze response can be used to activate a scanning electronic communication device.

Pull Switch

This interface can easily be used with the severely motorically involved student to develop eye-hand coordination, gross motor and fine motor skills such as reaching, grasping, and pulling. It encourages the student to interact with the environment and enhances the development of means-to-ends and cause-and-effect relationships.

Because of their disabilities, these students are frequently placed in a variety of therapeutic positions (e.g., sidelying, prone, and supported sitting) by their physical and occupational therapists. Such positioning strengthens muscle groups and neurological patterns. Campbell et al. (1977) depict and give the rationale for such positions. During these positioned times such students generally have nothing that they are able to do with their hands.

The pull switch can be suspended in front of the child while he or she is positioned over a bolster, on a wedge, prone, sitting or sidelying. In these positions the pull switch can encourage position maintenance, provide stimulation, structure time and provide environmental control. It can also provide an activity to continue the academic skill development previously interrupted during positioning. This interface helps to make the time spent in therapeutic positions more productive in terms of overall development; it also makes the positioned time more active and potentially pleasurable than the unstructured "dead time" that it used to be.

The reinforcing output device is activated when the student pulls down on an object suspended from a microswitch (see Figure 4). The suspended object may be selected on the bases of previously established educational objectives. The object can be a ring through which the child must place a finger and pull. The ring can initially be fairly large in terms of the diameter of the center hole. As the student becomes more proficient at the task, the ring can be replaced with one of several rings having successively smaller holes. Through this process the student could be taught more accurate control of a reaching or pointing response, eye-hand coordination, and general gross and fine motor control. As with most of the interfaces herein described, this unit encourages interaction with the environment. Another training application of this interface, depending upon the selection of the object to be suspended, could be color, shape, number or object labeling. The student could be made familiar with any of the above word object and concept relationships through such interaction. This might be accomplished in the following manner: When the teacher gives the command "show me the cup" (the cup being suspended from the microswitch), when the student touches or pulls the cup, it activates the selected output device (e.g., music, vibration, air movement, lights). Dubose and Deni (1980) illustrate a similar interface for stimulation and reinforcement of the same group of motor and cognitive skills.

Multiple Interface Application

Once a motoric response has been developed or strengthened with either the touch switch or the pull switch, it can be used to teach language skills through discrimination tasks. In this multiple interface application, two or more switches are connected parallel to one another; each one potentially activates the selected output device. Only one switch, however, can activate the reinforcer at any given time, and the instructor determines which one does. The instructor can therefore vary which one of the set of rings or touch switches activates the reinforcer.

For example, four pull switches could be placed in front of a positioning wedge so that a child in a prone position could easily reach and

PULL SWITCH

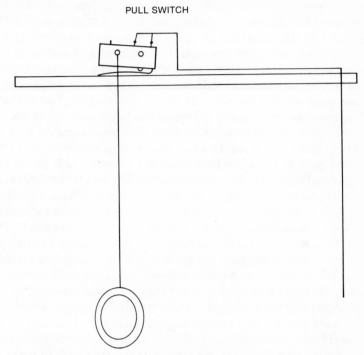

Figure 4.   A pull switch employing an oversized grip for easy use.

pull on one of the four suspended objects. If a student is working on shape discrimination, the objects suspended from the microswitches can be of the same color and size, varying only in shape. The instructor can set the discrimination switch so that downward pressure applied to the toilet shape alone activates the reinforcer. The student is then stimulated when the instructor explains "Show me the toilet. The toilet makes music [or other selected reinforcer]." If the student pulls on any other shape than the toilet, there is no reinforcement delivered by the output device. Once the student has been successful and reinforced for the selection, the instructor can use a shape suspended from another switch as the correct choice and begin the procedure again.

The same application holds for the use of several touch switches or several buttons mounted on a cigar box. Each button or touch switch could have the object, picture, symbol, word, or number to be trained placed on or beside it.

Head-Position Trainer   This interface was designed to train disabled students to hold their heads in an appropriate position more frequently and for greater lengths of time. This device was used with physically handicapped students who seldom held their heads in the normal midline position; when they did, it was only for brief periods of time. Many severely disabled students have difficulty holding their heads up. They frequently rest their heads on their chests, or the back of their chairs. The midline head position is addressed because it is an important prerequisite to the development of communication skills such as vocalization and language, as well as proper swallowing, chewing, and breathing patterns. Once these students are better able to support their heads in a more appropriate position they see more of their environments. The students therefore have greater exposure to experiences and knowledge of the environment. Through proper head position, they are allowed to have visual contact with elements of the environment. This adds meaning to the words they hear in reference to actions and objects. Such visual and meaningful auditory input increases the possibility that they might resultantly desire and request things from the environment. This new position also provides them with topics for conversation and information on how things work (means-to-ends and cause-and-effect relationships). The need for head-position training is seen in a broad variety of students ranging from developmentally immature children to cognitively aware high school students. It is therefore difficult to make a definitive list of the skills potentially developed through improved head position.

Subsequent to the inception, design, construction, and use of this device, several similar systems were discovered in the educational technology literature. The operating principles of and functions performed by these devices were essentially the same; however, the levels of sophistication regarding their construction and use were quite diverse. They ranged from a single mercury switch mounted on the top of a felt hat (Ross, 1976) to a system that automatically collected and recorded data for later retrieval (Mancino, 1977). Ross (1976) and this author suggest that cost alone might entice the classroom teacher to build, rather than purchase, such a device. The unit described by Mancino (1977) was priced at $400.00, the one built by Ross was only $5.00, and the one described here was built at a cost of approximately $15.00. The latter price difference is due to the fact that Ross's head-position trainer used only one mercury switch in 1976 while the one discussed below incorporates the use of three such switches at 1981 prices.

The mercury switch (see Figure 5) is the key to the position sensitivity of the head-position trainer as the microswitch was to the pressure sensitivity of the previously described interfaces. The mercury switch consists of a hermetically sealed tube containing mercury and having two wires exiting from one end. Mercury is a liquid metal and therefore has the properties of both a metal and a liquid. The fluid nature of this metal allows it to respond to the position of the sealed tube in relation to gravity. The mercury always seeks the lowest point of the tube and will therefore complete the electrical circuit when the tube is positioned so that the two wires are at the bottom. When tipped, the new position of the tube in

MERCURY SWITCH

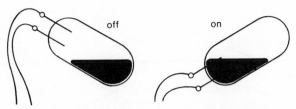

Figure 5.   The off and on states of the mercury switch.

relation to gravity will allow the mercury to flow away from the two poles and thereby break the electrical contact, stopping the action of any output device attached to it.

The position of the three mercury switches on the student's headband (see Figure 6) therefore determine the head position required for reinforcement. These three switches are connected in series, so that all of them must be activated simultaneously before the output device will be turned on. If any one of the three mercury switches is not activated, the circuit is not completed and the reinforcer will not start. By its position, each mercury switch monitors movement in one direction away from the desired midline position. The entire head-position trainer is, therefore, a position-sensitive switch. When the child's head position is appropriate, the circuit is completed and the reinforcer is activated. This device, therefore, provides immediate feedback and reinforcement to the student when his or her head moves into that area defined as acceptable midline head position.

Variability in the positioning of the mercury switches allows the instructor to use the device with several students during the same class period. This flexibility was initially used in shaping head position by gradually reducing the tolerated variance from an acceptable midline position. It became obvious, however, that the students acquired the skill much more rapidly when the criteria position was used from the onset of programming. This appeared to give the students a consistent set of parameters within which to develop head and neck control, rather than parameters that constantly became more rigid and required modification of the previously acquired·proprioceptive (position in space) limits. Programs and procedures for teaching associated clusters of head-control skills are discussed by Sternat, Messina, Lyon, and Nietupski (1977).

A tape player is one of the recommended forms of output for this particular training device because of the auditory feedback provided. A visual form of reinforcement can have a drawback for initial use, in that eye contact with an object is generally broken when their heads fall from the desired position. This means that they may not even realize that the

HEAD POSITION TRAINER

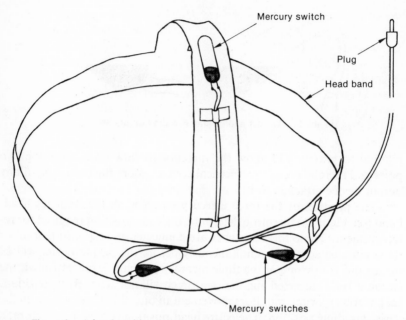

Figure 6.   A head-position trainer operating by the use of mercury switches.

visual display has stopped, as it is no longer within their visual field. Please note that even if the taped music chosen for initial use is not reinforcing to the student, the novelty of being able to control the tape player by merely holding the head in the desired position appears to act as a strong reinforcer. In later use, tactile or other nonauditory forms of stimulation might be considered to avoid providing competition to the student's development of vocalization. It should be noted that such vocalization has a greater probability of developing with the better alignment of the vocal mechanism and vocal track caused by the improved head position.

With such a device, a teacher can work with other children while monitoring visually and auditorially the progress made by a head-position trainee. The visual monitoring allows the teacher to ascertain that the device and the child are both in the proper position when the device turns the tape player on. The auditory monitoring allows the instructor to take both frequency and duration data based on the output of the tape player. Such data may also be based on the tape meter readings. This is not a substitute for instructor attention, but rather increases the attention and general instructional time for all students without decreasing the direct time committed to any individual student. The teacher should note that when recording tapes for playback as reinforcement with any of the aforementioned devices, the sound should be fairly continuous; that is, without pauses or gaps. This ensures that the child consistently receives reinforcement for performing the target behavior, rather than occasionally receiving only the "whurr" of a blank tape for his or her efforts. With the head-position trainer in particular, the teacher should further note that a physical therapist or occupational therapist should be consulted when determining an appropriate head position for training. These therapists are also able to provide input regarding the child's overall body position to provide the optimal skeletal and muscular support for appropriate head position.

Output Devices

The reinforcing output devices activated by the aforementioned interfaces were selected because they provide stimulation to the student's senses of hearing, vision, and touch. The current practice of using edible reinforcers for behavior modification is also a form of sensory stimulation in that it stimulates the senses of taste and smell. This form of stimulation may have some very severe limitations with severely disabled students, who very frequently have difficulty with tongue movement, chewing, and swallowing. These students "have extensive and, in some cases, life-threatening feeding problems" (Utley et al. 1977, p. 290).

The oral areas of such children are understandably a site of great anxiety and pain at every meal. They are often unable to feed themselves or verbally control the feeding process. The child's gums cannot escape being hit by the spoon and the feeder cannot always know when to give the next bite or drink. The mealtime is therefore a messy, awkward, and anxious time for these children. The resultant drooling and mess produce additional unpleasant sensations related to the oral area. With these poor chewing and swallowing abilities, an edible reinforcer can stay in the student's mouth for hours, reducing any directed reinforcing effect. As a result of the potentially stressful nature of feeding in general, foods may not have enough reinforcing quality to override the anxiety associated with the oral area. In addition to the difficulties that these students may have with the oral area, edibles have natural drawbacks in that they crumble, melt, go stale, and draw insects, which may also reduce any reinforcing effect. General health, weight control, and dental hygiene should also be considered before implementing edible reinforcement. Such problems are inherent with edible reinforcers and obviously limit their effectiveness with this seriously disabled student population. In fact, "with low functioning or physically disabled children, most reinforcers may be inappropriate or possibly even have no reinforcing value. Those that are effective may soon lead to satiation or may be impractical to administer" (Zucker, D'Alonzo, McMullen, & Williams, 1980).

These problems have prompted the use of hearing, vision, and touch as alternative sensory channels for rewarding behavior. These senses can easily be stimulated by elements of the environment with which these students have limited experience because of the severity of their disabilities. An instructor can provide sensory stimulation to a student directly contingent upon correct task completion (e.g., rubbing terrycloth on the skin, ringing a bell, shaking a rattle, blowing bubbles, and moving a pinwheel). There are, however, a number of environmental elements that are electrical or mechanical in nature and can therefore be activated by the child through interface operation. An additional benefit of this type of electrical or mechanical sensory stimulation is that the onset is immediate, upon activation of the interface, and continues only as long as the activation does. It also establishes a more direct relationship between the behavior and the reinforcing stimulation.

Contingent Music

This mode of auditory stimulation is readily accessable to most instructors, has inherent reinforcing qualities, and has potential as an auditory training tool. Additionally, it places an element of the student's natural environment under his or her control. The two methods for providing this auditory output are the use of a regular tape player or an easily adapted transistor radio. A student may enjoy listening to the radio or hearing favorite Sesame Street songs sung by his or her mother. Both the radio and the tape player can be activated when the targeted motor response is applied to the selected interface. This interface can be plugged into the "remote on" jack of any standard tape recorder. Once the tape recorder is set to play (or record), the student is in control of the off/on function of the tape. This output device and the other reinforcing devices to follow can be controlled by all of the previously described interfaces. When recorded for student playback, the music should be continuous so that the child never receives the sound of a blank tape for his or her efforts.

An easy method of interfacing the transistor (and other battery-powered reinforcing devices) involves the use of ZYGO's CA-9 cable (see Figure 7). This cable must be ordered with a plug compatible with the one on the selected interface. The CA-9 has two metal disks at one end. These disks are separated by a nonconductor. The set of disks is inserted between the batteries and permits the interface to start and stop the device when activated.

Contingent Toy Operation

The interface of choice becomes the off/on switch for operation of the selected battery-powered toy by connecting it to the wires on either side of the original off/on switch (or through the described use of ZYGO's CA-9).

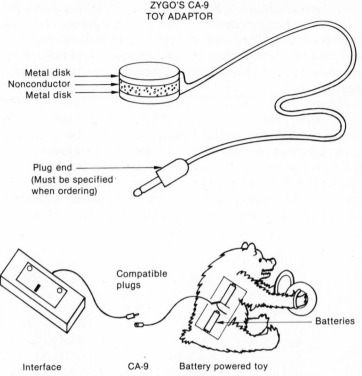

ZYGO'S CA-9
TOY ADAPTOR

Metal disk
Nonconductor
Metal disk

Plug end
(Must be specified
when ordering)

Compatible
plugs

Batteries

Interface   CA-9   Battery powered toy

Figure 7.   The universal adaptor used in ZYGO's CA-9 battery-powered toy.

Contingent Light

Light provides sensory stimulation for'reinforcement of visually limited students. This mode of stimulation can also be used with students experiencing other disabilities. The student can be seated in a dimly lit room or positioned so that reinforcing objects not easily controlled by an interface (i.e., mother's picture), placed in a dark area, can be illuminated by activation of the interface. Other forms of light potentially operable by an interface might be flashing Christmas lights, a flashlight, or a rotating color wheel.

By its very nature this form of sensory stimulation may be disruptive to a classroom. The instructor might consider using an empty classroom, office, or storage room for this type of sensory stimulation for training. The procedure is more effectively used in a room with shades or no windows.

Contingent Vibration and Contingent Fan Operation

These reinforcers provide tactile stimulation as a novel environmental contingency and could have applications in training the visually or auditorially impaired. Johnson, Firth, and Davey (1978) noted that they saw "preference. . .demonstrated for vibration reinforcement over praise/approval reinforcement" by eight of their nine severely retarded students. Zucker, D'Alonzo, McMullen, and Williams also noted that severely and profoundly mentally retarded children showed preference for vibratory stimulation over visual stimulation in several research studies (1980).

The vibrating stimuli may be attached to the child's chair, bed, positioning bolster, or even to some part of the body. The vibrator might also be covered in cloth to resemble a mouse, snake or other animal, and allowed to wiggle on the floor when activated. Successful activation of the individually selected interface could also activate a fan that blows air at the student or that flutters colored streamers or turns a pinwheel, producing a visual stimulus in conjunction with the tactile stimulation. The above examples of sensory stimulation provide additional potentially reinforcing events for student motivation.

Contingent Mobile or Kaleidoscope Action

These units provide visual stimulation incorporating movement and color, and yet have enough variation that the student would not tire of them quickly. Both of these output devices require a low RPM (revolutions per minute) motor that is activated by an interface (as seen in Figure 8). In the mobile application the motor is mounted in such a manner that objects suspended from a disk attached to the axis of the motor will hang parallel to the floor. Mounted on the kaleidoscope axis are two clear plastic coffee can lids attached lip to lip. Small, brightly colored objects varying in shape should be placed between the plastic disks. In this manner the movement of the axis will rotate the disks and cause the objects to move, falling over one another constantly varying the visual display presented. Either of these reinforcing devices could be placed beside a crib or therapeutic positioning area.

Rotary Dial Communication Device

This device (see Figure 8) provides a means for scanning and selecting from among several potential items; for use in testing, training, and/or communication. It can be used as an initial communication board surface for the student whose range of motion is too limited to benefit from the use of a conventional communication board surface. Devices such as this have been discussed by Lavoy (1957), Jones (1961), and Mancino (1977) as an alternative means for communication with and assessment of nonverbal students having a limited range of motion. (The construction and use of communication boards is described in detail in Chapter 7.)

The axis of a low RPM motor, as discussed with the mobile and kaleidoscope, rotates and moves a pointer around the clock-like display surface. Around the circumference of the course of the pointer are

ROTARY DIAL COMMUNICATOR

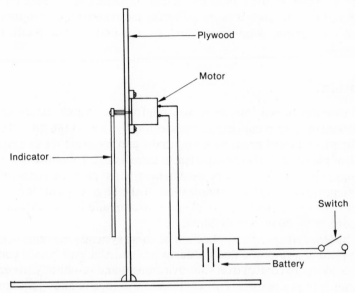

Figure 8.   Rotary dial communicator.

placed symbols, pictures, objects, or words for the student's communicative needs, training or skill testing tasks. By operating the interface, the student can cause the indicator to scan through a variety of messages until the one that he or she intends to communicate is located. The student then stops the movement of the pointer by deactivating the interface. This is generally done by releasing or breaking physical contact with the interface.

The mechanism of the unit is similar to the kaleidoscope previously noted in that the low RPM motor is activated by the student's interface. The difference, however, is that in place of a visual display an indicator has been attached to the axis of the motor. The axis passes through the display surface. Because the motor is mounted on the back, the indicator is the only part of the mechanism visible to the child, thus reducing any possible visual confusion.

Multiple Output Applications

With some students, a single output mode may not be sufficient to consistently elicit the desired response. In these cases two or more reinforcing stimuli may be paired for simultaneous presentation. For instance, a child's response can simultaneously activate a flashlight and a mobile or kaleidoscope. The flashlight can be aimed at the moving objects to focus the student's attention on them, and the room can be dimly lit to heighten the contrast with the rest of the room. Such pairing of reinforcers can be used to accentuate specific reinforcing qualities or help to draw the student's attention to the reinforcer. It can combine two or more minimal reinforcers to produce a more powerful motivator (e.g., auditory and visual localization). Reinforcers can also be paired to meet specific training goals.

SUMMARY

The aforementioned interfaces and reinforcing output stimuli can be combined in various configurations specifically to meet the student's particular physical and programmatic needs, and motivate his or her independent play and discovery experiences as well as performance in training settings. These devices may be used in data-based programs or as related experiences for building generalization of the targeted behavior. Teachers can use this technology to adapt classroom and home environments for control by disabled individuals.

In terms of specific application of these systems, the interface may be applied to a response that a student has under at least partial control, to provide more control over the environment and resultantly strengthen the motor response used. This environmental control allows the student to have some independence from others, assisting him or her to develop self-confidence and a concept of himself or herself as agent. The environmental control may only be the operation of a toy, film strip projector, tape player, motorized mobile, or communication system, but it still provides the student with more independence and experience. The interface may also be used to programmatically develop new motor skills, for example, by shaping the response required for interface activation by gradual changes in the form or position of the interface or both.

Regardless of the extent to which the above technology and ideas are used, it is the role of the classroom teacher to initiate the process, request the assistance, and coordinate the professionals needed for the actual construction of the devices. The classroom teacher is the one who must locate, procure, or develop the educational materials necessary for providing the individual student with an appropriate education.

The instructor may need to locate an interested electrical engineer, shop teacher, electronics class, or school maintenance person to actually construct the devices. The services of an occupational therapist or physical therapist will be required to determine the appropriate nonpathologic nature of the skills to be taught. The teacher can facilitate and mediate a team effort wherein the occupational and physical therapist, device constructor, and parent combine their varied and unique knowledge of the child to meet his or her training needs. The therapist knows and can best describe the motor responses that the student needs to develop and the most advantageous positions in which to work. This professional can also give meaningful precautions regarding interface placement movement and student body mechanics that can provide the greatest benefit when incorporated into the design of the training device and procedures. The parent and instructor are best suited to provide information on what the child will find reinforcing. The educational skills and concepts to be targeted are easily obtained from the coordinating instructor. With this informational input the device constructor can sketch, for the group's approval, ideas for a device that takes into account (1) the child's body position when in training, (2) the targeted motor response, (3) the educational objectives to be approached through the system, and (4) potentially reinforcing events contingent upon the student's emitted response. Once the group has discussed and refined the sketches, they become a blueprint for the educational system to be built.

Communication between the teacher, the therapist, and the person constructing the device is essential. In this coordinated manner the student will receive the most appropriately fitted interface and reinforcement system. The resulting system is therefore a feedback loop wherein the student is immediately informed of the acceptability and, perhaps, quality of each response.

The training team should ask the following questions regarding the student's training needs, abilities, and reinforcement preferences when designing the system.

1. Student response desired
   a. What skill has been difficult to train through typical methods that might be more easily taught through this technology?
   b. What is the closest approximation of the desired skill that the student produces from which the targeted response could be shaped?
   c. What position and manner of task performance best facilitates the desired response with the minimal stimulation of pathological neuromotor patterns?
2. Interface
   a. How can this approximation of the desired response be used to activate the reinforcing device and gradually be altered to require the targeted response for operation?
3. Reinforcement
   What sensory stimulation does the student find reinforcing and how can it be mechanically, electrically, or electromechanically produced as a result of the activation of an off/on switch?

Far too often, and quite understandably, the significant adults in these students' lives display an acquired acceptance of the child's disabilities. This is generally manifested by a limited expectation of skill performance and acquisition. Such students are frequently, therefore, found to be functioning well beneath their actual capabilities. It is because of this situation that the most important and difficult task before parents and educators is to look at the disabled child objectively. They must assume that any absent or weak response could conceivably be developed and put to some educational or functional use. It seems much easier to assume that improvement of a student's physical ability levels is impossible, and adapt their own behavior to compensate for the disability, than to adapt the environment to increase the student's ability to control it.

In essence, it is environmental design that ultimately labels one person as disabled and another as nondisabled. Engineers can easily design unadaptive interfaces requiring 2 tons of pressure for activation. In such an environment the previously nondisabled person would also be disabled. They would be unable to turn on the lights or television, operate elevators, type, and so forth. It is therefore important to remove the architectural and functional barriers that in part perpetuate the state of disability.

Throughout history humans have shown endless imagination in the invention of things to make the environment easier to cope with. To cross expanses of land and water, they invented cars, boats, and airplanes. To save the energy spent in climbing stairs, they invented elevators. To work into the dark of night, they invented artificial light. To speed communication across distances, they invented the telephone. It would take much less creativity to adapt elements of home, businesses and classrooms to extend some basic environmental control to the disabled. As it is, our total living and working environment has been engineered for manipulation by individuals having average responding capabilities. Such design includes the height of faucets, door knobs, and light switches, as well as the force and movements required for their operation. In essence, a handicapped person's primary disability is that he or she can not produce these average responses. In other words, the environmental design does not allow the disabled person an appropriate interface for control. These environmental adaptations, therefore, need to take place early in the disabled child's life, because without such technology these children will remain adrift in environments over which their limbs provide no control.

As can be seen from the variety of teacher-made educational materials presented in this chapter, the primary limitations to the development and use of such technology are the creativity and motivation of the instructor, builder, and consulting therapists. If, however, there is insufficient time to allow the instructor the luxury of constructing such devices as those described herein, the following appendices may be of some assistance. Appendices A through C contain information and sources of commercially available materials which can be used easily with these students, as described in this chapter. In the event that the instructor is interested in becoming involved in the construction of response-contingent educational materials, the remaining appendices will provide the necessary additional information.

APPENDIX A / Communication Systems

ZYGO Communication Systems and Prentke Romich Company offer a variety of interfaces that can be used as described in this chapter. Both companies sell communication systems operable via their own interfaces. The interfaces provided by Prentke Romich can also be used to operate the environmental control systems they sell. Both companies are currently working on providing disabled students with the ability to operate educational toys through the use of an interface. This means that the student does not need the fine motor control normally required to push specific buttons on a calculator-type keyboard. Instead, the student can make a single response on the interface and scan the available keys, selecting the needed key by activating the interface again. The electronic toys currently being used are the "Little Professor" (math), "Spelling Bee," and "Speak and Spell," all of which are manufactured initially by Texas Instruments (Romich, 1980).

Both of these companies are skillful at matching the disabled person with an appropriate interface. These interfaces range from $18.00 to $45.00 each. The interfaces available through Prentke Romich have a multiple prong plug while the ZYGO interfaces have a miniature-sized plug. In either case, for use with a standard tape recorder, the instructor must request a subminiature-sized plug rather than the one normally provided. ZYGO's miniature plug is, however, the correct size for use with the Library of Congress Tape Player discussed in Appendix B. Listed below are the companies' addresses.

ZYGO Communication Systems
ZYGO Industries, inc,
P.O. Box 1008
Portland, Oregon 97207
(503) 297-1724

Prentke Romich Co.
R.D. 2, Box 191
Shreve, Ohio 44676
(216) 567-2906

APPENDIX B / Free Materials

Library of Congress

It is with an eye to economy and the teacher's materials budget that the author presents the following sources of free materials. One such source is the Library of Congress, Division of Blind and Handicapped Services, that provides a variety of adaptive materials and services free of charge. These materials allow the blind or physically disabled to enjoy books, periodicals, and newspapers. The uses suggested in this chapter are not those for which the devices were originally intended. They are, however, as useful in the education of the severely disabled as they are in allowing disabled adults to "read" books. The Library of Congress is pleased to provide these devices to any disabled person who requests them. The creative teacher can find a variety of training uses for such materials beyond those suggested here. The generic term used by the Library of Congress to describe any device that brings the content of printed matter to the blind or disabled in a form useful to them is "*talking book*." There are two types of talking books currently available: the cassette tape player and the record player.

Tape Player   This tape player can easily be used with any of the aforementioned interfaces. This is done by plugging the interface into the "remote on" jack of the tape player. The remote on jack of the record player is compatible in size (miniature) with the ZYGO interfaces noted in the preceding appendix. The tape player has to be left in an on position for such an application, and will not operate until the student activates the interface. The Library of Congress will also supply extenders for the buttons of the tape player, which permit a greater surface area with a reduced pressure requirement for activation in the typical manner.

Record Player   This unit allows for the attachment of either a set of headphones or a pillow speaker. This permits the student to individually monitor the output of the record player and not disturb the other students. The private listening feature provides the teacher with a potential reinforcer for individual students. The pillow speaker can be mounted in the back of a chair to increase its special nature or it can be used as intended with bedbound students. An especially attractive feature of the record player is that it can be ordered with a remote control switch. This switch is sensitive to skin contact. No pressure is required for activation. This is of great value in training a variety of skills, ranging from pointing for early communication board skill training to teaching the concepts of environmental control. Both the tape player and record player are available on a loan basis to either groups or individual disabled students. If damaged, the Library of Congress will repair or replace either unit at no charge. Both the tape player and record player are available from regional offices that can be located by calling 1(800)-424-9100.

Telephone Pioneers

The Telephone Pioneers are another source of free materials and general assistance. They are a group of current and past employees of the Telephone company who dedicate their volunteer time to the service of their community. Each community has its own chapter and each chapter develops its own projects. The particular projects to be presented in this discussion are the audio ball and the VOX relay.

Audio Ball This device, built into a regulation size soft ball, emits an intermittent, high-frequency pure tone. It can be used to train auditory and visual localization, eye-hand coordination, visual or auditory tracking, and object permanence. It is a toy that stimulates curiosity, environmental interaction, general motor activity, or acts as a reinforcer for task completion. Although the audio ball was intended for use by the blind, it is available to individuals having any disability and to centers serving any population of disabled individuals.

VOX Relay This simple electronic interface is activated by sound and therefore operates in the presences of vocalization or sound production. The Telephone Pioneers donate the circuitry, a stuffed animal of the student's or instructor's selection, and the time required to implant the electronics into the stuffed toy. The end result is a toy with eyes (tiny lights) that blink off and on in response to the student's vocalizations. Although these toys were intended for use by the deaf, the Pioneers also provide them to hearing children with disabilities. The uses of these VOX (voice-activated) relay toys with the deaf overlap those for the handicapped and developmentally delayed students in that they reinforce vocalization. In addition, however, the VOX toys provide feedback from the environment. This is a basic concept needed to develop verbal communication, on the premise that if vocalizations or words have no influence or effect upon the environment, it is unlikely that much communication is generated. The VOX is helpful in teaching this concept, so crucial to the whole act of communication.

To contact the Telephone Pioneers:

1. Call the operator and ask for the phone number of the branch manager of the local office of the telephone company.
2. Request that either the operator or the branch manager of the phone company take your name and number and have the secretary or chairperson of the local chapter call you.
3. Describe your program needs to the chairperson or secretary, and he or she will assign some members of the pioneers to your project. If you are seeking either the audio ball or the VOX relay, the acquisition process will be greatly speeded up by providing them with the following information for locating the chapters responsible for the construction and distribution of these devices.

The audio ball and VOX relay can be obtained by contacting the following pioneer offices.

Rita Sweeney/Audio Ball
C/O Merrimack Valley Workers Chapter #78
Telephone Pioneers of America
1600 Osgood Street
North Andover, Massachusetts 01845
(617) 681-2310

Bob Wade
C/O Illinois Bell Telephone Co.
Telephone Pioneers of America
406 E. Monroe
3rd Floor West
Springfield, Illinois 62725
(217) 789-5438

The person in charge of the project then locates and purchases the materials, and donates them to the center or child indicated. It should be noted that the Pioneers have neither the educational background nor the experience required in selecting the stuffed toy in which the VOX relay is to be placed. The instructor must therefore provide considerations for selection or must select one for the student and give it to the pioneer responsible for the project. The criteria for selection are: small size; soft, washable exterior; and minimal distraction in color (i.e., a brown bear should be chosen rather than a zebra or tiger).

Another useful source of training materials is the IBM Corporation. Its services, however, apply to a much smaller segment of the disabled population. IBM offers reconditioned electric typewriters, at trade-in value, to disabled persons.

IBM also provides arm rests, keyboard templates, continuous-roll perforated paper, and cogwheel rollers to feed the paper into the machine. As many IBM employees do not know of this program, persistence is often required to locate a salesperson or an executive who can assist in the acquisition of the materials needed.

Sears and Radio Shack have recently started selling a mechanism that provides environmental control to the disabled. This unit is activated by the application of pressure to 1 of 16 small buttons. This unit can be used by a disabled person who has a good pointing response, even through the use of a head pointing apparatus. It is even possible to adapt this device for use through interface activation. There is no discount on cost to the disabled. It is, however, a potential training tool that could have broad application in placing more of the disabled person's world under his or her control.

RADIO SHACK ENVIRONMENTAL CONTROL UNIT (ECU)
PLUG 'N POWER SYSTEM

Control Center	61-2680	$39.95
Appliance switch	61-2681	$14.99
Dimmer switch	61-2682	$14.99
Wall switch	61-2683	$14.99

SEARS ECU
HOME CONTROL SYSTEM

Command Console	34AY 5456	$39.95
Cordless Controls	34AY 5457	$19.99
Lamp Module	34AY 5458	$14.99
Appliance Module	34AY 5459	$14.99
Wall Switch Module	34AY 5460	$14.99

APPENDIX C / Basic Electrical Considerations

The reader has thus far been exposed to the rationale for, and some applications of, the technology involved in using such educational materials with the handicapped. It seems appropriate that the reader also be made aware of the simple electrical building blocks involved in the process. This may better prepare the teacher to understand and use this form of educational materials.

Electric devices do not work without electricity, and to provide that electricity one must have a complete circuit or path from a power source to the device and back to the power source. The complete circuit is an unbroken path in which the electricity can travel. This pathway is broken and reestablished by any off/on switch. When a complete circuit is established, the electricity passes through all of the components which are connected into the circuit, providing the electricity required for operation.

There are two basic relationships that components in a circuit may hold to one another. These relationships permit the instructor to perform a variety of different functions with the same components. The components of a circuit can be arranged in either parallel, series, or a combination of the two.

Parallel

This method of connecting two or more components into an electrical circuit permits electricity to pass through all of the components regardless of the status of the other components.

Figure 9a illustrates three switches connected in parallel to a light bulb. Any of the three switches will operate the light bulb even if the other two switches are off. In other words, any of the switches individually can form a complete circuit from the battery to the light bulb and back to the battery. Another application of a parallel circuit is shown in

Figure 9b. In this particular application, three light bulbs have been connected in parallel with one switch. When the switch completes the circuit, all the bulbs will be illuminated. In the event that one or two bulbs are burned out, broken, or removed, the remaining bulb or bulbs will still be illuminated. This method of connecting components is frequently used with Christmas tree lights so that one inoperant bulb will not stop the electricity from lighting the other bulbs. Each component in a parallel circuit, therefore, has its own private pathway to the switch and power supply and is independent of the operational status of the other components in the circuit.

Series

In this method of connecting two or more components of an electrical circuit, the flow of the electricity is dependent upon the proper functioning of each component. Figures 9c and 9d present serial connections of three switches and three light bulbs respectively. If one of the compo-

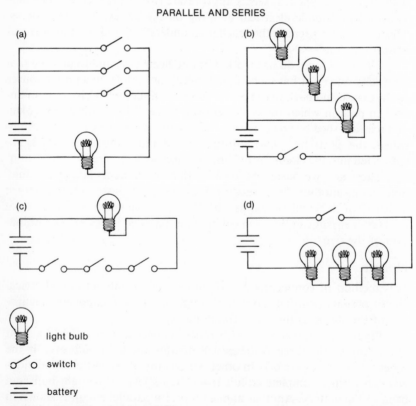

PARALLEL AND SERIES

light bulb

switch

battery

Figure 9.   Parallel and series switching.

nents connected in series fails to permit electricity to flow past it, the path of the electricity is broken. The remaining components do not receive the electricity they require to function. In Figure 9c all three of the switches must be closed to complete the circuit and activate the light bulb. If one switch remains open the circuit will not be complete, and the electricity will not reach the bulb. Figure 9d illustrates three light bulbs connected in series with one switch. When the switch is closed, the three bulbs are illuminated; if one bulb is out of the circuit, the remaining bulbs do not light up. The components of a series circuit are therefore dependent upon the functioning of the other components with which they are connected.

The parallel circuit allows the student to receive several reinforcing events for a single response as in Figure 9b. It also provides the student with the option of choosing from several switches for operation of the given reinforcing device as in Figure 9a. All of the interfaces discussed have been attached to the output devices in parallel to the normal off/on switch. The series circuit seen in Figure 9d permits the student to receive several reinforcing events contingent upon a single response as did the parallel circuit seen in Figure 9b, assuming that all components are in working order. The advantage of the series circuit is that it permits the teacher to require several concurrent components of a response for reinforcement as shown in Figure 9c. This arrangement was used in the head-position trainer discussed earlier in this chapter.

The switches most commonly used for interfacing students to reinforcing devices are the microswitch and mercury switch. They are generally adaptable to the process of interfacing, because they are tiny and sensitive to small amounts of pressure and movement respectively.

Both the microswitch and the mercury switch are momentary contact in nature. That is, they only complete the circuit while the student is operating them correctly, through application of pressure or by maintenance of the desired position. In both cases, once the student removes the pressure or moves from the desired position, the switch breaks the circuit and stops the flow of electricity.

Jacks and Plugs

This two component unit provides the teacher with the option of interchanging interfaces and reinforcers. These units are used as the connection between home stereos and earphones. Jacks and plugs present the option of using one reinforcing device with several students; each of them can use a different input interface specific to his or her particular disorder and training program. In essence, the jack and plug unit permits the teacher to plug and unplug the components, and thereby selectively combine interfaces and reinforcers specific to students' needs.

Indirect Switching

The relay and solenoid are two components that permit indirect switching. This is important in that the needed output device may require more voltage than the teacher thinks advisable for a student. Indirect switching is performed through the use of electromagnetism; the force generated around a wire when electricity is passed through it. When the wires are wound around a spool, the strength of this electromagnetic force (EMF) is greatly increased. The EMF arises with the onset of the flow of electricity and disappears when the electricity stops flowing. Although on a much smaller scale, the relay and solenoid operate on the same principles of electromagnetism as do the large magnets used to lift, move, and drop scrap metal and cars in junk yards. The large scrap movers pick up their load when the electricity is allowed to flow through huge coils of wire, thereby generating an EMF. The load is dropped when the electricity is stopped and the EMF resultantly disappears. The EMF, as used in the relay and solenoid, activates a switch directly linked to the output device. In other words, the student activates the relay or the solenoid through his or her interface, and it in turn activates the output device. By using such intermediate on/off switches as the relay and solenoid, the student is safely isolated from direct contact with a potentially hazardous power source needed for the output device.

Relay   The relay and microswitch are very similar in function; the only real difference is that the relay depends on an EMF to pull the points into contact for completion of the circuit.

Solenoid   The solenoid utilizes the EMF it generates to move an iron bar suspended through the center of its wire coil. The movement of the iron core, in turn, operates a microswitch.

Remote Control   To further insure the safety of the student, the relay and solenoid may be operated via remote control. This method of activation is used in both the talking-book record player and the environmental control units discussed in the preceding appendix. The use of remote control may require the assistance of an electronically sophisticated consultant. The parts for the remote control unit may be taken from a used remote control toy, and then adapted to the system needed by the student.

APPENDIX D / Materials list

If the team is interested in developing any of the described interface/reinforcement devices they can locate all of the needed components and technical advice at a local retail electronics store. Radio Shack and Lafayette Electronics are two such stores which are found in nearly every community. The materials needed are very basic and should be easy to locate. This Appendix presents the basic materials required for construction of the devices described in this chapter.

This chapter was not presented as a technical guide for construction, but rather as an idea book to stimulate the instructor's thought process and creative juices. The following materials list, therefore, does not contain specifications for any particular device. The dimensions are left to the team, as it is this group of individuals who best know the student's physical needs and abilities. The only precaution is that the device should be checked for safety by someone who understands electricity. For continued service of the system, it is also prudent to use wire of a multiple-strand type such as stereo wire, as it is more resistant to breakage from movement than wire of a single-strand type.

Touch Switch (Figures 1 & 2)
1. 1 microswitch* (Radio Shack #275-016)
2. 1 plug and wire
3. 1 block of wood (½" × 2" × 4")
4. 1 piece of lexan/trigger plate for activation**
    (small pieces can be obtained at local electronics stores)

Squeeze Switch (Figure 3)
1. 1 microswitch
2. 1 plug and wire
3. 1 piece of gauze
4. 1 thread to sew the gauze around the microswitch

Pull Switch (Figure 4)
1. 1 microswitch*
2. 1 plug and wire
3. 1 string*
4. 1 object for the student to grasp and pull*
    (curtain ring, macrame ring, shaped or colored black)

Head Position Trainer (Figure 6)
1. 4 mercury switches (Be certain that the mercury switches are child safe. Order plastic or unbreakable mercury switches with flexible wires attached at the end of the two metal poles. Look carefully at the pictures in the order catalogue.)
2. 1 plug and wire
3. 1 strip of material to go around the student's head front to back
4. 1 piece of elastic or other means of making the above strip adjustable
5. 1 piece of material to go across the top of the student's head ear to ear
6. 1 Velcro hook and loop strip for each mercury switch (to allow for adjustment of the position of the mercury switches).

---

*2 or more needed for the multiple switching application.
**Lexan is a polycarbonate that is less breakable than plexiglass but can't be heated or formed.

Sources of Material for Head Position Trainer
Velcro material:
"BE OK SELF-HELP AIDS"
Fred Sammons, inc.
Box 32
Brookfield, Illinois 60513
(312) 264-3216
Mercury switch (#7MP1-2) (It is sealed in a plastic tube, shatterproof and impact resistant, and comes with a bracket, and more durable, multiple strand wires. Approximately $4.00 each:
MICRO SWITCH (a division of HONEYWELL ELECTRONICS)
Freeport, Illinois 61032
Mercury switch (#U-24B mercury tilt switch)
Universal Security Instruments, Inc.
Owings Mills, Maryland 21117
Universal Adaptor (Figure 7)
1. jack and wire
2. 2 metal discs approximately the size of a nickel
3. 1 piece of foam rubber with glue on each side (the same size as the metal discs
NOTE: Double sided circuit board material can also be used for the adaptor
Kaleidoscope
1. 1 low-RPM (revolutions per minute), D.C. (direct current) motor
2. 1 battery supply appropriate to the requirements of the motor
3. 1 jack (allows the input from any of the above interfaces)
4. small, colorful objects of different shapes (to be placed between the disks for display).
5. 2 plastic lids (i.e., coffee can lids. Place the objects in the lids, glue the lids together, and attach them to the axis of the motor).
Source for the low RPM D.C. motor
Edmund Scientific Co.
1980 Edscorp Building
Barrington, N.J. 08007
1-rpm, 3-volt D.C. motor
41,327
$9.95
Mobile
1. 1 low-RPM, D.C. motor
2. 1 battery supply
3. 1 jack
4. 1 disk (to attach to the axis of the motor)
5. objects to attach to the disk
6. string to attach the objects to the disk (colorful yarn)

Rotary Dial Communication Device (Figure 8)
1. 1 low-RPM, D.C. motor
2. 1 battery supply (i.e. 4 "D" cell batteries)
3. 2 "D" cell battery holders
4. 1 jack and wire (to the interface)
5. 1 display surface
6. 1 flexible child-safe indicator (a plastic strap used to bundle telephone wires. Note: The wire bundle strap may be obtained from the Phone Company or someone who works with wires such as an instruction media repair person, electrician, or T.V. repair person).

REFERENCES

Arroyo, R. Control and communication devices for the severely disabled. *Bulletin of Prosthetics Research*, 1976, *10* (25), 25–37.
Aston, W., Bo the blinking dog helps children to speak. *Volta Review*, 1973, 75, 214–215.
Berenberg, W. Cerebral Palsy and the engineering sciences. *Developmental Medicine and Child Neurology*, 1968, 10(6), 195.
Campbell, P., Green, G., & Carlson, L. Approximating the norm through environmental and child-centered prosthetics and adaptive equipment. In E. Sontag, J. Smith, and N. Certo (Eds.), *Educational programming for the severely and profoundly handicapped*. Reston, Va.: Council for Exceptional Children, 1977.
Carbre, M., Johnson, A. R., McCann, E., Miller, J., Peterson, D., & Shervanian, A. *Development and evaluation of adaptive communication devices for the severely handicapped child*. (ERIC, ED-014 825, EC-000 097) pp 1–14, plus 14 appendices (1966).
Copeland, K. *Aids for the severely handicapped*. London: Sector Publishing, 1974.
Doughty, N. R. *Automated learning environments: Educational technology serving the multihandicapped. A systematic approach to the delivery of educational services to profoundly handicapped students*. Cambridge, Minn.: C.A.D.R.E. Center, undated.
Driscoll, M. C. Creative-technological aids for the learning disabled child: an interdisciplinary project. *American Journal of Occupational Therapy*, 1975, *29* (2), 102–105.
Dubose, R. F. and Deni, K. Easily constructed adaptive and assistive equipment. *Teaching Exceptional Children*, 1980 116–117.
Foulds, R. A., Crochetiere, W. J., Baletso, G., & Meyer, C. *The Tufts non-vocal communications program—Biomedical Engineering Center*. Boston, Mass.: Tufts University and New England Medical Center, undated.
Hagen, C., Porter, W., & Brink, J., Nonverbal communication: an alternative mode of communication for the child with severe cerebral palsy. *Journal of Speech and Hearing Disorders*, 1973, *38*, 448–455.
Hill, S. D., Campagna, J., Long, D., Munch, J., & Naecher, S. An exploratory study of the use of two response keyboards as a means of communication for the severely handicapped child. *Perceptual and Motor Skills*, 1968, *26*, 699–704.
Johnson, D., Firth, H., & Graham, C. Vibration and praise as reinforcers for mentally handicapped people. *Mental Retardation*, 1978, 9, 339–342.

Jones, M. V. Electrical communication devices. *American Journal of Occupational Therapy*, 1961, 15(3), 110–111.

Kavanagh, R. N. Holmlund, B. A., & Krause, A. E. *Communication systems for the physically disabled*. Digest of the first Canadian Medical and Biological Conference, Ottawa, Canada, 9, 8–9, 1966.

Lance, W. D. Technology and media for exceptional learners: looking ahead. *Exceptional Children*, 1977, 44(2), 92–96.

Lavoy, R. W. Rick's communicator. *Exceptional Children*, 1957, 23(7), 338–340.

Lipskin, R. An evaluation program for powered wheelchair control systems. *Bulletin of Prosthetics Research*, 1970, 10(14), 121–129.

Mancino, *Head position training through biofeedback*. Madison, Conn.: Adaptive Therapeutic Systems, 1977.

Mavilya, M. P., & Mignone, B. R. *Educational strategies for the youngest hearing impaired children (0–5 yrs. of age)*. Jackson Heights, N.Y.: The Lexington School for the Deaf, 1977.

Miller, J., & Carpenter, C. Electronics for Communication. *American Journal of Occupational Therapy*, 1964, 28 20–23.

Romich, B. The Scanning "Little Professor." In Y. Danjuma (Ed.), *Communication outlook*, 1980, 2(3), 6.

Ross, Head position monitor for under $5.00. *AAESPH Newsletter*, 1976, 5.

Sampson, D. A communication device for patients unable to speak. *Medical and Biological Engineering*, 1971, 8, 99–101.

Sheredos, S. Games for the severely disabled. *Bulletin of Prosthetics Research* 1973, 10(19), 130–137.

Sternat, J., Messina, R., Lyon, J., & Nietupske, J. Curricular suggestions for teaching severely handicapped students selected clusters of head control skills. In E. Sontag, J. Smith, and N. Certo (Eds), *Educational Programming for the Severely and Profoundly Handicapped*. Reston, Va.: Council for Exceptional Children, 1977.

Tawney, J. W., *Telecommunications for the severely handicapped*. Lexington, Ky.: U.S. Department of Health, Education, and Welfare, 1977.

Utley, B., Holvoet, J., and Barnes, K. Handling, positioning, and feeding the physically handicapped. In E. Sontag, J. Smith, and N. Certo (Eds.), *Educational programming for the severely and profoundly handicapped*. Reston, Va.: Council for Exceptional Children, 1977.

Vanderheiden, G. C., Volk, A. V. & Geisler, C. D. *An alternative interface to computers for the physically handicapped—the auto monitoring communication board*. Paper presented at the AFIPS National Computer Conference, 1974.

Wethered, C. E. *Hierarchies of operational efficiency and preference for interface selection for the physically disabled*. Master's thesis, Idaho State University, 1976.

Wethered, C. E. Teacher-made response-contingent training materials for the nonspeaking student, *Topics in Language Disorders*, 1982, 2(2).

White, S. D. A modular communication device for paralyzed patients. *Archives of Physical and Medical Rehabilitation*, 1974, 55, 94–95.

Wooldridge, C. P., & McLaurin, C. A. Biofeedback: Background and application to physical rehabilitation. *Bulletin of Prosthetics Research*, 1976, 10(25), 25–37.

Zucker, S. H., D'Alonzo, B. J., McMullen, M. R., & Williams, W. L. Training eye-pointing behavior in a nonambulatory profoundly retarded child using contingent vibratory stimulation. *Education and Training of the Mentally Retarded*, 1980, 15(1), 4–7.

Chapter 5

Motor Development

Barbara Connolly, Janice Schultz, and Bonnie B. Greer

INTRODUCTION

A significant proportion of the multiply handicapped population discussed in this chapter suffers from some type of motor development problem. Although individuals handicapped primarily by auditory and visual losses are typically less affected, the severely retarded and physically handicapped manifest a wider range of problems in this area. Whether the result of disease, paralysis, or an understimulating environment, such individuals are often frail and emaciated. Many are nonambulatory and some are almost completely paralyzed. Nearly all suffer from a general lack of coordination, poor posture, and an inability to do many of the basic daily activities that require a minimal level of gross and fine motor coordination. This presents a very serious challenge to those charged with the responsibility of educating the multiply handicapped. Real gains can only be made through carefully thought out, systematic motor development programs. A knowledge of correct therapeutic handling procedures, as well as of the sequence and content of activities appropriate for muscle and coordination development is essential.

In the past, when the vast majority of the multiply handicapped population was institutionalized, motor development activities and pro-

This chapter was adapted from material in *A Comprehensive Handbook for Management of Children with Developmental Disabilities*, edited by C. S. White, J. W. Minor, and B. Connolly. University of Tennessee Center for the Health Services: Child Development Center, 1977.

grams were typically provided by physical or occupational therapists, and were usually limited in scope. In the wake of recent legislation, especially P.L. 94-142, the legal right of the multiply handicapped to the physical and occupational therapy programs they need is guaranteed.

To guarantee rights is one thing. To deliver them is something else. The rapid changes demanded by law have produced more than a little confusion. As in other programming areas, many teachers and physical therapists have found themselves inadequately prepared to deal with the unique problems and needs of the multiply handicapped.

Physical therapists in public schools are accustomed to working with children who are functioning at levels of both normal intelligence and mild or moderate retardation. These, traditionally, have been the groups for which they have been trained. Now, because severely handicapped children are often unresponsive, nonverbal, and inactive, the techniques previously used with adult patients or mildly retarded children rarely work (Connolly & Anderson, 1978). Although various activities can be identified in the literature regarding physical therapy for children functioning at higher levels (Witengier, 1970; Tecklin & Holsclaw, 1973; Cronis & Gleeson, 1974; Harris & Cherry, 1974) there has been very little written about the role of the physical therapist and the severely handicapped child in the public schools. The assumption set forth in P.L. 94-142, that sufficient numbers of physical therapists have the training and experience required to work with these children, must clearly be questioned (Dehaven, 1974).

Most regular teachers, and many special teachers, are, no doubt, even less prepared to work with the multiply handicapped than are therapists in the area of motor development. Nevertheless, since such children are typically not seen on a daily basis by the physical therapist, the teacher must play a key role in stimulating muscle development and promoting independence in daily living activities. If he or she is unaware of basic handling and positioning techniques or of the activities that are being used in therapy, behaviors and postures inappropriate and inconsistent with the physical therapy program may unknowingly be reinforced (Connolly & Anderson, 1978).

Although there can be no quick solution to the lack of trained specialists, the optimum use of available personnel requires increased cooperation among all those involved in a physical development program for the severely handicapped. This may involve a role change for many physical therapists. Levangie (1980), in a survey of over three hundred physical therapists, found that they gave very low priority to such skills as developing or conducting in-service training programs for school personnel, consulting with physical education teachers on adaptive physical education programs, and writing and interpreting educational objectives. These skills, however, reflect important nontraditional functions that are increasingly determining the overall effectiveness of physical development programs. To properly carry out the therapy programs prepared for their students, teachers frequently need additional information. Physical therapists who actively share information with school personnel and who are readily accessible to teachers with questions or concerns will undoubtedly magnify the positive impact they are already having on handicapped youngsters.

The job of the physical therapist, with its added role of consultant or resource person, will be greatly facilitated as teachers gain a greater depth and understanding in basic physical development problems and the various techniques commonly used to remediate them. This chapter is designed to provide a practical introduction of this material to school personnel.

PRINCIPLES OF DEVELOPMENT

Before working with the child who has a motor or sensory disorder, one must first be aware of normal growth and development as well as deviations from normality. This will then make it possible to distinguish between significantly abnormal and normal behavior, to decide what to work on first with the child, and to promote normal development in an orderly sequence. Therefore, the following is a review of some principles of growth and development.

Development is from head to toe. The child first develops head control and then control over the lower part of the body. This is one reason why a therapist does not work on walking before the child masters head control. The child must first have head control for balance when on the elbows and in sitting and kneeling before learning balance standing up.

Development is from the middle of the body to the extremities. The child can control shoulders before fingers. A baby will wave his or her arms about in the air before picking objects up by hand. That is why we work on gross movements of the arms and legs before fine movements such as using hands and individual fingers.

Development occurs first generally and then specifically. The child may smile, laugh, and wiggle all over when seeing a toy. Later in development, he or she reaches out for it, and then waves, bangs, and mouths the toy. Later still, the child uses it purposefully.

Development is from simple to complex. The child learns very simple things at first and then moves on to more complex tasks: he or she sees, feels, tastes, smells, and handles objects before being able to tell the difference between them. The child uses a whole hand to grasp before using the fingers. He or she bangs and mouths blocks before starting to align, stack, and build with them imaginatively and learns the basic colors and how to match them before learning to say their names. Likewise, the child learns to put fingers in his or her mouth before learning to finger feed and to use a spoon.

Development is continuous. Development in one stage influences performance in the following stages. The baby begins learning certain skills in stomach and back lying, sitting and standing even from birth. As growth occurs he or she becomes more proficient in each position. For example, at 6–7 months of age a baby will bear a good deal of his or her own weight when you hold the baby in a standing position. This is a stage basic to the later development of standing and walking. A child must first bear weight before standing and walking alone. The same is true for hand skills. The infant will first probe with fingers before developing a pincer grasp.

Development is similar for all. The order of development varies little from child to child. Motor development occurs in a sequence, the rate and quality of which can be affected by various physical and environmental factors. Even a child who has motor problems must learn to hold his or her head up before being able to sit alone. The physically handicapped child may take longer to learn a skill but still learns it in the same order as the normal child.

When observing the gross motor development (use of large muscles) and fine motor development (use of small muscles) in a child, it is helpful to be familiar with the sequence that usually occurs. A brief overview of this sequence is included in Table 1.

In addition to the principles of sequence development previously discussed, development also occurs because of what is seen, heard, smelled, tasted, touched, and felt emotionally. The importance of the four senses of sight, hearing, smell, and taste is obvious. Individuals react to the world around them because of what their senses tell them, often because of past experience. From past experience it is possible to know what a food is going to taste like even before tasting it. From past experiences with objects it is possible to picture them in the mind even if they are not present in the room.

The sense of touch is especially important in the development process. People respond to objects that are hot or cold, rough or smooth, hard or soft because of their experiences with the sense of touch. The sense of touch is very important in moving about in the world. The sense of touch, together with another sense called the proprioceptive sense, are the two most important senses that enable the child to develop motor skills. The proprioceptive sense is the sense one has of movement or position of the body in space. There are receptors in the muscles and joints and in the inner ear that inform a person whether he is moving, standing

Table 1.   The normal developmental sequences for gross and fine motor skill development

Gross motor skill development	Fine motor skill development
1. Moves arms and legs on back	1. Has reflexive grasp (grasp upon contact with object)
2. Starts to roll over	
3. Lifts head while on stomach	2. Uses two-hand approach
4. Gets up on elbows	3. Uses one-hand approach
5. Pulls knees up under stomach	4. Has voluntary grasp
6. Gets up to kneeling	5. Transfers from hand to hand
7. Sits back on legs	6. Uses fingers and thumb movements
8. Can lie down and get up again	
9. Sits unsupported	7. Uses scissors grasp (between thumb and side of index finger)
10. Pulls up to knees	
11. Pulls up to feet	8. Has good pincer grasp (between thumb and tip of index finger)
12. Cruises holding onto furniture	
13. Walks independently	9. Grasps two objects at the same time
14. Creeps up stairs	
15. Seats self in small chair	10. Has good release; release is willful, not accidental
16. Runs, jumps, skips, hops, etc.	
	11. Hands coordinate action with what is seen
	12. Has refined skill and good use of hands

still, sitting, smiling, clapping hands, losing balance, standing upside-down, or waving a hand. By closing the eyes and having someone else move a person's arms in various positions, it is possible for that person to tell in what position his or her arms are without looking at them. There is a feeling for where our arms and legs are.

Each of the senses that have been mentioned work together to give people ideas about the world and help them respond to it. The control of all body movements comes from the brain, which responds because of the messages it receives from the eyes, nose, ears, skin, muscles, joints, and so forth. When there is normal brain control, movements will be normal. When there is damage to the brain, movements will be disturbed or retarded at an early age. Different areas of the brain have control over different functions. There is an area of the brain that has the greatest control over movement of the body. There is another area that has the greatest control over the sense of touch. Another area controls speech and still another hearing. Damage to the brain can affect some or all of these areas. It may result in a child being able to walk about but not hear, or not to be able to move about but to be able to hear and see. Whatever the case, the child will start by using the abilities he or she has, however abnormal they may be. This results in an uneven development, because many of the stages of normal motor development will be left out.

For instance, if a child does not experience lying on the stomach and lifting the head, he or she may not learn head control well enough to learn to sit, crawl, or walk. If a child turns only to one side and does not use the other side as much, he or she will develop fewer skills using that side. A child who can only stand by stiffening the legs and standing on the toes will become even stiffer and develop an awkward and unsteady gait. If a child is only able to sit with a curved back, he or she will eventually have difficulty in straightening the back for activities such as crawling and walking.

Because a child learns by feeling movement, the only movement an abnormal child may feel is abnormal movement. If this is all he or she can do, the child continues to do it, and the abnormal movement becomes so strong that it is difficult to change. The way to help these children is to provide an opportunity for them to move in a more normal way so that as they continue to move more normally they will be feeling and learning normal movement. Because learning comes through experience, if the experience is abnormal, the end result is abnormal. If the experiences of movement are normal, the end result will be normal movement. It is clear that if a child is not required to use a skill such as picking up the head or bringing the hands together, then that skill will not develop. The opportunity for experience in movement must be provided.

In order to foster more normal patterns of movement in a delayed child, a number of therapeutic handling and positioning techniques can be employed. When used skillfully, these procedures provide enough support to make the environment accessible for the child but not to create unnecessary dependence on the support systems. These therapeutic procedures encourage and facilitate experiences in movement for the child.

THERAPEUTIC HANDLING

General Considerations

Therapeutic handling is a broad term that covers a variety of methods and techniques. The most basic technique begins before a child is ever taken from the bed. Many children are unable to move themselves about in bed and rely upon others for their movement. A child left in one position receives very little stimulation. For example, a child who is left on his or her back sees primarily the ceiling. Children who respond to sound or movements can usually turn the head toward the stimulation. If the stimulation comes from only one side, a child may have the tendency to keep the head turned in that direction. Ultimately, that child may become unable to bring the head back to the midline or to the opposite side. If the child continues to keep his head turned to one side, serious problems such as deformities in the spine and hips can result. To prevent the child from continually turning to one side, either the bed can be moved so that stimulation (e.g., people moving, lighting, toys) comes from the neglected side or the child can be placed with the head at the opposite end of the bed. Ideally the child's position is alternated daily.

Back-lying is a position that is not beneficial for most children. If a child is spastic or has too much muscle tone, he or she has a tendency to press the head into the pillow, pull the arms out to the side, cross the legs and point the feet downward. The child may then be unable to initiate movements alone while in this position. The child who is "floppy" or has too little muscle tone may be unable to lift the head, arms, or legs against gravity while in the back-lying position. Neither the spastic nor the floppy child can experience such things as kicking the feet or bringing the hands to the mouth while in this position.

A side-lying position is probably the best position for any child. In this position, a child can bring the hands forward and reach for objects in front of him or her. In addition, the legs can relax and be bent to a comfortable position. If the child is unable to maintain the side-lying position alone, he or she can be propped with pillows until able to maintain side-lying. When the child lies comfortably on a side, encourage him or her to play in this position by placing toys within reach.

Stomach-lying should not be used during the night if the child cannot lift the head and turn it to the side. Under close supervision, however, stomach-lying during the day is good for relaxing of tight hips and knees and for facilitation of neck extension. A towel rolled up and placed under the child's chest will help make the child more comfortable while in this position and will help in lifting up the head.

The time that the child spends on the stomach should initially be short, with a gradual lengthening of the time. The duration of time in any one position is an important consideration when one is attempting to provide the optimal positioning. Most therapists feel that the child should not be left in the same position for longer than 30 minutes at a time, and for some children, a change should be made after 15 to 20 minutes.

Nighttime is a difficult time for many handicapped children. Because they may be unable to move themselves about in bed, they tend to become stiff and uncomfortable. Thus, the children who do not move freely about in the bed should be checked often and their positions in bed should be changed frequently during the night.

Children who have physical disabilities present special problems in their handling from the time they are lifted from the bed or floor until the time they are returned. Therefore, basic body mechanics should be employed whenever you attempt to work with the handicapped child. These techniques should be utilized when carrying, lifting and transferring the child from place to place. The following principles are especially important:

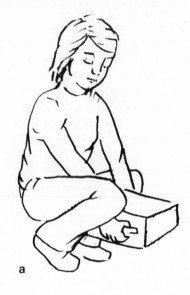

a

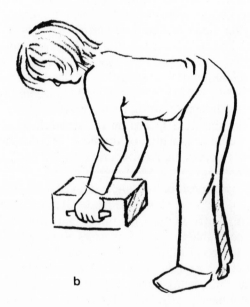

b

Figures 1a & 1b.

1. Do not bend forward with knee straight to pick up objects. Always squat (Figure 1).
2. Do not lift loads above the waist line. This puts too much strain on back muscles (Figure 2).
3. Never bend backward to carry. If an object is very heavy, try slinging it over your back or have another person aid in carrying (Figure 3).

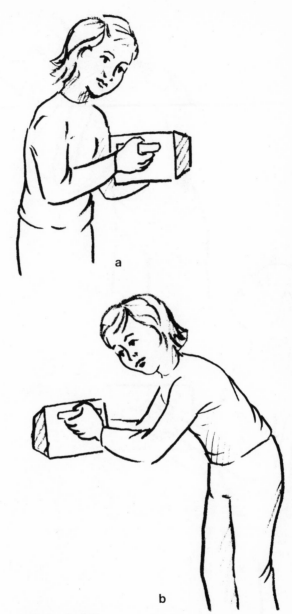

Figures 2a & 2b.

Key Areas of Control

There are certain key points used to manage a child with any type of abnormal muscle tone. These points are the head, neck, and spine. If their position is controlled, a child can be prevented from going into many of the abnormal body positions. For example, to get the head forward in a

Figures 3a & 3b.

child who tends to throw the head back, it can either be pressed forward at the base of the skull or by curling the shoulders forward. (Figures 4a, b).

Another example is a child who tends to allow the head to drop forward. By pulling the shoulder backward, head lifting will be facilitated (see Figure 5).

a

b

Figures 4a & 4b.

Maintaining the head in a midline position is important for control of the abnormal "fencer" position common to many children. The fencer position involves a primitive reflex that causes a child's arm to extend upon turning the head to the side, and the opposite arm to flex (Figure 6).

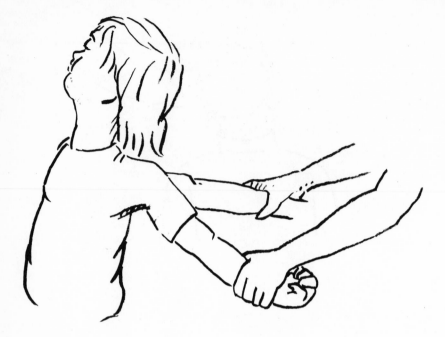

Figure 5.

Figure 6.

Figure 7.

Once a child is in this position, he or she has a difficult time moving out of it. By keeping the child's head in the midline position, the fencer position can be prevented and the child can use the arms more actively. The key areas of control should be kept in mind each time you attempt to work with the child in any type of activity.

Lifting

The best way to determine how to lift a child is to observe the reactions as you pick him or her up from the bed or floor. The child may stiffen, straighten up, or become floppy. In the following sketches, various ways to lift different types of children are illustrated.

A spastic child may be lifted from a back lying position by supporting him or her under the arms and pulling the child forward at the shoulders. This facilitates the bending of the head, arms, hips, and knees (Figure 7).

The spastic child can be turned to a side lying position, which will facilitate a bending of the hips and knees, and lifted while in the side lying position. The athetoid child can be handled in the same manner (Figure 8).

The floppy child can be lifted from various positions. However, a firm hold on the child's trunk and upper leg area should be maintained when lifting. *Never* pick the child up by the arms (Figure 9).

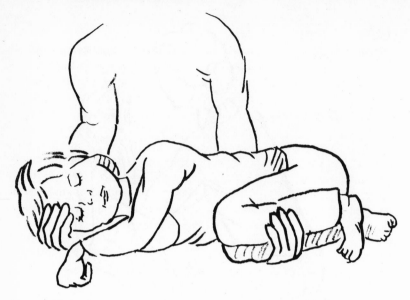

Figure 8.

Figure 9.

Carrying

The proper way to carry a child is determined by what type of muscle tone he or she has. There are a few basic points that are applicable, however, no matter what type of child you are handling. No child should be held so closely and firmly to the carrier's body as to be unable to see the surroundings. A child is stimulated by sound and sight while being carried. A child should also be allowed to use his or her own muscles as much as possible and not be completely supported by the carrier, especially for head control. If a child's shoulders and trunk are held properly, the child should be able to at least partially support the head.

For a child who is spastic or tends to completely straighten while carried, the following illustrations show several different methods of carrying. The child's arms should be laid over the carrier's shoulders and the legs parted and wrapped around the carrier's waist. Be sure that both the child's legs are kept bent. This position is good if the child tends to scissor the legs when being carried or picked up (Figure 10).

Figure 10.

Figure 11.

If the child is very heavy and spastic, Figure 11 shows a better way to carry the child because the weight is better distributed.

If the child is spastic but does not scissor the legs, he or she can be carried in the sidesaddle position if small (Figure 10) or in the swing position if large (see Figure 12). Both positions allow the child to be placed in a bent position that will break up the straight positioning.

If the child is floppy or athetoid, a variety of carrying positions can be utilized. In carrying the floppy child, trying to increase muscle tone and muscle strength is important. Floppy children can be handled quickly to increase muscle tone. A floppy child can be carried in the "football" position if he or she is small (Figure 13). This will encourage the child to lift the head and strengthen the neck muscles. The swing or saddle positions described for the spastic child can also be used with the floppy or athetoid child.

Figure 12.

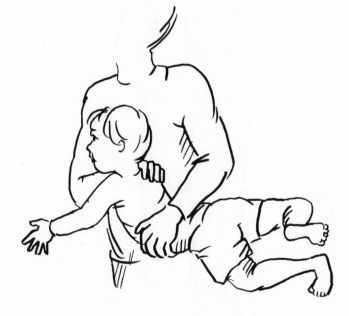

Figure 13.

Head Control

Head control is a basic necessity in the normal sequence of development. It is the first step toward more complex movements and skills. In the normal person it is the basis for all movements and activities, whether they be automatic and spontaneous movements of balance or voluntary movements.

Whenever a normal person moves, he or she adjusts the position of the head, holding it steady in midline to the body, which enables the person to focus properly. Thus, it is important to stimulate the handicapped child to place the head in midline whenever possible.

The following are instructions for how to improve head control:

1. The child can be suspended in space when held under the arms or at the waist. Then the child is gently and gradually tilted in all directions — sideways, forward, and backward. This gives the child the opportunity to pull the head back to an upright position (Figure 14).

Figure 14.

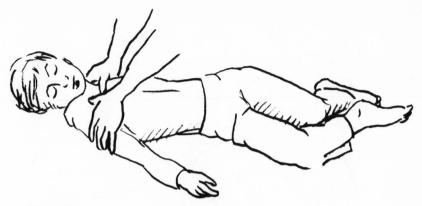

Figure 15.

2. It is difficult or impossible for some children to raise their heads up or to keep them in a midline position because they have poor muscle control and are referred to as being floppy. In order to assist such a child in raising the head up and to hold it in that position, place your hands on the front of the shoulders with your thumbs on the child's chest. By doing this, you can stabilize the child at the shoulders while he or she brings the head forward (Figure 15).

3. A child who throws the head, shoulders, and arms back while sitting on your lap should not be managed by pushing forward as shown in Figure 16a. The best technique is to put your forearm around the child's neck at the bottom of the head and then curl the shoulders forward while controlling them with your forearm and hand (Figure 16b).

4. Many children are unable to lift their heads when lying on their stomachs. If a child lies on the stomach supported by a bolster, roller, or on an incline, he or she will be able to lift the head and at the same time to straighten the back. The feet should not become stiff and pointed; when you are playing with the child, always spend a few minutes bending the ankles, with the feet up and legs turned out; also check to see that the hips are not stiff (Figure 17a, b).

    This position is not good for a child who thrusts the head back, arches the back, and straightens the legs tightly. Being supported on an incline only enhances any problems. The child should be placed over two bolsters with arms forward and legs bent on either side of the bolster. This will allow the child to support himself or herself on arms and knees and at the same time to raise the head. Try to interest the child in toys at this time (Figure 17c).

5. Lay the child on his or her back. Take hold of the child's arms just above the wrists, and with the child's knees bent and feet stabilized against your body, gently pull him to a sitting position (Figure 18).

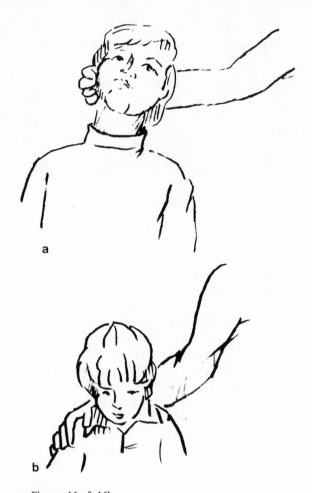

Figures 16a & 16b.

Do this slowly so that the child keeps the head in line with the body. If the head lags, wait for the child to bring the head up before continuing. Should the child lose head balance after starting the exercise, lower the child back to the mat and start over. If the child is very weak, hold him or her at the shoulders and gently rotate the body as you bring the child to a sitting position. As he or she gains head control, bring the child little by little to an upright position until head control without rotation is maintained.

Sitting Balance

Sitting is often a very difficult task for the handicapped child. With assistance from the instructor in controlling the key points, the child can

Figures 17a, 17b & 17c.

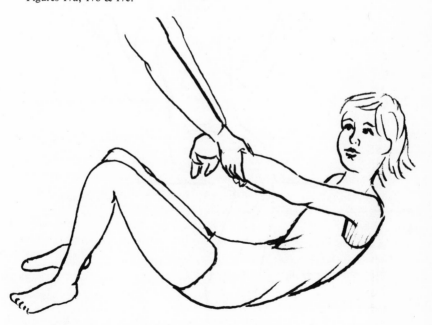

Figure 18.

maintain a sitting position for such things as feeding and improved visual stimulation. In deciding how to control the child for sitting, it should be determined whether or not the child is spastic, floppy, or athetoid. The child should sit in as normal a sitting position as possible, whether it be in a chair or on the floor. The following suggestions should help:

1. Figure 19 demonstrates the difficulties of a child with spasticity in a sitting position. The main problem is that the child is unable to bend at the hips because he or she:
    a.   pushes the head, trunk, and shoulders back.
    b.   puts pressure on the chair with the buttocks.
    c.   touches the floor with toes rather than the foot.
    d.   can't use hands for support or for reaching for objects.
    This problem can be reduced by lowering the back of the chair so that it touches at the shoulders; by bending the child at the hips before he or she sits well on the buttocks; and by having the chair low

Figure 19.

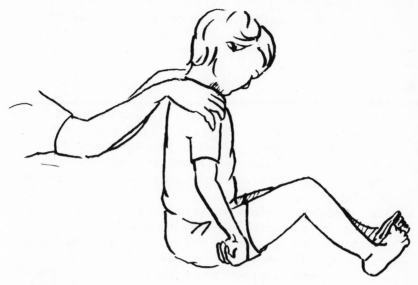

Figure 20.

enough so that the hips and knees are at right angles when the child is sitting.

2. For floor activities, sit the spastic child with legs together and bent. The shoulders should be turned in and pulled forward with steady pressure. This will place the child in a position to put the hands at his or her side for support (Figure 20).

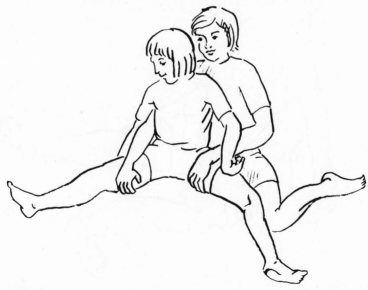

Figure 21.

3. The spastic child shown in Figure 21 is placed in this position by first pulling him or her toward you. By using your body to keep the child's body forward, you can use your hands to keep the legs apart and turned outward.

4. The child learns to sit forward alone, but you can assist by straightening the legs (Figure 22).

5. When seated, the hypotonic child cannot hold up the head and tends to round the back (Figure 23). In order to help straighten the back and to hold up the head, put both of your hands securely over the lower back and push down with thumbs on both sides of the spine (Figure 24). This method can also be used when the child sits on your lap (Figure 25).

6. Many handicapped children tend to turn their legs inward as they sit. However, if you attempt to correct this position by having them straddle your legs, the base may be too broad (Figure 26). The narrower base of only one leg will keep the legs apart and turned outward. This is also a good position for play with the child (Figure 27).

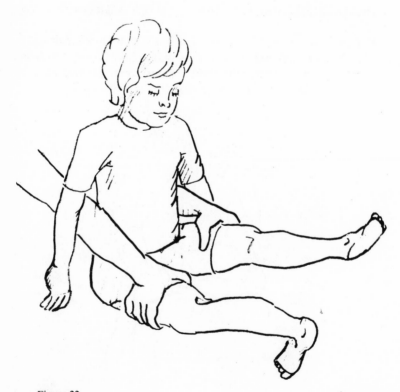

Figure 22.

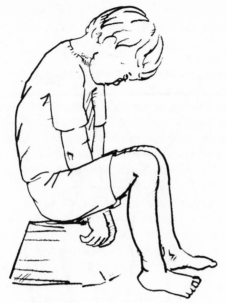

Figure 23.

Figure 24.

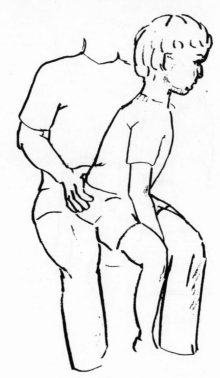

Figure 25.

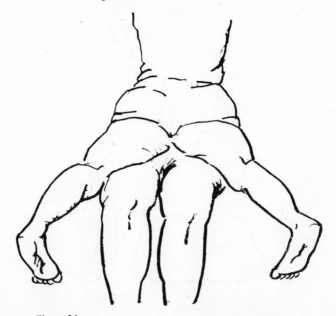

Figure 26.

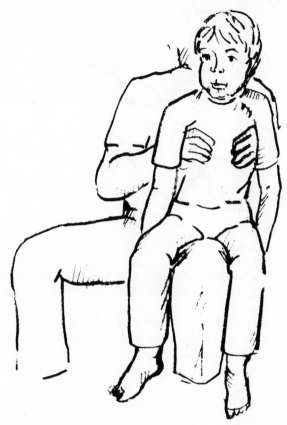

Figure 27.

Relaxation for the Spastic Child

Spastic children present unique problems for the teacher. Their muscles involuntarily contract when they are suddenly stretched, resulting in tenseness and difficult, inaccurate voluntary motion. The following suggestions should assist the teacher in relaxing the rigid, tense muscles of these children.

1. Never move the spastic child quickly. Fast movement only increases the spasticity. Move quietly and slowly. Avoid lifting, carrying, or positioning during which the child tends to tighten up muscles.
2. Immerse the child in warm water. Usually 5–10 minutes is a sufficient amount of time for obtaining relaxation.
3. Roll the child into a ball with the head forward and knees bent up on the chest.
4. Lay the child on the stomach with arms crossed over the chest and hips and knees bent. Place your hand over the child's crossed arms

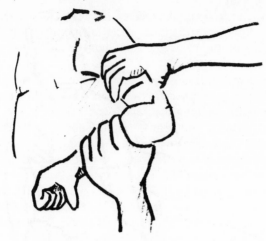

Figure 28.

and gently rock back and forth talking softly. As the child relaxes, slowly straighten the legs out and just rock with your hand over the crossed arms.

5. Slowly stroke the back in a nice rhythmical motion to relax the child. This can be done either with the child lying or sitting.

6. Have the child lie on the stomach. Straighten the arms out in front. Place your hands over the child's buttocks and gently rock the child

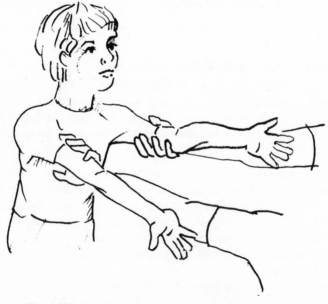

Figure 29.

back and forth. As he or she relaxes, the buttocks will go down to the floor and the legs straighten. After this point, move your hand to the middle of the back and continue rocking slowly until the child is relaxed.

7. For the child with increased extensor thrusting, do the same as in item 6; however, place the child over your lap with thighs and upper arms hanging down alongside your legs.

8. *Do not* straighten a bent arm by pulling above or below a joint. This will only cause more tightness (Figure 28).

9. By holding your hand over the joint, the leg or arm can be turned in or out in one movement (Figure 29).

10. Many handicapped children have tight arms, wrists, and hands (Figure 30a). To facilitate straightening of the wrist, fingers, and thumb, gradually lift the child's arm and straighten it while turning it out at the shoulder and elbow (Figure 30b & c).

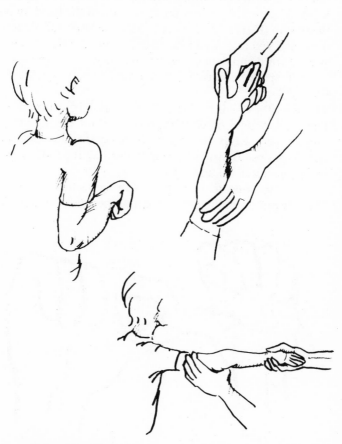

Figures 30a, 30b & 30c.

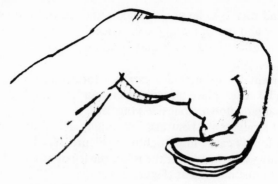

Figure 31.

11. The hand of a severely spastic child is usually characterized by flex-ion of the wrist and fingers with the thumb held in the palm of the hand. (Figure 31). *Do not* try to straighten the hand by pulling on the thumb (Figure 32). You can cause the wrist and fingers to bend more and you may injure the thumb joints. Straighten and turn the arm outward and then straighten the fingers. You can also massage the web space between the thumb and fingers to relax the thumb (Figure 33).

12. The legs of a severely spastic child are usually scissored or crossed. Putting any type of clothing on this child can be very difficult (Figure 34a). Relax the legs by bending the hips and parting the legs. This position will also help in bending the foot for putting on shoes and socks (Figure 34b).

13. When attempting to part the child's legs when scissored (Figure 35a), *do not* try pulling them apart at the ankle (Figure 35b). Place

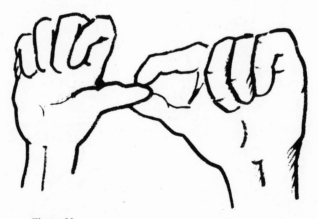

Figure 32.

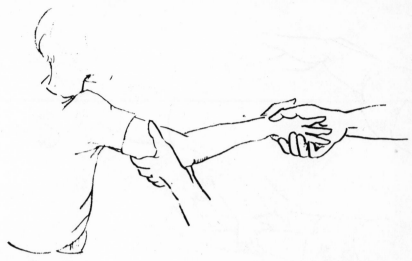

Figure 33.

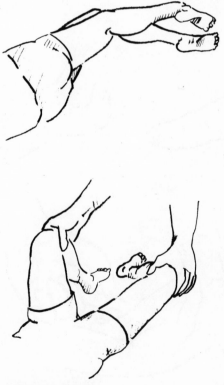

Figures 34a & 34b.

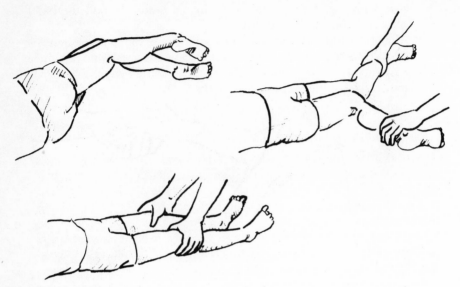

Figures 35a, 35b & 35c.

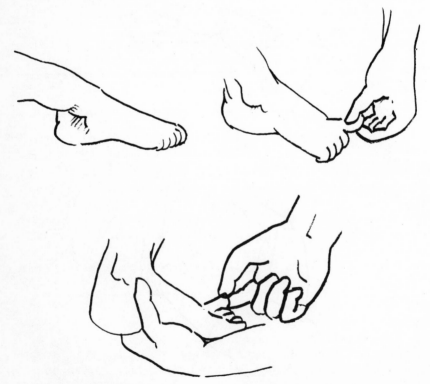

Figures 36a, 36b & 36c.

your hands over the child's knee joints, gradually pull the legs apart, and turn them out (Figure 35c).

14. Often the child's toes are curled under with the foot pointed downwards (Figure 36a). *Do not* try to straighten the toes by pulling upward on them (Figure 36b). Turn the leg outward, bend the foot up, and straighten the toes (Figure 36c).

GROSS MOTOR DEVELOPMENT

Gross motor activities refer to those activities that require the use of large muscle groups, such as postural reactions, head balance, sitting, creeping, standing, and walking. As stated previously, development is from head to toe. Therefore, the first goal in development of gross motor skills is the development of head control. Adequate head control must be obtained before a child can balance him- or herself in sitting or in any other activity.

However, there is a great deal of overlapping in the learning of skills. The normal child does not simply acquire one activity after the other. When the child is at the stage of lifting the head when back lying, he or she is already learning to sit. When still at the stage of creeping on the abdomen, the normal child begins to sit with little support and moves and practices balance in sitting at the same time as learning to stand. This means that instructors should not separate the various stages of development and try to make the child perfect one skill before going on to the next. In fact, the perfecting of one activity may only be reached by trying the next.

Crawling and Creeping

Crawling on the stomach and creeping on hands and knees must be preceded by several steps. The first is the ability of the child to lift the head and bear weight on the forearms. Next the child must be able to get to an extended arm position and finally to maintain a hands-and-knees position. Not all children learn how to creep. However, it is important that they learn to maintain an all-fours (hand-and-knees) position to help with stability at the shoulders and hips. If a child does not creep, exercises should be done to strengthen the muscles used in normal creeping. The following activities should be used in the development of crawling and creeping.

1. To encourage the child to take weight on the arms, place the child over a large towel roll that is high enough to allow resting the child's hands on the floor. Be sure to place the child's hands flat on the floor in front of him or her. Encourage the child to bear weight on the hands (Figure 37). With the child in this position, bounce him or her up and down on the elbows *gently*. The pressure into this joint

Figure 37.

will stimulate the child to hold the correct position. Place toys nearby which the child can see and reach. Once the child is able to support weight on the forearms, encourage reaching for the toys with one hand.

2. Place the child on the floor without the towel roll and dangle a toy above the head. Try to get him to lift up on his elbows. Tapping under the chin while the child is attempting to get to this position or slight pressure under the chin will aid your child in getting up on his or her elbows (Figure 38).

3. Slowly roll the child over a large ball or barrel and encourage him or her to lift the head. Also encourage propping up on the elbows (Figure 39).

4. Play wheelbarrow with your child. Hold him or her at first by the hips and let the child walk on the hands. As the child bears more weight, hold the feet and have the child straighten the legs (Figure 40).

5. Play "airplane" with your child with his or her hands down on the floor. Gradually allow the child to take on more weight. If you

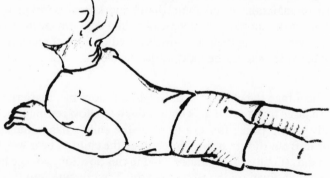

Figure 38.

Figure 39.

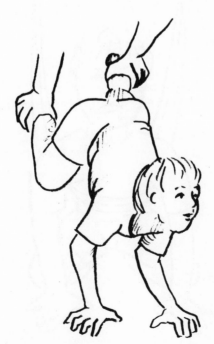

Figure 40.

Figure 41.

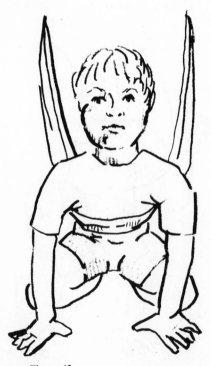

Figure 42.

have a large ball, try rolling the child out to catch weight on the hands (Figure 41).

6.   Place a diaper or towel under your child's chest and gently pull upward so that hands are flat on the floor and elbows straight. Gradually let the child support weight on the arms (Figure 42).

7.   To begin creeping, kneel behind your child (who should be lying on the stomach with arms on either side of the head). Hold the child's legs just above the ankles and gently push one leg forward and to the side. Encourage your child to move one hand forward and then repeat with the other leg. By placing a favorite toy or person in front of the child, you can encourage movement more readily. If the child is moving legs vigorously when lying on the stomach, kneel behind the child. Have him or her push against the resistance of your hand to move forward on the stomach.

8.   To begin getting your child up to a crawling position, place a towel under the chest, straddle the child and gently pull up until he or she is on all fours. Gradually reduce your assistance and have the child bear more weight. Encourage rocking back and forth when in this position (Figure 43).

9.   When the child is beginning to bear weight on all fours, kneel and give support with your hand under the stomach. Reduce your assistance so that the child is fully supporting the weight (Figure 44).

10.   To encourage crawling, again place a favorite toy or person in front of the child. You first will have to move one leg forward and then

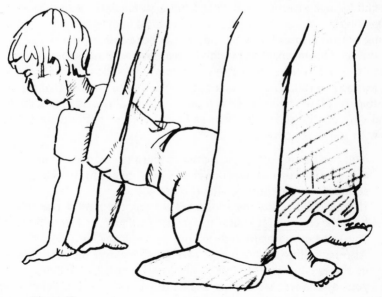

Figure 43.

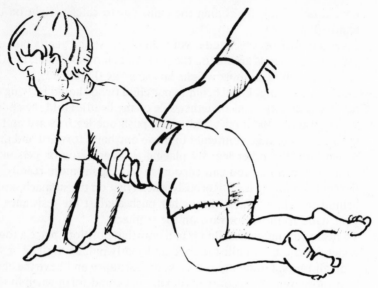

Figure 44.

have the child move one arm forward. Repeat with the other leg. Tell the child what you want done at all times. Praise the child when he or she has small successes in attempting to crawl.

Rolling Over

A child usually learns to roll first from a stomach-lying to a back-lying position. Usually the child lifts his or her head high while in the stomach-lying position, loses balance, and, as the head falls to the side, rolls to that side. This means that the child must have adequate extension of the head before he or she can roll over. In many cases the child will need help in learning to roll. The instructor can position the arms so that the child is able to roll over an arm or can place the child in a side-lying position and only require rolling halfway at first. Some suggestions for learning how to roll over follow.

1. You can begin helping your child to learn to roll over from an early age. At first, by turning your child's head gently to the side, you can stimulate turning to that side (Figure 45).
2. If your child resists the above, try turning the hips to one side and have the child roll to that side. At first you may need to roll the child yourself but gradually reduce your assistance (Figure 46).
3. Also try rolling the child by crossing one leg over the other when he or she is lying on the back. Then gently push to the side. Reduce your assistance as the child begins to roll (Figure 47). While doing the exercises, tell the child what you want done. Praise the child

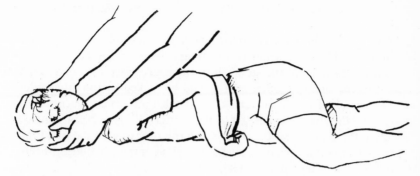

Figure 45.

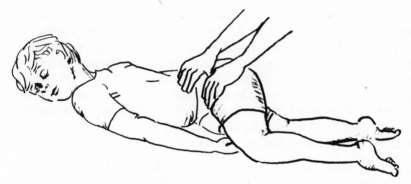

Figure 46.

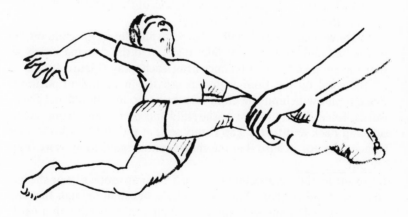

Figure 47.

when he or she succeeds even if at first it is only the turning of the head.

4. Roll your child both from stomach to back and from back to stomach. Have the child roll over and over on the bed or floor. When rolling from the stomach to the back, place the child's hand out to the side (the other arm should be tucked by the other side). Tell the child to push over. Repeat with both arms. Place toys in view so that the child can get to them after rolling over, or dangle a toy to the side so that the child has to roll over to grab the toy. Practice rolling on a variety of surfaces such as carpet, blankets, sheets, rubber pads, linoleum, and so forth.

Sitting

Sitting is an important step in the development of gross motor skills. Sitting is often a very difficult task for the handicapped child. With assistance in controlling the key points, the child can maintain a sitting position for such things as feeding and visual stimulation. In deciding how to control the child for sitting, it should be determined whether or not the child is spastic, floppy, or athetoid. The child should sit in as normal a sitting position as possible, whether it be in a chair or on the floor. Because the development of sitting was earlier discussed in relation to the spastic child, the following suggestions focus on the floppy child.

1. Sit the child on your lap facing away from you. The child who is floppy usually is unable to hold the head up or straighten the back (Figure 48a). Put your hands securely over the lower back and push down on both sides of the spine; this will give the child enough stimulation to raise the head and straighten the back (Figure 48b). If you have a vibrator, stroke down on both sides of the spine and down the nape of the neck to facilitate sitting.

2. If you have a large beach ball or barrel available, sit the child on top of the ball and sway it from side to side. Do the swaying slowly so that the child can regain balance after each sway (Figure 49).

3. Sit the child on the floor with legs crossed in an Indian position. Place a pillow behind the child in case he or she should fall backwards. Kneel down in front of the child and gently push from side to side and back and forth. Tap firmly so that the child begins to lose balance but not so hard that the child cannot regain composure (Figure 50).

4. Begin sitting the floppy child in a small chair as soon as he or she has adequate head control. The chair should be small enough that the feet rest on a flat surface. An adult chair can be used with a cardboard box for the feet support. This position helps to lessen the problems of lower extremity weakness in some children. Once your

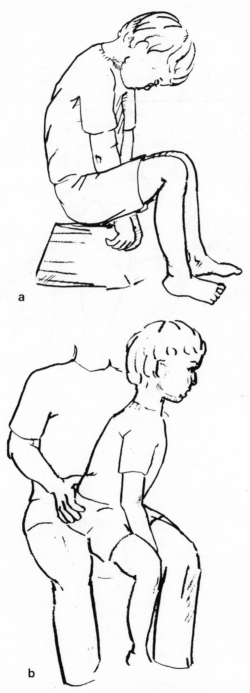

a

b

Figures 48a & 48b.

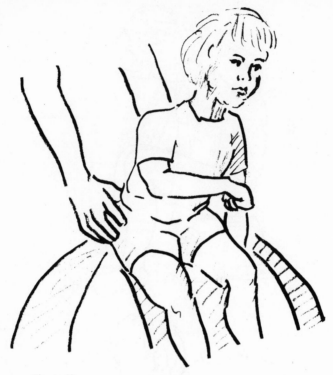

Figure 49.

Figure 50.

Figure 51.

child is sitting propped on the arms, encourage him or her to begin sitting erect. By dangling toys, you can entice the child to sit straighter and gradually obtain a full upright sitting position.

Standing

The activities used in teaching standing to the floppy child are slightly different from those used with the spastic child. For example, bouncing the floppy child on his or her feet usually causes an involuntary stiffening of the legs. For the spastic child, this stiffening is undesirable. For any type of child, the stance should be:

1. Legs slightly apart
2. Feet flat on the floor
3. Knees straight
4. Stomach out

Standing the child at a mirror is a good way to encourage the child to stand erect. In many cases placing the child in a prone stander is also of benefit, because the child is engaged in a fine motor skill at the same time he or she is standing (Figure 51). The following ideas can be used for teaching standing to a child who is developmentally delayed.

1. If the child resists standing or has difficulty in getting the knees straight, place the child leaning against a chair or couch. Grasp the child's legs at the knees and manually hold them straight. Gradually reduce your assistance as you feel the child controlling the legs.

2. Sit the child in a small chair (telephone books stacked together can also be used). The height of the seat should be such that when the child is seated, feet are flat on the floor. Place a towel around the child's chest and gently pull to a standing position. Practice standing up and sitting down with the child. Tell the child what you want done and have the child do as much of the work as possible. Encourage use of the legs to push up (Figure 51).

3. Place the child leaning against the wall or against the couch but facing out into the room. Kneel in front of the child and play. The child should begin momentarily pulling away from the wall and balancing alone. At first the child will only be able to balance for a few seconds before leaning back, but this time will gradually increase (Figure 52).

4. Support the child at the hips. Have the child lean forward to touch toes or gently push the child over into position (Figure 53a). Hold tight at the hips and across the knees to keep them straight. Encourage the child to come to a standing position alone. If the child is un-

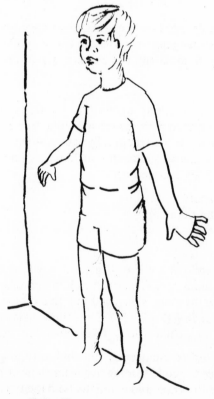

Figure 52.

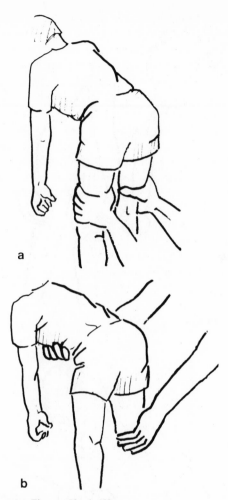

Figures 53a & 53b.

able to do this at first, give a slight push upward to the chest (Figure 53b).

5. Hold the child by the knees while standing erect. Sway the child from side to side but do this slowly enough that he or she can remain balanced (Figure 54).

6. If you have a vibrator, stroke the child on the upper thighs and over the buttocks before you practice standing (Figure 55). This should be done only under the direction of the physical therapist if the child is spastic or has a tendency to stand on the toes.

7. If you have a large beach ball or barrel, have the child stand holding on to the ball with only minimal assistance from you to prevent the ball from rolling away (Figure 56).

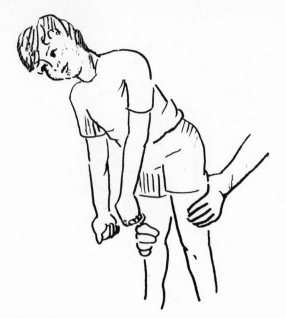

Figure 54.

Figure 55.

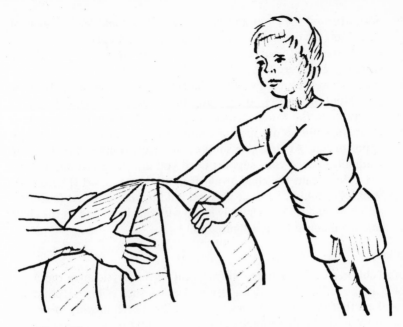

Figure 56.

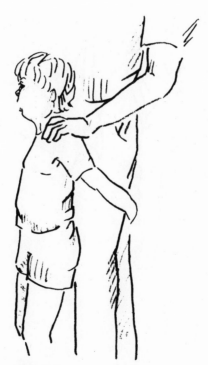

Figure 57.

8. Stand behind the child and have him or her stand leaning against your legs (the back resting against your legs). Occasionally bounce the child against your legs gently so that at times he or she is self-supporting (Figure 57).

9. Place a towel around the child's chest and stand him or her in front of you. Hold the towel near the body at first but, as the child becomes steady, hold the towel further away from the body (Figure 58).

10. Have the child hold a stick or object in one hand and you hold the opposite end. At first give support by firmly holding the stick but gradually reduce your support until you are just touching the object. This weans the child away from needing support (Figure 59).

11. Stand the child in front of you and hold by the waist. At first hold with both hands. Momentarily let go with one hand and let the child balance independently (Figure 60).

Walking

Not all children can walk independently. Either the physician or therapist should advise the instructor about assistive devices such as braces, crutches, or walkers that may be necessary for the child. The following ideas can be used to teach the developmentally delayed child to walk.

Figure 58.

Figure 59.

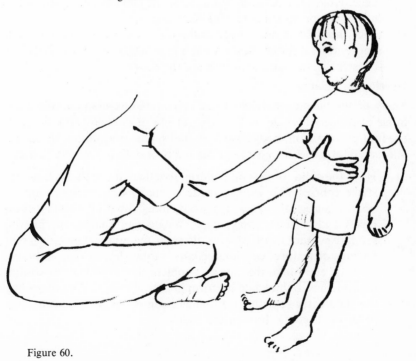

Figure 60.

1. Place the child at the couch (or have him or her pull up to a standing position at the couch). Place a toy on the couch just out of reach. Kneel down behind the child and urge him or her to go for the toy. At first you should move one leg to the side and then urge moving the other leg. Tell the child what you want done and praise the child for attempting to take a step.

2. Hold the child under the arms and "walk" him or her. At first you should allow the child to lean against your legs. Move each leg forward with your own. Then let the child move each leg as you gently push the shoulder forward on the side that is to be moved. Encourage the child to pick the feet up.

3. Place a diaper around the child's chest and walk him or her by holding on to the diaper. Place a favorite toy on the couch or chair so that the child is stimulated to move forward. You can also do this by holding on to the back of the child's clothing.

4. If your child will hold on to your hands and walk, do this walking often. Decrease your assistance by substituting a stick for your hand. Slowly decrease your amount of support using the stick until you are only touching the stick while the child is walking.

5. Have the child walk between two people. Only allow the child to take two to three steps at first and then gradually increase the distance. Hold your outstretched arms to the child or hold a toy out so that he or she attempts to take the steps.

6. Place the child standing against the wall or a couch and hold your arms out. Urge him or her to walk to you. Only have the child take a few steps at first and then increase the distance.

Developing Balance

Many of the balance activities listed below also develop coordination. Some of the activities aid in the improvement of eye-hand coordination, eye-foot coordination, body awareness and spatial orientation. By careful selection of activities the instructor can improve skills in a variety of areas.

1. Have the child (or several children together) move through an obstacle course. This can be made of many objects. Use ladders, boards, sheets of plywood, barrels, inner tubes of all sizes, tires, boxes and cartons, ropes, pipe, jungle-gym equipment, blocks, sandboxes, sacks stuffed with different materials to give different feelings of texture, cushions, chairs, tables, hoses, rugs, brooms, buckets, etc. Make the courses problem-solving situations so that the child has to think and perform in a flexible way. Vary by having the child carry something or balance something on the head while he or she is going through the course.

2. Balance the child in a sitting position on top of large beach ball or on top of a vestibular board.

3. Use balance-beam activities such as:
    a. Walking forward, backward, and sidewise
    b. Walking forward, backward, and sidewise with weight in one hand or both hands
    c. Ball-bouncing and tossing while crossing beam
    d. Walking on elevated beam
    e. Walking on tiptoe

4. Have the child place feet in a box or on a spot on the floor. Toss a soft ball to the child. The child must duck to avoid the ball, yet maintain balance to stay on the spot on the floor or keep feet in the box.

5. Draw footprints on paper and place on the floor. The child must place feet on the prints and walk without losing balance. Begin by drawing the footprints approximately one foot apart and gradually bring the footprints closer and closer together so that they are only several inches apart. Finally, place the footprints so that one foot is placed directly in front of the other, with no space between.

6. For all tiptoe positions, the heels should be raised from the floor as far as possible. Have the child stand, take a tiptoe position, hold for 3 to 5 seconds, and then return to standing position.

7. Implement animal imitations:
    a. Bear walk: The child bends over from the waist and touches the floor with the hands, keeping legs stiff. He or she moves forward, walking the hands and plodding the feet behind in a cross-lateral fashion. The head must be kept up.
    b. Ostrich walk: The child bends forward at the waist and grasps the ankles. See that knees are as stiff as possible. The child then walks forward, stretching the neck in and out.
    c. Frog walk: Have the child do a deep knee bend with hands on hips. The child extends one leg to the side and brings it back.
    d. Measuring worm walk: The child supports the body on hands and toes. The arms are held straight, a shoulder-width apart and directly under the shoulders. The body is kept in a straight line from head to toe. With the hands remaining stationary, the child walks the feet up as close to the hands as possible, taking tiny steps. The body should not sag. Next, keeping the feet stationary, the child walks the hands forward in tiny steps until the first position is reached.
    e. Dog run: Have the child gallop by running forward with both hands on the floor and knees slightly bent.

8. The child knee-walks on carpet-strip pathways, pillow courses, and so forth.

9. The child walks barefoot on pillows spaced on the floor and at various levels.

10. To develop the child's ability to roll (like a log), have him or her lie in a blanket. Pull on one edge of it and roll the child off. Also have the child roll down hills and over inclined places.

11. The child walks erect, arms at sides, balancing an object on top of his head. If the object falls off, the player must stop, replace it, and then continue. The child returns to the starting point and touches the second player, who then takes a turn.

12. Design an obstacle course using blocks that are at least 4 inches in width. Begin by using two parallel rows of blocks, the left side for the left foot and the right side for the right foot. Increase the complexity of this design so that it resembles a hopscotch game. The child can vary the activity by touching the floor with the feet as he or she maneuvers over the course, or by keeping the feet on the blocks and not touching the floor with either foot. This can become more complicated by changing the spacing of the blocks as the child progresses through the course.

13. A "walking box" is made for each of the child's feet. The boxes must be sturdy enough to hold the child's weight and each one large enough to fit under one foot. A hole is drilled in each side of the box and a rope attached with which the child holds the box against each foot. The length of the rope will vary with the size of the child. The object is for the child to stand on the boxes, hold on to the rope, and walk in a coordinated manner.

14. Have the child sit, kneel, and stand in and on inner tubes. He or she may also straddle-bounce on them or crawl around the edges and through a tire tunnel. Following are other variations.

> The child can walk around a group of tubes using makeshift ski poles for support.
> Place side planks between the tubes and have the child traverse across them using a variety of body positions.
> Have the child walk with one foot on and the other foot off the tubes.
> Have the child jump in and out of the tubes without touching the edges.

15. Games of hopscotch can be played and varied depending on the child's abilities.

16. Put a straight line down on the floor and have the child try to walk on it without stepping off. Later the child can place things along the way. This could be varied later by making a large circle to follow.

Develop Total Body Coordination

The following are just a few of the activities instructors can use with the children. Simple activities should be used in the beginning and complexity increased slowly.

Variety is important. The child should not become skillful in only one activity but should develop flexibility of movement.

1. Have the child practice starting and stopping on command (as in the game "red light"). This can be done for a variety of movements — running, jumping, hopping, etc. Have the child perform the activities while blindfolded so that he or she relies entirely on an auditory cue.

2. Teach the child to bowl using plastic milk bottles as targets and any type of ball that is easy to handle. Vary the distance the child stands from the bottles to throw the ball. Begin with a large ball and as skill increases use a smaller and smaller ball.

3. Have the child (or children) crawl, walk, march, jump, and climb over, under, around, and through chairs, tables, cartons, cylinder drums, ropes tied between chairs, and so forth as in "Simon says" or "Follow the Leader." This is a good time to name body parts and point to them. If a child is functioning on a higher level, begin right and left discrimination.

4. Using balls, bean bags, etc., have the child shoot at targets on the wall, into boxes and baskets of varying sizes, and from varying distances. Throw and toss at graduated circles on floor.

5. Beanbag and ball games provide excellent training in eye-hand coordination and kicking games stimulate eye-foot coordination. Little agility is involved when an object is thrown or caught in a standing position. To incorporate agility, movements such as running and jumping should be included as the beanbag or ball is caught or avoided. Because beanbags are easier to handle, they should be used first.

6. Use bicycles and other riding toys in which the feet move back and forth for improvement of coordination.

7. Use rhythm-band instruments, hands, feet, and total body to teach rhythm. Have the child jump to rhythm, hop, and so forth. You can also have the child exercise to music by kicking legs, bending the torso, raising the arms, etc.

8. Have a group of children gallop in a circle as if they are circus horses and then change direction at the beat of an instrument. Also have them move individually, changing from galloping to trotting, running, or walking, as they choose. Encourage them to demonstrate their movement sequences to each other. You may have the

children perform any of the steps in pairs, holding hands or with arms crossed behind their backs. If a child has difficulty galloping, he or she may practice by lying on the back and making a bicycling movement with the legs in a one-two, one-two rhythm. If necessary, you can guide the legs.

9. Have the children step through the spaces in a ladder when it is lying on the floor. You can also use lines on the floor, hula hoops, and so forth.

10. As agility increases, try somersault, jumping, hopping, skipping, leapfrog, and mat activities.

Fine Motor Development

Fine motor skills refer to hand skills. It is the small muscles of the hand that enable people to do very intricate tasks such as threading a needle, playing the piano, buttoning buttons, and picking up tiny objects with the thumb and index finger.

One very important way a child learns about the world is by reaching out, picking up, manipulating, and purposefully using toys and objects. A normal infant gets to know hands and fingers by putting them in the mouth and by bringing them together and playing with them. A child learns about the shape, texture, size, and temperature of objects in this fashion. He or she learns different sounds by banging, squeezing, shaking, and throwing objects that are hard or soft, metal or plastic. A child learns about distance by reaching for both near and far objects and by throwing. In all these ways and many more, a child learns about the world because he or she can experience it through touch and muscle movement.

Some children do not reach out and handle toys and objects because they are not motivated to do so. These children may not see well or they may be oversensitive to touch so that contact with objects can be disturbing. These children may withdraw and avoid touching objects. Increased contact with objects and toys helps these children to be less sensitive and to discriminate better between those objects that are sharp, rough, or prickly and those which are smooth and pleasant to touch.

Some children may touch objects but their experience is meaningless. Because they do not get any satisfaction from touching, they do not continue to reach out and explore. They often wander aimlessly, just looking and watching. These children also benefit from a stimulation program aimed at increasing contact with toys and objects. After many experiences with toys and objects they begin to connect some meaning to the objects and gain pleasure in using them. They begin to learn that if they shake a rattle it makes a pleasant sound and if they pick up a piece of food and put it up to the mouth, they will be rewarded with food. This will then encourage them to reach out and explore further.

Beginning Activities

The following activities have been found to be useful in stimulating a child to be alert to the environment, become more aware of hands and body, and to reach out and grasp.

1. Gently rub the child's hands, arms, legs and feet with a variety of textured materials such as a terrycloth wash cloth, a sponge, a piece of carpet, and ice.
2. Tie bells on the child's shoes or sew bells on elastic wristlets.
3. Engage the child in sand and water play. Place ice cubes or toys in the water and encourage the child to reach in and pick them up. Use food coloring to color the water or add bubbles for a variation.
4. Bury objects in sand and help the child find them. Sit the child in the sand so he or she can feel the sand on the feet and legs as well as on the hands.
5. Drape a diaper or piece of material over the child's head and face and encourage him to pull it off (as in "peek-a-boo").
6. Lightly wrap brightly colored yarn around and in between the child's fingers of one hand and encourage him or her to pull it off with the other hand. Alternate hands.
7. Put mittens, puppets, thimbles, etc., on the child's hands and encourage him or her to pull them off.
8. Provide small grasping toys or parts of toys for the child to grasp and examine: e.g., rattles, bells, squeeze toys, pop beads, a plastic ring with string attached, blocks, nesting cups, etc. If the child sits in a chair with a tray, attach toys to the tray. If there is no tray, make a table out of a cardboard box. String toys on a string and attach to the top of the box. This will provide a source of stimulation through objects at times when you are not able to work with the child.

Developing the Pincer Grasp

After the child has learned to reach directly, grasp with all fingers, and hold and manipulate objects, he or she begins to use the fingers individually. One of the first signs of this development is the child's poking at objects with an index finger. Soon the child begins to use the thumb and index finger to pick up objects. This is called *pincer grasp*. He or she begins by picking up an object with the thumb and all fingers, then the thumb and two or three fingers, and finally the thumb and index finger. When this skill is fully developed, the child will be able to manipulate very small objects. The average child has developed a good pincer grasp by 12 months of age.

A child who has not developed a pincer grasp but is able to reach directly, grasp with a full hand, and hold and manipulate objects should be encouraged to develop the pincer grasp with the following activities.

1. Provide dry cereal, raisins, or other small finger foods at meals and snacks to encourage finger feeding.
2. Tie brightly colored yarn onto small toys for the child to manipulate.
3. Provide toys with buttons to push, dials to turn, and strings to pull, such as a toy telephone, a toy cash register, a talking doll or other toy with pull string, busy box, Jack-in-the-box, or toy piano. Show the child how to use the toys if he or she does not appear interested. Take the child's hands through the motions, then let the child try himself.
4. Bury small blocks or favorite objects in sand and encourage the child to find them.
5. Provide finger paints. Show the child how to make designs with the fingers. Take his or her hands through motions if necessary.
6. Encourage the child to scribble on paper with a crayon.
7. Provide soft dough or clay for the child to pinch and poke holes in with the fingers.

Children should be encouraged to reach and grasp with both hands individually. However, a child may prefer one hand over the other. This is appropriate if the child is developing hand dominance. It is not appropriate if he or she ignores the other hand and does not use it together with the dominant hand. In such cases, provide large toys that require the use of two hands.

It is also good to encourage the child to transfer objects from one hand to the other. Developmentally, this skill is seen at approximately 7 months of age.

Improving Eye-Hand Coordination

As a child is reaching and grasping with a whole hand and a pincer grasp, he is developing accuracy of eye-hand coordination. Some handicapped children, however, continue to have limited or poor arm and hand control in reaching and placing objects. In order to improve accuracy of eye-hand coordination:

1. Begin with activities that require reach and placement at close range such as building block towers, placing forms in formboard or shape sorting box, placing rings on ring stack, or placing pegs in pegboard.
2. Use activities that require the child to reach and place a hand on distant objects. Have the child point to the eyes, nose, and mouth on the image in a mirror. Have the child poke at bubbles blown in the air. Hold pegs, blocks, or rings at different positions in front, to the side, and above the child and encourage the child to reach before placing them.
3. Following the above activities, have the child aim and throw at targets. As skill develops, move the targets further away from the child or make the targets smaller.

All these activities may be done with each hand alternately. A higher level of accuracy can be achieved by introducing activities that require the two hands to work together. First, a child has one hand holding or supporting an object while the other hand works, so that the child is, for example, holding paper with one hand while the other colors or holding a jack-in-the-box with one hand while the other turns the handle. Activities that require more refined manipulation of objects by both hands can be used. In these activities, both hands are working but performing different tasks. Examples are stringing beads, unscrewing barrel kegs, cutting with scissors, playing toy xylophone, and interlocking blocks.

REFERENCES

Bobath, B. The very early treatment of cerebral palsy. *Developmental Medicine and child neurology*, 1967, *9*(4), 373–390.

Bobath, B. Motor development: its effect on general development and application to the treatment of cerebral palsy. *Physiotherapy*, 1971, *57*(11), 526–532.

Bobath, K., & Bobath, B. The facilitation of normal postural reactions and movements in the treatment of cerebral palsy. *Physiotherapy*, 1964, *50*(8), 246–262.

Connolly, B. H., & Anderson, R. M. Severely handicapped children in the public schools: A new frontier for the physical therapist. *Physical Therapy*, 1978, *58*(4), 433–438.

Cronis, S., & Gleeson, A. W. Orthopedic screening of school children in Delaware. *Physical Therapy*, 1974, *54*, 1080–1083.

Dehaven, G. E. Is selective hearing an occupational hazard in physical therapy? *Physical Therapy*, 1974, *54*, 1301–1305.

Finnie, N. *Handling the young cerebral palsied child at home.* New York: E. P. Dutton, 1970.

Gesell, A., & Amatruda, C. S. *Developmental diagnosis* (3rd ed.). New York: Harper & Row, 1974.

Gordon, I. J. *Baby learning through baby play.* New York: St. Martin's Press, 1970.

Gordon, I. J., Guinagh, B., & Jester, R. E. *Child learning through child play.* New York: St. Martin's Press, 1972.

Harris, S. E., & Cherry, D. B. Childhood progressive muscular dystrophy and the role of physical therapy. *Physical Therapy*, 1974, *54*, 4–12.

Levangie, P. K. Public school physical therapists. *Physical Therapy*, 1980, *60*, 774–779.

Pearson, P. H. & Williams, C. E. (Eds.). *Physical therapy services in the developmental disabilities.* Springfield, Illinois: C. C. Thomas, 1972.

Tecklin, S. J., & Holsclaw, D. W. Cystic fibrosis and the role of the physical therapist in its management. *Physical Therapy*, 1973, *53*, 388–394.

United Cerebral Palsy of Central Indiana, Inc. *Play together, parents and babies.* Indianapolis: United Cerebral Palsy of Central Indiana, 1972.

U.S. Department of Health, Education and Welfare. *The child with nervous system deficit* (No. 432). Report on two symposiums, 1965.

Witengier, M. An adaptive playground for physically handicapped children. *Physical Therapy*, 1970, *50*, 821–826.

Chapter 6

Self-Help Training

Bonnie B. Greer and Chris E. Wethered

Many of the severely handicapped students entering the public schools as a result of P.L. 94-142 have training needs in the area of self-help skills. If a child needs to learn dressing, self-feeding, and bathing, then these become realistic curricular content areas to be addressed in providing the student with mandated appropriate education. Such students require a highly structured, systematic, behavioral approach to learn the self-help skills acquired so automatically by the nonhandicapped child (Azrin et al., 1976). These skills must be taught to the disabled child or he or she will become a dependent adult. The process of skill acquisition begins in infancy, but training is generally not delivered until some arbitrary chronological age. As a result these children are exposed to years of disability-based failure, prior to any attempts at habilitation. Early intervention provides the disabled child with better overall chances of coping in society. This training in self-help skills makes the residential student more independent and, therefore, a better candidate for placement. Such a child might eventually live in a family unit or a group home and his or her degree of self-sufficiency would determine many of the responsibilities imposed upon the other individuals in that group or family constellation.

These impositions could, therefore, greatly affect the cohabitants' feelings for and treatment of the individual.

Self-help training would involve teaching the child to perform, independently, as many activities of daily living as possible (i.e., toileting, eating with utensils, taking off and putting on articles of clothing, personal hygiene, bathing, and tooth brushing). It becomes obvious, therefore, that this new student population has a unique and specific need for a specialized curriculum, different even from that used with the less retarded students previously served by public education. As the literature review indicates, this curriculum, to be effective with a severely handicapped population, must start at very low developmental levels, rely heavily on a structured use of behavior modification techniques, and seriously address the need for developing self-help skills.

On a large scale, educators have only recently attempted to train such students in the performance of self-help skills. Part of this failure to train was based on the prevailing impression of this population's learning capacity. Dunn and Capobianco noted, in 1959, that at that time educators assumed that retarded individual's with IQ scores below 30 would be unlikely to master self-care skills. Current research, however, clearly invalidates this negative assumption, indicating that, in fact, such students can be taught to meet their self-care needs. This research indicates that profoundly retarded students can be taught to eat appropriately (Azrin & Armstrong, 1973), stop bed wetting (Azrin, Sneed, & Foxx, 1974) and in fact learn to use the toilet by themselves (Azrin & Foxx, 1971; Foxx & Azrin, 1973). Similar rapid and effective training has been done in other self-help areas including buttoning (Adelson-Bernstein & Sandow, 1978), dressing and undressing (Azrin, Schaeffer, & Wesolowski, 1976), and self-feeding (O'Brian, Bugle, & Azrin, 1972; Nelson, Cone, & Hanson, 1975; Albin, 1977).

Self-help skills "can most easily be taught to the child by using established principles of behavior modification, especially prompting, shaping, cueing, fading, chaining, modeling, and overlearning," (Edgar et al, 1978). The science of behavior modification presents the principles that are the foundation of all human learning. It is, therefore, crucial that teachers of the multiply handicapped make use of these same basic principles to produce effective learning in their students.

DEVELOPMENTAL PROGRAMS

Meyen and Altman state that "there is evidence that public schools are moving forward in meeting legislative commitment to the severely and profoundly handicapped" (1976, p. 40). They also note, however, that because these students have entered the schools suddenly, due to legislation, rather than "as the result of an evolutionary process" (Meyen & Altman, 1976, p. 40), the schools have been frequently ill prepared to instruct them. Nonetheless, there is an immediate need for appropriate assessments and curriculum. Litton (1978) has reported that the acquisition of self-help skills follows a general developmental sequence in both retarded and nonretarded individuals. Because this general progression exists, the most appropriate assessment for self-help skills is the developmental sequence of those skills. This naturally occurring developmental sequence, used as both an assessment and a curriculum guide, can be clearly seen in the Radea Programs (Ort, 1976), the Portage Project (Bluma, Sheare, Frohman, & Hilliard, 1976), and the Project MEMPHIS Developmental Program for Severely and Profoundly Handicapped. These three programs, in addition to the Brigance Diagnostic Inventory of Early Development (Brigance, 1978), provide the foundation of a hierarchy of tools for varied instructional orientations and needs.

The Radea Program

This program provides curricular support in the areas of auditory, visual, language, perceptual motor, and functional living/socialization. It offers a developmental sequence in each of the above areas from approximately 0–6 months of age to 7 years. The stated objective is to train students who are functioning developmentally between the ages of 0–7 years (Ort, 1976). This curriculum includes 564 cards that are color coded into the five content areas listed above. Each card presents 2 content area and skills to be taught. It also lists a backward chaining sequence of the task-analyzed steps required to teach the skill. The card specifies the materials for instruction and the criterion performance level for mastery. This program provides the instructor with a highly structured set of materials and procedures of great value to a teacher unfamiliar with this population. As the instructor becomes more skillful in using the teaching strategies espoused, he or she can use the program as a guide. Concerns expressed by professionals who have used this kit include the amount of paper work, the amount of time required for assessment, several questionable skill sequences, and some unrealistic mastery criteria (e.g., a student is to take 20 sips of a fluid correctly in 20 trials for skill mastery). This program would best be used in a center or school-based situation with trained instructors new to the severely and profoundly handicapped population. The associated forms, manipulative materials, and assessments would, in their current state, probably prove unwieldy for application in a home-based program. However, with modification of the materials and parent training, this tool could provide a structured and effective curriculum for home-based programming.

Portage Program

The package for this program consists primarily of a box of color-coded file cards. The content areas include infant stimulation, and cognitive, motor, self-help, and language skills (Bluma et al., 1976). This package was designed for use in both home and classroom. The content cards list the skill to be taught and several general suggestions to stimulate acquisition of the skill. Bluma et al. report that the Portage Program encompasses skills from a developmental age of under 6 weeks to a developmental age of 5 or 6 years of age. The Portage Program starts with very low self-help skill levels, such as "stimulate the suck-swallow pattern," and progresses in 105 small steps along a developmental sequence to much higher skills, such as "buckle own car seatbelt." Professionals who have used this program note that it allows them flexibility in teaching. They report having used this tool as a source of general ideas for training. With the Portage Program, the instructor is left with the responsibilities of task analysis, selection of the appropriate chaining process to use, and development of a training sequence to fit the needs of the child. This program has direct applicability for use with the severely and profoundly retarded. The manual states that the curriculum is designed for use by parents, teachers, nurses, psychologists, and institutional aides.

Brigance Diagnostic Inventory of Early Development

The third instrument in this sequence of progressively less structured programs is the Brigance Diagnostic Inventory of Early Development. There is no pretense that this developmentally sequenced assessment was meant to be a curriculum. Experienced professionals can use this as a framework for programming. They can draw upon their own skills to determine what to teach and how to teach it at each developmental level. As in the first two models of intervention, this program illustrates varying levels of structure for the classroom instructor that can be applied, with parent training, for use in a home-based program.

Project MEMPHIS

The Project MEMPHIS Developmental Program for the Severely and Profoundly Handicapped presents a center-based model that strongly encourages consultation with the family for carry-over into the home environment. It addresses 111 skills in each of five areas: gross motor, fine motor, language, perceptual-cognitive, and personal-social. There are also 555 structured lesson plans covering a developmental age range from birth to 36 months (Quick & Campbell, 1977, 1981). The skills are arranged in sequential order and provide a format for training parents to teach their own children. After an initial assessment is completed, skills are assigned for the child and the parent is shown how to encourage the development of those skills while in the home environment.

The prospects for appropriate self-help training of the severely and profoundly retarded seems to be improving in the public schools. Meyer and Altman were initially concerned because, until recently, only institutions had any experience with these students (1976). One concern was that "in many institutions personnel either [tried] to 'get the child ready for education' or [tended] to wait until he [had] a mental age of three or a chronological age of eight (to meet the [old] requirements in public school classes). In many cases the most precious learning periods in the lives of these children [were] being wasted" (Baumgartner, 1971, p. 247). In addition to losing the early "learning periods," Meyer and Altman also noted the extreme philosophical difference between institutions and public schools. "Residential centers, by design, have assumed a total care posture in programming for this population, whereas public schools are oriented toward meeting the educational and social needs of a population of independent learners." Time has shown that the public schools have not accepted the institutional posture of fostered dependence but have been training these students to function as independently as possible. As evidenced by the developmental curricula described earlier, public schools are currently capable of programming for students with developmental ages of just a few weeks or months. Because of P.L. 94-142, these students, at a chronological age of 3 years, are now able to enter public schools to receive training.

TRAINING

A very important first step in developing the training program for teaching self-help skills to severely and profoundly retarded learners is finding out what the learner is already capable of doing. This eliminates confusing duplications of training and saves valuable learning time for the student. Numerous standardized instruments and informal developmental check lists are available to the teacher in evaluating the student's functional level in the self-help area. Some of the more widely used published instruments include the Brigance Inventory of Early Development, the AAMD Adaptive Behavior Scale, the Portage Guide to Early Education, the Radea Program, and the Project Memphis Developmental Program for the Severely and Profoundly Handicapped. Depending upon the particular scale, the teacher can ascertain, to a fairly accurate degree, where the learner's strengths and weaknesses are.

The second step is evaluating a student's basic readiness to learn. Activities such as attending, imitation, following directions, and fine motor and eye-motor skills are interdependent when learning new tasks.

The severely and profoundly retarded learner must be able to attend to what is being said and to comprehend communications before learning can progress in a systematic way. This requires eye contact and some degree of concentration. Attending is a prerequisite to any communication process, and its absence automatically signals a need for training in this area first. Imitation moves one step further in necessitating that the student physically accomplish what is being modeled by the instructor. Obvious motor activities such as handclapping and arm, leg, and head movements are useful for quickly checking imitation skills. Once past these hurdles, the learner must independently follow one-step directions before beginning to sequence several of these one-step directions into the completion of a self-help task. This is basically what is involved in learning any self-help skill.

After initial assessment is made, and it is determined that the learner has achieved at least minimal abilities in communication and following directions, the instructor should make a priority listing of skills that need to be learned on an individualized basis. Not all severely and profoundly retarded persons can learn the same skills at the same rate. Therefore, it is important to determine what skill each learner needs to use most frequently in his or her given lifestyle, and make an individual plan with self-help skills sequenced in order of need. Then it must be determined what prerequisite skills are needed for learning the chosen self-help skill. For example, before beginning instruction on buttoning, the learner should have developmentally progressed through palmar and scissors grasps to the pincer grasp and should be able to perform a task using both hands simultaneously in different motions. Ideally, instructors can, before instruction is begun, assess the physical characteristics of the learner and make modifications in the teaching strategy to accommodate any physical disabilities or preference for learning modalities.

Most severely and profoundly retarded learners have limited verbal skills, both expressive and receptive, and this prohibits the teacher from simply explaining the procedures for a skill and expecting compliance. Modeling, physical guidance, and repeated drilling of a task, using established behavior modification techniques, have been effective teaching tools.

Peers, aides, and volunteers can be utilized in carrying out these training procedures with severely and profoundly retarded learners as long as the approach and language cues are standardized. It is confusing to have different people teaching the same skills in different ways with different instructions when the learner is so cognitively limited. Conceptually he or she has no way to generalize that putting on an undershirt head first and putting it on arms first are essentially the same act, and that an instruction to pick up a shoe and an instruction to pick up a loafer, or to bend a knee and to raise a leg, are also the same. To the low-functioning learner, these are different and confusing directions that appear to be totally unrelated. This confusion makes the learning process more complicated and often results in failure. Repeatedly going through the exact same sequence of steps with the same commands each time will eliminate distracting factors for the learner by allowing different people to teach the same self-help skill with equal ease.

General training approaches such as task analysis and reverse chaining further facilitate this standardized method. Task analysis provides a consistent, sequentially developed breakdown of measurable steps that must be learned in order for a task to be completed. When preparing a task analysis to be used with the severely and profoundly handicapped population, it is important to break these sequential steps down into very small, observable increments so that student progress can be monitored accurately each time the task is attempted. Figure 1 illustrates how a simple task analysis inventory can be converted into a monitoring format to be used with each instruction. This format also provides immediate feedback to the teacher, by showing where the student is failing skills, which in turn prevents successful completion of the task. In some instances it is helpful to pinpoint skills in which the student is failing and to teach them

Task: To push a button

	10/1	10/2	10/3	10/6	10/7	10/8
1. Locate button	✔	✔	✔	+	+	+
2. Move hand to button	✔	✔	✔	+	+	+
3. Extend pointer finger (or thumb)	—	✔	✔	✔	✔	+
4. Place finger on button	—	✔	✔	✔	+	✔
5. Exert pressure for 3″	—	—	✔	✔	✔	✔
6. Remove finger from bell	✔	✔	✔	+	+	+

+ = Can Do Without Assistance
✔ = Can Do With Assistance
— = Cannot Do

Figure 1.   Example of a task analysis inventory.

in isolation. Once mastered, these skills can be placed back into the sequence necessary for task completion. For example, when teaching a severely or profoundly retarded learner to open a jar, it may be necessary to isolate the skill that requires a modified pincer grasp of the lid, and to strengthen the learner's hand and finger muscles doing several activities that require this same skill (e.g., using clickers, spring clothes pins, and play dough). When the student is able to do these activities, the teacher once again asks him or her to open a jar and should find improved performance on this skill due to the extra practice and resulting muscle strength.

Reverse chaining has proven to be a very good technique to use when teaching self-help skills to moderately, severely and profoundly retarded persons. The reason for this can be traced to the intrinsic reward system built into the process. Basically, this involves taking a task analysis inventory and assisting the learner through each of the steps until the end, at which the learner is asked to complete the last step (then the last two, then the last three, etc.) alone. In this way, he or she independently finishes the task each time and receives appropriate rewards for successfully being able to do what was required. This approach has been particularly useful in teaching dressing skills to lower functioning students. Tasks such as putting on a shirt or tying shoes can take months to teach, which is frustrating to the student. With the help of reverse chaining, the student is rewarded at the beginning for the entire act of putting a shirt on when he or she only straightens the lower part of the shirt around the waist at the end of the process.

Figure 2 summarizes some of the suggestions that have been made to facilitate the training of severely and profoundly retarded learners in initial training situations.

CURRICULUM

For the purposes of this chapter, the areas of feeding, toileting, grooming, and dressing skills are considered under the self-help curriculum. A

—Standardize the approach
—Standardize the language cues
—Break skills into small sequential steps
—Use short, frequent teaching sessions
—Consistently reinforce approximations
—Utilize reverse-chaining when appropriate
—Provide actual objects to train for skills (not toys)

Figure 2.   Suggestions for training self-help skills.

range of skills is offered for teaching in each area, with the understanding that not every severely or profoundly retarded learner can master each skill, depending upon the individual's intellectual and motor abilities. The skills presented are not a comprehensive listing of all self-help skills to be mastered by the severely and profoundly retarded population. Rather, a teacher can use this listing as a suggested guide for developing the self-help curriculum and then further define, through diagnostic evaluations, skills that should be assigned to given individuals. The training principles that have been discussed in the previous section should be applied when teaching these skills.

Feeding

Major Skills to be Developed

1. Sucking
2. Swallowing soft foods
3. Closing mouth to retain liquids and food while swallowing
4. Using tongue to move food in mouth
5. Cooperating with feeding
6. Drinking from spout cup
7. Finger feeding small pieces
8. Eating with spoon
9. Asking for food or drink
10. Chewing
11. Biting off pieces of food
12. Sucking liquids with straw
13. Eating with fork
14. Using fork to cut
15. Eating without drooling or spilling
16. Using knife to spread
17. Using knife to cut
18. Pouring liquid into cup from container
19. Preparing dry cereal
20. Fixing own sandwich or drink
21. Retrieving ingredients for making sandwich and other simple foods

Suggestions for Implementation   There are many adaptive devices and techniques that can be utilized in training severely and profoundly retarded learners to eat. An occupational therapist (O.T.) is a very good asset to school systems that are providing on-the-job training for teachers who have never worked with this population. The O.T. can give in-service training programs and on-site assistance with identified special cases.

The area of eating is of primary concern to parents, physicians and teachers alike, because of the implications involved for the child's health, development, and safety. If a child has no suck-swallow reflex pattern when he or she is born, this will have a profound effect upon the child, family, and school for many years. Force-feeders such as an enlarged eyedropper and an infant feeder are used with some success. However, these devices do not promote eating skills. They merely help satisfy the requirement of getting food and liquids into the child. One adaptive device that can promote independence in feeding when there is no suck-swallow reflex is a straw bottle. When made properly (with clear squeeze bottle and aquarium tubing) so that a vacuum is formed when the lid is tightened, the bottle can be used to teach sucking and can facilitate the feeding of individuals who have great difficulty drinking from a cup. Those who have no ability to suck can have small amounts of liquid squeezed into their mouths at controlled intervals, allowing time to swallow. The straw can be placed in the side of the mouth for those persons who have tongue-thrust or bite-reflex patterns. An additional benefit of this device is that the child's head can and should be in an upright, midline position, which keeps the throat open and inhibits unwanted motor reflex patterns. By manually holding the child's lips closed around the straw (see Figure 3), liquid can be kept in the mouth until the child has a chance to swallow (voluntarily or by inducement). It is possible to induce swallowing by firmly rubbing two fingers in a repeated downward motion on the throat of the individual (see Figure 4).

Once a student is more advanced, liquid can be squeezed to the end of the straw and maintained there while the child is encouraged to suck, thus providing many opportunities for learning this missing skill. Eventually the child should learn to hold his or her own bottle and self-feed

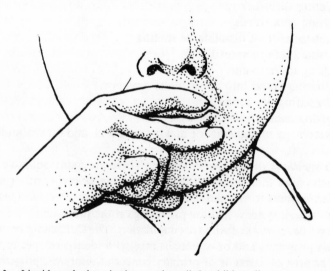

Figure 3.   Liquid can be kept in the mouth until the child swallows.

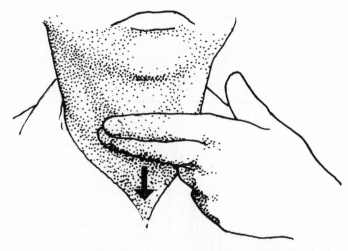

Figure 4. Swallowing can be induced by firmly rubbing two fingers in a downward repeated motion on the throat.

liquids at will, gradually moving from the straw bottle to more traditional drinking devices.

Whether assisting young children in drinking liquids or teaching older students to feed themselves, the trainer often overlooks two areas: (1) positioning and (2) the comfort and security of the child. If a child is too young to sit, he or she should be held in the lap at an angle that supports the head at a level higher than the body. It is nearly impossible for a child to swallow anything while in a back-lying, completely horizontal position because the throat muscles are closed. For this reason, a child's head should never be tilted back to keep liquid from running out of the mouth. A straw bottle can be used instead. With an older child, care should be taken to support the shoulders, spine, and feet while he or she is eating. It is very unnerving for a child to try to maintain an upright position in a chair and attend to all the stimuli involved in the eating process. In a school or home situation where adaptive seating systems are not readily available, cardboard boxes can be used to stabilize the child (see Figure 5). If a child does not have to worry about falling out of a seat, more attention can be focused upon the training process.

The eating environment should be pleasant and relaxed. Calm, firm directions, manual assistance when required, and lavish praise for attempted compliance are useful approaches. Task analysis and behavior modification principles should be employed by the trainer.

Two common difficulties for children who may already be feeding themselves are biting and chewing. Biting off bits of food can be taught using pieces of cracker, chips, or zwieback and placing the food in the front of the mouth. By quickly pushing down the child's chin and releas-

Figure 5.   Cardboard boxes can be used to stabilize the legs of a child learning to sit.

ing it, the natural bite reflex will be stimulated. Biting food between the front teeth rather than the molars should be encouraged. Chewing is a little more complicated because it involves several skills, and some children merely gum their food between the tongue and the roof of the mouth and then swallow it nearly whole. This interferes with obtaining nutritional benefits from the food and causes digestive problems. In fact, some parents and teachers are completely unaware that this is occurring until they take time to carefully observe the eating process. One common reason why chewing is a problem is the limited ability of the child to move the food from the front of the mouth to the side with the tongue. In some cases doing so is a physical impossibility, but sometimes the reason is a lack of training. A quick way of checking the physical ability to move the tongue from side to side is to place honey or jelly on the outside corners of the child's mouth and to ask him or her to lick it off. This will provide some information about tongue control. If a child cannot move the food to the side of the mouth because of physical limitations, he or she should be fed to the side of the mouth by placing the food inside the cheek next to the molars on alternate sides. This stimulates the chewing reflex by putting food where it can be easily chewed and then swallowed. With younger children a vinyl-coated, small-bowl spoon should be used to place the food inside the cheek. Older children can learn to do this for themselves.

If a child does not chew because of a lack of training, there are a few approaches that can be tried. Only small bites should be taken, and the child should be encouraged to move the food over between the molars. If chewing is not spontaneous, the process can be modelled by manually moving the child's lower jaw in a rotating, side-to-side manner that results in the grinding pattern. Initially, the trainer may have to prompt a learner throughout the entire process for each bite, but gradually this becomes a habit that requires little supervision.

Children who have motor problems can usually master eating with the assistance of adaptive devices. Grasping problems can be accommodated by built-up handles, velcro straps or even by adding a plastic bottle handle to the handle of a spoon. A swivel spoon will sometimes add stability to moving food when the child has uncontrolled hand movements. High-sided plates, nonslip surfaces, and even a self-contained adaptive feeding system can also contribute to the development of independent eating.

As the severely or profoundly involved child matures and learns to eat with a fork, cut with a knife, and prepare his or her own food, the trainer should continue to utilize the same systematic procedures and refrain from interfering unless it is a matter of safety. Obviously, it is easier for an instructor to pour a glass of juice for the child than to silently watch the prolonged struggle that sometimes results, but if the severely or profoundly involved child is to master such a skill he or she must have many opportunities to practice.

Toileting

Major Skills to be Developed

1. Being aware of wet or soiled diaper
2. Indicating awareness of wet or soiled diaper
3. Staying dryer 1½ to 2½ hours at a time
4. Unintentionally urinating on toilet
5. Urinating in toilet at consistent intervals
6. Cooperating with toileting procedures
7. Flushing toilet
8. Making bowel movements in toilet
9. Washing hands independently after using toilet
10. Asking to use bathroom
11. Pulling down pants when using toilet
12. Controlling daytime bladder and bowel movements
13. Independently using toilet with aid in personal hygiene
14. Controlling nighttime bladder and bowel movements

Suggestions for Implementation.   Toilet training should be a cooperative arrangement between the educational facility and the home (whether a traditional home, a group home, or an institutional ward). Because the severely or profoundly retarded learner spends a significant amount of time in both situations, the training procedures for toileting must be standardized. Therefore, the first step in beginning a toileting program is a sharing of information. Inquiries should be made as to the medical condition of the child to determine if any chronic infections, tumors, paralysis, or other disorders are present. The trainer should not begin a toileting program without this information, because to do so could result in many months of futile efforts to train a child who is not ready or able to be trained. Another factor to consider is the length of time between the child's urinations. The muscles used to control bladder and bowel movements must be strong enough to retain pressure for moderate lengths of time so that the child can learn to hold back until placed on the toilet. If a child still urinates every 20 to 30 minutes, the instructor should consider waiting for maturational growth to occur before starting to toilet train. If toilet training has been previously attempted, a trainer should determine the methods tried and the reactions of the child.

Once it is determined that the child is physically ready to begin a toileting program, the trainer must decide upon an approach. There are several methods that can be employed, ranging from one-day training (Azrin & Foxx, 1971) to the more gradual phasing-in strategy. One of the more traditional options, which most classroom teachers use out of necessity, is to determine a schedule for toileting, by setting regular intervals during the day when all children will sit on toilets. Some of the more usual times are upon arrival at school, midmorning, before lunch, and midafternoon. An alternate method is to set up individualized times for toileting based upon each child's usual elimination patterns. This initially requires considerable time on the part of the teacher, but ultimately becomes a matter of scheduling.

For about 2 weeks, the teacher and aides check each child every 10 to 15 minutes to see if he or she is dry. The results of each check are recorded on the child's time sheet (see Figure 6). This information is summarized at the end of a 2-week period in order to outline a toileting schedule for each child, which must then be followed by the trainer. Although more time-consuming, this individual scheduling is more efficient in training young children because based upon this information the trainer can often arrange for the child to use the toilet successfully and then lavishly praise him or her.

Even with the most conscientious scheduling, a child will have accidents in the beginning. Sometimes this is because the learner is still unsure exactly what is expected, and sometimes it is because he or she forgets

NAME: _____   Week # _____

Time*	11/2		11/3		11/4		11/5		11/6	
	Wet	Dry	Wet	Dry	Wet	Dry	Wet	Dry	Wet	Dry
8:00										
8:15										
8:30										
8:45										
9:00										
9:15										
9:30										
9:45										
ETC.										

*Mark with B for bowel movement

Figure 6.   An example of a toileting schedule time sheet.

until too late. The consistent use of behavior modification principles is important in both the initial training and the follow-through. When accidents occur, the child should participate in cleaning up. Angry accusations, shaming, or yelling should be avoided by the trainer, who should let him or her know of any inappropriate behavior. If the child rebels at cleaning up, he or she should be physically assisted in helping. Overcorrection can be used when other milder forms of training have been unsuccessful.

Consistency and persistence are cornerstones in the toilet training process. Good communication with the home helps maintain a consistent approach throughout the training and enhances the child's chances of success. In some cases, the toilet training process becomes a contest of wills between the severely or profoundly retarded learner and the trainer. This often leads to emotional upheaval on both sides that is counterproductive to the toilet-training goal. Strict adherence to behavioral principles and sometimes a switch in trainers helps to alleviate this confrontation.

Eventually the child will assume more and more of the responsibility for toileting until daytime independence is achieved. As he or she begins consistently to tell the trainer of the need to use the toilet, and then becomes able to go as needed with minimal assistance with clothing, the trainer may begin to concentrate more heavily on nighttime control. Communication between home and school is stressed as the toilet training progresses toward completion of the goal.

Grooming
Major Skills to be Developed

1. Cooperating in personal hygiene activities
2. Drying hands
3. Washing and drying hands
4. Using soap independently
5. Washing and drying face
6. Controlling drooling
7. Blowing nose as needed
8. Adjusting hot and cold water temperature
9. Rinsing teeth and expelling water
10. Brushing teeth unassisted
11. Combing and brushing hair
12. Bathing or showering independently
13. Cleaning nails
14. Using deodorant
15. Caring for self during menstruation
16. Applying makeup or aftershave
17. Putting hair in rollers
18. Shampooing hair

19. Choosing appropriate clothing
20. Using electric shaver
21. Repairing clothing, shining shoes, etc. when directed
22. Using washing machine and dryer

Suggestions for implementation   How a person looks is very important. If the severely or profoundly involved person is unkempt or in soiled, rumpled clothing with a runny nose and drooling mouth, an onlooker will often reject the individual, even though no personal interaction has yet occurred. Thus, the area of grooming is not only important from a health standpoint, but is also a key factor in the socialization of the severely and profoundly retarded.

Modeling plays an important role in the acquisition of many grooming skills. As the learner sees others in the environment washing their hands and faces, combing their hair, applying makeup, and so forth, he or she develops an awareness of these activities. It becomes routine to have his or her hands held under water and rubbed together with soap before assistance is given with drying the hands. Eventually, less and less physical guidance is given, and verbal prompts are later replaced by a single command. When training a severely or profoundly involved person to independently wash and dry his or her hands or face, one of the most difficult tasks is teaching the use of soap, unless a pump-action dispenser is used. A slippery bar of soap often ends up in the basin or on the floor. Use of a suctional soap holder will eliminate this problem by securely anchoring the soap to the sink, allowing the learner to rub his or her hands or a washrag on the surface of the soap without dislodging it. Another method is to slit a sponge, place a bar of soap inside, and close the sponge with nylon thread. This is a great help to severely and profoundly retarded learners when they begin to bathe or shower themselves.

The problem of drooling is quite prevalent among severely and profoundly involved learners. Sometimes, the child has trouble keeping his or her mouth closed because the tongue is enlarged, and this subsequently leads to drooling. In cerebral palsied persons, drooling is often related to a lack of muscular control. Another common cause of drooling is simply habit. The severely or profoundly involved child may be used to sitting with his or her mouth open, which leads to drooling. Also, if the child is a mouth breather, he or she has a tendency to drool because the mouth is left open.

To discourage drooling, several approaches can be tried. The child should be reminded to swallow and to keep the mouth closed. If there is a physical reason why the child cannot keep the mouth closed, or swallow, he or she should be taught to wipe the chin often. Behavior modification strategies should be used in either situation to help ensure consistency and follow-through even when the child is not with the trainer. Eventu-

ally, verbal prompting is faded out, and drooling becomes fully controlled by the learner. Similar types of training can be used to teach a
child to blow his or her nose rather than sniffing or just letting the nose
run.

Toothbrushing is a necessary skill that severely and profoundly
handicapped persons should learn to do independently. It ensures good
physical health as well as preventing offensive odors caused by poor dental hygiene. In some cases the child resists toothbrushing because of
discomfort in having a brush put inside the mouth. This can usually be
overcome by putting jelly on the toothbrush and requiring the child to
put the brush in the front of the mouth to lick it off. Eventually tooth-
paste is substituted and the front teeth are brushed. The brush is then
gradually moved further and further back in the mouth until all teeth are
brushed with some assistance. Modeling is an important teaching tool for
this procedure. The child is systematically able to take over more and
more of the responsibilities until the task becomes independent.

When teaching older severely and profoundly handicapped persons
grooming skills in a.school situation, it is important to confer with the
parents about the types of skills that are being introduced. Many professionals require signed permission forms before giving instruction in bathing, makeup, shaving, hairstyling, and so forth. There are some families
who strenuously object to training in these areas on the basis of cultural,
religious, or moral beliefs. When instruction is begun, it is desirable to
have the learners participate in each of the skills, which means the trainer
often models the skills along with each handicapped person. In some
cases this may require special effort on the part of the trainer, who may
need to don a swimsuit to get in the shower with a student.

Overall, the acquisition of grooming skills can be a lifetime endeavor on the part of a severely and profoundly handicapped learner. By
consistently applying behavioral principles during the training process
and carefully sequencing and breaking down the skills, the trainer can
help ensure that the learner is given an opportunity to achieve his or her
maximum performance as rapidly as possible.

Dressing

Major Skills to be Developed

1. Cooperating in undressing and dressing
2. Removing clothing
3. Untying bow
4. Unsnapping
5. Unzipping
6. Removing pulldown clothing
7. Unbuttoning

8. Zipping
9. Buttoning large buttons
10. Undressing except for pullover clothing
11. Putting on coat (overhead method)
12. Putting on shoes
13. Snapping
14. Identifying front and back of clothing
15. Identifying that clothing is inside out
16. Removing pullover clothing
17. Putting on socks, pulling up clothing
18. Buckling belt
19. Lacing shoes
20. Putting on pullover clothing
21. Dressing self (minimal assistance)
22. Tying shoes
23. Fastening back of clothing
24. Tying a necktie
25. Fastening jewelry

Suggestions for Implementation   Children learn to undress before
they are able to put clothes on. Just as it is easier to remove puzzle pieces
from their inserts on a board than to find the right fit when trying to replace them, children have difficulty finding the right fit when putting on
their clothing. Thus, the obvious place for the trainer to begin dressing
skills with severely handicapped learners is with undressing.

Fastening skills should be taught separately from the dressing process and then added into the skill sequence. Practice on dressing frames
(see Figure 7) would be a good initial learning exposure for a child. When
the child becomes proficient at fastening on the frame, he or she should
move to fastening on other students' clothing or on dressing vests. The
ultimate objective is requiring the learner to fasten his or her own cloth-

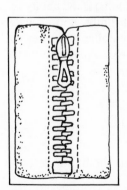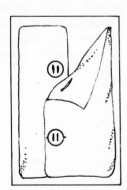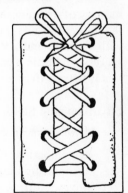

Figure 7.   Examples of dressing frames.

ing, which involves transferring skills learned on a frame to the upside-down positioning on himself or herself. If a child is learning to take off a coat, unzipping is taught as a separate skill and then put into the sequence of tasks required to remove the coat independently.

During the evaluation process, before assigning the student skills, the trainer should observe the learner while he or she is using both hands simultaneously to perform a task. This is a fairly complicated request that combines manual dexterity and visual motor coordination and requires that the learner perform two different actions at the same time to successfully complete a task. Two-handed manipulations are prerequisite to mastering most of the fastening skills, but this is sometimes overlooked, especially when attempting to teach a child to tie shoes. By not checking this particular prerequisite, many professionals devote years of futile effort trying to teach children to tie their shoes when they do not yet have the component skills.

There are a few teaching methods trainers can use when attempting to help handicapped learners become independent dressers. Velcro material can be substituted for buttons or snaps to assist a child who has little fine motor ability. For a child who always puts shoes on the wrong feet, matching dots can be painted on the inside top of the shoe soles. Small fabric squares sewn into the back of clothing can help the learner to orient clothing in the proper direction and can also provide reference points for a young learner to put on a jacket using the over-the-head approach. (A coat is placed open on the floor with the top of the coat, showing the fabric square, nearest to a learner. The learner slides both arms into the sleeves simultaneously and flings coat up and backwards over the head). Many children can learn to tie shoes with the "rabbit ears" approach when more traditional methods have failed. The learner makes two identical loops with the shoelaces and then wraps one "ear" around the other, pulling tight to fasten (see Figure 8).

One of the most important factors in the handicapped learner's mastery of dressing skills (in fact, in most self-help skills) is the ability of the trainer to wait. It takes patience to watch a child fumble and struggle with clothing and not to intervene. But learning by doing is the key to success, and little is gained if the instructor always helps. An exception to this is when safety is involved.

Environmental Skills

Major Skills to be Developed

1. Remembering where things are kept
2. Recognizing dangerous situations (fire, poisons, boiling water, knives, etc.)
3. Caring for simple injury

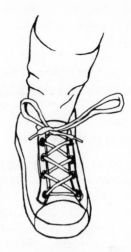

Figure 8.   Examples of dressing approaches: fabric squares sewn into the inside of clothing can help the learner identify clothing orientation and "rabbit ears" are a helpful mneumonic in teaching shoe tying.

4.   Waiting for assistance to cross busy intersection
5.   Helping put away toys and clothing
6.   Describing illness or injury
7.   Obtaining emergency help
8.   Dusting and operating vacuum cleaner
9.   Washing dishes
10.   Crossing street unassisted
11.   Using telephone

Suggestions for Implementation   The same principles apply to teaching environmental skills to a severely and multiply handicapped learner as have been previously discussed in this section. Prerequisite skills should be determined before training begins. Task analysis and behavior modification procedures should follow. Some of the skills listed above can be taught in conjunction with other self-help skills, such as recognizing boiling water and knives as dangerous while learning to cook.

In some instances, visual prompts are useful in simplifying the training process, for example, sticking picture labels on containers to warn of poisons and color-coding the telephone can familiarize a learner with a new process using learned skills. Identifying pictures can be placed on shelves or drawers to indicate where things are kept. Over a period of time, most learners will be able to succeed at these same tasks without depending upon the visual prompts.

Implicit in all of the self-help curricula is the crucial need for generalization skills on the part of a severely handicapped learner. It is not enough for the person to be able to perform a skill, in a given environment, with a given trainer observing. In order for these skills to have real import and usefulness, they must be transferred to the daily living needs of the learner no matter where he or she is. Generalization must be an inherent part of the training once the initial skills are mastered.

GENERALIZATION

Attention to generalization and maintenance of the student's newly acquired skills is a crucial element of any program. It makes no sense to invest time and energy in training, if a student is not taught to use the skill outside of the training room. Self-help skills taught through the structured, systematic approach necessary for initial learning are not readily generalizable without direct training. This direct training must include systematic variation of important parameters, such as changing the trainers and having them provide different verbal cues in several situations, and varying times with appropriate materials. It must be emphasized that the generalization element of the training is only presented once the skill has been mastered to some minimum level of proficiency. At that point, the "instructional environments should be consistently inconsistent or systematically varied" (Brown, Nietupski, & Hamre-Nietupski, 1976, p. 14). Any variable that might influence task performance outside of training should be introduced in training to better prepare the student for skill maintenance.

Special educators must remember what the severely or multiply handicapped student learns in training situations. He or she not only learns how to perform the targeted task, but also where to do it, who to do it for, when, and contingent upon what verbal cues. This is another reason why generalization of skills has been a problem in the past. "Teachers of the severely handicapped can rarely assume that because a student performs a particular skill in an artificial setting, that he or she can also perform that skill in other more natural settings" (Brown, et al.). An instructor may use artificial settings and contrived or adaptive materials to speed a student's progress in the initial stages of training. When the student reaches criteria skill performance levels, however, he or she should be moved into training for generalization with realistic settings and materials. The "criterion of ultimate functioning" is the rule presented by Brown, et al. to govern generalization considerations in programming for the severely and profoundly handicapped. The criterion educators should use for the ultimate success of a student's training is the actual performance of a skill in a natural setting with natural materials and under naturally occurring conditions.

Verbal cues are very important in relation to skill generalization and maintenance. Language skills of retarded students are frequently very low, and as a result students are generally only exposed to short, specific verbal cues to stimulate the performance of a targeted skill. These cues are important in the initial stages of training. The problem, however, arises well after training ends. Everyone involved with a particular student after that point may not know the magical "open sesame" phrase that tells the student what skill sequence to perform. The solution, as suggested by Brown, et al., is to provide a variety of paired verbal cues as the stimulus for skill performance. Azrin et al. (1976) state that the training situation can also be used to develop the student's language lexicon regarding the self-help skill being taught. They propose that the instructor continually describe what the student is doing to the student and use this as a component in the reinforcement procedure.

This process may be observed in the following sequence of directions: "Take off your pants," "Push them down to your knees," "Good, you're pushing them down"; "Now push them to your feet," "Good, you're pushing them"; "Get your foot out," "Good, you're pulling your foot out of your pants" (Azrin, et al., 1976).

Further success in skill generalization and maintenance is derived from appropriate manipulation of the reinforcers. This manipulation affects the ratio, interval, and nature of the reinforcers administered. The training variable must be gradually altered so that the student continues to emit the desired response correctly in the absence of continuous reinforcement. Thus, the student should eventually be able to continue to respond with a low level of reinforcement naturally available in the world outside of the training room. He or she must also be capable of working in an environment that utilizes social reinforcers (Gold, 1980).

Utilizing adapted materials in the initial training process is both necessary and desirable. The adaptive materials are of even greater value when they can be gradually modified to approximate those materials normally found outside the training situation. These adaptive features can later be faded out as the student develops the competencies required to manipulate clothing, buttons, or other self-help material commonly used. In a dressing program, for example, the clothing used might be several sizes too large for the student.

Other adaptations of the training material might include the use of elastic waist bands, short-sleeved shirts and cut-off pants, no buttons, and suspenders. The instructor must gradually change the characteristics of the adaptive training materials until they closely conform to those of articles commonly used out of training. As the student meets the performance criterion, therefore, these other clothing variables must be systematically introduced into the training setting. This process helps ensure the principles of generalization as the learner moves from adapted to standard materials while in training. In addition, the student should have an opportunity to practice the newly acquired skills in the appropriate environment, under conditions that normally accompany the skill.

A creative use of shaping the characteristics of adaptive materials is clearly seen in the self-feeding study done by Carr (1976). In this study Carr taught a student to drink from a cup. The student was able to use a spoon, but refused to drink from a cup. Through the use of a moldable material such as orthoplast, a spoon was gradually reshaped into a cup. The "bowl" of the spoon was enlarged and then deepened, and finally the handle was progressively turned into a cup handle.

The technology necessary for teaching skills to the severely, profoundly and multiply handicapped presently exists. Behavioral techniques provide for developing skill generalization, but instructors often fail to incorporate these procedures into skill training. Provision for training for generalization of skills is an essential part of each student's program.

ADAPTIVE MATERIALS

This section provides a sampling of adaptive and assistive materials that can be used to train self-help skills. The illustrations have been divided into the self-help domains discussed in this chapter: feeding, dressing, grooming, and toileting. The adaptive materials presented in each domain are representative of the type and variety available for such skill development. These materials can be used to train normal performance of self-help skills. Some of the items can be used sequentially (as in training drinking from a cup) to gradually give the student more responsibility for independent skill performance.

A selection of auxiliary materials are also presented for each domain. These have been included because the physical limitations that commonly accompany severe retardation frequently prohibit normal performance of self-help skills. In such cases, therefore, alterations must be made in both the task and the equipment used for performance of the skills involved. It is important that the student develop a set of skills to independently perform the task, even if it is greatly modified. The independence that comes with the ability to tend to one's own self-care needs is important, especially to a physically disabled person who is dependent in so many other ways.

Although a student's physical condition may necessitate the use of assistive materials and modified techniques, he or she should be reevaluated periodically for entry into training for normal self-help skill performance, as the condition that initially required the use of modifications may have altered through practice in self-care. Through the use of the assistive devices, for example, the student might improve his or her range of motion. This improvement can, in turn, facilitate the execution of the prerequisite movements needed for some of the self-help skills. At this point, without reevaluation for entry into normal self-care training, the assistive materials can become roadblocks to progress rather than bridges to skill performance.

The materials that follow have been sequenced logically, and this ordering may have no relation to the actual developmental sequence for the skills they represent. These items are intended to illustrate the generic types and variety of articles available through purchase or construction. Several of the adaptive materials can be located in the child-care products sections of drugstores (e.g., The First Year, Tommee Tippee, and Disney Products). The majority of the assistive materials, however, are available only through specialty outlets (e.g., Help Yourself Aids and J. A. Preston).

Feeding

Straw Bottle   A clear bottle marked in ounces and fitted with a straw can be used to develop a suck & swallow response. The student can obtain the fluid by either sucking on the straw or squeezing on the bottle (Figure 9).

Vacuum Cup   This cup permits the student to receive fluid for a sucking response. A small amount of liquid can also be released by applying pressure to the button on the lid. This cup is also available with two handles. Because of the suction requirement, this utensil is useful for

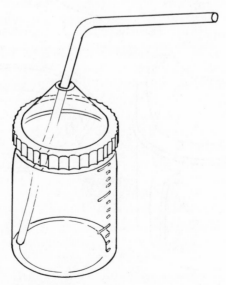

Figure 9.

students whose condition requires that they drink while laying down (Figure 10).

Infant Training Cup   This item is commonly used in training non-retarded children to drink from a cup. It is available from several child-care product companies. The lid permits a free flow of liquid through the mouth piece when the cup is tipped. The alternate lid, pictured, allows a small amount of fluid to collect at the upper level of the cup, for drinking in the manner that adults do. Both of these lids allow the student to drink without spilling (Figure 11).

Cut-Out Cup   The cut-out section of this cup permits the student to drink without tipping the head back. It also allows the glass to be tipped to a greater angle than the standard glass, since it does not hit the nose or forehead when tipped (Figure 12).

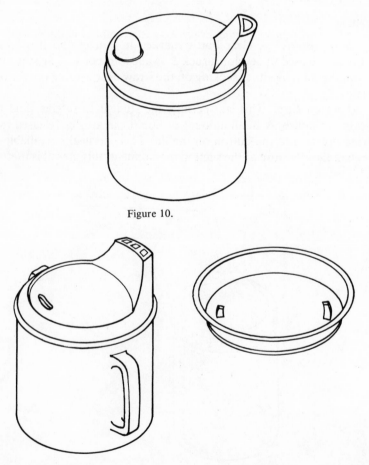

Figure 10.

Figure 11.

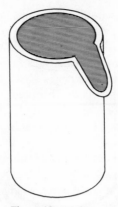

Figure 12.

Improved Grip   The adhesive-backed, nonslip strips and designs used in bathtubs make cups and glasses easier to hold by increasing the friction of typically slick container surfaces. The nonslip strip is spiralled around the cup, and a decorative nonslip design is placed where the student is to hold the cup or glass (Figure 13).

Suction-Cup Base   A cup may be securely attached to a surface by a suction cup. This item provides stable support for a cup-and-straw arrangement. This device might be used in conjunction with straw clips (Figure 14).

Straw Clip   Both of the illustrated straw holders (Figure 15) will maintain the disabled student's straw in a position maximally useful to him or her. The holder on the left consists of an alligator clip and a per-

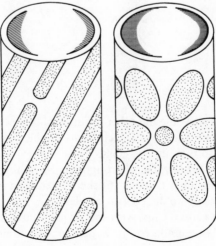

Figure 13.

Figure 14.

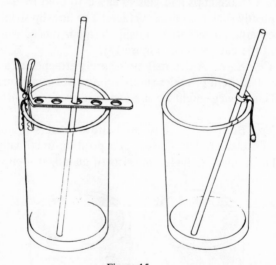

Figure 15.

forated metal strip, while the other requires only a pencil clip positioned around the straw. The use of such items enables the student to drink without having to pick up the glass.

Adjustable Cup Handle   Through the use of either a double- or single-handled attachment (Figure 16) the student can have an improved, adjustable means of holding a cup or glass.

Easy Grasp Cups   Cups with special grips have been designed to be easily held and manipulated by a person with limited manual skills (Figure 17).

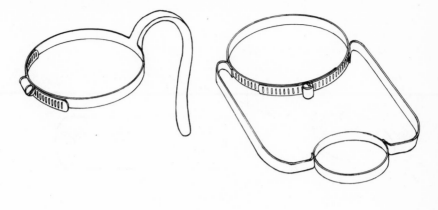

Figure 16.

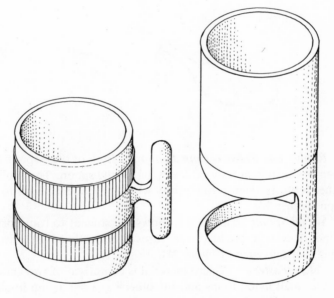

Figure 17.

Large-Handled Eating Utensil   A foam rubber tube (Figure 18) can be used to increase the diameter of a spoon, knife, or fork handle. This spongy material provides a more easily grasped, nonslip surface to facilitate the student's ability to hold eating utensils. This type of tube can be used to increase the diameter of other utensils (e.g., tooth brush, comb, and hair brush) and thereby make them easier to use.

Adjustable Diameter Spoon Handle   The malleable metal on the handle of this spoon can be bent to meet the needs of the student's hand (Figure 19).

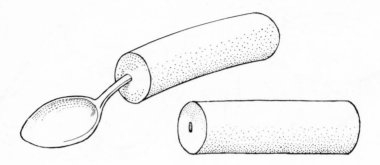

Figure 18.

Figure 19.

Rubber and Rubber-Tipped Spoons   Both of these spoons limit the self-injury a student may inflict by biting the spoon. The rubber spoon further protects against gum injury when the student begins to pilot the spoon (Figure 20).

Swivel Spoon   This spoon allows the student to transport food to the mouth even before he or she learns to correctly adjust wrist position during that movement (Figure 21).

Velcro Fastener   Velcro material is comprised of two components: one has small nylon loops and the other has small nylon hooks. When touched together, they adhere to one another but are easily disconnected. This material is very useful in dressing but has also been applied to both grooming and eating through use of the universal cuff (see below) (Figure 22).

Universal Cuff   The utensil or grooming tool is placed in the pocket (a) attached to a velcro strap, the strap is then placed around the student's hand so that the utensil or tool is in the student's palm (b), the velcro strap is looped through a ring, (c) and the strap attaches to itself (Figure 23).

Wooden Handle with Velcro Strap   This utensil incorporates a velcro attachment that fits onto an enlarged handle (Figure 24).

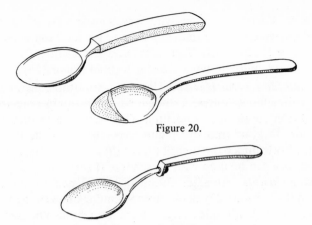

Figure 20.

Figure 21.

Figure 22.

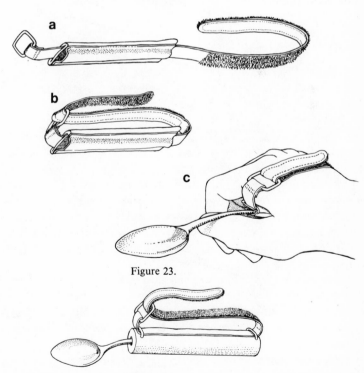

a

b

c

Figure 23.

Figure 24.

Bent Spoon   Forks and spoons with curved necks alleviate the need for controlled movement of the student's wrist to get food to the mouth. They are available for both left- and right-handed students. The spoon also has a built-up handle to make it easier to hold (Figure 25).

Vertical and Horizontal Handled Utensils   Adjustable material on the end of an eating utensil allows a student with limited grasping ability and wrist position to eat independently. The vertical grip utensil (a) places the spoon, fork, or knife in a plane perpendicular to the student's palm, while the horizontal palm utensil (b) is held parallel to the palm. A bent spoon or fork can be used with these units (Figure 26).

Finger Ring Utensils   An adjustable utensil attachment (seen in illustrations (a) and (b) of Figure 27) allows for positioning of an eating utensil along the disabled student's index finger. Here it might also be useful to attach a bent utensil to aid in performing needed actions (Figure 27).

Elongated Utensil   This attachment produces a longer eating utensil and increases the student's reach (Figure 28).

Rocker Knife   The rocker knife, the rocker knife-fork, and the side-cutting fork were designed for use by individuals with only one hand. They are also very useful to students having adequate control over only one hand (Figure 29).

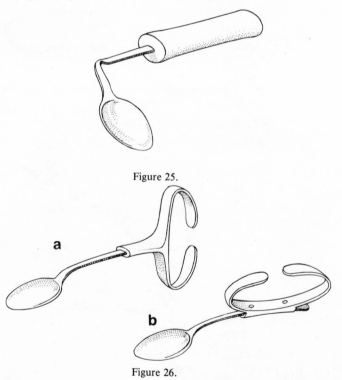

Figure 25.

a

b

Figure 26.

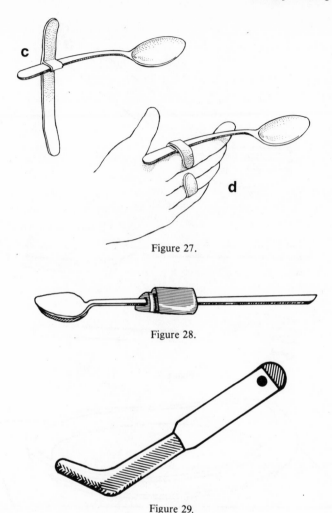

Figure 27.

Figure 28.

Figure 29.

Rocker Knife-Fork   This utensil provides a bent fork built into the rocker knife (Figure 30).

Side-Cutting Fork   This fork has a knife edge along one of its outside tines (Figure 31).

Spork   A combination of a spoon and a fork, the spork eliminates the need for balancing forked foods (Figure 32).

Round Scoop Dish   This aid helps in teaching the student to get food on a spoon. He or she need only move the spoon toward the elevated end of the bowl. The curved, elevated part of the bowl causes the food pushed by the student's spoon to move up and fall back onto that utensil (Figure 33).

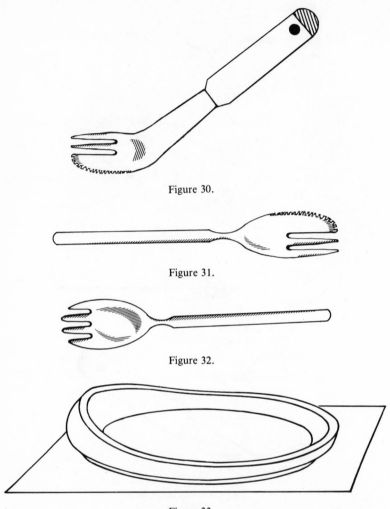

Figure 30.

Figure 31.

Figure 32.

Figure 33.

Scoop Dish   The scoop dish has a higher edge at one end. This elevated edge is straight rather than curved. This means that the student must cause the food to move onto the spoon more voluntarily (Figure 34).

Food Guards   There are two food guards (Figure 35a & b) that perform the same function as the scoop dish. The food guards are removable. One (a) has three hooks that attach to the rim of the plate. The other food guard (b) has a groove that also hooks onto a plate rim.

Food Warmer Plate   This commercially available child-care product is hollow. Food is kept warm during feeding training by the hot water contained within the plate. The plate surface is divided into sections and is attached to the table by suction cups on the bottom (Figure 36).

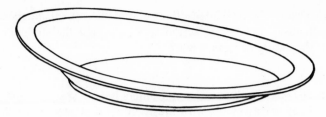

Figure 34.

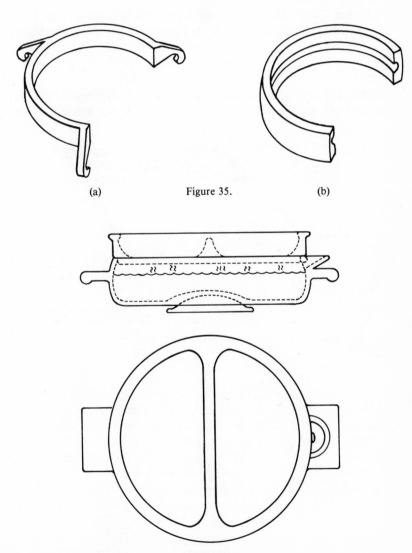

(a)   Figure 35.   (b)

Figure 36.

Self-Feeder   With limited effort a student can eat independently. This mechanism uses spring action to supplement the student's movements in the eating process (Figure 37).

Toileting

Kiddie Toilet Trainers   These trainers have a seat belt and a back support. They are available with music boxes that play when the child uses the toilet. An adapter may be affixed to an adult toilet for advanced training (Figure 38).

Adapted Toilet   This set of supportive bars is commercially available. It provides assistance to a disabled person in maneuvering (Figure 39).

Grooming

Hair Brush Straps   A velcro strip, as used in the universal cuff, can be attached to a regular hair brush (Figure 40a). A hair brush outfitted

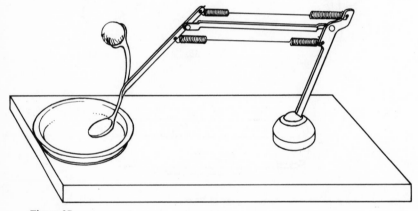

Figure 37.

Figure 38.

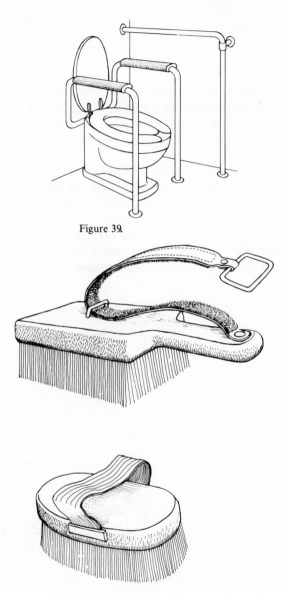

Figure 39.

Figure 40.

with a strap that fits across the students knuckles also provides a firm grip for the student (Figure 40b).

Electric Toothbrush   A student may be able to use an electric toothbrush. For training purposes, the use of a child-care toothbrush with a rattle in the handle introduces an auditory stimulus into the training as a potential reinforcer (Figure 41).

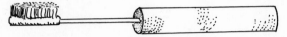

Figure 41.

Toenail Clipper   A modified unit that involves a pulling skill allows for toenail clipping by those with limited ability (Figure 42).

Fingernail Clipper   An adapted fingernail clipper with extended grips enables the student with limited fine motor control to clip fingernails (Figure 43).

Extension Combs and Brushes   These long-handled devices allow the student with a limited range of motion to comb or brush hair (Figure 44).

No-Hands Mirror   The curved end of this device hooks around the neck and the mirror rests in front of the face. This unit provides the student with the freedom to use both hands (Figure 45).

Washcloth Mitt   A velcro strap can be used to hold a terrycloth mitt to the student's hand for washing purposes (Figure 46).

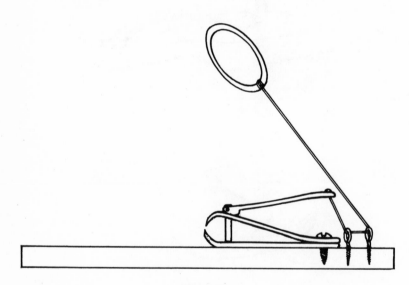

Figure 42.

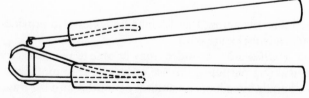

Figure 43.

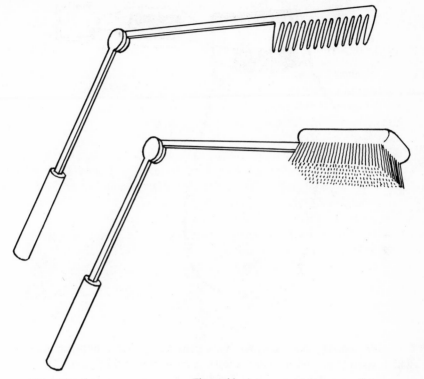

Figure 44.

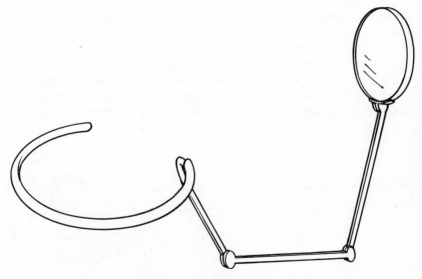

Figure 45.

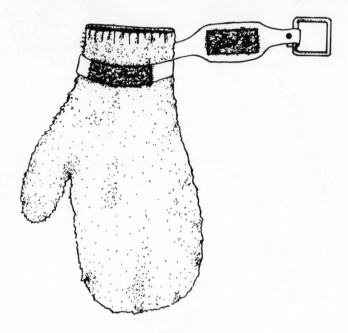

Figure 46

Self-Soaping Back Brush   This back brush has a compartment in which soap is placed in contact with sponge material (Figure 47).

Extension Brushes   Extended back brushes allow a person with a limited range of motion to scrub his or her own back (Figure 48).

Aerosol Trigger   A homemade unit enables a disabled individual to use aerosol products dispensed into one hand as the other hand pushes down a large, spring-hinged block of wood to activate aerosol sprayer beneath it (Figure 49).

Faucet Extender   The nozzle of this hose aid can be wall-mounted at any point that proves to be efficient for the disabled bather (Figure 50).

Lever-Operated Faucets   Faucets with levers are easily operated with limited motor control, range of motion, or muscle strength. The ease of

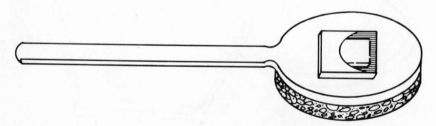

Figure 47

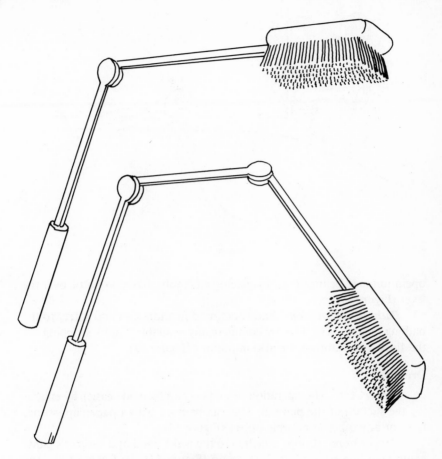

Figure 48

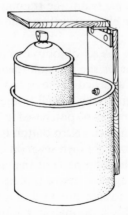

Figure 49

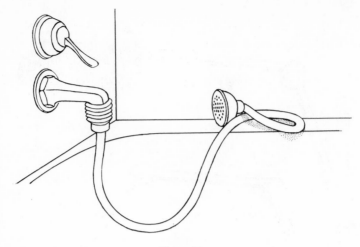

Figure 50.

operation may be improved by placing an empty shampoo bottle over the lever (Figure 51).

Bathtub Adaptation   Bathroom modifications can add safety to the bathing process. The bars are commercially available. Safety stripping for the floor and bathtubs are also important (Figure 52).

Dressing

Zipper Aid   The operation of zippers can be made easier by enlarging the surface of the pull tab. This can be done with a paperclip, string, ring, or any other attachable object (Figure 53).

Pants Loops   Loops attached to the waist band of a student's pants could help him or her to pull them up (Figure 54). To further assist the student in learning to put pants on, the training pants might be several sizes too large, and have an elastic waistband, no fasteners, and shortened pants legs.

Multiple Pants Loops   A set of loops can be attached to a disabled person's pants, whereby he or she can pull them on alone (Figure 55a). Multiple loops can also be attached to the belt loop (Figure 55b). The student can use the loops sequentially to pull trousers on.

Velcro Buttons   Velcro can be purchased in button-sized circles. One half (i.e., the hook part) of each velcro button is sewn on in place of the original buttons. The buttons are then sewn on over the button hole and the remaining half (i.e., the loop part) of the velcro buttons is sewn on behind the buttons. Through the above process the student can merely touch the button to the velcro spot and it will stay there. The button movement discussed above yields a normal appearance on the shirt surface (Figure 56).

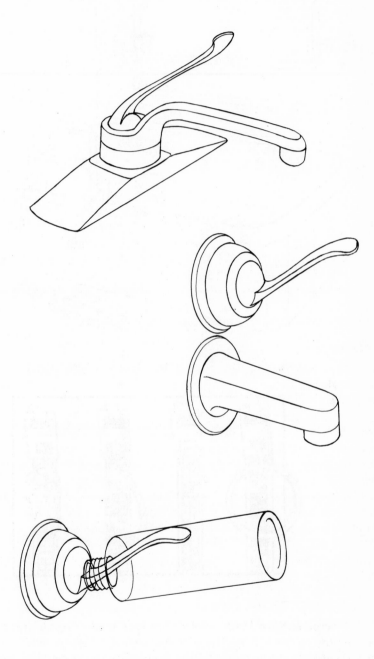

Figure 51.

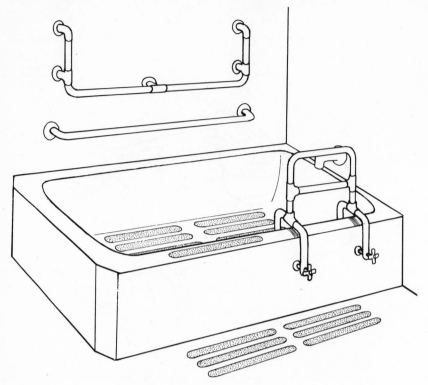

Figure 52.

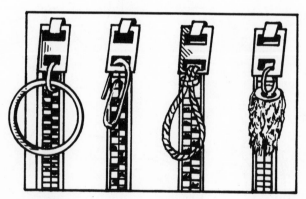

Figure 53.

Velcro-Modified Pants   Velcro has been used to replace the zipper and button on these pants. The pants legs have also been modified through the use of velcro to better enable the disabled student to get his or her feet through the pants cuffs (Figure 57).

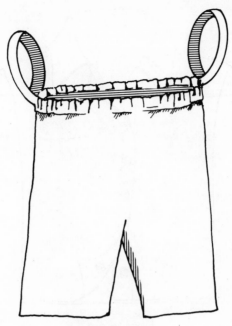

Figure 54.

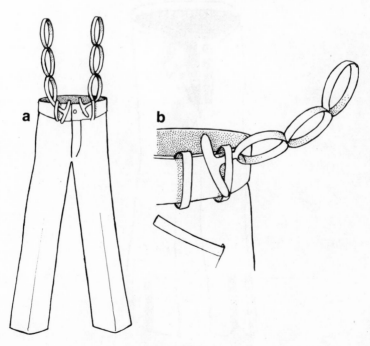

Figure 55.

Figure 56.

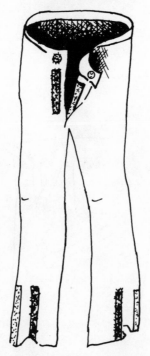

Figure 57.

Figure 58.

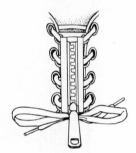

Figure 59.

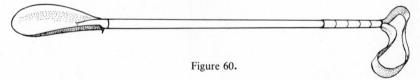

Figure 60.

Velcro-Modified Shoe   Shoe fasteners and buckles can often be adapted by the use of velcro for closure (Figure 58).

Shoestring Zipper   If this device is laced into the front of the shoe, the student can zip the shoe to tighten the laces (Figure 59). A zipper hook can be used to allow the student to grip and pull the zipper more easily.

Long-Handled Shoe Horn   A shoe horn provides assistance for the student who has difficulty with balance or in reaching shoes when dressing (Figure 60).

Environmental Skills

Drawer Grip   Attaching a cloth loop to drawer handles aids the student in opening drawers (Figure 61).

Door Lever   A commercially available rubber door knob attachment allows for easier operation by a person with limited grasp and range of motion. With this adapter, the door knob can be turned with a simple downward pressure (Figure 62).

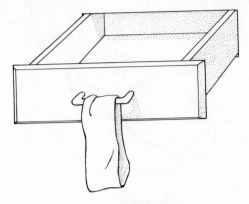

Figure 61.

Figure 62.

SUMMARY

The aforementioned curricula and materials provide for severely and profoundly and multiply handicapped students identified even at an early chronological age. The public schools, in addition to reaching the very young student, must expand current educational services into the home. Wehman and Goodwyn stress that the "success of training [self-help] skills will depend upon the effectiveness with which parents can follow through, as well as implement, self-help programs" (1978, p. 159). The public schools should, therefore, teach parents to train their children and thereby provide a home environment consistent with the skills taught in school. It is through this consistent follow-through at home that self-help skills are generalized for use in natural settings. All described curricula can be easily used for such home-based programs. The curricula selected might depend upon the training provided for the parent and the frequency of consultation available from the schools over a predetermined time. Wehman and Goodwyn note that in selecting the correct teaching procedure the most important factor is the uniqueness of each child's needs. This is important in terms of both behavioral and physical needs. For more physically involved students, many self-help procedures must be adapted on an individual basis, contingent upon the absence and presence of various prerequisite motor skills. The instructor of the physically disabled must be able to apply the described techniques with any necessary individualized adaptations of the basic self-help skills being taught. A new emphasis is being placed on normalization and deinstitutionalization, fueled by the implementation of P.L. 94-142; as a result, educational services in the public schools are increasing in both kind and complexity. The creativity and adaptability of public school teachers is being put to the ultimate test. These instructors are having to reevaluate their educational philosophies, as they must provide nontraditional, individualized, curricular content to meet specific and unique life needs of the relatively new student population appearing in the public schools. The behavioral and curricular technologies currently exist; it rests upon the shoulders of the public schools to apply them in order to best serve the severely and multiply handicapped citizen.

APPENDIX A / Sources of Equipment for Severely/Multiply Handicapped

Aids For the Disabled
Help Yourself Aids
Post Office Box 192
Hinsdale, IL 60521

B. And L. Engineering
Orthopedic Supplies Co.
9126 E. Firestone Blvd.
Downey, CA 90200

Child Care Products
The First Years
Avon, MA 02322

The Cleveland Orthopedic Co.
3957 Mayfield Avenue
Cleveland, Ohio 44121

Fred Sammons, Inc.
(formerly B-K Sales Co.)
Box 32, Brookfield, IL 60513
    also
Box 5173, Inglewood, CA 90303

G. E. Miller, Inc.
484 South Broadway
Yonkers, NY 10705

Hospac Corp.
31–35 61st Street
Woodside, NY 11377

J. A. Preston
71 Fifth Avenue
New York, NY 10003

Jaeco Orthopedic Specialties
Box 616 M-R5
Hot Springs, AR 71719

MEDCO
Rehabilitation Aids Company
Post Office Box 146
East Rockaway, NY 11518

Rehab Aids
Post Office Box 612
Miami, FL 33144

Rehabilitation Products
Division Amer. Hosp. Supply
40–05 168th Street
Flushing, L.I., NY 11300
Rehabilitation Technical
  Components
625 Pennsylvania Avenue
Elizabeth, NJ 07201

Stauffer Wood Products
R. D. #1, Box 65
Tower City, PA 17980
United Cerebral Palsy Associa-
  tions, Inc.
66 E. 34th Street
New York, NY 10016

REFERENCES

Adelson-Bernstein, N., & Sandow, L. Teaching buttoning to severely/profoundly retarded multihandicapped children. *Education and Training of the Mentally Retarded*, 1978, 13(2), 178–183.

Albin, J. B. Some variables influencing the maintenance of acquired self-feeding behavior in profoundly retarded children. *Mental Retardation*, 1977, 15(5), 49–52.

Azrin, N. H., & Armstrong, P. M. The "mini-meal": A method for teaching eating skills to the profoundly retarded. *Mental Retardation*, 1973, 11(1), 9–11.

Azrin, N. H., & Foxx, R. M. A rapid method of toilet training the institutionalized. *Journal of Applied Behavior Analysis*, 1971, 4(2), 89–99.

Azrin, N. H., Schaeffer, R. M., & Wesolowski, M. D. A rapid method of teaching profoundly retarded persons to dress by a reinforcement – Guidance method. *Mental Retardation*, 1976, 14(6), 29–33.

Azrin, N. H., Sneed, T. J., & Foxx, R. N. Dry-bed training: Rapid elimination of childhood enuresis. *Behavior Research and Therapy*, 1974, 12(3), 147–156.

Baumgartner, B. B. Goals for independence. In B. Stephens (Ed.). *Training the developmentally young*. New York: John Day Company, 1971.

Berdine, W. H., Murphy, M., & Roller, J. D. A criterion referenced training program based on the ABS: The Oakwood Scale for training and evaluating programs. *Mental Retardation*, 1977, 15(6), 19–22.

Bluma, S., Shearer, M., Frohman, A., & Hilliard, J. *Portage guide to early education*. Portage, Wisc. Cooperative Educational Services, 1976.

Brigance, A. L. *Brigance diagnostic inventory of early development*. Woburn, Massachusetts. Curriculum Associates, 1978.

Brown, L., Nietupski, J., & Hamre-Nietupski, S. Criterion of ultimate functioning. In M. A. Thomas (Ed.), *Hey, don't forget about me!* Reston, Va. Council for Exceptional Children, 1976.

Carr, J. The severely retarded autistic child. In L. Wing (Ed)., *Early childhood autism*. New York: Pergamon Press, 1976.

Dunn, L., & Capobianco, R. J. Mental retardation. *Review of Educational Research*, 1959, 29(5), 451–465.

Edgar, E., Maser, J., Deutch Smith, D., & Haring, N. G. Developing an instructional sequence for teaching a self-help skill. *Education and Training of the Mentally Retarded*, 1977, 12(1), 42–51.

Fredrics, H. D. B., Baldwin, V. L., Grove, D., Riggs, C., Furey, V., & Moore, W. Curriculum for the severely handicapped. *Education and Training of the Mentally Retarded*, 1977, 12(4), 316–324.

Foxx, R. M., & Azrin, N. H. Toilet training the retarded: A rapid program for day and nightime independent toileting. Research Press, Champaign, Ill: Research Press, 1973.

Gold, M. W. *"Did I say that": Articles and comments on the try another way system.* Champaign, Ill. Research Press, 1980.

Litton, F. W. *Education of the trainable mentally retarded, curriculum, methods, materials.* Saint Louis: C. V. Mosby, 1978.

Mercer, C. D., & Algozzine, B. Observational learning and the retarded: Teaching implications. *Education and Training of the Mentally Retarded*, 1977, 12(4), 345–353.

Mayen, E. L., & Altman, R. Public school programming for the severely/profoundly handicapped: Some research problems. *Education and Training of the Mentally Retarded*, 1976, *11*(1), 40–45.

Nelson, G., Cone, J. D., & Hanson, C. R. Training correct utensil use in retarded children: Modeling vs. physical guidance. *American Journal of Mental Deficiency*, 1975, *80*, 114–122.

O'Brien, F., Bugle, C., & Azrin, N. H. Training and maintaining a retarded child's proper eating. *Journal of Applied Behavior Analysis* 1972. *5*, 67–72.

O'Donnell, P. A., & Bigge, J. L. *Teaching individuals with physical and multiple disabilities.* Columbus, Ohio: Charles E. Merrill, 1976.

Ort, E. S. (Ed.). *The Radea Program Manual.* Dallas, Tx.: Melton Book Co., 1976.

Quick A. D., & Campbell, A. A. A model for preschool curriculum: Project MEMPHIS. *Mental Retardation*, 1977, *15*(2), 42–46.

Quick A. D., & Campbell, A. A. *The project MEMPHIS developmental program for the severely and profoundly handicapped.* Unpublished manuscript, 1981.

Schedgick, B., & Deschapelles, A. Curriculum for the severely handicapped: Focus on the generalization process. *Education and Training of the Mentally Retarded*, 1978, *13*(4), 389–393.

Wehman, P., & Goodwyn, R. L. Self-help skill development. In N. H. Fallen and J. E. McGovern (Eds.), *Young children with special needs.* Columbus, Oh.: Charles E. Merrill, 1978.

Chapter 7

Communication Skills

Sara J. Odle, Chris E. Wethered, and Suzanne Selph

Deficiencies in communication skills are present, in some degree, in almost all of the severely/multiply handicapped population. These deficits vary in type and severity and arise from a number of causes. These communication deficiencies directly affect the handicapped student's ability to interact with others, follow directions, express wants and needs, demonstrate cognitive ability, and participate in the learning process.

Our language is a rule-governed system of words (signs, symbols), the meanings of which we agree upon, by means of which we interact. Language training for the severely/multiply handicapped must not only increase their understanding (convey the meaning) of these symbols, but also encourage use of the learned symbols to influence what happens to them — in other words, to have more control over their environment. It is often necessary to program for their understanding of the *usefulness* of communication as well as for their acquisition of a vocabulary. Another dimension of language that must receive special consideration in the training programs for this population is that of *pragmatics*, which Bates (1976) defined as "rules governing the use of language in context" (p. 420).

Use of the word "child" in this chapter is obviously inappropriate when the discussion is meant to apply to language acquisition by older severely and multiply handicapped persons, even though cognitively they may be functioning at the early childhood level. The word child, however, is used in portions of this chapter for the sake of simplicity. General principles of communication training for the normal child are applicable to many adults in the target population. However, the age of the person being programmed for must be taken into consideration. Do not let the term child lead you to disregard this very important factor.

Use of appropriate language in specific contexts must be taught to those persons lacking adaptive behaviors. Students must learn when and where to say what to whom.

The need to emphasize speech and language development throughout the total program for the severely handicapped assumes even higher priority as more and more members of this population, both children and adults, are placed in less restrictive educational, vocational and residential settings. One of the primary requirements for successful functioning in these settings is the ability to communicate with others. The presence of language is almost a prerequisite for any approximation of normalization (Anderson & Greer, 1976).

Although communication is equated with verbal language by many educators, development of communication skills for the severely/multiply handicapped cannot be restricted to this one modality. To do so would be a denial of the right of every child—or adult—to an appropriate education. Achievement of desired goals for many multiply handicapped persons can be reached only through provision of alternative forms of communication. This chapter therefore describes various nonverbal communication systems and devices currently available, as well as methods for development of oral language skills.

Deficits in Language Development

Three types of language deficits were described by Schiefelbusch (1978): delayed language, communication problems (interpersonal), and speech disorders.

Delayed Language   The optimum time for a child to acquire language is from 1 to 4 years of age. When he or she does not acquire the ability to communicate meaningfully "on schedule," we say that he has delayed language. The child or adult may have little or no speech or a restricted pattern of use. This condition usually accompanies mental retardation or a severe developmental delay.

Early intervention is extremely important for correction or amelioration of this problem. Language programs are usually developmental or functional in approach. Researchers have found that most children acquire the various features of their native language in generally the same order, with each new element building on previous ones (Brown, 1973). Given this assumption, the way to design a language intervention program is to discover a child's linguistic level and train the next structures a normal child would acquire. This is especially indicated when the child is young and has the potential for language learning (i.e., the child has intact speech and hearing mechanisms).

The case of a severely involved older child, teenager, or adult who has not acquired language presents different programming needs. Because the learner did not develop language at the optimum acquisition time, priorities as well as procedures may change. Many trainers find it difficult to justify spending valuable training time on syntactical structures when the student simply needs to communicate well enough to have more control over the environment. In this case the preferred approach is to train functional language, the specific, easily acquired structures and essential vocabulary the handicapped person will need in his or her daily environment. Training in alternate forms of communication is often indicated. Such forms are described in this chapter.

It is important that the language strategy used be appropriate to each student's specific needs. Basic objectives of language programs are to provide the person with a means of expressing desires and needs, the ability to manipulate the environment, and training for communication in settings other than the teaching situation. Methods for reaching these goals vary depending on the student's age, cognitive level, learning style, environmental requirements, and other factors.

Communication Disorders   Problems for some persons may lie in the area of *semantics*, in using language meaningfully for communication. The person may merely repeat whatever he or she hears, with no apparent attempt at communication. Such a problem may be seen in autistic children or in those with other severe emotional disorders. Other children and adults may have difficulty putting ideas into words, even though they may know the appropriate words. Other communication problems may be in the use of language in context, or *pragmatics*. Words selected may be inappropriate for the situation. Often deficits in other adaptive behaviors will accompany these communication problems.

Speech Disorders   Such disorders include articulation errors, stuttering, and other problems in the production of correct speech sounds. In some cases, especially with the cerebral palsied, correct articulation is a physical impossibility.

Planning for Intervention

Schiefelbusch (1978) listed six generally accepted guidelines for planning a language training program:

1. An essential outcome of language intervention training should be functional communication.
2. Low functioning children learn language best in a context in which *simple, stable,* and *useful* features are taught.
3. A combined system of language (both nonspeech and speech) may facilitate acquisition for many multiply handicapped children.
4. Early language intervention is preferred to all other time-related strategies.
5. For most children a natural environment provides the greatest range of functional language stimulation.
6. Home-based programs monitored and taught by parents often show the greatest gains and the most lasting effects. (p. 15)

Most of the guidelines listed by Schiefelbusch are relevant to planning any language development program. An appropriately designed and applied language program can enrich the life of the severely handicapped individual, whatever his or her age. A brief review of the program planning procedures described in Chapter 2 may be helpful at this point. There are five basic steps in the planning of any program: 1) assessment, 2) program development, 3) program implementation, 4) evaluation, and 5) generalization. The initial assessment or evaluation identifies the individual's current level of functioning, and provides a foundation for further planning. Next, the program is designed. Utilizing the evaluation information, a sequential series of units and behavioral objectives is developed, or a specific program is selected for use. Program implementation includes the selection and use of specific stimuli that are reinforcing to the individual and are available for natural reinforcement in his environment. Techniques for behavior management may need to be provided. Program evaluation will include both short-term probes and evaluation at specified longer intervals to determine the effectiveness of the instructional strategies and the progress of the individual, and allow for revision of the program when necessary. The last aspect of the language training program may be the most important. This involves the generalization of training stimuli to use in other contexts. Such generalization ensures that the use of language has been integrated in the learner's behavior. The following sections of this chapter explain these five steps in greater detail.

THE LANGUAGE PROGRAM

Assessment

Both language assessment and program development are most effective when carried out by a multidisciplinary team. Prior to any language assessment, it must be determined whether the learner's vision, hearing, and speech mechanisms are adequate or in need of compensation. Formal language assessment and diagnosis are best handled by a speech and language pathologist, although teachers play an important role in the informal assessment of the student's functional level. In addition to initial data collection, continuous informal assessment and periodic formal probes provide progress data and criteria for movement to the next level.

In assessing language for an intervention program, it is most helpful both to look at what the individual can presently do and to estimate what he will need to be able to do in the future. The person's age and cognitive level can give information about both. The prognosis for developing adequate language for a child under the age of 5 is much better than for a person 20 years of age.

Formal Assessment Tools   Formal tests that measure various elements of language acquisition may be appropriate for some members of the severely/multiply handicapped population. Selection of any test should be on the basis of determined *need* for the information and the planned *use* of the test results. There are a number of assessment tools available to the speech/language pathologist or the special educator who has experience in their administration and in interpretation of the results. A listing of the more commonly used tests follows, grouped according to the language-related area being tested:

Language Processing
> *Boehm Test of Basic Concepts* (Boehm, 1970) — Measures abstract concepts occurring frequently in preschool and primary level curricula.
>
> *Northwestern Syntax Screening Test* (Lee, 1969) — Individually administered; screening instrument to discover children with possible problems in areas of expressive or receptive morphology or syntax.
>
> *Peabody Picture Vocabulary Test-Revised* (Dunn, 1980) — Individually administered, norm-referenced measure of receptive (hearing) vocabulary; shows extent of vocabulary acquisition.
>
> *Test for Auditory Comprehension of Language* (Carrow, 1973) — Individually administered; measures child's auditory comprehension abilities and determines specific content areas of language difficulty.

Perception
> *Auditory Discrimination Test* (Wepman, 1958) — Individually administered, norm-referenced; measures auditory discrimination abilities of children 5- to 8-years-old.
>
> *Illinois Test of Psycholinguistic Abilities (Visual Closure Subtest)* (Kirk, McCarthy, & Kirk, 1968) — Individually administered, norm-referenced; designed to measure child's ability to understand, process, and produce language, both verbal and nonverbal. In the *Visual Closure Subtest*, the child is to recognize familiar objects when only part of the object is seen.

Memory
> *Illinois Test of Psycholinguistic Abilities (Visual Sequential Memory)* — A sequence of abstract designs is shown for 5 seconds; the child is then to use chips, each containing one design, to reproduce the sequence.

Information on available tests, their use and appropriateness can be secured from the speech therapist serving one's school system, or from local speech and hearing centers. The reader is also referred to Carrow (1972), who categorized various instruments of speech and language assessment in regard to particular functions measured and responses required by the task. Appropriate uses for the tests, their levels of difficulty, and cautions for their use were provided by the author. The difficulty of assessing communication problems in any area and for any population was emphasized by Carrow, who stated ". . . fully appropriate and accurate tools for measuring the specific functions which must be considered in speech and language assessment have not yet been developed; most of the existing tests are too global" (p. 85). The *appropriate* assessment of speech and language problems required for development of an *appropriate* educational/habilitation program will require more than routine application of a screening test.

Informal Assessment   Specific areas to be assessed are comprehension, production, and use of language. In each area we will use both formal and informal assessment methods. We can first look at the student's level of acquisition of words, semantic relations and grammatical morphemes. We then need to evaluate his pattern of language use. Is it restricted in terms of the variety of words or types of sentence constructions? Does he use language spontaneously in appropriate settings? Is the language he uses meaningful or is it mainly jargon or echolalia (parrot-like repeating of what is said by others)?

There are two main ways to evaluate the learner's production of language. The first is through elicited language. We can ask questions ("What's this?"), show him pictures and ask him about them ("What boy doing?"), or ask that he repeat words or sentences. The reason that we use a shortened form to ask our question ("What boy doing?"), as opposed to a fully grammatically correct sentence ("Tell me what you think the boy is doing"), is that we want to use sentences only a word or two longer than those which the student is using. Use of this "telegraphic language" aids in student comprehension of our meaning. It is also important to use telegraphic speech when responding to the learner's initial utterances. This will increase his attention, thus maximizing his opportunity for learning (Miller and Yoder, 1972).

The second way to evaluate production is to study the learner's spontaneous language in the natural setting. We record a sample of the language he uses, writing down the context in which each utterance is spoken. This sample is analyzed for communication intent, syntactic and semantic categories, vocabulary, and the mean length of utterance (MLU; the average length of a child's sentences).

With this latter method, you get a better estimate of the student's actual use of language; with the elicited method, you may get a more complete assessment. However, the accuracy of information obtained in the elicited situation also depends on other skills the learner has: being able to sit still, follow directions, etc. If the amount of time available for assessment is adequate, it is best to use both methods together. If we discover through elicitation that a student knows some forms that he is not using, this can have implications for the training program.

We also want to assess the learner's comprehension of language. In addition to the formal tests which may be used by the speech pathologist, informal assessment of comprehension can take place in the classroom every day. When you ask a child to point to the blue block, you determine whether he can follow directions, recognize the color blue, *and* comprehend your language. The teacher (or other person) who has worked with a child for some time will be familiar both with the student's receptive vocabulary (the words he understands) and with the form communication with him must take.

Informal assessment of the learner's use of language may be carried out either by observing him in a natural setting or by arranging a particular social context. Does he use language to interact with peers or caregivers? To request that others meet his needs? To follow directions? How does he utilize gestures to aid in communication?

In addition to language assessment, it is important to do a behavioral assessment. Does the learner attend and have adequate eye contact for initiation of a training program? How long can he work on a task? Does he have adequate motor imitation and vocalization to be able to proceed with verbal imitation? Does he have an awareness of the interactive nature of language and its usefulness, and therefore have the motivation to learn? All these are prerequisite to our teaching the person to talk.

We must also investigate the reinforcements most meaningful to the learner, seeking those which are most likely to be found in the natural environment. Part of this process is to investigate each setting in which the person spends a large amount of time, asking those working with him about his interests, routines, etc. What are his needs for language? What types of reinforcement are available? How can we set up the language intervention program so that it is most compatible with these other settings, thus increasing the chance for generalization to occur? The best route to take is to investigate ways that the program can be implemented in these other settings.

Components of the Language Program

Guidelines of state and federal legislation in regard to responsibilities of the placement committee dictate that the communication specialist assess those clients needing speech and language training and, as a member of the placement team, have the responsibility of writing the communication objectives of the individual education program (IEP) (Stremel-Campbell, 1977). The severity and complexity of the speech and language problems of the multiply handicapped dictate the further involvement of a specialist in the actual training through an interdisciplinary team effort. As emphasized by Nietupski, Scheutz, and Oakwood (1980), language therapy should not be carried out solely by the speech pathologist, nor should it be provided in an isolated physical setting. These authors proposed that language training is most effective when carried out in the person's natural environment throughout the day, in the context of purposeful activities. This requires the cooperation of different professionals and paraprofessionals who work with the person in the various settings. The speech therapist, in addition to working directly with the student, can give other team members suggestions for program development and implementation. Effective language instruction in the context of purposeful activities can be carried out only if there is continued and cooperative interdisciplinary communication.

Designing a language program without the assistance of a communication specialist is not recommended. Prudent selection of a packaged program ensures appropriate scope and sequence for language development and provides suitable teaching activities. Individualization for a specific learner can be done within the parameters of the program.

There are teacher-related considerations for the choice of a language program: How does the program under consideration relate to the instructor's philosophy about the nature of children and their learning? Does the instructor look at learning as the changing of specific behaviors or as an interrelated part of the student's movement through developmental stages? Philosophical orientation and preferred style of teaching will have a strong influence on the type of program a teacher selects and whether he or she will be comfortable with the selection.

It is therefore important that the teacher have a clear understanding of the theoretical backgrounds of the programs under consideration. He or she should also be familiar with the various approaches to language learning so as to be able to choose those which will have optimum effect on the student's learning. The teacher must have goals for the student clearly in mind in making program selection. The student's needs should take priority over personal preferences.

Whatever type of intervention program is selected, determination of the person's program entry level is the first step. Most packaged programs include a means of assessing for this entry level and for the presence of prerequisite skills. Once the entry level is established, the target behaviors (i.e., words or structures to be trained) are decided upon. Decisions to be made at this point include selection of training procedures and materials, methods of reinforcement, and forms of data collection. Several widely used programs are described later in this chapter as examples of different approaches to language training.

Selecting an Initial Lexicon for Training   A crucial step in any training program, whether for the very young or the adult, is the selection of the words to be taught (i.e., the *lexicon* or vocabulary). There are many suggestions in the literature available as to what words, or types of words, to teach first. Schiefelbusch (1978) stated that the selection should be based on the person's probable need to use a word. Words should be chosen that are reinforcing to the individual and available in the various settings of the person's life. Most authors recommend that one start with labels for objects. When the student can label a certain number of nouns, verbs are introduced. Holland (1975) emphasized that the core lexicon should reflect the child's "here-and-now" frame of reference. An example of a developmental core lexicon for a young child, together with the rationale for each word choice, is presented in Table 1. No preferential rank order is implied by the listing.

Table 1.   A core lexicon for Susie

1. *Me* (or *I* initially as interchangeable equivalents). This word was chosen for frequency of usage in early normal language, and because it is essential if one is ever to learn to include oneself in verbal communication.

2. *You*. This word was chosen because it greatly simplifies teaching *me* as it contrasts with it. It is also essential for verbal self-other differentiation.

3. *Child's own name*. This was chosen because it is essential for self-esteem. (In this case, she's Susie.)

4-6. *The names of "significant others" in a given child's life*. The arbitrary number was set at three in order to illustrate that there is at least one more than the obvious candidates, Mommy and Daddy. Perhaps it's the family dog, or a brother or sister. This is obviously an expandable lexical category. "Significant others" can be significant for either high-positive or high-negative affect reasons, of course. "Significant others" were chosen for relevance to a child's life. (Here consider Mommy, Daddy, and Fido, the family dog.)

7. *Kiss*. This word was chosen as an active verb closest to describing a basic emotional condition (love) and because, in this lexicon at least, it is an active affective verb. It relates to the organicity context.

8. *Hate*. The rationale for *kiss* applies here.

9. *Gimme (wanna)*. This word was chosen for several reasons: it relates to a basic or perceived deprivational condition; its use brings a natural environmental contingency into play; it is an active verb; and it is potentially organic.

10. *Scared*. This word was chosen for organicity. It is also a potential modifying word.

11. *Wash*. Water play provides an excellent therapeutic environment. Children's early language includes comment on recurring activities. *Wash* is a verb with recurrent possibilities; hence, its choice here.

12. *More*. This word was chosen for its frequency of occurrence in normal-child lexicons and for its recurrent possibilities.

13. *Go*. This word was chosen because it represents a typical child activity and because it is an action verb.

14. *No*. This word was chosen because of its role in stating nonexistence, rejection, and denial. In communication, it functions as a major step in using language to send and receive information.

15. *Yes*. The communication role as outlined for *no* applies here as well. *Yes* is the major exception to the combining rule previously identified.

Reprinted by permission from A. Holland, "Language Therapy for Children: Some Thoughts on Context and Content." In *Journal of Speech and Hearing Disorders*, 1975, *40*, pp. 521–522.

Table 1. A core lexicon for Susie (Continued)

16. *The name of a favorite food.* a favorite food name has natural contingency possibilities. It was also chosen for its tangibility. (Here consider *Fruitloops.*)
17. *The name of a least favorite food.* The same rationale as for Number 16 applies here. (Here consider *pickles*).
18. *A very angry word.* This word was chosen without regard to its combinational possibilities. While it does indeed combine, if carefully chosen, this is quite secondary to its inclusion here. Language deficiency is a profoundly frustrating problem to its owner. It is crucial to be able to express some of the frustration verbally. The ideal choice is the strongest angry word a child's parents can be counseled to tolerate. (Here consider [*expletive deleted*]).
19. *Allgone.* This word was chosen for its symbolic play possibilities, for its object-constancy usage, and for its use with other words in signaling nonexistence verbally.
20. *The name of a loved activity.* This word should be, preferably, an active word such as *throw* rather than a passive word such as *TV*. It was chosen for its relevance to the child's life.
21. *Up.* This word was chosen to represent activity and positionality, even perhaps simultaneously. It is a simple word to use in action-talking activities.
22. *Down.* The rationale replicates the rationale for *up.*
23. *There.* This word was chosen for its high frequency of occurrence in young children's speech and its locative role in two-word grammars.
24. *That.* This word was chosen for frequency of occurrence and for usefulness in combining.
25. *Hi.* When spoken to, most people respond. This word was chosen to assure verbal interaction and to teach the child that he can be noticed verbally.
26. *My (mine).* This word was chosen for early introduction of possession.
27. *Your.* The same rationale as for *my* applies here. Note that both also strengthen self-other differentiation.

The final words in this lexicon are possibly more representative of clinically appropriate language environments than of core lexical words. They grew out of linguistic combination possibilities primarily, and clinical good sense secondarily. In short, these words represent classes of traditional clinical activities and clinical accoutrements and, as lexical terms, are even less sacrosanct than those already listed. They are:

28-29. *Big* and *little.* These words are here for combinational, perceptual, conceptual, and cognitive reasons.
30-32. *Ball, block,* and *car.* Ball playing and building big blocks and car going are excellent big-motor activities for clinical language use. Thus it seems natural to teach their names here.
33. *Beads.* In various sizes and shapes, beads are clinically useful for teaching size differentiation and linguistic recurrence. It again seems natural to teach their name.
34. *Doll or stuffed cuddly toy.* Who could be a clinician without at least one of them? Might as well teach their names. (Here consider *Dolly*).
35. *Clinician's name.* This name is included here to ensure active role in therapy. (In this case consider *Audrey*).

Bloom and Lahey (1976) offer further guidelines for selection of a lexicon. Their suggestions may be summarized as follows:

1. Select words that can be acted out or pointed to.
2. Select words that can be illustrated in a variety of contexts.
3. Select verbs and adjectives which have general functions, such as "give" or "want."
4. Use child's name rather than "I" or "me" at the single-word stage.
5. Avoid affirmative words, colors and opposites, and words that apply to internal states at the single-word stage.

It cannot be emphasized too strongly that the lexicon must include words to further the independence of the individual. Often the words taught to an individual are chosen solely to make service provision easier for attendants, teachers and parents. Failure to include environment-controlling language in the lexicon can only reinforce the "outer-directed-ness" described by researchers as characteristic of the mentally retarded, especially the institutionalized.

Teaching the Lexicon in Appropriate Context   Once the learner can imitate the trainer, it is important to provide contexts meaningful to him in which to teach each word. Such contexts may occur naturally but not often enough to ensure that the desired learning takes place. Provision of the appropriate situation is included in the case study. Examples of training the learner to say a word in the appropriate context are provided in Table 2.

Generalization   A most important part of any program is the plan for generalization. Generalization has traditionally been a problem for trainers of the severely handicapped, and it is particularly difficult to achieve with language training programs. "It appears to be easier to *establish* a rudimentary language repertoire in language-deficient children than it is to teach *spontaneous use* of the skills in nontraining situations" (Guess, Keogh, & Sailor, 1978, p. 375). Much too frequently, language learning is an isolated experience, and no effort is made to provide the learner with opportunities to use the new skills in other settings; the language learned may not even be useful in those settings.

There are two types of generalization a teacher must plan for. *Stimulus* generalization refers to a language skill that is to be used in a non-training situation with other similar stimuli, such as a response made to the parent at home. *Response* generalization, or differentation, refers to a similar language behavior that will be used in the same setting. For example, if the learner correctly pluralized a new noun after being trained on one set of nouns, this would indicate that the learner had internalized the rule (i.e., integrated this rule into his or her system of rules) and could respond similarly with members of the same response class. Since using language spontaneously depends on the learner's understanding of

Table 2. Provision of appropriate context

Function of word	Present context	Verbal stimulus	Imitative prompt (to be faded)*	Desired response
Naming	Point to truck	"What's this?"	"Say 'truck.' "	"Truck"
Rejection	Present noxious stimulus (cold greens)	"Have some greens."	"Say 'no.' "	"No"
Recurrance	Give potato chip, keeping more in sight	"Want another one?"	"Say 'more.' "	"More"
Request	Hold up milk	"Want some?"	"Say 'milk.' "	"Milk"
Noticing	Person will enter room and wave	"Here's Bill!"	"Say 'hi.' "	"Hi"
Locative	Place ball in truck	"Where ball?"	"Say 'truck.' "	"Truck"

*Fade the directive "Say" first; fade the entire prompt as soon as possible.

the usefulness of language and on his or her learning rules, this is very important. "The efficiency of the intervention process itself must be judged by how well it teaches generalized language use" (Guess et al., 1978, p. 376).

The more language a person learns, the more opportunities there will be for him or her to generalize. The environment must provide opportunities for the person to use language in order for generalization to occur. Training must focus on the natural environment. Stokes and Baer (1977), in their review of the technology of generalization, described situations in which it is more likely to occur. When training takes place across different settings, with different trainers, the person is more likely to generalize. A teacher can also transfer behavioral control to natural contingencies in the environment. Especially in the institutional setting, the natural environment may have to be rearranged to accommodate the person's new learning, or the learner may be taught to request reinforcement ("Look what I did.") Another way to teach a rule such as agent and action is to train many examples of it utilizing various nouns and verbs in that form until the learner generalizes. The training situation is usually structured carefully with standardized stimulus and response, but Stokes and Baer described lessons taught under looser, more variable conditions as contributing to wider generalization. Finally, generalization may depend on how similar the training and natural settings are and whether there are similar contingencies in both. If the trainer can eventually make the reinforcement similar to that found in other settings (i.e., intermittent social reinforcement) the behavior will be better maintained.

An example of initial planning for program implementation follows. This plan for Karen, a 3-year-old language-delayed child, describes the language therapist's interaction with the child in the isolated training setting of the therapy room. It therefore represents only one aspect of the total training program, which should be carried out in various settings.

Language Program for Karen

Karen is at the prelinguistic stage of development, with a questionable understanding of the usefulness of communication. She also seems to have a limited repertoire of play behaviors. The general goal is to train a core vocabulary of 8 to 10 words initially, with training beginning on four prerequisite subgoals. We will be seeing Karen in a clinical setting five days per week for 50 minutes per session. The play therapy room will initially contain many different toys, which will be decreased once training on the core vocabulary begins. Each session will be videotaped to facilitate data collection on behaviors being monitored. A multiple baseline paradigm will be utilized to determine the effectiveness of the clinician. Data will be collected on all goals from the start. The first two goals will be trained simultaneously. When both goals have reached criterion, training will commence on Goal 3. When criterion is reached on Goal 3, the following list of core vocabulary words will be reevaluated. They are listed now to provide a framework for the trainer's verbal behavior in the training setting.

Lexical Item	Rationale
"Karen"	She evidenced considerable interest in looking at herself in mirror.
Preferred food(s)	
Preferred toy(s)	Naming, in context of their being used.
Preferred activities and actions	
"More"	She uses some vocalization to express this concept at home.
"Look"	Useful indicator that can be used with mirror.
"Bye-bye"	Disappearance of people and things is a familiar occurrence.
"Mama"	Her mother is a familiar, important person.

Goals	Rationale	Procedures
1. Karen will initiate eye contact with the trainer 5 times per session for 3 consecutive days.	To establish an interactive relationship with trainer helpful in subsequent goals.	A. Reinforcement of eye contact, however brief, with a smile and a nod. Modelling of the behavior by seeking Karen's attention. B. Verbal prompt ("Karen, look at me"), Physical prompt, if necessary, or edible reinforcer, held near eye if necessary.
2. Karen will initiate play with a toy 5 times per session for 3 consecutive sessions.	To provide action setting for trainer's comments. To identify potential words for initial vocabulary. To stimulate symbolic play.	A. Imitating of Karen's behavior, using single words to comment about anything Karen shows interest in. B. Shaping successive approximations by: 1. Reinforcing looking at toy 2. Reinforcing touching toy

1. Karen will evidence use of proto-declarative and/or protoimperative statements 5 times per session for 3 consecutive sessions.

To establish her understanding of the interactive nature of communication and its usefulness to her.

3. Reinforcing engaging in activity with toy for longer than 10 seconds

A. Making favorite toys (identified in Goal 2) visible but unavailable without assistance from trainer. Trainer will:

1. Reinforce any signal from Karen by providing assistance, comment or attention.

2. Delay response until Karen actually establishes eye contact.

3. Delay response until Karen points or moves in trainer's direction.

4. Delay response until Karen uses an object or a vocalization to obtain the trainer's attention.

B. Shaping behavior as above, with more rigid training situation: Child and trainer sit at table with desirable items out of reach. If child does not make movement or vocalization toward item, trainer helps model motor behavior by reinforcing successive approximations of target behavior.

Data Collection

Behavior:	Session Date:							
Eye Contact								
Play with Toy								
Protodeclaratives Protoimperatives								
Words: 1.								
2.								
3.								
4.								
5.								
6.								
7.								
8.								
9.								
10.								

Data represent frequency of behavior
Ø indicates criterion

ORAL LANGUAGE TRAINING

Training Prerequisite Skills.

Many of the severely and profoundly handicapped who lack language skills also lack the prerequisites for language learning. Although most of the better-known language programs list immediate prerequisite skills for each unit or sequential level, few provide procedures for training these skills. Even fewer have been designed for use with very low-functioning individuals.

One program that does deal with prelanguage skills, developed by Van Dijk (1965) to meet prelanguage programming needs of deaf and blind children, begins with development of awareness of the self and nonself, the realization by the child that he or she is separate from the environment. Sternberg, Battle, and Hill (1980) examined the Van Dijk procedures in regard to their applicability to other severely and profoundly handicapped and described the approach as needed and useful for the population. The program, widely used in the Netherlands, is little known in the United States but, as described by Sternberg et al., seems worthy of investigation.

Bricker and Dennison (1978) also addressed the need for acquisition of prerequisite sensorimotor skills, describing a training program for such skill development. These authors stated that the target audience for their presentation of the program was "any professional, paraprofessional, parent, or student who is involved in the direct application of a language program to the developmentally young" (p. 157). The "developmentally young" were defined as "young children who are significantly delayed in acquiring early forms of behavior necessary for the acquisition of language and older severely/profoundly handicapped children who have multiple problems that hinder their acquisition of necessary sensorimotor prerequisites for language" (p. 157).

The four major objectives of the program were defined by Bricker and Dennison as follows:

1. On-task behavior
   Definition: Child can consistently focus attention on selected tasks for a reasonable, predetermined time period.
2. Imitation
   Definition: Child can reproduce vocal sounds and gestures produced by a model.
3. Discriminative use of objects
   Definition: Child can carry out activities with objects generally considered relevant to the characteristics of an object (e.g., pound with a hammer, eat with a spoon).
4. Word recognition
   Definition: Child can associate meaningful auditory signals with appropriate events. (p. 162)

Acquisition of each of these behaviors is prerequisite to training on formal linguistic skills. Specific procedures for training each of the steps in the sequence of acquisition are described by Bricker and Dennison with such clarity that they can be easily implemented. We recommend that each member of the target audience become familiar with this program.

Development of Formal Linguistic Comprehension and Production Skills

Programs appropriate for use after prerequisite skills have been acquired include those developed by Guess, Sailor, Keogh, and Baer (1976), Bricker, Dennison, and Bricker (1976), Kent (1974), and Miller and Yoder (1974).

The Guess et al. program, like that of Bricker et al., has sufficient detail for use by a trainer who has little experience in designing, adapting, or applying a language program. Changes necessary for adaptation to special handicapping conditions are easily introduced. Inclusion of spe-cific planning for generalization makes this program especially desirable.

Control of the environment by language is the key concept of this program, which is designed to teach expressive language, in contrast to the normal sequence of language acquisition that dictates that receptive language should come first. The authors argue that receptive language is the means by which the person is controlled by the environment; there-fore, teaching expressive language will give the person a means by which he or she can achieve some personal control of others. The program is designed to establish the elements of language that the learner finds most useful for interaction outside the teaching situation.

There are prerequisite skills that must be evaluated prior to initiating this program. Necessary sensory and motor abilities include hearing at a conversational level (with or without a hearing aid), the ability to identify objects and actions visually, and an adequate physiological speech mechanism. The program could probably be adapted to communication boards or signing if these prerequisites are absent. Another prequisite is verbal imitation: the ability to hear, discriminate sounds, and reproduce the sounds heard. Operant conditioning has traditionally been used to train verbal imitation, but a possible alternative is the method described by Bricker et al. (1976) in which spontaneously occurring verbalizations are reinforced by the trainer.

Also suggested as a helpful technique for training verbal imitation is the use of functional responses. If a response produces an immediate nat-ural consequence for the learner, such as saying "juice" and getting some, then the rate of acquisition will be higher. The natural consequence must be potentially reinforcing (something the learner often desires) and spe-cific to the response (the learner gets juice when he or she says "juice" and a ball when he or she says "ball"). Finally, the response should be natural to the learner's interaction with the environment. If the learner can get juice upon saying "juice" in places other than the training situation, then the usefulness of the learner's utterance is a motivation for further learning.

The Language Acquisition Program (Kent, 1974) was designed pri-marily for severely retarded children with normal hearing and vision, but may be adapted for the multiply impaired. Directions for its adaptation to use with sign language and total communication programs are included. This strictly operant program is based on reinforcement theory and programmed instruction.

The program includes preverbal, verbal-receptive and verbal-expressive sections. The preverbal section includes attending and motor imitation phases, thus providing these important prerequisites to the actual teaching of language. Unlike the Guess et al. program discussed above, the Language Acquisition Program teaches receptive language before expressive. The program is very well organized, and provides a good system of record keeping. A major shortcoming is that it provides no training for generalization. It seems possible that a learner could spend much time in the program without becoming aware of the usefulness of language.

The Syntax Teaching Program (STP) was designed by Miller and Yoder (1972). The authors give the following description of the program:

1. The child for whom this program is designed is not developing the language code of the mainstream of the linguistic community at a rate commensurate with his age;
2. The child comprehends a number of referent and relational terms and may be using a limited number of these in his speech;
3. The child can appropriately answer a *yes*-or-*no* question and has limited understanding of *wh* questions;
4. The clinician's concern is to teach the child the use (oral/verbal) of the terms he comprehends, following a developmental hierarchy:
   a. single words,
   b. syntactic constructions,
   c. expanded syntactic constructions;
5. The teaching environment is structured to deal with those experiences which aid the child to learn and talk about his most relevant needs and interests;
6. The materials within the teaching environment are those which the child can handle, manipulate, and involve himself with personally;
7. The child has been formally evaluated and a complete baseline of language functioning behavior is available in the following areas:
   a. comprehension of single referents,
   b. comprehension of relational terms,
   c. comprehension of simple commands,
   d. comprehension of *yes-no* and *wh* questions,
   e. use of gestures,
   f. use of verbals;
8. All words initially selected for use in the program will be taken from the child's comprehension repertoire; new words may be taught on a selected individual basis but only through the use of expansion and modeling techniques discussed herein. (pp. 199–200)

The technique of expansion involves taking a word spoken by the learner and adding to it. For example, if the child says "Ball!," the adult could say "Ball roll" or "Your ball" or whatever the adult interprets as being the child's semantic intent. The learner often tries to imitate the expansion, thus accelerating or expanding grammatical development. Modeling is introduced when the child has begun using two-word combinations. Models are well-formed sentences that expand on the child's previous utterance but do not contain the content words of that utterance. The child might say "Bobby bath"; a modeled response is "Feel clean" or "Wash," thus providing additional linguistic information to the child.

Miller and Yoder also believe that adults interacting with the child should reduce their syntax to telegraphic speech. The use of telegraphic speech, which presents the content words to the child in phrases or two-word combinations, simplifies the task of linguistic decoding. More fully grammatical sentences will be used as the child develops syntactically.

A final important principle in the Miller and Yoder program is that children are more likely to talk about what they are interested in and what they are doing. The adult should talk to the child (using telegraphic speech, expansion, and modeling) about what is happening at the moment. That is when the child is most likely to be paying attention to the meaning of what is said.

Table 3, a sequence from the Syntax Teaching Program (STP) illustrates a child's progress through various stages of the program.

Table 3.   Example of an STP sequence.

Target sentence: *Jon is sitting on the chair.*

1. Teacher:	*Sitting* (while going through the act of sitting)	Single-word stimulus
Child:	*Sitting**	Imitated response
Teacher:	*Jon sitting.*	Simple expansion
2. Teacher:	*What is Jon doing? Sitting.*	*wh* question stimulus and stimulus word
Child:	*Sitting**	Imitated single-word response
Teacher:	*Yes. Jon is sitting.*	Longer expansion
3. Teacher:	*What is Jon doing?*	*wh* question without stimulus word
Child:	*Sitting. **	Desired nonimitated response
Teacher:	*Very good, Jon is sitting on the chair.*	Complex expansion
4. Teacher:	*Is Jon walking?*	Question for comprehension
Child:	*No. **	Desired negative response
Teacher:	*No, Jon is sitting on the chair.*	Imitated response *no* and repeated target sentence
5. Teacher:	*Where is Jon sitting?*	Question for expanded response
Child:	*Sitting.*	Incorrect single-word response

*Indicates consumable reinforcement.

Reprinted by permission from J. F. Miller and D. E. Yoder "A Syntax Teaching Program." In J. E. McLean, D. E. Yoder, and R. L. Schiefelbusch (Eds.), *Language Intervention with the Retarded: Developing Strategies.* Baltimore: University Park Press, 1972.

Table 3.   Example of an STP sequence. (Continued)

Target sentence: *Jon is sitting on the chair.*

	Teacher:	*Sitting chair.*	Desired response as stimulus
	Child:	*Sitting chair.**	Imitated two-word response
6.	Teacher:	*It's a big chair.*	Modeled stimulus
	Child:	(Reinforced for any response related to *Chair* or *Sitting*.)	
7.	Teacher:	*Where is Jon sitting?*	Question for expanded response
	Child:	*Sitting chair.**	Correct two-word response
	Teacher:	*Good, sitting on the chair.*	Complex expansion
	Child:	*Sitting on chair** or *on the chair.**	Imitated or spontaneous three-word response
8.	Teacher:	*Who is sitting on the chair?*	Question for comprehension
	Child:	*Jon.*	Correct response
	Teacher:	*Yes, Jon is sitting on the chair.*	Complex expansion
	Child:	*Jon sitting on chair.**	Expanded four-word response

9. The clinician continues to expand the child's responses to questions and picture stimuli until the desired phrases are uttered by the child.

	Teacher:	*What is happening in the picture?*	Question for comprehension
	Child:	*Boy sitting.**	Correct two-word response
	Teacher:	*The boy is sitting on the chair.*	Complex expansion
	Child:	*Boy on chair** or *boy sitting on chair** or *sitting on the chair.**	Three- and four-word responses
10.	Teacher:	*The boy was tired.*	Modeled stimulus
	Child:	(Reinforced for any verbal response which is not a simple imitation.)	

The speech/language clinician and any other communication trainers should know the rationale that underlies the selected training program. The training personnel should also be aware of research that provides successful techniques or modifications of procedures related to the selected language training program.

Because the severely and multiply handicapped student population has extraordinary needs uniquely compounded by the restrictions the environment imposes, language trainers must place added emphasis on the training instruments. The speech and language therapist must be aware of the program limitations and potential and combination with other techniques for adaptation to better meet the unique training needs for the student (Siegel & Spradlin, 1978).

Selection of the appropriate language training program requires more than mere determination of the current developmental status or communication disorder exhibited by the student. Each individual's present and future communication needs and living and working environments must also be considered. This, in combination with the student's age and general abilities or disabilities must be considered when selecting and implementing any language training program.

NONORAL LANGUAGE TRAINING

Thus far, the focus of this discussion has been on the development of oral language. Alternative means of communication also need to be addressed, because this population's diversity calls for equal diversity in individualizing the provision of treatment. In a nondisabled population, it is assumed that oral communication will be the means of expressing ideas. This is a fair assumption for the nondisabled, but what of the student who has no reliable voluntary control over his or her oral mechanism? Does this student do without communication?

> The development of communication skills is crucial for this population, as it is the...child's primary means of interaction and the process through which his educational and communication competence, social adjustment, and vocational potential are measured (Harris-Vanderheiden & Vanderheiden, 1977, p. 232).

A further statement of need for the training of communication skills for the handicapped was made by Hollis, Carrier, and Spradlin (1976), who stated that regardless of what the "handicapping condition may be, in order for teachers to be effective, they must be able to locate or develop at least one functional communication channel" (p. 268). Many severely and multiply handicapped students will develop intelligible speech/communication skills with training (Hagen, Porter, & Brink, 1973). In the area of the severely physically involved, however, there is a significant proportion for whom a prognosis of adequate speech is poor at best. Sayre (1963) noted that many

> ...handicapped children give evidence which suggests that they should be able to learn to talk but after many years of intensive therapy they acquire no oral speech for any practical purpose. These children are left with no adequate communication system with which to function in our society. Therefore it may be more practical to provide the children with some other expressive communication system rather than oral articulated speech (p. 3).

When the prognosis for speech acquisition is limited, prolonged or doubtful, it may be more realistic to initially develop some means of nonspeech communication, such as a communication board, finger spelling, sign language, gestures, mime, reading, or writing. The important point is that the person is communicating, not whether he or she is signing, pointing or speaking. "As long as the communicatively handicapped person is able to transmit information and express ideas, it only matters that the most efficient channel of output is used. The selection of this mode of output is often further limited by a given physical disability" (Wethered, 1976, p. 2).

The two nonspeech techniques that have generally been used with nonspeaking students for the development of communication are sign language and the communication board, which presents a display of the student's vocabulary from which he or she may select the elements to be expressed. Both of these systems permit communication, and in addition often stimulate the development of communication through more conventional channels. The same prerequisite skills apply to the potential signer and communication board user. The primary reason for placement in a communication board program rather than a signing program is the student's physical disability. The greater the student's limitation is, the more artificial or mechanized his or her communication system must become.

The general principles for development of language given in the first portion of this chapter have equal application with the child using either of these two communication systems. Chapman and Miller summarized:

> Children whose language acquisition has been studied showed a number of similarities in the way their language and communication skills develop (Brown, 1973). Similar sequences are found across language (Bowerman, 1973), across cultures (Mitchell-Kernan, 1971), in children learning to sign (Bellugi, 1972), and in developmentally delayed children (Lackner, 1968; Larson, 1974; Coggins, 1973). The rate at which individual children learn to communicate varies, but the ordering of major milestones in syntax, semantics, phonology and pragmatics appears invariant (1980, p. 162).

Criteria for Beginning Use of Nonspeech Programs. Scheuerman, Baumgart, Sipsma, and Brown (1976) suggested general criteria for the initiation of a nonspeech communication program. If the nonspeaking student is beyond an age where verbal language should have developed, and verbal language programming has been unsuccessful, these authors suggest the use of some nonspeech communication system. Chapman and Miller (1977) noted that the "age" referred to above should relate to a cognitive/developmental age; otherwise all retarded students would meet the criterion for a nonspeech system. They indicate, therefore, that a disparity should be between speech language production and a developmental age above the chronological age at which the average student begins to produce the same elements.

A second criterion for usage of a nonspeech communication system was also presented by Chapman and Miller (1977). That criterion is the acquisition of stage VI of sensorimotor development (the child looks at a mentioned object; understands words when their referents are absent). These authors pointed out that although a child may be able to use a non-verbal communication system prior to attaining that level of sensorimotor development, performance will be far superior once he or she reaches stage VI functioning. It was also suggested by Stremel-Campbell, Cantrell, and Halle (1977) that, specific to sign language, a certain attention span was necessary. In addition to attention span, Stremel-Campbell et al. also mention that the child should have sufficient receptive language to follow simple directions, be able to imitate, and have enough motoric control to produce at least a gross approximation of the desired signs. The latter skill, motoric control, is the primary element that separates the signer from the communication board user. The teacher-made electric devices described in Chapter 4 can aid in developing readiness for use of these communication systems.

Sign Language

The past decade has seen a significant increase in the clinical and educational use of manual signs, gestures and mime with autistic, retarded, aphasic, and other individuals with severe communication disorders. Such unaided systems have been found to be effective as a temporary means of communication until such time as oral communication can be established, as the principal means of communication for individuals who are unable to produce oral speech, and in some cases as a facilitator of the development of spoken communication (Lloyd, 1980).

There are a number of manual sign systems. The best known, American Sign Language (ASL or Ameslan), is the language that ranks fourth in use in the United States, after English, Spanish, and Italian (Fristoe & Lloyd, 1977). Several dictionaries and workbooks on ASL are available, including those by Babbini (1974) and Christopher (1976). Several North American systems have been developed from ASL, among them being Seeing Essential English (Anthony & Associates, 1971) and Signed English (Bornstein, Kannapell, Saulnier, Hamilton, & Roy, 1973). These systems all owe their basic vocabulary to ASL but complement it by including missing components and using spoken English word order.

The pros and cons of sign language usage were presented by Stremel-Campbell, Cantrell, and Halle (1977). Sign language provides the user with an unlimited vocabulary that is completely portable and does not interfere with mobility, and "labels" the user only when he or she is signing. Two problems with signing are that the "listening" audience is limited to those persons who know the signed system, and the signer must have a certain level of digital/motor control.

Hamre-Nietupskie, Stoll, Fullerton, Flottum-Ryan, and Brown (1977) discussed the rationale for starting sign language training with motorically simple signs and then progressing to signs requiring more complex motor movements. These authors have further suggested a pairing of the spoken word and presentation of the sign with the actual referent. The child is in essence being trained to understand both the signed and the spoken word. It is also recommended that the system be used in a variety of settings, using varied stimuli, with different trainers to enhance the probability of generalization of the signed behavior. Holland (1975) stressed the need for illustrating the semantics of the utterance being signed. She noted that the meaning should be made clear to the child as he or she produces the utterance in the language training setting. For example, when teaching the word "drink," a drink should be given the child. Although Holland's work was done in reference to verbal language development it should be applicable to nonverbal forms of language, as the underlying structures are similar. This was also the contention of Guess, Sailor, and Baer (1978) when they discussed the application of their language curriculum to the training procedures for communication board users. Chapman and Miller (1980), as previously stated, stress the universal nature of language development across all mankind. A synthesis of the above compatible considerations, procedures, and technology could be utilized in constructing a viable program for instructing a nonspeaking child in the initial stages of sign language or in the use of other communication aids.

Communication Boards

Problems that interfere with the use of sign language, such as lack of motor/digit coordination, can be solved:

> In the past several years professional therapeutic objectives have shifted from the development of speech as the primary communication mode to the development of nonspeech communication for the severely physically handicapped whose neuromuscular dysfunction prevents functional speech. Numerous communication aids and techniques for indicating and transmitting messages are rapidly becoming available. (Elder & Bergman, 1978, p. 107)

The communication board provides physically disabled students whose speech is unintelligible or slow in development with the ability to express their ideas and needs to others, and actively participate in conversation. Beyond the obvious benefits of increased stimulation from the environment and the ability to interact more efficiently with other people, the communication board user may concurrently improve oral speech abilities (McDonald & Schultz, 1973). Communication device users generally experience reduced tension with the lessened frustration of aided communication (McDonald & Schultz, 1973); this reduction is frequently seen to facilitate oral speech development. The reduced tension also makes the child easier to care for physically. In combination with a more efficient means of communication, requiring less guessing, the reduced effort in child care brings attitude changes in the people caring for them. "The majority (begin) to view the children as more intelligent and more as persons than they (have) previously" (Hagen, Porter, & Brink, 1973, p. 453). This reaction was seen by other researchers who noted that the caregivers spent more time relating to the people using communication boards than they had before use of the communication board was initiated (Feallock, 1958; Goldberg & Fenton, 1960; Vanderheiden, Raitzer, & Kelso, 1974).

Many parents become alarmed at the suggestion of an alternate form of communication for their children. They are concerned because their child would be using a language different from their own. This concern is unfounded because the child is not being deprived of the language mode used by his or her family and world (McDonald & Schultz, 1973; Vicker, 1974). In fact, the communication system will provide the child with the closest possible approximation to the language of society and family. This approximation is more efficient than the communication system he or she has been using. The communication device also helps the person learn his or her native language rather than preventing its acquisition. Vicker adds that "...the ability to speak a language is not crucial for development of its understanding" (1974, p. 19). Lenneberg (1971) concluded that acquisition of the organizing principles of language is more important to knowing that language than is the ability to produce oral skills.

Prerequisite Skills   Several prerequisite skills must be present for successful use of the communication board. The child must have a means of pointing; therefore he or she must have voluntary control of the muscles involved in at least one type of pointing response. This response might be developed via response contingent materials described in Chapter 4. He or she must be able to select and visually monitor the response, so eye-hand coordination, visual acuity, and figure-ground discrimination are needed. Attention span and cognitive development need to be sufficient for training and use of the communication system (Miller, 1974). It was noted by McDonald and Schultz (1973) that the evaluation should assess the child's ability to recognize pictures when named, recognize simple printed words, and sound out words. Vicker recommended that the student reach a mental age of 3 years before a communication board is considered (1974). This mental age was selected because Gesell (1940) found it to be the lowest age at which normal children could identify action pictures. Obviously, tests used in assessment of the child must be those that can be administered to nonspeaking subjects. Several such tests were listed earlier in this chapter.

In addition to having a certain level of cognitive development, visual acuity and visual discrimination skill, the child needs adequate motor and neural function to produce a good pointing response. McDonald and Schultz (1973) stressed the importance of having an occupational therapist evaluate the student's neurological development and motoric abilities. Muscle function should be assessed to determine range of motion and the synergistic actions of the muscles required in the proposed pointing responses.

The occupational therapist is the appropriate person to assess the individual's strength, range of motion, and ease of fatigue. The pointing response to be used may be developed by the occupational therapist. It can be enhanced, (strengthened, made more accurate, or more frequently exhibited) through the use of specialized training materials, as discussed elsewhere in the book. The variety of possible pointing responses is limited only by the imagination of the classroom teacher, speech therapist, and occupational therapist. Many disabled students use head sticks; others use mouth sticks, the tip of a finger, a bent knuckle, a dowel or pencil held in their hand, and others even use their feet. The important thing is to find a response that the child can control reliably.

> The child must be able to make some type of pointing response for the communication board to be functional. . . Certain electrical or gadget type modifications may be utilized in cases of catastrophically handicapped individuals (Dixon & Curry, 1965, p. 12).

The student's range of motion, general physical condition, and type of pointing response will affect the size of the vocabulary and the position of frequently used words, and thereby limit the complexity of the child's responses (McDonald & Schultz, 1973; Vicker, 1974) when using a non-commercial/non-electronic communications device. Technology discussed in this chapter provides the user having limited responding capabilities with an almost limitless vocabulary and the access thereto. For instance, one communication system requires only directional eye movement for its implementation.

It is often necessary to back up formal testing with diagnostic training. The child's actual ability to function in training with use of the communication device is more relevant than performance on formalized tests standardized on a nonhandicapped population. This diagnostic training informally assesses the student's present ability, potential capability, ease in learning concepts, and carryover into spontaneous usage (McDonald & Schultz, 1973).

Meeting the Student's Personal and Environmental Needs.   The actual construction of the communication board should be suited to the individual needs of each child. The board should be useful in more than just one situation. The student will need words to refer to all of the places that he or she goes and the things done there. When vocabulary for any one place is excessively large and unused outside of that situation, a separate board may be devised specifically for that place. For example, the vocabulary for school may be full of terms and concepts virtually unused out of the school building.

Vicker (1974) listed several points to consider in construction of the board and development of the vocabulary, including portability, flexibility of use, accuracy of the pointing response, vision, general language level, reading and spelling level, ease of modification (as the child develops), ease of operation, and the ease with which others can understand the message. The board must be portable and yet not limit the child's means of movement. The child needs to be able to communicate at any location, not only when he or she is near a stationary communication board. The ambulatory child might use a notebook or the folder system that McDonald and Schultz suggest to be hung from the child's neck (1973). The student confined to a wheelchair would be able to use a lapboard, or notebook format, neither of which would interfere with the operation of the chair.

A noncommercial, nonelectric (homemade) communication device should be covered with a clear, protective material for maximum protection and visibility. This covering should not prohibit alteration of the vocabulary: removing unused words and adding new ones, and changing word positions as required by the student's changing physical and/or intellectual status. The placement of words or symbols, and their size, will be determined by the student's visual acuity, figure-ground discriminations, the accuracy of the pointing response and the range of motion (McDonald & Schultz, 1973). These authors reported on a boy whose range of motion was confined to one corner of his lapboard; his communication system was therefore placed on a flip chart in that corner. They also suggested that there are certain range of motion restrictions specific to particular modes of indication. For example, people who use a headstick cannot point to symbols positioned near their stomach; such symbols must therefore be placed where they are easily accessible. When extraneous movement makes accurate pointing difficult the teacher/therapist can separate the words with small ridges against which the student may brace his hand (Feallock, 1958).

The Symbol Communication Board   The simplest form of communication system involves pointing to pictures to convey ideas and wants. The picture board is used with children too young to read and with older students who are unable to read or spell. The pictures used can be photographs from the child's home environment or cut out from magazines. These photographs should be of people, places, things, and actions that the student may wish to express. It is important to note that for lower functioning students, the pictures used should closely resemble the object or concept they represent (McDonald & Schultz, 1973). In choosing pictures for individuals having visual perception problems, figure-ground confusion should be reduced whenever possible.

The choice of pictures, symbols, words or alphabet as a medium of display depends upon the child's ability to read, spell, and pair meaning with symbols or pictures. Pictures and symbols are very useful for the non-reading student's communications needs. Symbols are not as descriptive as photographs, but they carry more meaning per unit than do the letters of the alphabet. On both the picture and symbol boards the word depicted appears beneath the symbol or picture. This allows the person unfamiliar with the symbols to communicate with the child. The child is therefore not limited to using the communication system only with those people trained in its use. The words beneath the picture or symbol also help develop the child's sight vocabulary for possible later use of a wordboard (McDonald & Schultz, 1973), which presents words and phrases the child needs for communication. The word board can hold more words in the same space consumed by the pictures or symbols; it is also more efficient as a lexicon.

The symbol systems most commonly used are the pictographic rebuses from the Peabody Rebus Reading Program (Woodcock, Clark, & Davis, 1967, 1969, 1979) and Blissymbolics (Silverman, McNaughton, & Kates, 1978). The Rebus program includes a reference book (glossary) containing over 2,000 words derived from 818 individual rebus symbols. Vicker (1974) suggested that before the Rebus symbols are used, the teacher or therapist should consider the level of abstraction involved in their usage, the similarity of some of the Rebus symbols, and the recognition-retrieval problems involved (1974). Rebus symbols are less abstract than Blissymbolics. Many are relatively complete pictures of their referents. However, these more complex visual images may be confusing for those children with problems in visual perception.

Blissymbolics are a widely used form of symbolic representation. Some of the symbols are pictographic, resembling the objects or concepts for which they stand. Others are abstract, some being ideographic (symbolizing the idea of a thing, but not its actual name), some arbitrary, and some being internationally accepted symbols.

Silverman, McNaughton, and Kates (1978) discussed adaptation of Blissymbol syntax to different ages and populations, including the more severely handicapped, stating, "An immediate need is apparent for a special style of communication for the severely disabled. . . . They require development and refinement of further Blissymbolic sentence forms which can provide effective communication with a minimum number of symbols" (p. 34). These authors explored factors to be considered in adaptation of Blissymbolics to use by the severely and multiply handicapped. These factors are equally applicable to any other communication system. As with any planning for instructional purposes, the teacher must be familiar with the handicapped person, the environment(s) in which he or she will function, the persons with whom he or she will interact, and with the program under consideration. The instructor should know the characteristics, strengths, and weaknesses of any symbol system, as well as the learning characteristics of the student, in order to appropriately match the student and the learning system.

The Lexicon for the Communication Board   Once a mode of representation has been chosen, the words or symbols to be used and their arrangement must be decided upon. The considerations for such vocabulary selection are the same for the nonoral as those for the oral child, which were presented earlier in this chapter. Their importance bears repeating. McDonald and Schultz (1973) suggested the following criteria for selecting the words for the nonspeaking child's initial vocabulary:

1. Frequency of occurrence in the child's environment
2. Availability to the child
3. Reinforcing value of the referent to the child
4. Basic human needs filled by the element

Scheuerman, Baumgart, Sipsma, and Brown (1976) reiterated that initially students should be taught to refer to things which they liked and wanted to obtain. It is imperative that the board be individualized to the communicative needs and interests or the child will not use it. Sayre (1963) commented that

> ...if a most-frequently-spoken word list is not included in teaching, the child's vocabulary will immediately be inadequate in view of the fact that we spend 45% of our time...in listening to the oral communication of other people (p. 4).

Items from any lexicon of most frequently used words should be added to the board as the child has a need for them or becomes developmentally ready to use them. Goldberg and Fenton (1960) made an important point:

> A child should never be presented with a conversation board that has been completed with all sections filled with words or symbols...the teacher and child should start with a blank board and together, over a period of time, develop the unit section by section (p. 4).

The child may use the communication device only temporarily or for the rest of his or her life. In either case, great care should be exercised in its design, construction or selection, and use, because it is the child's sole avenue of expression. The child can express ideas only through the words on the board. The communication device should change as the child's expressive needs change. This artificial language must keep pace with the child's development, just as the nonhandicapped child's language develops with maturation. Dixon and Curry (1965) emphasized an often overlooked point in regard to the maturation of the severely handicapped:

It should be stressed that periodic re-evaluation of the child's abilities at oral speech should be made concomitantly with communication board use. It is this writer's bias that many severely handicapped individuals that we have given up on from the standpoint of oral speech should have another try as young adults (p. 13).

Limitations of the Conventional Communication Board   There are some inherent difficulties that naturally accompany the use of communication boards. Children fail due to unreliable word or symbol recognition, because of inadequate or insuffient teaching, or because of insufficient coordination to perform reliable pointing (Feallock, 1958). Others may prefer to use their limited speech, gestures, or eye movements, which they have always used, feeling no need for further communication. Hagen, Porter, & Brink (1973) concluded that for the communication board to be successful the child must have some intrinsic need to communicate, as well as want to meet some social or physical needs.

Admittedly, the communication process with the board is a slow and laborious one, as the child individually points to each symbol, letter or word to express the meaning. A further limitation is that in order to receive his or her message, an observer must be willing to devote full attention to the pointing process. In addition, the nonspeaking population

includes a significant number whose limbs are weak, incoordinated, or paralysed to such an extent that they cannot write, sign, or use a conventional communication board. Thus, this population of non-vocal physically handicapped individuals are in reality prisoners of their own disabilities, in that they have no readily available avenue of communication (Vanderheiden, Volk, & Geisler, 1974, p. 2).

Electronic Communication Devices

The introduction of electronics into communication board technology has greatly lessened the problems inherent with a limited range of motion. These devices allow the means of indication to be breaking a light beam, producing a sound, or even an eye blink, a muscle contraction, or through respiratory control (Copeland, 1974). Electronic alternatives have also been devised that release the message receiver from constant observation of the pointing responses. Printed readouts and television screens are included in these time-saving introductions to communication board technology.

Electric communication devices have been described by several writers (Harris & Vanderheiden, 1980; Danjuma, 1979, 1980). These devices include the Canon Communicator, which is essentially a calculator-sized electronic typewriter that can be attached to the student's belt or wrist. This portable means of communication would not interfere with the mobility of the ambulatory student. This unit prints out a strip of paper with the student's message on it, thus eliminating the requirement that the "listener" watch while the student points to letters on an alphabet board.

The Autocom (Harris & Vanderheiden, 1980) is a laptray sized electric communication device. Mounted across the arms of the wheelchair, it does not interfere with the operation of the chair. This unit is programmed with words, numbers, and the alphabet. Additional information (words, phrases) may be programmed into the unit. This preprogrammed and user-programmed information is retrieved through movement of a magnet to specified locations on the board surface. This may be done through the use of a head stick, ring, wristlet, or handheld mechanism. The piece of information, once selected, may be displayed on a television screen, in a small window on the device, on an adding machine sized strip of paper, or may feed directly into a computer on teletype for long distance communication. The surface of the Autocom has recently been adapted to provide the student with control of the movement of his or her chair via the same magnet moving procedure used for communication.

The Handivoice (Harris & Vanderheiden, 1980) is a portable communication device that speaks for itself through an electronic voice. By selecting the words or phrases, the student can speak aloud via this type of unit. Words that are not included in the preprogrammed vocabulary can be built by the user on a phoneme-by-phoneme basis of selection.

Zygo Industries produces a scanning communication board (Zygo, 1980) that is portable and provides the user with control over the scanning process through any of several specialized on/off switches. These switches were designed for easy activation with the range of typical residual responding capabilities of the disabled. Pictures, drawings, or words may be attached to an acetate sheet placed on the front of the scanning device. The student then initiates a process wherein small lights in the corner of each of the 200 grids sequentially light up and then shift off. When the light is lit in the square containing the concept that the student wishes to express, he or she stops the scanning process. The acetate sheets may be changed, thereby multiplying the number of elements in the student's vocabulary.

Several training centers across the United States are using computer and Cathode Ray Tube (CRT) displays for training and communication purposes (Danjuma, 1979–1980). Such computerized systems can be controlled via any adaptive on/off switch operable by the student.

In the near future a "talking wheelchair" will be on the market. The prototype of this unit has a small computer built into the back. This computer provides the student with control of a voice synthesizer, so that he or she can speak aloud. The computer has a memory and will therefore store messages for later retrieval. This electronic marvel can be controlled by either a conventional typewriter keyboard or the slightest responding capability that the student can reliably produce.

SUMMARY

The final section of this chapter focuses on the general considerations and decisions necessary in selecting and developing a nonspeech method of communication. Use of communication boards was emphasized because of the many severely/multiply handicapped whose physical involvement precludes the use of sign language. The brief sampling of electronic communication systems indicates the progress made in recent years in providing a means of communication to the most severely physically involved.

The appropriate method of communication and the program for language training will be selected by the communication disorders specialist (speech/language therapist). Information presented in this chapter should enable other personnel working with the student to better understand and manage the selected system. The basic principles of oral language development also apply to the nonspeaking child and training in use of nonoral communication devices. The lexicon (vocabulary) must be chosen to meet the child's specific communicative needs. Everyone in the child's total environment should be familiar with the communication system and encourage its use. It is crucial that these communication skills become generalized to use with all the people the child meets, in all probable environments.

REFERENCES

Anderson, R. M., & Greer, J. G. (Eds.). *Educating the severely and profoundly retarded.* Baltimore: University Park Press, 1976.

Anthony, D. A., & Associates (Eds.) *Seeing Essential English.* Anaheim, Calif.: Educational Services Division, Anaheim Union High School District, 1971.

Babbini, B. E. *Manual communication: Fingerspelling and the language of signs.* Urbana: University of Illinois Press, 1974.

Bates, E. *Language and context: The acquisition of pragmatics.* New York: Academic Press, 1976.

Bloom, L., & Lahey, M. *Language development and language disorders.* New York: Wiley & Sons, 1976.

Boehm, A. E. *Boehm test of basic concepts.* New York: Psychological Corp., 1970.

Bornstein, H., Kannapell, B. M., Saulnier, K. L., Hamilton, L. B., & Roy, H. L. *Signed English series: The basic pre-school signed english dictionary.* Washington, D.C.: Gallaudet College, 1973.

Bricker, D., & Dennison, L. Training prequisites to verbal behavior. In M. E. Snell (Ed.), *Systematic instruction of the moderately and severely handicapped.* Columbus, Oh.: Charles E. Merrill, 1978.

Bricker, D., Dennison, L., & Bricker, W. A. A language intervention program for developmentally young children (no. 1). Miami: *Mailman center for child development Monograph Series, 1976, #1.* Miami: University of Miami.

Brown, R. *A first language: The early stages.* Cambridge: Harvard Press, 1973.

Carrow, E. Assessment of speech and language in children. In J. E. McLean, D. E. Yoder, & R. L. Schiefelbusch (Eds.), *Language intervention with the retarded.* Baltimore: University Park Press, 1972.

Carrow, E. *Test for auditory comprehension of language.* Austin, Texas: Educational Concepts, 1973.

Chapman, R. S., & Miller, J. *Analyzing language and communication in the child.* Paper presented at the Conference on Nonspeech Language Intervention, Gulf State Park, Alabama, March, 1977.

Chapman, R. S., & Miller, J. F. Analyzing language communication in the child. In R. L. Schiefelbush (Ed.), *Nonspeech language and communication: Analysis and intervention.* Baltimore: University Park Press, 1980.

Christopher, D. A. *Manual communication.* Baltimore: University Park Press, 1976.

Copeland K. *Aids for the severely handicapped.* London: Sector Publishing, 1974.

Danjuma, Y. (Ed.). *Communication outlook.* Michigan State University, East Lansing, Michigan, 1979–1980.

Dixon, C., & Curry, B. Some thoughts on the communication board. *Cerebral Palsy Journal,* 1965, *26,* 12–13.

Dunn, L. M. *Peabody picture vocabulary test-R.* Circle Pines, Minnesota: American Guidance Service, 1980.

Elder, P. S., & Bergman, J. S. Visual symbol communication instruction with nonverbal, multiply-handicapped individuals. *Mental Retardation,* 1978, 16, 107–117.

Feallock, B. Communication for the non-verbal individual. *American Journal of Occupational Therapy,* 1958, *12,* 60.

Fristoe, M., & Lloyd, L. L. Manual communication for the retarded and others with severe communication impairment: A resource list. *Mental Retardation,* 1977, *15* (5), 18–21.

Gesell, A., *The first five years of life: A guide to the study of the preschool child.* New York: Harper & Brothers, 1940.

Goldberg, H. R., & Fenton, J. *Aphonic communication for those with cerebral palsy: Guide for development and use of a conversation board.* New York: United Cerebral Palsy of New York State, 1960.

Guess, D., Keogh, W., & Sailor, W. Generalization of speech and language behavior: Measurement and training tactics. In R. L. Schiefelbush (Ed.) *Bases of language intervention.* Baltimore: University Park Press, 1978.

Guess, D., Sailor, W., & Baer, D. M. Children with limited language. In R. L. Schiefelbusch (Ed.), *Language intervention strategies.* Baltimore: University Park Press, 1978.

Guess, D., Sailor, W., Keogh, B., & Baer, D. Language development programs for severely handicapped children. In N. Haring & L. Brown (Eds.), *Teaching the severely handicapped.* New York: Grune & Stratton, 1976.

Hagen, C., Porter, W., & Brink, J. Non-verbal communication: An alternate mode of communication for the child with severe cerebral palsy. *Journal of Speech and Hearing Disorders,* 1973, *38,* 448–455.

Hamre-Nietupskie, S., Stoll, A., Fullerton, P., Flottum-Ryan, M., & Brown, L. Curricular strategies for teaching severely handicapped students. In L. Brown, J. Nietupskie, S. Lyon, S. Hamre-Nietupskie, T. Crowner, & L. Gruenewald (Eds.). *Curricular strategies for teaching functional object use, nonverbal communication and problem solving and mealtime skills to severely handicapped students,* Vol. 7. Madison, Wisc.: University of Wisconsin-Madison and Madison Metropolitan School District, 1977.

Harris D., & Vanderheiden, G. C. Augmentative communication techniques. In R. L. Schiefelbush (Ed.), *Nonspeech language and communication: Analysis and intervention.* Baltimore: University Park Press, 1980.

Harris-Vanderheiden, D. Blissymbols and the mentally retarded. In G. Vanderheiden & K. Grilley (Eds.), *Nonvocal communication techniques and aids for the severely physically handicapped.* Baltimore: University Park Press, 1976.

Harris-Vanderheiden, D., Brown, W. P., Mackenzie, P., Reinen, S., & Scheibel, C. Symbol communication for the mentally handicapped. *Mental Retardation*, 1975, *13*, 34–37.

Harris-Vanderheiden, D., & Vanderheiden, G. Basic considerations in the development of communicative and interactive skills for non-vocal severely handicapped children. In E. Sontag, J. Smith, & N. Certo (Eds.), *Educational programming for the severely and profoundly handicapped.* Reston, Va.: Division on Mental Retardation, Council for Exceptional Children, 1977.

Holland, A. Language therapy for children: Some thoughts on context and content. *Journal of Speech and Hearing Disorders*, 1975, *40*, 514–523.

Hollis, J., Carrier, J., & Spradlin, J. An approach to remediation of communication and learning deficiencies. In L. Lloyd (Ed.), *Communication assessment and intervention strategies.* Baltimore: University Park Press, 1976.

Kent, L. R. *Language acquisition program for the retarded or multiply impaired.* Champaign, Ill.: Research Press, 1974.

Lee, L. *Northwestern syntax screening test.* Evanston, Ill.: Northwestern University Press, 1969.

Lenneberg, E., Understanding language without ability to speak: A case report. In A. Ban Ardon and W. Leopold (Eds.), *Child language: A book of readings.* Englewood Cliffs, N.J.: Prentice-Hall, 1971.

Lloyd, L. L. Unaided nonspeech communication for severely handicapped individuals: An extensive bibliography. *Education and Training of the Mentally Retarded*, 1980, *15* (1), 15–34.

McDonald, E., & Schultz, A. Communication boards for cerebral palsied children. *Journal of Speech and Hearing Disorders*, 1973, *38*, 73–88.

McLean, J. E., Yoder, D. E., & Schiefelbusch, R. L. *Language intervention with the retarded: Developing strategies.* Baltimore: University Park Press, 1972.

Miller, J. (Ed.) *A developmental approach toward assessing communication behavior in children.* Madison, Wisc.: Waisman Center on Mental Retardation and Human Development, University of Wisconsin, 1974.

Miller, J., & McMillen, M. Cognitive development. In J. Miller (Ed.), *A developmental approach toward assessing communication behavior in children.* Madison, Wisc.: Waisman Center on Mental Retardation and Human Development, University of Wisconsin, 1974.

Miller, J. F., & Yoder, D., An otogenetic language teaching strategy for retarded children. In R. L. Schiefelbusch and L. L. Lloyd (Eds.), *Language perspectives: Acquistion, retardation, and intervention.* Baltimore: University Park Press, 1974.

Miller, J. F., & Yoder, D. E. A syntax teaching program. In J. E. McLean, D. E. Yoder, & R. L. Schiefelbusch (Eds.) *Language intervention with the retarded: Developing strategies.* Baltimore: University Park Press, 1972.

Nietupski, J., Scheutz, G., & Ockwood, L. The delivery of communication therapy services to severely handicapped students: A plan for change. *Journal of the Association for the Severely Handicapped* (JASH), 1980, *5*, 13–23.

Sayre, J. Communication for the non-verbal cerebral palsied. *Cerebral Palsy Review*, 1963, *24*.

Scheuerman, N., Baumgart, D., Sipsma, K., & Brown, L., Toward the development of a curriculum for teaching nonverbal communication skills to severely handicapped students: Teaching basic tracking, scanning and selection skills. In

N. Scheuerman, L. Brown, & T. Crowner (Eds.), *Toward an integrated therapy model for teaching motor, tracking, and scanning skills to severely handicapped students*, Vol. 4. Madison, Wi.: Madison Metropolitan School District, 1976.

Schiefelbusch, R. L. (Ed.), *Language intervention strategies*. Baltimore: University Park Press, 1978.

Siegel, G. M., & Spradlin, J. E. Programming for language and communication therapy. In R. L. Schiefelbusch (Ed.) *Language intervention strategies*. Baltimore: University Park Press, 1978.

Silverman, H., McNaughton, S., & Kates, B. *Handbook of Blissymbolics*. Toronto, Ontario, Canada: Blissymbolics Communication Institute, 1978.

Sternberg, L., Battle, C., & Hill, J. Prelanguage communication programming for the severely and profoundly handicapped. *Journal of the Association for the Severely Handicapped*, 1980, *5*, 224–233.

Stokes, T. S., & Baer, D. M. An implicit technology of generalization. *Journal of Applied Behavior Analysis*, 1977, *10*, 349–367.

Stremel-Campbell, K. Communication skills. In N. G. Haring (Ed.), *Developing effective individualized education programs*. Washington, D.C.: Department of HEW, Office of Education, Bureau of Education for the Handicapped, 1977.

Stremel-Campbell, K., Cantrell, D., & Halle, J. Manual signing as a speech initiator for the non-verbal severely handicapped student. In E. Sontag, J. Smith, & N. Certo (Eds.), *Educational programming for the severely and profoundly handicapped*. Reston, Va.: Division on Mental Retardation, Council for Exceptional Children, 1977.

Vanderheiden, G., Raitzer, G., & Kelso, D. A portable non-vocal communications prosthesis for the severely physically handicapped, the Portable Autocom/ Wordmaster. Madison, Wisc.: Trace Research and Development Center for the Severely Communicatively Impaired, University of Wisconsin, 1974.

Vanderheiden, G., Volk, A., & Geisler, C. An alternate interface to computers for the physically handicapped: The Auto-Monitoring Communication Board. Paper presented at the National Computer Conference, 1974.

Van Dijk, J. The first steps of the deaf/blind child towards language. *Proceedings of the conference on the deaf/blind, Refsnes, Denmark*. Boston: Perkins School for the Blind. 1965.

Vicker, B. (Ed.). *Non oral Systems Project 1964/1973*. Iowa City, Iowa: University Hospital School, 1974.

Wepman, J. M. *Auditory discrimination test*. Chicago: Language Research Assn., 1958.

Wethered, C. E. *Hierarchies of operational efficiency preference for interface selection for the physically disabled*. Unpublished master's thesis, Idaho State University, 1976.

Woodcock, R. W., Clark, C. R., & Davies, C. O. *Peabody rebus reading program*. Circle Pines, Minn.: American Guidance Service, 1979.

Zygo. *Zygo 100 Communicator*. Portland, Oregon: Zygo Industries, Inc., 1980.

Chapter 8

Treating Maladaptive Behaviors

Chris E. Wethered, Anne C. Troutman, and Nancy P. Wilder

Imagine that you are observing a class of severely retarded students through a one-way mirror. You see a child biting himself. The teacher walks over to him and shouts, "Stop it!" The child stops immediately and goes back to his task. The teacher pats his shoulder and praises him for good work. As she turns away, the child next to him pulls his hair. The teacher takes the hair puller firmly by the arm and removes her to a small room adjacent to the classroom saying, "Time-out, Sherri, don't pull hair." In a few minutes the teacher returns Sherri to the classroom.

Meanwhile another child is waving his hands in front of his face. An aide is sitting at the table with him. She pays no attention to him as long as he persists in this behavior, but whenever he stops for a few seconds she gives him a small piece of a pretzel.

The teacher has begun working on a language task with three students. One of the students slides off his chair and begins crawling on the floor. To your surprise, the teacher pays no attention to him, but gives each of the others a raisin, saying, "Good staying in your seat."

At the conclusion of the language lesson the teacher takes the three students to another area of the classroom. You notice that there is a puddle around one child's chair. The teacher takes the student to the bathroom, guides him as he removes and changes his clothes, assists him in washing out his soiled ones, and hands him a mop. She directs him as he mops up the puddle, then provides him with a pail of soapy water and requires him to mop the entire classroom floor.

After the children have gone, you ask the teacher about what you have seen. She explains that she uses behavior modification techniques, and what you have observed includes: punishment, time-out, differential reinforcement of other behavior (DRO), extinction, positive reinforcement, and overcorrection.

Classroom teachers have found behavior modification techniques to be efficacious in providing classroom management in general and control over individual students in particular. Because severely and multiply handicapped students are characterized by a variety of maladaptive behaviors, their teachers are particularly dependent upon efficient teaching strategies. When working with such students, the use of behavior modification techniques is not a nicety but a necessity.

Because of the number of different behaviors displayed by severely handicapped students, it is helpful to consider these behaviors in groups or categories rather than individually. In an analysis of 56 studies done between 1971 and 1975, Bates and Wehman (1977) defined six general classes of maladaptive behaviors displayed by the severely handicapped. These classes were:

1. Self-injurious behavior, including voluntary falling, face hitting, scratching, eye gouging, biting, and head banging.
2. Aggressive behaviors, including damaging furniture, biting, choking, throwing, hitting, and verbal aggression.
3. Stereotypical behaviors, including bizarre gestures, hand flicking, hand staring, mouthing of objects, body rocking, and verbal repetitions.
4. Classroom disruptive behaviors, including impulsive respondency, talking out, arguing, obscene vocalizations, and out-of-seat behaviors.
5. Noncompliance behaviors, including bickering, jumping on furniture, persistent crawling, and playing with doors and windows.
6. Inappropriate social behaviors, including behavior problems such as pica, stealing, enuresis, encopresis, nasal discharge, self-exposure, and chronic regurgitation.

Obviously these are unacceptable classroom behaviors. They are unacceptable because the teacher's role is to teach, and these behaviors interfere with teaching and learning. They distract students from learning tasks; students cannot learn while they are engaged in such behaviors. Inappropriate behaviors provide a source of positive reinforcement for students — their teachers and peers pay attention when they display such behaviors. Students who display maladaptive behavior serve as models for other students. If one student receives attention because of some startling behavior, other students may imitate him or her in order to get the same attention. Some such behaviors threaten the safety of students or teachers; they all steal the instructor's attention from the remainder of the class. These behaviors are, therefore, incompatible with the transmission of the curricular content, that is, teaching the targeted tasks.

In this chapter approaches to the elimination of maladaptive behavior are discussed. In addition to effective procedures discussed by researchers, step-by-step instructions for the teacher who wants to use the most efficient techniques to decrease students' inappropriate behavior patterns are provided. The procedures discussed are useful with any stated population. They are therefore appropriate for dealing with behaviors such as those listed above, regardless of whether the student is retarded, physically handicapped, and/or sensorially impaired.

The efficacy of behavior modification procedures in the elimination of maladaptive behaviors has been demonstrated. Instructors using behavior modification techniques have achieved speedy elimination of self-stimulation (Azrin, Kaplin, & Foxx, 1973), self-injury (Azrin, Gottlieb, Hughart, Wesolowski, & Rahn, 1975), and aggressive/disruptive behaviors (Foxx & Azrin, 1972). Researchers have also successfully eliminated classroom disruptive behaviors (Repp & Deitz, 1974; Foxx, 1976; Foxx & Shapiro, 1978), noncompliance behaviors (Forehand and Baumeister, 1976; Cuvo, 1976), and have either eliminated or radically modified inappropriate social behaviors (Azrin and Foxx, 1971; Foxx and Azrin, 1972).

THE ELIMINATION OF MALADAPTIVE BEHAVIOR

Behavior management skills are critical for teachers of severely and multiply handicapped students. Socially maladaptive behavior prevents such students' integration into community living facilities, discourages attempts at mainstreaming and deinstitutionalization, and interferes with opportunities for meaningful employment (Bates & Wehman, 1977). According to special educators responding to a survey conducted by Wehman and McLaughlin (1979), stereotypic behavior is most difficult to manage. Temper tantrums, noncompliance, self-abuse, and aggression toward others are considered progressively easier to control. Ease of control, however, is by no means the primary concern when targeting behaviors for elimination. In this review, maladaptive behaviors are discussed in a sequence based on their potential for preventing students' learning, ranging from those that are dangerous or even life-threatening to those that simply lessen students' acceptability in the home, school, and community. Maladaptive behaviors are considered in the following order: self-injurious behavior, aggression, self-stimulation (stereotypy), classroom disruption, noncompliance, and socially inappropriate behavior.

Self-Injurious Behavior

Many severely and multiply handicapped individuals display repetitive behaviors that result in injury to themselves. Such forms of self-injury include, but are not limited to, head banging, face slapping, fist-to-head movements, beating and scratching the body, and hair pulling (deCatanzaro and Baldwin, 1978). Preventing self-injurious behavior (SIB) takes precedence over other goals since physical injury is inevitable and permanent damage not unlikely. It is therefore important that an efficient method for elimination be applied, especially to the potentially life-endangering behaviors. In the past, such behavior often resulted in the use of straitjackets and other restraining devices. More recently, contingent electric shock has been applied using a portable battery-operated device that delivers a painful but not dangerous electrical current (Lovaas, Schaeffer & Simmons, 1965; Risley, 1968; Yeakel, Salisbury, Greer, & Marcus, 1970). The contingent electric shock results in rapid elimination of self-injurious behavior. It has been justified on the grounds that because of the immediacy of its effects, it results in less injury in the long run than milder forms of intervention. However, because of ethical concerns about the application of shock, particularly its potential for abuse when used by untrained persons, its use to control such behavior has been limited (Mayhew & Harris, 1979).

Less drastic forms of punishment have been successful in reducing or eliminating self-injurious behavior. Promising results have been reported with the use of aromatic ammonia. Either a capsule of the ammonia or a bottle of smelling salts is held under a student's nose following the behavior (Tanner & Zeiler, 1975; Altman, Haavik, & Cook, 1978). Other successful techniques reported include the contingent application of citric acid to the student's tongue (Mayhew & Harris, 1979) and aversive tickling (Green & Hoats, 1971). The reader is referred to Chapter 3 for a more extended discussion of punishment procedures.

Punishment is not the only alternative available for dealing with self-injurious behavior. Successful results have been reported using overcorrection. Azrin et al. (1975) required a student to go to bed and to keep the hands to the sides (forced relaxation), as soon as the behavior was initiated. Physical guidance was used if necessary. De Catanzaro and Baldwin (1978) used a contingent forced-arm exercise, moving a student's arm rapidly up and down at his or her side.

Time-out has also been used to eliminate self-injurious behavior. Because of the danger to the student when traditional time-out procedures such as isolation are used, alternative ways of preventing positive reinforcement are used. Lutzger (1978) reported successful results using a piece of terrycloth to cover the faces of the students exhibiting self-injurious behavior. It is interesting to note that this strategy was effective even though immediate application of the terrycloth was not always possible.

Differential reinforcement of other behaviors (DRO) is yet another way to reduce SIB. This should not be confused with the reinforcement of incompatible behaviors (described in Chapter 3), which is the reinforcement of a specific behavior that is incompatible with the SIB. For example, if a child displays a behavior such as hitting the head, the instructor using DRO would reinforce the student at intervals for not displaying the behavior. The teacher reinforcing incompatible behaviors would select a behavior such as "student's hand held below shoulder level; at belt level; arms on table; or on task."

In using DRO, positive reinforcement is delivered at intervals if the student has not displayed self-injurious behavior. Attempts are usually made to engage the student's attention in some activity other than SIB in order to increase the opportunities for positive reinforcement (Corte, Wolf, & Locke, 1971; Lovaas, Freitag, Gold, & Kassorla, 1965; Peterson & Peterson, 1968). The physical restraints traditionally used to prevent SIB were used as positive reinforcement by Favell, McGimsey, & Jones (1978). Noting that their subjects seemed to enjoy being returned to their restraints, these authors expressed the concern that the restraints might function as positive reinforcement for SIB. They therefore devised a procedure wherein restraints were applied contingent upon an interval without SIB. This seemingly paradoxical procedure successfully reduced rates of self-injurious behavior, and ultimately resulted in the students spending less time in restraints as the rate of SIB decreased.

Promising results have been reported using relaxation training. Steen and Zuriff (1977) taught a profoundly retarded woman to relax her arms and hands while still in full restraints. The restraints were then gradually removed and the woman was able to maintain the relaxed state and refrain from SIB.

Finally, for behaviors that are not life-threatening and do not result in disfigurement, extinction may be employed (Lovaas & Simmons, 1969). Some SIB is apparently maintained by attention from adults who are understandably upset when children hurt themselves. If this attention is withdrawn, however, the behavior, being no longer reinforced, undergoes extinction. Thus, ignoring SIB, although not recommended in all cases, may be an effective strategy. Extinction would not be recommended for such behaviors as head-banging, eye-gouging, and biting, because serious and perhaps permanent injury to the student might occur before the behavior was extinguished.

Aggression

Some severely and multiply handicapped students hurt others instead of, or in addition to, themselves. Such aggression may take the form of hitting, biting, choking, pinching, hair pulling, or throwing things at other students or teachers. Controlling such behaviors is necessary to ensure the safety of staff and students. Unless effective measures are taken to prevent them, managing these behaviors requires an inordinate amount of the teachers' time and thus interferes with instruction.

Although punishment may effectively eliminate or reduce aggressive behavior (Bucher & Lovaas, 1968), there are a number of disadvantages to its use for this purpose. Punishment may increase aggression by the offender (Ulrich & Azrin, 1962). The person administering the punishment may serve as a model for future aggression (Bandura, 1969). Also, the teacher who is authorized to use punishment as a consequence for aggression may do so in anger, particularly if the aggression is directed toward her (Azrin & Holz, 1966). Thus, other procedures are recommended when attempting to eliminate aggressive behavior.

One such procedure is Time-out, which has been used successfully in treating aggressive behavior (Wolf, Risley, & Mees, 1964; Bostow & Bailey, 1969; Calhoun & Matherne, 1975). Isolation is more appropriate for aggressive behaviors than for self-injurious ones because the student cannot hurt anyone else when alone in a time-out room. This period of isolation should be limited to a very few minutes and the procedure must be applied consistently in order to be effective.

Another procedure used to eliminate aggressive behavior is differential reinforcement of other behavior (Repp & Dietz, 1974; Repp, Dietz, & Deitz, 1976). An even more effective intervention technique combines this technique with other procedures (Repp & Dietz, 1975). The authors combined it with time-out, verbal reprimand, and response cost. In the first procedure, a severely retarded child received positive reinforcers for other behavior when not performing aggressive acts. The child also received a 30-second time-out whenever an assaultive act occurred. The second procedure combined earning puzzle pieces for periods of time without inappropriate responses and the instructor's saying the word "no" when an aggressive behavior was demonstrated. A third subject earned tokens for 15-minute periods without aggressive behavior, but lost all tokens subsequent to performing an aggressive act. All three strategies proved effective in reducing aggressive behavior.

Martin and Foxx (1975) successfully applied a unique form of extinction in treating an aggressive resident of an institution. The salient feature of this treatment was that certain staff members subjected themselves to the aggression of the resident; aggressive attacks were limited to these staff members rather than to all individuals with whom the resident came in contact. The victims of the aggression were not to do or say anything that might reinforce the subject's aggression. The disadvantage of this procedure is of course the inordinate demand made on the stoicism of staff members, and it must certainly be limited to relatively mild forms of aggression.

Self-stimulation (Stereotypy)

Self-stimulation has been defined as "highly idiosyncratic stereotyped responses that appear to provide the performer with sensory input but have no obvious social consequences" (Koegel, Firestone, Kramme, & Dunlap, 1974). Self-stimulation is characterized by the repeated performance of motor patterns having no apparent influence on the environment.

Examples of self-stimulatory behavior, as presented in the available literature, include mouthing or spinning of objects (Hutt & Hutt, 1965; Kaufman, 1967; Campbell, 1968; Lovaas, Litrownik, & Mann, 1971), rocking, hand waving, and head waving (Berkson & Mason, 1964; Hollis, 1965; Hutt & Hutt, 1965). Self-stimulatory behavior is also referred to as stereotypy or stereotypic behavior, but the most common working term for it is *self-stim*. Although stereotypic behavior does not produce physical injury, it is a major concern for those who work with the severely and multiply handicapped. As has previously been noted, this behavior is the most difficult to eliminate of all maladaptive behaviors.

Worley (1978) suggests that this resistance to treatment arises from the very nature of the behavior of self-stimulation. There appears to be some quality of the behavior that has a strong reinforcing value for these children. The reinforcing quality is so strong, in fact, that some students refuse food, drink, and social interaction rather than interrupt their self-stimulatory behavior. The self-stimulatory behavior is, therefore, a reinforcer that competes with other potentially reinforcing stimuli (Lovaas, Litrownik, & Mann, 1971). The teacher must isolate a more powerful reward, which can be used to reinforce nonperformance of the stereotypic behaviors.

In an effort to isolate an effective reinforcer to use in eliminating self-stim behavior, it is possible to employ a literal interpretation of the Premack Principle. The Premack Principle (also discussed in Chapter 3) proposes that low-probability behaviors occur more frequently when followed immediately by high-probability behaviors (Premack, 1959). Application of this principle can be seen daily (e.g., "Eat your spinach and you can have a cookie" and "Finish your homework and then go out to play"). In each case, a behavior that has a high probability of occurrence in a free-choice situation is made contingent upon the performance of a behavior that has a very low probability of occurrence in the same free-choice situation. Guess and Rutherford (1967) have noted that for autistic and multihandicapped mentally retarded children, the high-probability behavior, the preferred behavior, is a self-stimulatory behavior. Worley (1978) analyzed the self-stim behaviors exhibited by his students and selected a component from each as the student's reinforcer. One student intently patted her leg, twirled objects, and rocked, while another rubbed his arms together, rocked, and flapped his arms. The reinforcers selected were, therefore, leg patting and arm rubbing, respectively. These physical reinforcers were delivered by the teacher, contingent upon correct student response in the absence of self-stimulation. The results of Worley's study suggest that a reinforcer similar to some component of a child's self-stimulation may be competitive with that self-stimulation.

Other researchers have indicated that allowing a child to engage in self-stimulation for a short period of time following a desired response may make the performance of that response more likely (Mira & Hoffman, 1974; Hargrave & Swisher, 1975; Lovaas, 1975).

The development of alternative responses is an important component in the elimination of self-stim behavior. Foxx and Azrin (1973) have proposed that both inward-directed and outward-directed responses can bring reinforcement to the student. In the absence of reinforcement for outward-directed responses, the repetition of inward-directed responses may dominate. It is for this reason that several researchers (Foxx & Azrin, 1973; Cuvo, 1976; Repp, Deitz & Deitz, 1976) have suggested that reinforcement of competing, outward-directed responses, incompatible with the maladaptive behavior, would be effective in reducing inappropriate behaviors.

Overcorrection procedures have been successfully applied in the treatment of self-stimulatory behavior (Foxx & Azrin, 1973). Several researchers have successfully reduced the frequency and variability of such repeated response with positive reinforcement administered through a schedule based on differential reinforcement of other behavior (Cuvo, 1976; Repp, Deitz, & Deitz, 1976).

Although no extensive body of research was identified, it is the authors' experience that self-stimulatory behavior increases in the absence of structured activities or appropriate alternate avenues of stimulation. Variation of the stimulation received by institutionalized persons is therefore suggested as a way to reduce the display of self-stimulatory behaviors.

Such added stimulation and reinforcement may be readily provided through the training of appropriate skills incompatible with the response targeted for elimination. Creative environmental design or manipulation may also provide the needed stimulation to reduce the display of undesirable responses. Skill training may be tied to contingent environmental stimulation, as discussed in Chapter 4 of this book. Use of such response-contingent environmental stimulation provides for both the development of incompatible motor schemes and the presentation of varied environmental stimulation. In addition, these devices encourage functional skills that provide the student with actual control over some element of the environment.

Classroom Disruption

Classroom disruptive behaviors include, but are not limited to, talking out, obscene vocalizations, arguing, and out-of-seat behaviors. These acts keep the performer, other students, and the instructor from pursuing classroom goals. Behaviors of this type place a barrier of distraction between the students and the task at hand.

Many such behaviors are maintained by teacher attention and may be eliminated simply by withdrawal of attention (Madsen, Becker, & Thomas, 1968), particularly if the extinction procedure is accompanied by reinforcement of appropriate behavior.

When extinction is insufficient to eliminate disruptive behavior or when, as Sulzer-Azaroff, and Mayer (1977) suggest, such a procedure might drive a teacher to desperation as high rates of disruption rise even higher, other intervention techniques may be necessary.

When strategies other than extinction are necessary to eliminate classroom disruptive behaviors, other options are available to the teacher. Porterfield, Herbert-Jackson, and Risley (1976) described a procedure in which students who were disruptive were told what they were doing wrong and then required to observe other students engaged in appropriate activities. This strategy is somewhat similar to time-out, but differs in that the instructor asked the disrupters frequently if they were ready to rejoin the group. This technique proved more successful than a previously used redirection procedure.

Time-out, often combined with positive reinforcement of appropriate behavior, can be used to reduce disruptive behavior (Bostow & Bailey, 1969). Because such behavior is neither as dangerous as self-injurious behavior or aggression nor as resistant to treatment as self-stim, nonexclusionary time-out strategies are particularly appropriate. Browning (1980) has described a time-out procedure that provides immediate isolation with a minimum of social interaction and no physical contact. In use, this procedure calls for the teacher to give a hand signal or a verbal cue to the student when he or she exhibits an undesirable behavior. Upon receiving this signal, the student has to time him- or herself out by sitting on the floor and tucking the head between the knees and arms. If the student fails to do so, the teacher physically moves him or her to a time-out room. Obviously, this would be difficult with larger students, and assistance from other staff would be required.

Foxx and Shapiro (1978) used a time-out ribbon, which provided time-out without exclusion. Each student in the class wore a colored ribbon around his or her neck; when it was in place, the student was a class member. When a student misbehaved, the ribbon was removed for a predetermined period of time. Although still in the room, the student was totally ignored by the teacher and students, as if removal of the ribbon had made the student invisible. This strategy successfully reduced rates of disruptive behavior. Foxx and Shapiro suggest several advantages of this procedure over traditional time-out:

1. During time-out students view the reinforcers and activities enjoyed by other students.

2. This time-out can be implemented immediately, as opposed to isolated time-out, in which a student must be escorted to a room that might be located some distance away.
3. The continuity of the group's activities is interrupted less than by the removal of the misbehaver to another place.
4. Inappropriate behavior in time-out, such as self-abuse or stripping, can be interrupted earlier in the response chain because the teacher is in the same room.

The authors note that in the event of continued major disruption a backup procedure such as isolation would be required.

Differential reinforcement of other behavior has been used successfully to reduce classroom disruption (Repp and Deitz, 1976). When the behavior is only mildly disruptive, a more tolerant procedure known as differential reinforcement of low rates (DRL) is also appropriate. Deitz and Repp (1973) employed such a procedure to reduce talk-out behavior with a group of mentally retarded children. If the group made fewer than five talk-outs in fifty minutes, each member earned two pieces of candy. It should also be noted that a group contingency was used in this instance. Such a procedure increases cooperation among students and promotes appropriate socialization while diminishing maladaptive behavior.

Noncompliance

Noncompliance is the failure to follow instructions. The student who is told to do something and does not do it exhibits noncompliance. Conversely, a student told to stop performing some inappropriate behavior but refuses to do so is equally noncompliant.

Behavioral techniques discussed in the literature as useful in treating this maladaptive behavior include time-out (MacMillan, Forness, & Trumbull, 1973; Forehand & Baumeister, 1976), overcorrection (Foxx and Azrin, 1973; Azrin and Wesolowski, 1974), DRO (Cuvo, 1976; Browning, 1980), and social punishment (Moore & Bailey, 1976; Forehand, Roberts, Doleys, Hobbs, & Resick, 1975; Doleys, Wells, Hobbs, Roberts, & Cartelli, 1976). The social punishment used by Doleys et al. deserves special note. The researchers approached each child exhibiting maladaptive behavior, firmly held him or her by the shoulders, and loudly scolded the child for not complying with a command within 10 seconds of its issuance. The subject was told that he or she had not obeyed the teacher immediately and that such nonresponding displeased the researcher. This verbal reprimand was then followed by a 40-second silent glare. While maintaining a fixed stare on the child, the researchers held their hands on their hips.

These researchers claim that social punishment, as defined above, was more efficient and had longer residual effects in the reduction and elimination of noncompliance than either time-out or overcorrection procedures.

The teacher who wants students to comply with instructions is referred to the section later in this chapter that deals with teaching this behavior. Generally, positive reinforcement for compliance is an alternative to, or can be used in conjunction with, the aforementioned procedures.

Socially Inappropriate Behavior

Inappropriate social behaviors include stealing, nasal discharge, chronic regurgitation, self-exposure, enuresis (urinating in inappropriate places), encopresis (defecating in inappropriate places), and pica (ingestion of nonfood substances). In addition to these, public masturbation should also be noted as an inappropriate social behavior frequently displayed by the severely and multiply handicapped students. Such behaviors, although neither dangerous nor necessarily disruptive to the learning process, are certainly unpleasant. They are also resistant to change because many have elements of intrinsic positive reinforcement. Eliminating such behaviors is necessary, however, if students are to be acceptable to parents, teachers, and other caregivers. Inappropriate social behaviors have been successfully treated by differential reinforcement of other behaviors (Zeilburger, Sampen, & Sloan, 1968), overcorrection (Foxx & Azrin, 1972), and a combination of these two procedures (Carroll, Sloop, Mutter, & Prince, 1978).

Restitutional overcorrection was successfully applied by Azrin and Wesolowski (1974) to a food-stealing behavior seen in the profoundly retarded. In this application, the thief not only had to return the stolen article, but also had to give the victim another article identical to the one stolen. The stealing behavior was eliminated in 3 days and maintained for the following 16 days of observation. A simple correction procedure, involving only the return of stolen articles, had been ineffective when applied for 5 days prior to the use of the overcorrection procedure. Azrin and Foxx (1971) used overcorrection principles in toilet training retarded adults. The subjects were required to clean up all traces of their accidents, disinfect the area of the accident, wash their soiled clothes, shower themselves, clean under their fingernails, wash their hands thoroughly, and locate and dress in clean clothes without assistance. Rapid, enduring behavioral change was achieved. The advantages of overcorrection include its direct relationship to the nature of the inappropriate behavior. In effect, the instructor is imposing on the student an extreme of the natural consequences of the behavior. The procedure provides reeducation, removal of reinforcement for the offense, and time-out from general positive reinforcement, as well as requiring considerable expenditure of energy as a consequence of misbehavior (Foxx & Azrin, 1972).

PROCEDURES TO DECREASE INAPPROPRIATE BEHAVIORS

In the following section, a number of sample strategies are provided. In each example a particular maladaptive behavior is paired with an intervention technique frequently used to decrease its rate of occurrence. In many cases the suggested sample programs, with minor alterations, may be used to decrease a variety of different behaviors. The more intrusive procedures, particularly those using punishment, should be reserved for potentially harmful behaviors. Such behaviors endanger either the physical well-being of the student engaged in the behavior or the safety of other students.

A specific intervention procedure, as well as the behaviors to be eliminated or decreased, must be included in each student's Individualized Educational Program (IEP). The multidisciplinary team responsible for each student's IEP must determine the maladaptive behaviors that should be eliminated. Dangerous behaviors and those that interfere with learning or disrupt the classroom are frequently targeted. Inappropriate behaviors that make the child unacceptable or unwelcome in the community may also be of concern. The decision on specific behavior modification strategies must be made based partly on the reported efficacy of that procedure in eliminating that behavior. However, an equally important consideration is the reinforcement history of the child in question and the contingencies maintaining his or her current behavior. The rationale for using a given procedure with a specific student must be based on information about both the procedure and the child.

Self-Injurious Behavior

Students who hurt themselves seriously must be stopped from doing so. Traditionally, physical or chemical restraints have been used. Such restraints, often necessary for the safety of students, make participation in learning activities impossible. The goal of behavior modification strategies for the elimination of self-injury is to enable the student to remain free of restraints and able to participate actively in learning. The use of some form of aversive consequence appears justified in light of such a goal.

One type of aversive stimulus that can be used to interrupt and eliminate self-injurious behavior is a loud noise such as a bicycle horn, a handclap, or a shout. It may be necessary to try several of these with a student before an effective punisher is isolated. A suggested format for a program using loud noise as a punisher is described in detail below.

1. The target behavior, such as head banging, face scratching, or hand biting, should be carefully defined. The teacher must have exact criteria for determining whether or not the specified behavior has actually occurred.
2. Initial stages of training should be carried out in a relatively isolated area. The same instructor should conduct all initial sessions.
3. The child should be removed from any restraining device used to eliminate self-injurious behavior.
4. As soon as the child performs the target behavior, the teacher presents the selected aversive stimulus. It is important to reiterate that, to be maximally effective, punishment must be applied as soon as possible following the onset of the self-injury.
5. The noise must be repeated at the onset of each display of SIB.

Additional considerations include the following:

1. If the child fails to respond to the aversive stimulus within a short period of time, the session must be terminated so that he or she will not do serious damage to himself or herself. Other aversive stimuli may be tried to see if one will actually function as a punisher.
2. Although the behavior may decrease dramatically or even disappear completely within minutes, it will almost certainly reappear in the absence of the instructor and in other settings. Additional training, using several different adults in a variety of settings, are required before a general and durable behavioral change can be achieved.
3. The self-injurious behavior may recur when the student is under stress. In such cases, the aversive stimulus may need to be reintroduced. Every effort should be made to pair the stimulus with a verbal command so that the original punisher will not have to be used indefinitely. (See the procedure for compliance training later in this chapter.)
4. As soon as possible, the child should be taught to perform behaviors for which he or she can receive positive reinforcement. A child who has alternate methods of receiving reinforcement is less likely to resort to self-injury in search for reinforcement.

Aggression

Behavior which results in injury to teachers or other students rather than to the instigator of the response is termed aggressive behavior. Aggressive behavior may range from life-threatening acts such as choking, to merely painful or annoying behaviors such as pinching and hair pulling. Aggressive behavior is often dealt with through the use of a time-out procedure. An example of this procedure follows:

1. As with self-injury, the target behavior must be clearly defined.
2. When an aggressive act occurs, the child should be moved to the area designated for time-out. A small, separate room with no furniture is preferred, but a corner of a room separated by furniture may also be used.
3. As the child is taken to time-out, the adult should say "Don't hit people. Go to time-out." The verbalization is not necessary to the success of the procedure. It will, however, facilitate eventual transfer from physical removal to compliance with the verbal instruction "Go to time-out."
4. The child should stay in time-out for some predetermined interval of time (usually about 5 minutes).
5. The child should be released from time-out and returned to the activity in a matter-of-fact manner.

Additional considerations include the following:

1. A kitchen timer is helpful in keeping track of how long a child has been timed out. It can also prevent a student timed-out at 9:15 from spending the day forgotten in the time-out room.
2. A child who tantrums or creates some other disturbance while in time-out should be required to stay for the predetermined interval after he or she becomes quiet.
3. Except for a simple statement of the reason for time-out and such physical guidance as is necessary to ensure compliance, the child should be given no extra attention before, during, and after time-out. Lecturing the child about the behavior or attempting to elicit promises of improvement provide the child with a great deal of adult attention. Such attention may serve as a positive reinforcer for the aggressive behavior.
4. Teachers often wonder what to do when the time-out room is occupied and a second student needs to be timed-out. In such cases an auxiliary area such as a corner behind a bookcase may be used. Another alternative is one of the nonexclusionary time-out procedures described earlier in the chapter. If more than two students simultaneously need time-out, the teacher should reevaluate her classroom management plan.
5. Students who are too large for their teachers to physically move to time-out must be taught to comply with the verbal instruction "Go to time out." It may be necessary to use an aversive stimulus to punish noncompliance until the student reliably goes to the time-out room when told to do so. In emergencies such students can be timed out by removing all other students and adults from the area.

Self-Stimulation (Stereotypy)

Behaviors such as body rocking, hand flapping, and twirling are familiar to teachers of the severely and multiply handicapped. Such behaviors, although not harmful to the physical well-being of students, certainly interfere with their learning. Self-stim behaviors including screaming, humming, or verbalizing for no apparent reason may be efficiently decelerated using positive reinforcement contingent upon the performance of any behavior other than the one targeted for elimination. The student receives a reinforcer at specified intervals as long as he or she has not performed the inappropriate behavior. A sample procedure for reducing self-stim behavior using DRO follows:

1. The training can take place either in the classroom or in a small area designed for one-to-one instruction.
2. The teacher should choose a food reinforcer that the child likes and that can be delivered in small pieces.
3. The teacher gives the child a piece of the edible reinforcer at the end of every interval during which the self-stimulatory behavior is not displayed.

Initially, the intervals may have to be very short; 1 or 2 seconds is not unreasonable. The teacher may time the intervals by counting silently. Absolute precision in timing is not necessary. Intervals may be gradually lengthened until the behavior occurs very infrequently.

Additional considerations include the following:

1. Absolute elimination of self-stimulatory behavior is unlikely. It is apt to recur when the child is not actively engaged in a learning or recreational activity. It is of primary importance to reduce self-stimulatory behavior during teaching activities. It may, thereafter, be kept at a low level by keeping the child involved in activities.
2. It takes experience, even with carefully defined behaviors, to determine whether a particular self-stimulatory behavior has indeed occurred. In addition, as in any shaping procedure, the decision regarding how quickly to lengthen the intervals is difficult to make, especially when watching a child closely and counting busily. The novice teacher should not become discouraged if the first few attempts are unsuccessful or even laughable. Observation of an expert, if one is available, is a big help in learning this as well as many other procedures.

Classroom Disruption

Behaviors that are dangerous, such as self-injurious behavior and aggression, call for relatively intrusive procedures such as punishment or time-out. The elimination of self-stim behaviors, because they occur with such frequency, requires intensive intervention by the teacher. Classroom disruptive behavior such as out-of-seat behavior, talking out, arguing, or creating some other disturbance usually does not cause physical harm or occur continuously. It can therefore be dealt with by either of two relatively nonintrusive procedures, neither of which requires one-to-one involvement. The two procedures are extinction — withdrawing all attention from the inappropriate behavior — and the reinforcement of incompatible behavior. A program combining these two procedures to reduce out-of-seat behavior follows.

1. When the child is in his or her seat the teacher should provide frequent primary or social reinforcement. Being in the proper seat is a behavior incompatible with being out-of-seat.
2. When the child leaves his or her seat, the teacher withdraws all reinforcement. She must not attend to the child in any way.
3. Other students may receive tangible or social reinforcement for demonstrating the target behavior. They will thereby serve as models for the disruptive student.
4. This reinforcement may also be contingent upon whether the other students ignore the inappropriate behavior.

Additional considerations include the following:

1. As soon as possible, the teacher should choose an incompatible behavior to be reinforced that involves some aspect of task attention or task completion. Such behavior is usually equally incompatible with out-of-seat behavior, though some imaginative students may manage to complete tasks while continuing this and other disruptive behaviors.
2. Whenever a previously reinforced behavior is ignored, an initial increase in the rate of that behavior may be expected. This phemonenon is fully explained in Chapter 3, in which extinction is discussed. The teacher must be prepared to endure the period when the behavior seems to be getting worse.

Socially Inappropriate Behavior

Behaviors such as pica, enuresis, encopresis, and public masturbation make a student intolerable to many people. Because these behaviors, by their nature, produce such immediate and strong reactions from others, they are inevitably positively reinforced. Over a period of time, they can develop into firmly established habits. In addition, these behaviors have intrinsic reinforcing qualities for many students. They are often very difficult to alter. For this reason a relatively intrusive procedure, overcorrection, is often employed to eliminate them. An example of the use of this procedure to decrease inappropriate toileting behavior follows:

1. The child who has had ample opportunity to use the toilet but who wets or soils his or her pants is required to remove the soiled clothing, wash up (shower or bathe if necessary), redress in clean clothes, and wash and hang up the soiled clothing. This may be accomplished through verbal instruction if possible or physical guidance when necessary.

2. The child should also be required to clean any urine or feces from the floors or other surfaces soiled either in the original accident or in the cleaning process. The teacher should then state several times during the procedure, "You messed your pants. You have to clean up the mess."

3. With extremely recalcitrant children, a more extensive procedure may be needed during which the child might be required to mop the entire classroom floor, wash down walls, or scrub the bathroom. The underlying assumption is that the mess becomes more work than it is worth.

Other considerations include the following:

1. In instances where physical guidance is needed, the teacher should take care to use the least guidance necessary to ensure that the student complies with the requirements of the procedure.

2. Overcorrection is a difficult, tedious, time-consuming procedure. It should be used only when positive reinforcement for the appropriate behavior has failed.

The examples provided above explain in detail the management and reduction of several maladaptive behaviors displayed by severely and profoundly handicapped children. Any of the procedures described can be applied, with a little adaptation, to many behaviors. The imaginative teacher should be able to use one of them, or a combination of several, to reduce virtually any maladaptive behavior displayed by his or her students. No attempt has been made to list every bizarre, maladaptive, or inappropriate response likely to be exhibited by handicapped students. Such an attempt would be doomed to failure; in any event, somewhere in the world at this very moment a teacher is asking an aide, "Good grief, have you ever seen a kid do that before?"

SOCIAL SKILL DEVELOPMENT

Little research has been done in the area of development of appropriate social behaviors for severely and multiply handicapped students. The disparity between the amount of reported research concerning the elimination of inappropriate behavior and research concerning the development of socially adaptable behavior reflects the focus of attention imposed on instructors by the behavior of this population. A student who bites himself or herself, hits people, screams continuously or lacks bowel control presents problems that automatically take priority over social isolation or lack of cooperative play. The literature reflects this unavoidable emphasis on the behaviors most urgently in need of change.

The development of socially appropriate behaviors is, however, an important task for the teacher of the severely and multiply handicapped. It is one method of providing these students with stimulation and reinforcement for something other than maladaptive behavior. Essentially, it gives them an avenue for behavioral expression that is environmentally reinforced and that is incompatible with such behaviors. Therefore, we shall also provide explicit instructions for teaching this population basic social interaction skills.

The development of appropriate social skills in the severely and multiply handicapped should parallel the elimination of maladaptive responses. Appropriate behaviors provide a vehicle for acquiring positive reinforcement from peers and adults. Suggested skills include sharing roles in a structured activity, building on the same structure, taking turns, holding hands, handing an object to a peer (Strain, 1975), and vocalizations or gestures directed at peers (Peterson et al., 1979). The development of these social skills depends on whether the students have acquired certain prerequisite behaviors. These presocial skills include attention to an instructor, compliance, and imitation.

It is important to teach skills that will prompt continued socialization from the students' peers and nonhandicapped associates (Gable, Hendrickson, & Strain, 1978). Several authors have noted that trained social behaviors are maintained only if continued reinforcement is provided (Whitman, Mercurio, & Caponigii, 1970; Paloutzian, Hasazi, Streifoe & Edgar, 1971; Peterson, Austin & Lang, 1979; Gable et al., 1978). Peterson et al. demonstrated that social activity among severely and multiply handicapped students can be increased and expected to generalize to free-play settings in which no reinforcers are given and the trainer is not present. This potential for generalization may be increased by training such behaviors in the settings in which they should be demonstrated.

As previously indicated, the primary purpose for eliminating behaviors such as aggression towards others, self-injury, and self-stimulation is to facilitate the teaching of appropriate behavior. Discussed here are specific procedures for the development of basic skills such as eye contact, imitation, compliance, and rudimentary play interactions with both peers and teachers. In teaching such skills to severely and multiply handicapped students, most professionals rely on the basic techniques of behavior modification. Most frequently used is some combination of stimulus control, shaping, and positive reinforcement.

Eye Contact

In order to teach students, it is necessary to get their attention. Severely and multiply handicapped students characteristically do not attend to verbal or visual stimuli presented by their teachers. Behavior modification procedures have been successfully used to train these students to attend either to their names or to some other cue. A commonly used cue is "Look at me" (Marr, Miller, & Straub, 1966; McConnell, 1967; Simmons & Lovaas, 1969; Ricks & Wing, 1975). This training is not an end in itself, but a foundation for teaching virtually all other skills — cognitive, language, motor and social. Based on procedures reported in the literature, a suggested program for training eye contact is as follows.

1. The instructor and student should be seated facing one another in close proximity, preferably in a fairly confined space. This will minimize distractions and the potential for student escape. In the early stages of training, a one-to-one ratio between student and instructor is virtually a necessity. The instructor should have an ample supply of the selected primary reinforcer on hand at the onset of training. The reinforcer should be one that can be delivered in small pieces and is easily administered by the instructor. Small bits of dry cereal, salty snacks, or dried fruit are suggested. The instructor should hold a bit of the reinforcer in front of his or her own eyes and say either the student's name or "Look at me." The choice of which stimulus to use first is arbitrary; eventually, however, the instructor wants eye contact from the student in response to either command. Some instructors may want to begin with both (e.g., "John, look at me"). If even a flicker of eye contact occurs as the student looks at the food, the instructor delivers the reinforcement. In addition to the primary reinforcer the teacher might deliver some social reinforcer such as praise (e.g., "Good looking, John") or physical contact (e.g., a pat, hug or tickle). If the student fails to look at the trainer a physical prompt (gently turning the student's head so that he faces the instructor) may be used as needed. Such a prompt should be faded as soon as possible.

2. When the student reliably responds to the instruction, the position of the reinforcer is gradually moved from in front of the instructor's eyes until eventually it is held out of sight. This effect can be easily produced by gradually turning the wrist of the hand holding the edible reinforcer. When held between the thumb and forefinger, this action places the back of the instructor's hand between the edible and the student, effectively blocking the student's view of the reinforcer. Once out of sight, the instructor should gradually move the hand holding the obscured reinforcer from eye level to approximately waist level. The student still earns the reinforcer for eye contact, but

now there is no visible cue held near the instructor's eyes to prompt the student's response. These steps should be initiated as quickly as possible or the instructor will find that the student responds to the stimulus "Look at me" as if it were "Look at the raisin."

3. Once under stimulus control, the response may be shaped so that eye contact is held for several seconds. .The goal is to maintain attention long enough to deliver some instruction related to a learning task.

4. The response must now be maintained by intermittent reinforcement and generalized to other instructors and settings. The student is required to give several seconds of eye contact when any instructor says his or her name or "Look at me." It is now possible to work with several students simultaneously, reinforcing each student responding to his or her name and all students when they respond to "Look at me." This ultimately makes it possible to carry out small-group instruction for learning tasks. The duration of the eye contact is of some significance in that prolonged eye contact can be as socially maladaptive as no eye contact at all. Two seconds of eye contact should be sufficient for training purposes. In addition to eye contact, eye-to-object contact should also be developed: similar procedures may be employed for such training.

5. For many students it is necessary to shape the eye-contact response so that it occurs at gradually increasing distances. Beginning with the original arrangement, in which the student is seated facing the instructor, the response may be required from several feet away and eventually from across the classroom. Ultimately the student should respond to his or her name by turning to look at the instructor even when engaged in some other activity at a considerable distance. This will facilitate classroom management enormously, making it possible to stop inappropriate behaviors without actual physical intervention.

The procedure described above may be complicated by the recurrence of inappropriate behaviors such as aggression or self-stimulation. It may be necessary for the instructor to reinstate the procedures initially used to eliminate those behaviors. It is important that the student not be allowed to escape the training situation through inappropriate behavior. Such an occurrence will almost certainly result in an increase in this maladaptive behavior.

Imitation

Normal children learn a great many things through imitation. They imitate their parents, teachers, and peers without specifically being taught to do so. Indeed, the tendency to imitate frequently results in the acquisition of behaviors that parents and teachers prefer that the youngsters did not perform. Most severely handicapped students do not imitate (Garcia, Bacon, & Firestone, 1971). The failure to benefit from incidental learning makes it very difficult to teach many skills. Students, however, can be taught to imitate behaviors demonstrated by teachers (Lovaas, Berberich, Perloff, & Schaeffer, 1966; Baer, Peterson, & Sherman, 1967). It has been determined that, once a number of imitative responses have been established, a generalized imitative response occurs. In other words, when students are taught to imitate specific behaviors by a process of positive reinforcement, they will also imitate behaviors that have never been reinforced. It is apparent that imitation of an instructor's behavior provides a foundation for many learning tasks, ranging from self-care to language. A procedure for teaching students to imitate is described below.

1. The initial setting should be similar to that in which eye-contact training was undertaken. Such training is prerequisite to imitation training. The instructor says the child's name or "Look at me." When eye contact is established she says "Do this" and performs some simple motor action such as touching his or her head or clapping hands. The specific action is irrelevant; the goal is for the child to respond to the instruction "Do this" by imitating the teacher. If the child fails to respond within a few seconds, the action may be physically prompted, and the guidance is gradually faded. Correct responses should be followed by primary and social reinforcers.
2. When a number of motor responses are reliably imitated, vocal stimuli should be introduced so that the instructor can be sure that imitation is under stimulus control of the instruction "Do this."
3. For some children, vocal imitation may also be introduced. Imitation of the instructor's vocalizations serves as a foundation for vocal language training for such children.
4. Once the imitative response has been established, it must be generalized to other instructors' cues and settings. As with eye-contact training, it will eventually be possible to work with children in small groups. Emphasis at this point is placed on teaching the child to respond to his or her name and to the teacher's instruction.
5. A simplified form of the game "Simon Says" will help a group of children to maintain these skills. The teacher says, "Look at me. John, do this. Mary and Susan, do this." Each student is expected to perform the action that is mentioned after his or her name but not the actions that accompany other students' names.

Compliance Training

When working with severely handicapped students, it is extremely helpful to teach them to follow certain very simple verbal instructions. If some behaviors can be brought under verbal control, the children will be much easier to manage both at school and at home, thus increasing their acceptability in a potentially less restrictive environment. It is advisable for parents, or direct care personnel, and teachers to work together to individually determine the most important instructions for each child. The most frequently suggested basic compliance instructions follow.

Negatives	Positives
No	Come here.
Stop it.	Stay there.
	Give it to me.

For some youngsters other instructions are equally important. A specific example might be "Drop it" for a child who picks everything up, including potentially dangerous objects. Another cue might be "Spit it out" for a child who puts nonfood items in his or her mouth. It is important to emphasize that these instructions are not arbitrary demonstrations of authority. They help the child to be more tolerable, more pleasant to live with, and safer. The child who responds to "No" or "Stop it" may be prevented from putting a metal object into a wall socket. The child who has been taught "Give it to me" will hand his or her mother the light bulb retrieved from the garbage can, before accidently cutting him- or herself. The child who reacts to "Stay there" may be prevented from running into the street.

Teaching children to comply with instructions is essentially the same as teaching eye contact and imitation. In the case of "No" and "Stop it," the instructions are simply paired with one of the procedures described earlier to decrease inappropriate behavior. When the child has some receptive language ability the teacher may say, "I said 'Stop it'. You didn't stop it. You go to time-out," but such verbalization is by no means necessary. Consistent pairing of the verbal stimulus with the aversive consequences will ensure the eventual effectiveness of the procedure. The positive compliance instructions may be taught using positive reinforcement. An example follows.

1. The teacher stands close to the child, holding a bit of a primary reinforcer and says, "John, come here." If John fails to move, physical guidance may be used. When he does approach the teacher the behavior is reinforced.
2. The teacher gradually moves away from the child so that the distance the child must move is sequentially increased.
3. A "come here" game is a good practice activity. The teacher calls a child's name and adds "Come here." A hug, tickling, or swing of the body is given along with praise when the child complies. If several

adults are available, each may sit or stand in a corner of the room and call children so that each child moves from adult to adult.

4. Care must be taken that no adult uses the instruction to get a child to approach him or her in order to administer punishment. A child who expects a hug and gets a slap may decide that the best response to "Come here" is to move rapidly in the opposite direction. The teacher may find that a child appears to have forgotten the response. In this case he or she should investigate this possibility and repeat the training procedures.

Other instructions may be taught the same way. A practice activity for "stay there" is similar to the game of "statues" which is popular among nonhandicapped children. When the teacher says, "Stay there," everybody freezes in position. Again, there is the danger that some adults may misuse the cue and require a child to remain in a chair for long periods of time to keep the child out of the way.

Compliance with instructions, however, may serve as a foundation for management and social interaction. Teaching severely handicapped students to interact with others is described in the following section.

Play

Observation of a group of severely handicapped children usually shows that, except in the case of aggressive acts, they appear generally unaware of one another. They do not play together or cooperate to perform tasks. Such play or cooperative behavior can be taught using imitation and compliance. Suggestions for a few activities are given; the imaginative teacher will be able to think of many others.

"Roll the Ball" The instruction "Give it to me" serves as the basis of this activity. The teacher sits close to the child, facing him or her, and pushes a large, soft ball to him. She then says, "Give it to me," and when the child returns the ball, the instructor repeats the sequence, gradually moving farther away so that the child must roll the ball. The instruction "Stay there" may be useful if the child's response to the game is to move himself closer to the teacher rather than to roll the ball. The verbal instruction may eventually be dropped and children can be taught to play together rather than with a teacher.

"Give it to Me" Children who imitate the teacher and who respond to the instruction "Give it to me" can be taught to give objects to one another. The teacher says, "John, do this. Give it to Mary," and demonstrates. The demonstration is faded and the instruction will eventually acquire controls over the behavior. The children thus learn one another's names and some interaction occurs. This activity is particularly effective when used with edibles, such as during the midmorning snack. Children become very aware of one another when foods are involved.

The teacher should be aware that it requires considerable restraint to "Give it to Mary" when "it" is a cookie. Occasional lapses are inevitable. One of the authors has observed a teacher handing a basket of cookies to a student for distribution to the class. Before she could begin the "Give it to..." instructions, a minor crisis occurred. The basket was empty and the student had a cookie-crumb-encrusted smile on his face. Therefore, nonedible materials such as puzzle pieces may initially be better for training cooperative play.

Puzzle If students can put together simple wooden puzzles or form-boards, several students may work together. The teacher hands each student a piece and has him or her in turn "give it to another student," who fits that piece into the board. Alternately, each student may put his or her own piece in as the teacher says "Now it's John's turn, then Mary's turn." The concept of "turns" may be used for many other activities.

The development of appropriate social behaviors in severely and multiply handicapped students is one of the most important and challenging tasks that teachers undertake. Maladaptive behaviors interfere with instruction in all areas for all students. The behavior exhibited by one child interferes with the other students for whom the teacher is unavailable due to the misbehaving student. Children who behave appropriately are accessible to instruction. They can be taught skills that enhance the quality of their lives and make them as competent and independent as possible. Of equal importance, appropriate social behavior makes such children more acceptable to their communities, schools, and families. This enhanced acceptability maximizes their chances of functioning outside institutional environments.

REFERENCES

Altman, K., Haavik, S., & Cook, J. W. Punishment of self-injurious behavior in natural settings using a contingent aromatic ammonia. *Behaviour Research and Therapy*, 1978, *16*, 85–96.
Azrin, N. H., & Foxx, R. M. A rapid method of toilet training the institutionalized retarded. *Journal of Applied Behavior Analysis*, 1971, *4*, 89–99.
Azrin, N. H., Gottlieb, L., Hughart, L., Wesolowski, M. D., & Rahn, T. Eliminating self-injurious behavior by educative procedures. *Behaviour Research and Therapy*, 1975, *13*, 101–111.
Azrin, N. H., & Holz, W. C. Punishment. In W. K. Honig (Ed.), *Operant behavior: Areas of research and application.* New York: Appleton-Century-Crofts, 1966.
Azrin, N., Kaplan, S., & Foxx, R. Autism reversal: Eliminating stereotyped self-stimulation of retarded individuals. *American Journal of Mental Deficiency*, 1973, *78*, 241–248.
Azrin, N. H., & Wesolowski, M. D. Theft reversal: An overcorrection procedure for eliminating stealing by retarded persons. *Journal of Applied Behavior Analysis*, 1974, *4*, 577–581.

Baer, D.M., Peterson, R.F., & Sherman, J.A. The development of imitation by reinforcing behavioral similarity to a model. *Journal of the Experimental Analysis of Behavior*, 1967, *10*, 405–416.

Bandura, A. *Principles of behavior modification*. New York: Holt, Rinehart & Winston, 1969.

Bates, P., & Wehman, P. Behavior management with the mentally retarded: An empirical analysis of the research. *Mental Retardation*, 1977, *15*, 3–12.

Berkson, G., & Mason, W. A. Stereotyped movements of mental defectives. Part 4: The effects of toys and the character of the acts. *American Journal of Mental Deficiency*, 1964, *68*, 511–524.

Bostow, D. E., & Bailey, J. B. Modification of disruptive and aggressive behavior using brief time-out and reinforcement procedures. *Journal of Applied Behavior Analysis*, 1969, *2*, 31–37.

Browning, R. M. *Teaching the severely handicapped child: Basic skills for the developmentally disabled*. Boston: Allyn & Bacon, 1980.

Bucher, B., & Lovaas, O. I. Use of aversive stimulation in behavior modification. In M. R. Jones (Ed.), *Miami Symposium on the prediction of behavior, 1967: Aversive behavior*. Coral Gables: University of Miami Press, 1968.

Calhoun, K. S., & Matherne, P. The effect of varying schedules of time-out on aggressive behavior of a retarded girl. *Journal of Behavior Therapy and Experimental Psychiatry*, 1975, *6*, 139–143.

Campbell, C. M. Stereotyped and expressive movements in imbeciles. *American Journal of Mental Deficiency*, 1968, *73*, 187–194.

Carroll, S. W., Sloop, W. E., Mutter, S., & Prince, D. L. The elimination of chronic clothes ripping in retarded people through a combination of procedures. *Mental Retardation*, 1978, *16*, 246–249.

Corte, H. E., Wolf, M. M., & Locke, J. B. A comparison of procedures for eliminating self-injurious behavior of retarded adolescents. *Journal of Applied Behavior Analysis*, 1971, *4*, 201–213.

Cuvo, A. J. Decreasing repetitive behavior in an institutionalized mentally retarded resident. *Mental Retardation*, 1976, *14*, 22–25.

de Catanzaro, D. A., & Baldwin, G. Effective treatment of self-injurious behavior through a forced arm exercise. *American Journal of Mental Deficiency*, 1978, *82*, 433–439.

Dietz, S. M., & Repp, A. C. Decreasing classroom misbehavior through the use of DRL schedules of reinforcement. *Journal of Applied Behavior Analysis*, 1973, *6*, 457–463.

Doleys, D., Wells, K., Hobbs, S., Roberts, M., & Cartelli, L. The effects of social punishment on non-compliance: A comparison with time-out and positive practice. *Journal of Applied Behavior Analysis*, 1976, *4*, 471–482.

Favell, J. E., McGimsey, J. F., & Jones, M. L. The use of physical restraint in the treatment of self injury and as a positive reinforcement. *Journal of Applied Behavior Analysis*, 1978, *11*, 225–241.

Forehand, R., & Baumeister, A. Deceleration of aberrant behavior among retarded individuals. In M. Hersen, R. M. Eisler, & P. M. Miller (Eds.), *Progress in behavior modification*. New York: Academic Press, 1976.

Forehand, R., Roberts, M., Doleys, D., Hobbs, S., & Resick, P. An examination of disciplinary procedures with children. *Journal of Experimental Child Psychology*, 1975, *4*, 95–100.

Foxx, R. M. The use of overcorrection to eliminate the public disrobing (stripping) of retarded women. *Behavior Research & Therapy*, 1976, *14*, 53–61.

Foxx, R. M., & Azrin, N. H. Restitution: A method of eliminating aggressive-disruptive behaviour of retarded and brain-damaged patients. *Behaviour Research and Therapy*, 1972, *10*, 15–27.

Foxx, R. M., & Azrin, N. H. The elimination of autistic and self stimulatory behavior by overcorrection. *Journal of Applied Behavior Analysis*, 1973, *6*, 1–14.

Foxx, R. M., & Shapiro, S. T. The time out ribbon: A non-exclusionary time out procedure. *Journal of Applied Behavior Analysis*, 1978, *11*, 125–136.

Gable, R. A., Hendrickson, J. M., & Strain, P. S. Assessment, modification, and generalization of social interaction among severely retarded, multihandicapped children. *Education and Training of the Mentally Retarded*, 1978, *13*, 279–286.

Garcia, E., Baer, D. M., & Firestone, I. The development of generalized imitation within topographically determined boundaries. *Journal of Applied Behavior Analysis*, 1971, *4*, 101–112.

Green, R. J., & Hoats, D. L. Aversive tickling: A simple conditioning technique. *Behavior Therapy*, 1971, *2*, 389–393.

Guess, D., & Rutherford, G. Experimental attempts to reduce stereotyping among blind retardates. *American Journal of Mental Deficiency*, 1967, *71*, 984–986.

Hargrave, E., & Swisher, L. Modifying the verbal expression of a child with autistic behaviors. *Journal of Autism and Childhood Schizophrenia*, 1975, *5*, 147–154.

Hollis, J. H. The effects of social and nonsocial stimuli on the behavior of profoundly retarded children, Part 1. *American Journal of Mental Deficiency*, 1965, *69*, 755–771.

Hutt, C., & Hutt, S. J. Effects of environmental complexity on stereotyped behaviors of children. *Animal Behavior*, 1965, *13*, 1–4.

Kaufman, M. E. The effects of institutionalization on development of stereotyped and social behaviors in mental defectives. *American Journal of Mental Deficiency*, 1967, *71*, 581–585.

Koegel, R. L., Firestone, P. B., Kramme, K. W., & Dunlap, G. Increasing spontaneous play by suppressing self-stimulation in autistic children. *Journal of Applied Behavior Analysis*, 1974, *7*, 521–528.

Lovaas, O. I. *Recent developments in behavior modification with autistic children.* Paper presented at the Annual Meeting of the National Society for Autistic Children, 1975.

Lovaas, O.I., Berberich, J.P., Perloff, B.F., & Schaeffer, B. Acquisition of imitative speech by schizophrenic children. *Science*, 1966, *151*, 705–707.

Lovaas, O. I., Freitag, G., Gold, U. J., & Kassorla, I. C. Experimental studies in childhood schizophrenia: Analysis of self-destructive behavior. *Journal of Experimental Child Psychology*, 1965, *2*, 67–84.

Lovaas, O. I., Litrownik, A., & Mann, R. Response latencies to auditory stimuli of autistic children engaged in self-stimulatory behavior. *Behaviour Research and Therapy*, 1971, *9*, 39–49.

Lovaas, O. I., Schaeffer, B., & Simmons, J. Q. Building social behavior in autistic children by use of electric shock. *Journal of Experimental Research in Personality*, 1965, *1*, 99–109.

Lovaas, O. I., & Simmons, J. Q. Manipulation of self-destruction in three retarded children. *Journal of Applied Behavior Analysis*, 1969, *2*, 143–157.

Lutzker, J. R. Reduction in self-injurious behavior by facial screening. *American Journal of Mental Deficiency*, 1978, *5*, 510–513.

McConnell, O. L. Control of eye contact in an autistic child. *Journal of Child Psychology and Psychiatry*, 1967, *8*, 249–255.

MacMillen, D., Forness, S., & Trumbull, B. The role of punishment in the classroom. *Exceptional Children*, 1973, *40*, 85–96.

Madsen, C. H., Becker, W. C., & Thomas, D. Rules, praise and ignoring: Elements of elementary classroom control. *Journal of Applied Behavior Analysis*, 1968, *1*, 139–150.

Marr, J. N., Miller, E. R., & Straub, R. Operant conditioning of attention with a psychotic girl. *Behaviour Research and Therapy*, 1966, *4*, 85–87.

Martin, D., & Foxx, R. Victim control of the aggression of an institutionalized retardate. *Journal of Behavior Therapy and Experimental Psychiatry*, 1975, *4*, 161–165.

Mayhew, G., & Harris, F. Decreasing self-injurious behavior: Punishment with citric acid and positive reinforcement of alternative behavior. *Behavior Modification*, 1979, *3*, 322–336.

Mira, M., & Hoffman, S. Educational programming for multihandicapped deafblind children. *Exceptional Children*, 1974, *40*, 513–514.

Moore, B., & Bailey, J. Social punishment in the modification of a preschool child's "autistic-like" behavior with a mother as therapist. *Journal of Applied Behavior Analysis*, 1973, *6*, 497–507.

Paloutzian, R., Hasazi, J., Streifel, J., & Edgar, C. Promotion of positive social interaction in severely retarded young children. *American Journal of Mental Deficiency*, 1971, *75*, 519–524.

Peterson, G. A., Austin, G. J., & Lang, R. P. Use of teacher prompts to increase social behavior: Generalization effects with severely and profoundly retarded adolescents. *American Journal of Mental Deficiency*, 1979, *84*, 82–86.

Peterson, R. F., & Peterson, L. R. The use of positive reinforcement in the control of self-destructive behavior in a retarded boy. *Journal of Experimental Psychology*, 1968, *6*, 351–360.

Porterfield, J. K., Herbert-Jackson, E., & Risley, T. R. Contingent observation: An effective and acceptable procedure for reducing disruptive behavior of young children in a group setting. *Journal of Applied Behavior Analysis*, 1976, *9*, 55–64.

Premack, D. Toward empirical behavior laws: 1. Positive reinforcement. *Psychological Review*, 1959, *66*, 219–233.

Repp, A. C., & Deitz, S. M. Reducing aggressive and self-injurious behavior through reinforcement of other behaviors. *Journal of Applied Behavior Analysis*, 1977, *7*, 313–325.

Repp, A. C., Deitz, S. M., & Deitz, D. E. Reducing inappropriate behaviors in classrooms and in individual sessions through DRO schedules of reinforcement. *Mental Retardation*, 1976, *14*, 11–15.

Ricks, D. M., & Wing, C. Language, communication and the use of symbols in normal and autistic children. *Journal of Autism and Childhood Schizophrenia*, 1975, *5*, 191–221.

Risley, T. R. The effects and side effects of punishing the autistic behaviors of a deviant child. *Journal of Applied Behavior Analysis*, 1968, *1*, 21–34.

Simmons, J. O., & Lovaas, O. I. Use of pain and punishment as treatment techniques with childhood schizophrenics. *American Journal of Psychotherapy*, 1969, *23*, 23–25.

Steen, P. L., & Zuriff, G. E. The use of relaxation in the treatment of self-injurious behavior. *Journal of Behavior Therapy and Experimental Psychiatry*, 1977, *8*, 447–448.

Strain, P. Increasing social play of severely retarded preschoolers with socio-dramatic activities. *Mental Retardation*, 1975, *13*, 7–9.

Sulzer-Azaroff, B., & Mayer, G. R. *Applying behavior analysis procedures with children and youth.* New York: Holt, Rinehart & Winston, 1977.

Tanner, B. A., & Zeiler, M. Punishment of self-injurious behavior using aromatic ammonia as the aversive stimulus. *Journal of Applied Behavior Analysis*, 1975, *8*, 53–57.

Ulrich, R. E., & Azrin, N. H. Reflexive fighting in response to aversive stimulation. *Journal of the Experimental Analysis of Behavior*, 1962, *5*, 511-520.

Wehman, P., & McLaughlin, P. J. Teacher's perceptions of behavior problems with severely and profoundly handicapped students. *Mental Retardation*, 1979, *17*, 20-21.

Whitman, T., Mercurio, J., & Caponigii, V. Development of social responses in two severely retarded children. *Journal of Applied Behavior Analysis*, 1970, *3*, 133-138.

Wolf, M. M., Risley, T. & Mees, H. Application of operant conditioning principles to the behavior problems of an autistic child. *Behavior Research and Therapy*, 1964, *1*, 305-312.

Worley, M. R. Self-stimulatory behavior as a basis for devising reinforcers. AAESPH Review, 1978, *3*, 23-29.

Yeakel, M. H., Salisbury, L. L., Greer, S. L., & Marcus, L. F. An appliance for autoinduced adverse control of self-injurious behavior. *Journal of Experimental Child Psychology*, 1970, *10*, 159-169.

Zeilburger J., Sampen, S. E., & Sloane, H. N. Modification of a child's problem behaviors at home with the mother as therapist. *Journal of Applied Behavior Analysis*, 1968, *1*, 47-53.

Chapter 9

Adaptations for the Sensorially Handicapped

Sheldon Maron

This chapter focuses on severely and multiply handicapped individuals with sensory deficits (i.e., visual handicaps, hearing impairments, or a combination of both). These learners represent a population generally exhibiting significant delays in many, if not most, areas of human growth and development (e.g., daily living skills, motor development, communication and socialization skills, etc.). They require a comprehensive, individualized education plan in order to reach the highest level of independence of which they are capable. Traditional assessment tools and curricular packages need substantial modification if they are to be useful for this group of handicapped students.

The prevalence and incidence of blind and deaf multihandicapped persons has been increasing for some time, especially since the rubella epidemic of 1963 to 1965. Wolf (1965) estimated that one-third of the blind population he observed had additional handicaps. Craig and Craig (1975) found that 21% of 53,009 deaf students studied were multiply handicapped, while Ries (1973) reported that 25% of the hearing-impaired children and youth sampled had at least one additional handicap. Medical advances, special education legislation, federal funding priorities, and more optimistic educational philosophies have been the primary factors responsible for the emergence of these subgroups both in residential and public school programs. Overall, these individuals could be best characterized by their relatively small numbers and extreme heterogeneity.

Sensorially handicapped children and adults with concomitant disabilities represent a low-incidence group fraught with stereotypes and misconceptions. Until recently, they were commonly excluded from programs in most public school systems as well as from many workshop opportunities. The public, including many educators, has had little contact with, and knowledge of, these people, and so are less likely to be supportive of establishing programs for them. In fact, many parents complain that despite the mandates of P.L. 94-142, their small numbers act as a deterrent to the development of programs and services for their children. Exclusionary policies still continue to be a significant problem for special educators and parents alike.

The notion that severely and multiply handicapped individuals cannot learn or do not belong in public schools has resulted in a host of self-fulfilling prophecies (Haring & Bricker, 1976). When individualized instruction is withheld for this reason, a vicious circle develops, further reinforcing the low expectation levels, reduced expenditures, and low service priorities. In the long run, it costs far more to do nothing than to provide quality programs and services. Not only does it make good sense, but P.L. 94-142 and Section 504 of the Rehabilitation Act of 1973 mandate that this be the case.

Professionals from numerous disciplines have expressed the feeling that medical and psychological diagnoses do not necessarily have substantial predictive validity for the teacher, parent, or employer. Diagnostic labels such as "legal blindness," "deafness," and "severely and multiply handicapped" often have little direct correspondence to people in "the real world." For example, there is little compelling evidence that demonstrates a strong link between IQ scores and the development of orientation and mobility skills, vocational success, or socialization skills in visually handicapped people. Similarly, audiometric evaluations of hearing-impaired children without their aids on are generally poor indicators and predictors of hearing ability (Pollack, 1964). Reliance on unaided audiograms can thus give misleading information about how a person's hearing is utilized in everyday life, lead to serious errors in program placement, and generate negative expectations of future performance.

Labels, although enabling funding by category, do not necessarily reflect or predict ability in the classroom, at home, or in the community (Hobbs, 1975). Labels are often not only misleading and counterproductive, but they do not address the basic instructional concerns of teachers: What do I teach? How do I teach it? How do I know when it is adequately learned?

The ability to see or hear is a function of many factors and because of this can fluctuate greatly. Motivation, stability of condition, experiential opportunities, intelligence, additional handicaps, and instructional strategies are but some considerations that must be taken into account. When evaluated by individuals with limited experience in working with sensorially handicapped students, it is not surprising to find that many have been misdiagnosed as autistic, mentally retarded, emotionally disturbed, or learning disabled (although these conditions may exist in combination with a vision or hearing difficulty).

Those who work with the multihandicapped must carefully analyze the interacting effects of multiple disabilities. When one handicap is complicated by another, the resulting problems (both in teaching and learning) are not additive, but probably increase exponentially. For example, in Usher's Syndrome, in which congenital deafness is followed by the visual difficulties of retinitis pigmentosa, many of the educational techniques used with the deaf become increasingly less applicable (e.g., sign language, color-coded instructional materials, etc.). As vision progressively deteriorates, these compensatory techniques are no longer appropriate, and the number of proven alternative approaches is significantly reduced. To give another example, as the communication problems of deafness are compounded by the mobility problems of blindness, resulting social, cognitive, self-help, academic, and vocational difficulties are often intensified.

It is essential to remember that many disciplines have a vested interest in sensorially handicapped individuals. Effective instruction requires strong ancillary support from audiologists, optometrists, speech pathologists, ophthalmologists, social workers, physical therapists, orientation and mobility specialists, physical educators, and so forth. Professional alliances and multidisciplinary (or transdisciplinary) delivery systems require a sharing of turf in the formation of a treatment plan with clear-cut lines of involvement and responsibility. Teachers must become thoroughly familiar with the spectrum of programs and services available not only in their communities but also those funded by state and national agencies, such as the American Foundation for the Blind, The Alexander Graham Bell Association for the Deaf, and the Helen Keller National Center for Deaf-Blind Youths and Adults.

Teachers and other interested professionals will be called upon increasingly to serve as advocates and case managers for these students. This is especially true in these times of rapid technological advances and changing delivery systems. It becomes crucial, therefore, that these workers not only have opportunities to update their skills, but also receive ongoing support and encouragement from their program administrators in this endeavor.

CURRICULUM AND INSTRUCTIONAL GUIDELINES

When planning educational programs, counseling parents, or evaluating performance, the following guidelines should be considered.

1. Sensorially handicapped students learn best by direct, first-hand experiences with real-life situations. Although models, replicas, and verbal explanations are sometimes appropriate or mandatory, they do not always convey the dynamic, ever-changing relationships of stimuli. In short, learning by doing is an essential way of compensating for reduced visual and auditory input. Just as important, teachers and parents must encourage active exploration of the environment as early as possible. Overprotective parents, although well intentioned, may unknowingly reduce the already meager stimuli available, placing the student at a further disadvantage.

2. Hearing-impaired and visually handicapped students must develop their auditory abilities as early as possible. Pollack's unisensory approach (1970), as well as many multisensory programs for hearing-impaired infants and children, stresses auditory training, early fitting with hearing aids, and close cooperation from parents. Even severe hearing losses usually leave individuals with some residual hearing that can be used for everyday functioning. Activities that promote awareness, localization, discrimination, and recognition of sounds should play a central role in the curriculum.

   For the visually handicapped student, these same principles also apply, especially for the congenitally blind child. Often, many deaf and blind students have significant amounts of usable hearing and vision. The definition of deaf-blindness (see *The Deaf-Blind Student*) is a functional one — it is not linked to any specific level of vision or hearing ability. It is also imperative that these students have their hearing tested annually and especially when a change in hearing acuity is observed.

3. Students with sensory difficulties must be taught to develop their vision to its utmost. Room lighting, seating arrangements, low-vision aids, enlarged print, and vision-stimulation programs are all important considerations in improving a child's visual efficiency (how well vision is used for everyday purposes). No prosthetic sensory system can even remotely approximate the sensitivity and resiliency of the eyes, and the presence of residual vision makes the teachers' and learners' options significantly greater. As with hearing visual ability should be regularly assessed by an optometrist or ophthalmologist.

4. Adapted or constructed materials for students should be:
   a. simple and uncluttered with extraneous information.
   b. durable enough so that they can withstand rough handling.
   c. made of nontoxic materials in case they are put in the mouth.
   d. free of sharp or jagged edges.
   e. easily discriminated or highlighted against a given background (i.e., consider contrast, color, texture, size, shape, etc.).

    f.   of a size and shape that facilitates ease of manipulation.

    g.   stimulating, interesting, and geared for the student's developmental needs.

    h.   without extraneous cues that detract from the critical elements of the instructional objectives.

    i.   easily understood and capable of being used by a variety of instructors.

5.   A wide range and variety of experiences should be provided (Lowenfeld, 1973), especially in the formative years. Trips to the supermarket and department store are excellent teaching opportunities. The use of residual vision, hearing, touch, smell, and taste should be stimulated. The students should be provided with constant communication (verbal or manual), and encouraged in self-initiated activity. For the preschool child, the importance of conversation cannot be overestimated. Communication should center around the following (Northcott, 1972).

    a.   accepting the child's conversation, however imperfect.

    b.   linking messages with meaningful activities.

    c.   speaking naturally and having the child focus attention on the teacher or parent.

    d.   basing communication on the child's experiential world.

6.   Instructors should work coactively with students. Often it is advantageous to work from behind the student, especially when body control is essential (e.g., when teaching feeding or dressing skills).

7.   Careful task analysis of situations is important for avoidance of a cookbook format of instruction. Each learner needs an individualized program of direct instruction. Two multihandicapped students learning the same skill may require two significantly different behavioral sequences.

8.   At the outset of instruction, a highly structured environment may provide the best setting for mastering daily tasks. As competence develops, more natural settings can be incorporated into the overall program.

9.   Instructional programs should be developed in a logical, orderly progression corresponding to the same developmental milestones seen in normal students (i.e., from simple to complex, from more concrete to less concrete, in order of functional value to the student, etc.).

10.   Some students may engage in mannerisms (ritualistic behaviors such as rocking, flicking of the fingers in front of the eyes, eye poking, etc.). This is more likely to occur in situations in which meaningful stimulation is lacking. These unacceptable behaviors can be best dealt with by providing sensory stimulation activities and by rewarding incompatible behaviors that are more socially acceptable.

11. In order to develop or modify a curriculum for the severely handi-
     capped, it is important to determine first the range of possible future
     placements for each learner, and then the environmental demands
     that these settings require for successful functioning (White, 1980).
     Placement possibilities, however, that are both reasonable and real-
     istic can sometimes be difficult to pinpoint. Despite this potential
     uncertainty, the following suggestions may prove helpful (White,
     pp. 63–67).
     a. Consider the general skills that will be needed for successful
         functioning in a given setting. Most often this will include sur-
         vival skills for improving independence in everyday situations.
         Adaptations of existing curricula should also be contemplated.
     b. Weigh the essential components of each skill and how they
         must be broken down for each student.
     c. Consider specific adaptations that may be needed for those with
         senory deficits (e.g., group hearing aids, glare-free pictures,
         low-vision aids, seating arrangements, etc.). This can include
         modification of materials, equipment, and environments.
     d. Plan a systematic way of recording and evaluating behaviors.
         This should include both gradations of skill levels (e.g., un-
         aided, verbally prompted, physically prompted, no response,
         etc.) and predetermined criteria for judging acceptable perfor-
         mance of the assigned task.
12. Like all other students, the severely handicapped respond best to a
     disciplinary program in which the behavioral limits are clearly artic-
     ulated and appropriate behavior consistently rewarded. Acknowl-
     edgment of acceptable and unacceptable behavior must show con-
     sistency from teacher to teacher as well as across learning situations.
13. Specialized equipment or specialized techniques should not be over-
     emphasized, but placed in proper perspective. Successful programs
     are largely based on the quality of interaction between teacher and
     pupil, and that consideration should serve as the core of the instruc-
     tional program. Equipment and techniques are only a means to an
     end and not ends in themselves.
14. Although highly important in teaching compensatory skills, the
     senses of hearing and touch have limitations that must be recog-
     nized. Tactual exploration is a much slower process than visual
     searching and is limited by the complexity of the stimulus. It re-
     quires a piecemeal construction of units into wholes, the inverse of
     visual processing. Hearing, on the other hand, is a long-distance
     sense dependent on the production of sounds that (1) may be masked
     by other sounds, (2) may be intermittent, and (3) do not necessarily
     give information about the essential properties of objects per se.
     Despite these drawbacks, however, auditory training and tactual

discrimination skills should play a key role in readiness training, which in turn leads to basic skill acquisition.

SPECIAL ADAPTATIONS IN SCHOOL

Visual Assessment

The sense of vision is highly complex and has many different functional parameters. Detail resolution at a distance (acuity) and closeup (near vision) are key components, and both must be evaluated to give an accurate profile of visual abilities. It should be noted that in many low-vision individuals, distance and near vision do not necessarily correspond. Binocularity (both eyes working together), visual field (area seen by the fixed eye or eyes), night vision, and color vision are other visual functions that must be regularly evaluated by eye specialists. By definition, low-vision patients are those who, even with the best correction possible (i.e. through medicine, surgery, low-vision aids, or a combination of treatments), have subnormal vision.

Teachers, on the other hand, as well as other personnel working with the visually handicapped, can play an important role in assessing visual skills for programming needs. They also should initiate referrals for additional testing when specific behaviors are noted. Below are listed visual behaviors and parameters of vision that require assessment in order to generate a more precise record of visual abilities (Ficociello, 1976; Kaplan, 1976; Langley & Dubose, 1976). The following areas should be carefully observed:

I.   General conditon of the eyes and visual behaviors.
    a.   Inappropriate behaviors (eye poking, fixation on lights, etc.).
    b.   Nystagmus — rapid oscillations (vertical or horizontal) or "dancing" of the eyes.
    c.   Head or body tilting to see better.
    d.   Crusting, burning, itching, or watering of the eyes.
    e.   Pupillary reaction. Focus a penlight flashlight into the eyes from about 12 inches away. Observe constriction of the pupil as well as dilation when the light is removed.
    f.   Blink reflex. Note eye blinking in response to an object passing in the field of view, or moving directly toward the student.
    g.   Eye deviation. Note simultaneous movement of both eyes, especially when an object is brought up close. Observe whether light is centered in the pupils of both eyes.
    h.   Visual fields. Working behind the student, slowly bring a penlight around the right and the left visual field and then from above and below. Note when the student first notices the light.

      i.   Eye preference. Provide preferred objects such as toys to the student in both right and left visual fields. Carefully observe if he or she consistently prefers to play with objects on one side more so than the other.

      j.   Color vision. Does the student respond to all or only some colors?

      k.   Acuity. How far away must objects be in order to be seen clearly? How large must objects be in order to be seen clearly?

II.   Visual skills.

      a.   Attending and shifting attention. Shine a penlight into each eye, then both eyes, from 10 to 12 inches away. Check to see whether the student watches the light and for how long, and whether the student tries to grasp the light.

      b.   Fixation. Using a favorite toy or a light, determine how long the student can selectively focus on the stimulus and assess fixating ability with each eye as well as with both eyes.

      c.   Tracking. Using a penlight, note whether the student can follow a moving light horizontally, vertically, and obliquely.

      d.   Scanning. Placing preferred toys in front of the student, note the frequency and regularity of attending powers as the gaze is shifted from one toy to another.

      e.   Auditory-visual reflex. Using an auditory stimulus (bell or buzzer), observe whether the student looks in the direction of the sound.

III. Motor performance utilizing vision.

      a.   Eye-hand coordination (gross and fine motor).

         1.   gross—observe skills in bouncing a ball, balancing, and imitating body movements.

         2.   fine—observe bead stringing, block building, cutting, etc.

      b.   Eye-foot coordination. Observe skills in walking, kicking a ball, and jumping over an obstacle.

      c.   Body movement and body image. Check for identification of body parts, balance on one foot, rhythmic hopping, control over body movement, etc.

      d.   Laterality and directionality. Assess discrimination skills between left and right, up and down, front and back, etc. This can be done verbally or nonverbally.

      e.   Functional movement. Note ease and independence of travel, overall coordination, and facility in getting about in familiar and nonfamiliar settings.

IV. Visual perceptual skills.

      a.   Discrimination of shapes, sizes, and colors (depending on residual vision). Utilize matching activities, sorting and classifying, and sequencing activities.

    b.   Figure-ground discrimination. Present cards with objects either inside others or overlapping others. Dark line drawings with high contrast are preferred.

    c.   Visual memory. Ask the student to imitate simple patterns of colored cubes, blocks, or designs (visually or tactually).

    d.   Spatial relationships. Using toys or other preferred objects, the teacher probes for recognition when objects have been rotated in space, viewed from different vantage points, or both.

V.   Visual-cognitive processing.

    a.   Object permanence. The teacher shows the child a favorite object and then removes it from view, watching to see whether he or she searches for it. More complex variations upon this theme can be developed (e.g., hiding one object within another).

    b.   Anticipation. The teacher runs a toy train through a tunnel and has the student watch until it appears on the other side. After a few trials, it is noted whether the student moves to the other side of the tunnel waiting for the train to appear.

    c.   Causality. The teacher has the child watch various pull or wind-up toys in action. It is noted whether the child attempts to perform the same activity with the toy.

    d.   Object constancy. The teacher carefully observes recognition of favorite objects despite being placed at varying distances and in different spatial orientations.

    e.   Means-ends relationships. The student watches the activity of an action toy, and then the teacher places it out of sight. When placed back into view, the teacher observes whether the student attempts to activate the toy.

Object permanence, anticipation, causality, object constancy, and means-ends relationships are key developmental milestones. They normally appear or begin to emerge within the first two years of life. They are not only dependent to a large degree on the ability to see and hear, but are also key determinants of reasoning abilities. These relationships are a primary reason why blind students, especially the congenitally blind, generally fall behind their normally sighted peers on Piagetian scales of cognitive functioning. Furthermore, Bricker and Bricker (1970) have suggested that these same developmental benchmarks (including purposeful activity with objects) are prerequisites for language development as well.

Auditory Assessment

Most traditional tests of auditory function such as pure-tone audiometry are often inappropriate for multihandicapped deaf children (Franklin, 1977). In fact, Eisenberg (1976) concluded that no sensitive battery of tests exists for infants (and correspondingly for those who function at this level). Below are listed some auditory behaviors that teachers and parents should look for and report to the audiologist or otolaryngologist when hearing is evaluated.

1. Auditory behaviors
   a. awareness of sounds. For many children, certain sounds may lose their novelty readily through habituation. To reduce stimulus adaptation, note awareness and response to a number of different auditory stimuli.
   b. response to environmental sounds, especially those heard around the home. As with all responses listed here and below, watch for a head turn, eye blink, change of activity, startle, reaching for the sound source, etc.
   c. response to musical sounds and sound toys, such as drums, clackers, and cowbells.
   d. response to loud noises and loud voices (familiar and nonfamiliar).
   e. response to his or her own name (spoken and tape recorded).
   f. response to simple commands.
   g. attending to sounds in purposeful activity.
   h. attempting to localize the source of sounds (e.g., looking for or moving in the direction of the sound's origin).
   i. spontaneous vocalizing or imitating. Observe response when the teacher's or parent's face is present as a visual cue and when it is absent (reliance on auditory and visual input). Note the differences in each situation.
   j. discriminating between sounds.
   k. associating sounds with meaning. Use sound stimuli to probe for (1) object permanence and (2) anticipation.
      Test from both left and right sides, front and rear. Sounds should be of 4 to 5 seconds duration and located no more than 12 inches from the head. Alternate presentations 3 to 4 inches on either side of the posterior midline (Sailor et al., 1980a).
2. Some behaviors may signal a change in auditory acuity. The following behaviors usually indicate that a comprehensive hearing evaluation should be performed:
   a. increased difficulty in hearing distant or close-up sounds. Note hearing changes for speech in the conversational range.
   b. lack of or change in response to loud sounds.
   c. inability to screen out extraneous or background sounds.
   d. complaints of ringing or pain in the ears.
   e. consistent head or body tilting to hear better.
   f. wide fluctuations in hearing ability from day to day.

    g.   tendency to become more dependent on vision in learning situations.

    h.   aggressive and "acting out" behavior or withdrawn, passive, and submissive behavior. Increased amount of time spent daydreaming.

    i.   decreased ability to coordinate visual and auditory clues.

    j.   problems monitoring his or her voice and speech.

    k.   speech or language regression.

    l.   decreased interest in social interaction.

3.   Sailor et al. (1980b) have developed two stimulus shift paradigms to prepare some severely handicapped students for formal audiological assessment. The programs involve transferring stimulus control from one set of stimuli that determined a response to a second set that initially did not control that behavior.

    A motor response (head turning, reaching for an object, etc.) is first linked to a light stimulus. The light is then paired with an auditory cue, and the light source is gradually faded in intensity until the motor response occurs as a result of the auditory stimulus alone. If such a shift occurs, then the audiologist has a starting point for testing. Care should be taken with some low vision and deaf-blind students that the light stimulus does not increase stereotypic behaviors.

    For a totally blind child, a motor response such as grasping may be initiated in response to a tangible stimulus, paired with an auditory cue, that is later faded. It is essential that the paired stimuli have reinforcing value and that the response mode already exist in the student's behavioral repertoire.

4.   Audiological assessment of newborn infants using the crib-o-gram technique has been demonstrated by Simmons (1977). Amplified sounds are presented at regularly scheduled intervals. Sensors attached to the crib detect the infant's movement responses seconds before and after the presentations of these sound stimuli. This approach, however, is useful only for the detection of significant hearing losses. With continued refinements to produce increased sensitivity, this technique represents a potential breakthrough for early identification of mild to moderate hearing losses. At this age, intervention procedures may have even greater therapeutic effects.

Classroom Management

The ultimate goal of those who teach developmentally delayed students with visual and hearing problems is the students' attainment of skills that allow independent functioning in a wide variety of settings. Mastery of these skills, however, requires that they be broken down into a series of simpler tasks that can be taught separately and then be recombined until the overall skill is learned. Although such a task-analytic approach is effective, some cautions need to be emphasized.

1. Severely handicapped individuals often have great difficulty in transferring and generalizing skills learned in the classroom to novel settings (Williams, Brown, & Certo, 1975a; Brown, Nietupske, & Hamre-Wietupske, 1976). One common problem with behavioral chaining (sequencing skills together to form more complex behaviors) is the limited ability of students to connect discrete behaviors in an artificial environment. Even when skills are task analyzed into simpler steps, students often cannot make appropriate associations so that the behavior has functional value outside the classroom. This is why a greater emphasis should be placed on (a) teaching in natural settings, such as home and community-based environments and (b) using the actual materials likely to be encountered in real-life situations.

2. A second potential problem with the skill-oriented approach is that students may not get sufficient opportunity or encouragement to initiate behaviors. Mere replication of teacher-initiated skills is often marked by a rote, mechanical appearance that has limited functional value at home or in the community (Maron, 1979; Krug, Rosenblum, Almond, & Arrick, 1980).

3. Another possible problem that requires closer scrutiny by teachers is the selection and use of reinforcers. Although tokens and social praise may be employed in school for such activities as toilet training or shoe tying, these skills are expected in other settings, and rewards are rarely given for their performance. Teachers must be willing to fade out artificial rewards as soon as possible in favor of natural reinforcers. For a task to be replicated successfully and independently, it must have meaning for the student. In the long run, motivation to learn a task because of its perceived value must be at the core of the learning process. Eventually, the student must understand the connection between the actual carrying out of an activity and its consequences (Krug et al., 1980). As this occurs, transference, generalization, and retention will be improved. To see more rapid gains, teachers should require their students to complete tasks:
    a. in response to a number of different instructors.
    b. in response to different verbal and nonverbal cues.
    c. in different environments, preferably natural settings, where the specified behavior commonly takes place.

4. A fourth potential difficulty lies in the determination of criteria for successful performance levels. Achievement of arbitrarily chosen response rates does not necessarily indicate that a given skill has been mastered. It may be quite disconcerting for both teacher and student to find that appropriate response rates (and the intensity or duration

of responses) in the classroom meet with frustration in community settings or at home.

Vision and hearing impairments do affect response occurrences, often significantly (e.g., time taken to locate clothing or master a list of signs, etc.). It is desirable to reach the highest responding levels possible, especially with developmental skills, because they involve cumulative activity. Performance criteria must be situation specific; that is, they must be tied to the broader environment in which they are likely to occur.

5. Teachers must develop a data collection and evaluation system to verify that a given skill has been mastered (Williams et al., 1975b). Systematic recording of performance levels is essential for the determination of student competence. Program planning, modification, evaluation, and justification all hinge on this empirical data.

Direct measurement is also important when teaching cumulative skills, and most developmental skills are taught and learned in this fashion (Brown, 1976). A well-organized data-collection and retrieval schedule is essential, and it must not interfere with the daily instructional program. Teachers are urged to investigate many different measurement designs (e.g., multiple baseline, trials to criterion, ABAB, etc.) when searching for the one (or ones) that most appropriately meet their needs. Perhaps even more basic than design selection is the development of a clearly articulated rationale for measuring the relationships between student behaviors and performance objectives.

When vision and hearing problems are compounded by other handicaps, serious developmental lags often surface. As the severity of the handicaps increase and their interactive effects become more evident, the learner's world becomes more chaotic. Environmental contact takes on a more haphazard, less predictable pattern. Control over everyday events becomes difficult, with corresponding problems in systematic coping strategies.

To combat this problem, classroom settings should follow a more structured format. Under such a controlled situation, clear-cut behavioral limits are established, and extraneous environmental stimuli are minimized to a greater degree. A framework is thus established whereby mastery of basic skills can easily be achieved and performance is more easily monitored by the instructor. Success in this endeavor serves as an impetus for further exploration and mastery, and so begins a cyclical process of developmental progression. Although classroom settings by no means represent learning in the real world, they signal a beginning from which an adaptive behavioral repertoire can be built.

Teachers at the initial stage must be willing to accept small gains in performance that come at the expense of much repetition. The routine, structure, and slow progress may pose a problem for some teachers, especially those who become frustrated by the significant discrepancy between their expectations and the relatively slow rate of student achievement. Other sources of frustration include (1) limited interaction opportunities with colleagues and other interested workers to share concerns and needs, (2) lack of support from administrators or supervisors, and (3) limited opportunities for in-service training to update skills. Perhaps these are some reasons contributing to the high rate of "burnout" and staff turnover among teachers of the severely and profoundly handicapped.

From direct observations and assessment instruments come data for determining annual goals. These goals are then translated into a series of long- and short-term objectives that target specific skills to be developed or modified (e.g., self-help skills, grooming, and toothbrushing). Behavioral objectives must be written in clear, operationally defined, and measurable terms. They should also include a statement of the criterion level for task mastery, together with the conditions under which the learning is to occur. Once an instructional objective is isolated, the process of task analysis can be used to pinpoint the target behavior stated in the objective and to break it down into a series of interdependent activities (see Table 1). Behavioral objectives should serve to provide (Ryan et al., 1977):

1. a mechanism for the assessment and evaluation of student performance. Guidelines are designated for minimal acceptable performance levels that can be determined by specific test instruments.
2. a framework for curriculum usage. Curricula and materials can be selected with greater assurance that they are appropriate for a particular student.
3. an easily discernible level of competency from which to evaluate successful performance as well as guidelines to indicate when to proceed with further stages of instruction.
4. a clearly articulated statement of expectations and required achievement levels.
5. a well-organized efficient system of performance criteria that meet the requirements of P.L. 94-142.

Examples of behavioral objectives written for sensorially handicapped individuals are listed below.

I. *Goal*: To improve sound-localization skills.
 A. *Long-term objective*: When presented with four different sounds (bell, drum, cymbals, and human voice) at 4-second durations, the student begins moving toward the source of each sound within 10 seconds.
 B. *Short-term objective*: When presented with the sound of a bell at a 6-second duration, the student begins to move in the direction of that sound within 10 seconds.

Table 1. Comparison of Rubella and Usher's syndromes.

	Rubella Syndrome (German Measles)	Usher's Syndrome
Cause	Virus contracted in the first trimester of pregnancy	Unknown; inherited as an autosomal recessive
Occurrence	Present at birth; a cyclical disease (6 to 7 year intervals)	Congenital deafness complicated by retinitis pigmentosa in teenage years or later
Sites potentially affected	Eyes (e.g., congenital cataracts); ears (sensorineural loss); cardiovascular system; musculoskeletal system; central nervous system	Eyes (deterioration of vision from peripheral to central); ears; central nervous system
Treatment (medical)	Surgical removal of cataracts and fitting with eyeglasses; hearing aids; cardiovascular and orthopedic surgery; effective vaccine available for young girls (preventative)	Experimental treatment available for retinitis pigmentosa; no cure known; premium must be placed on prevention
Treatment (psychoeducational)	Visual and auditory stimulation programs; academic and vocational programs, as well as those to improve developmental skills	Genetic counseling and rehabilitation services (orientation and mobility training, braille instruction, communication skills, etc.); career counseling and psychological services
Risk	15% of women in child-bearing years; once contracted in first trimester, risk is 15% to 20%	3% to 6% of congenitally deaf children in the U.S.
Mechanism of action	Virus blocks cell division	Unknown

II. *Goal*: To develop manual communication skills.
   A. *Long-term objective*: When presented with pictures of family members, the student makes the correct sign for mother, father, and brother with 100% accuracy for six consecutive trials (two trials daily).
   B. *Short-term objective*: When presented with a picture of his or her mother, the student will make the correct sign with 100% accuracy for six consecutive trials (two trials daily).
III. *Goal*: To develop braille readiness skills.
   A. *Long-term objective*: When presented with five 3-inch squares of various textures, the student correctly identifies the two that are identical in all six trials.
   B. *Short-term objective*: When presented with three 4-inch squares of various textures, the student correctly identifies the two identical textures in five of six trials.
IV. *Goal*: To improve independent travel skills.
   A. *Long-term objective*: Upon leaving the dormitory room, the student walks unaided to the classroom on the first floor of the school building within 15 minutes for 6 consecutive school days.
   B. *Short-term objective*: The student travels unaided from the dormitory room to the stairway leading to the front hallway of the building with 100% accuracy for 4 consecutive days.

In developing behavioral and instructional objectives, the following points should be kept in mind (Van Etten, Arkell, & Van Etten, 1980).

1. Tasks must have meaning for the student. For example, deaf students must make the connection between a sign, its referent, and its action sequence as early as possible.
2. Skills must have functional value to the student. Hearing-impaired students learning new words or signs must have opportunities outside the classroom to use them. Similarly, a blind child must have opportunities to practice and use the orientation and mobility techniques taught at school. Feedback in the form of positive reinforcement from significant others tends to increase the probability that these behaviors are demonstrated again.
3. Skills must be functionally related to each other. Competencies are not fragmented in real life, only in textbooks. Survival skills require an interdependency of skills (e.g., motor, communication, and cognitive).
4. Instructional objectives must be related to the nature and severity of the visual or auditory problem. For example, the presence of a potentially progressive and unstable eye disease such as diabetic retinopathy may contraindicate a vision stimulation program. When

possible, it is essential to determine the prognosis of eye function prior to the formulation of specific objectives.

5. Sufficient instructional time must be allocated for teaching and learning skills. A skill priority list should be established, because the constraints of time often play an important role in determining what can be realistically taught and learned.

6. Skills must be appropriate to the overall instructional sequence designed by the teacher. For example, independent travel skills must be taught after the basic functions of balance, coordination, and concept formation are well established.

7. Skill development must bear a close relationship to the student's needs and opportunities outside of school. Parents, ward staff, and other interested individuals must be willing to follow through on the programming begun at school. Their encouragement, enthusiasm, and visitations to the school make a significant impact on school performance.

Once short-term objectives are formulated, they must then be task analyzed into a sequence of simpler steps (see Figures 1 and 2). Often they are further subdivided, since severely handicapped students will progress in smaller increments over longer periods of time. A plan is then devised that details how each step is to be accomplished (Snell, 1978).

In designing instructional programs, a strong rationale must be developed in response to the following question: Why is it important that this student perform this particular skill? This key question must be related to other concerns: 1) What materials are to be used? 2) What strategies are to be employed? 3) What prerequisite skills are needed? 4) What is the setting in which the activities will occur? and 5) What are the minimal acceptable performance levels for this task?

The Deaf-Blind Student

The deaf-blind are generally defined as having both visual and auditory difficulties the combination of which precludes accommodation in programs solely for the visually handicapped or hearing impaired. The vast majority of deaf-blind people in this country have become sensorially impaired due to either German measles (rubella virus) or Usher's syndrome (see Table 1 for a description of these conditions). The rubella epidemic of 1963 to 1965 was responsible for the birth of children with both visual and auditory handicaps, as well as many other combinations of physical and psychological abnormalities. The term *deaf-blind*, for the rubella children at least, is largely a misnomer. Many of these individuals have considerable amounts of residual vision and hearing, and it is essential that they develop these learning channels as early as possible.

Student: Robert C., a student with a severe hearing loss and
            spina bifida.

Short-term objective: When given a physical prompt
                         (touching shoulder), Robert will attend
                         to the movements of a hand puppet for
                         20 seconds without looking away.

Prerequisite skills: 1. head control
                      2. maintenance of eye contact
                      3. visual searching and tracking skills
                      4. social responsiveness and response
                          to simple commands (e.g., his name,
                          "look", etc.)

Task sequence
                      1. Attends to physical prompt
                      2. Demonstrates fixed head position
                      3. Demonstrates eye contact with teacher
                          in sequences of 3, 5, 8, and 10 seconds
                      4. Visually fixates on familiar objects
                          straight ahead in sequences of 5, 8, and
                          10 seconds
                      5. Demonstrates searching and tracking
                          eye movements
                      6. Fixates on objects in all four quadrants
                          of right and left visual fields in se-
                          quences of 5, 8, and 10 seconds
                      7. Tracks movements of familiar objects
                          and people for 8, 10, and 15 seconds
                      8. Can fixate on stationary hand puppet in
                          sequences of 8, 10, and 15 seconds
                      9. Follows movements of hand puppet
                          across both visual fields in sequences of
                          10, 15, and 20 seconds

Figure 1.   Task analysis for developing attending skills.

Certainly the most famous deaf-blind person was Helen Keller.
Despite her blindness and deafness, she was able to lead a remarkable life
and serve as a model of accomplishment for countless individuals, handicapped and otherwise. Much of this success was due to the tireless work
of Anne Sullivan and Helen's other teachers.

It would be a misconception, however, to equate the deaf-blind
child of today with the story of Helen Keller. These students are multiply
handicapped with a wide range of disabling conditions that may be su-
perimposed on their visual and auditory problems. They often are from
the lower socioeconomic strata with fewer opportunities for gaining access to early intervention programs. With the rapidly escalating costs of
educating children today, it is highly unlikely that these students receive
the intense, one-to-one instruction that was afforded the gifted Miss
Keller.

Programs and services for deaf-blind children and youth are provided through regional centers serving all fifty states. Diagnostic, vocational, and social services are also provided by the Helen Keller National Center for Deaf-Blind Youths and Adults in Sands Point, New York. A comprehensive program for deaf-blind individuals should include training in the following areas:

1. *Communication skills.* Possible approaches include:
   A. Oral (speech, Tadoma method, speechreading)
   B. Manual (gestures, signs, fingerspelling, tellatouch, palmwriting, wrist-com)
   C. Combination of oral and manual (total communication, Rochester method, cued speech)
   D. Written (regular and large print, braille, telebraille, Blissymbolics, rebus method)
2. *Orientation and mobility skills.* Some students will have sufficient vision to travel independently. It is also essential to improve motivation to travel as independently as possible. This is especially true of adolescents and adults with the progressive vision deterioration of Usher's syndrome. Some deaf-blind require assistance and must communicate these needs to the public through written cards, printing letters on the palm, and so forth. Some may learn cane skills. Before this occurs, however, training must be provided to improve (Burke, 1976):
   A. Awareness of spatial relationships
   B. Kinesthetic memory
   C. Balance and coordination
   D. Cognitive skills
   E. Residual vision and hearing
   F. Tactile sensitivity
   G. Smell and taste
3. *Daily living skills.* Training areas involve eating skills, dressing and grooming skills, toileting, personal hygiene, interpersonal and social adjustment skills, food preparation, home management, shopping, and leisure and recreational skills.
4. *Prevocational and vocational skills.* This includes work readiness skills, vocational assessment and evaluation, career counseling, career exploration, occupational training and retraining, awareness of local, state, and national rehabilitation agencies, both public and private.
5. *Coping skills and emotional well being.* This will include opportunities for:
   A. Individual and family genetic counseling
   B. Psychological counseling and support services

C. Social contact and interaction with family, peers, neighborhood and community citizenry, and so forth.

Specialized and Modified Curricula

Severely handicapped individuals represent an extremely diverse and heterogeneous group. As such, no curriculum guide can possibly furnish a self-contained package that has all the education solutions to instructional needs. At best, these guides provide a resource for teachers who must make modifications to suit their unique program needs.

When using any of these approaches, it is important to remember that developmental skills evolve in a logical, orderly progression and interact with one another. For example, communication and socialization skills are interdependent and mutually reinforcing, while also sharing a common core of prerequisite behaviors. A number of commercially available curricula which, with modification, may prove helpful to those who work with severely/profoundly handicapped students having sensory deficits are listed in Appendix A.

Specialized Equipment and Techniques

In order to compensate for a visual or hearing loss, special equipment may be necessary. While this equipment is important, it should not take precedence over direct instructional practices. The successful use of these aids depends largely on practice, opportunities for use, level of motivation, and abilities — all of which take time to develop.

Low-Vision Aids Some of the most efficient low-vision aids are the simplest and easiest to obtain. Proper room lighting, glare-free surfaces, and enlarged print should be very helpful. Tensor lamps, adjustable reading stands, and hand-held or mounted magnifying glasses should also be considered for close-up work. For other students, closed-circuit television (e.g., Apollo Laser and Visualtek) may provide significant help, but these aids are much more expensive.

Telescopic lenses often greatly improve distance vision. As the strength of these lenses increases, however, the visual fields correspondingly constrict (as type size increases, for example, less can be seen with a single gaze), so that the amount of information presented for processing at any given time is reduced. This in turn decreases the speed of visual learning and may be fatiguing for the student. Some students may not tolerate eyeglasses or contact lenses, especially when first prescribed. Teachers and others should develop a shaping program of gradually increasing periods when these aids are worn while simultaneously rewarding the required behavior. The same is true of adjusting to any other prosthetic device.

Hearing Aids For many hearing-impaired students, amplification is often of significant help, whether it be used for recognition of environmental sounds or for speech and language usage. Individual and group aids are available. Hearing aids make sounds louder nonselectively, so that distortion commonly occurs. This can be particularly annoying and frustrating when communicating and in social settings. Aids must be worn as much as possible to be most beneficial, and this will take a period of adjustment and encouragement. Those who work with the hearing impaired should be sensitive to these potential problems, particularly encouraging them to wear their aids, and help them maintain the device properly.

Communication Boards   Some multihandicapped students have significant speech and language problems (e.g., those with cerebral palsy, mental retardation, etc.). They can use communication boards by pointing to a word, picture, group of letters, or special symbols that are based on some predetermined rules of communication. These aids provide 1) accessibility to two-way communication, 2) language experiences, 3) enhanced opportunities for social interaction, 4) a vehicle for organizing thoughts, and 5) a source of minimizing the stress and anxiety brought on by poor speech, perhaps leading to improved vocal ability later (Von Bruns-Connolly & Shane, 1978).

Some boards have highly sophisticated circuitry, but to be effective, each must be individualized to represent situations and content that the student is likely to encounter. For the visually handicapped, labels for visual symbols can be easily modified (e.g., using enlarged print or regular print with low-vision aids). Important considerations for the use of communication boards include a design that is flexible to allow for increasing the complexity of the messages at a later time as well as making allowances for the student's range of motion in reaching for commonly needed messages.

Direct selection boards are the simplest to operate, and are often used with Blissymbols, pictographs, or rebuses. Motor responses can be made with a head pointer, eye movements, and so forth. Extensive preplanning should go into format and content selection, a response mode, and discrimination training — all matched to the learner's needs and abilities. In addition, pretraining should include improving visual, auditory, and tactile attending skills.

Braille   Many functionally blind students with additional disabilities depend on braille as a method of communication. For them, the course of instruction may require a slower rate of presentation and more repetition. The Mangold Program (Mangold, 1977) is recommended, since it places strong emphasis on developing proper fundamental touch techniques. It has also given close scrutiny to the sequencing and teaching of the progression of letters and contractions, so that reversals, scrubbing, and other common problems can be minimized.

Talking Book Machines, Records, and Auditory Trainers   Students with visual, orthopedic, neurological, and other chronic health impairments may have difficulty in scanning or turning pages, necessitating the use of the talking book machine. This is a specially designed phonograph that uses long-playing records, and is available on extended loan from the regional library for the blind as part of the Library of Congress program. Books, magazines, and other materials are reproduced and shipped free of charge. Title selections are printed and regularly updated in the publications *Talking Book Topics* and *Braille Book Review*.

Special phonographs with amplifiers also serve as auditory trainers. This device enables a hearing-impaired child to make better use of his or her residual hearing. With microphones and wireless headsets, the child and teacher are able to move freely about the room. In addition, captioned films (messages added to films or filmstrips) are available in a wide variety of topical areas and levels of sophistication.

Mobility Aids   Wheelchairs, braces, crutches, ramps, and canes are devices essential for independent travel and overall functioning. Although prescription and evaluation of their use is determined by physicians, physical therapists, and orientation and mobility specialists, teachers should be well versed in the proper use of this equipment (Heward Orlansky, 1980). Very importantly, parents, teachers, and employers should check for architectural barriers and try to eliminate them. It is essential to encourage independent movement, as it builds increased positive interactions with the environment that in turn lead to the development of a healthier self-concept.

Some individuals may require highly sophisticated prosthetic devices and mobility aids such as artificial limbs and automated wheelchairs. They can be most helpful in integrating the severely handicapped person into the mainstream of society.

There appears to be little evidence that directly links intelligence (as measured by traditional paper and pencil IQ tests) with success in the development of orientation and mobility skills. Thus, even when medical evaluations indicate significant problems (e.g., when wheelchairs or braces have been prescribed), students should still be encouraged to travel as independently as possible. Movement programs for multihandicapped blind students designed by orientation and mobility specialists continue to represent an unmet challenge for the future. Greater resources from the organizations for the blind must be focused on this area of need. Whatever the level of motor ability, the handicapped person must be motivated and must understand the critical importance of moving and living in the greater world of seeing people.

Self-Help Aids   Many self-help and safety aids are available commercially or can be made by local craftsmen or volunteers. The reader is directed to the International Association of Parents of the Deaf, the American Foundation for the Blind (see their aids and appliances catalog), and the American Printing House for the Blind. Examples of equipment include a specially designed syringe for the administration of insulin, special labels for clothing, and modified cookware. Other agencies for the handicapped also provide resources and materials such as special eating utensils, oversized fasteners, and special clothing. Development of basic self-help skills is especially vital for all handicapped people, since it frequently serves as a prerequisite for gaining admission to educational, vocational, and recreational programs.

SPECIAL ADAPTATIONS AT HOME

A number of studies have indicated that parents can make significant inroads in developing basic skills in their handicapped children through home teaching (Karnes, Wollersheim, Stoneburner, Hofgins, & Teska, 1968; Baker & Heifetz, 1976). As a result of P.L. 94-142, which mandated the formulation of an Individualized Education Program (IEP), parents now have the opportunity to shape curriculum objectives by participating in the IEP conference (Snell, 1978). These meetings also enable parents to furnish critical information to teachers about their children's behavior at home, as well as sharing in placement and intervention decisions. Parents of severely handicapped children are thus given greater access to information that will enable them to determine the least restrictive environment for their children. In some instances, this is a public school program, in others it is a residential school program. Whatever the setting, it is essential that students have access to a stimulating environment where sufficient time is devoted to developmental skill acquisition such as daily living skills, sensory and perceptual stimulation, and communication and socialization skills.

Daily Living Skills

When vision or hearing is either reduced, absent, or accompanied by additional handicaps, skills in feeding, dressing, grooming, and toileting are often delayed. In initiating a daily living skills program, many prerequisite skills must be considered—attending, gross, and fine motor imitation, comprehension of verbal or nonverbal cues, and compliance with simple commands. Tasks should be divided into a series of smaller subtasks that can later be recombined to gradually approximate the overall behavior to be learned.

A loss of sight prevents or minimizes learning through visual imitation (depending upon when vision was lost), and the lack of visual feedback can increase laxness about personal appearance. Likewise, a hearing problem can lead to difficulties in social interaction and a lack of oppor-

Student: Jean B., a deaf-blind student

Short-term objective: When given the sign for "washing hands," Jean will find the restroom independently, wash her hands unaided with 100% accuracy for 6 consecutive days.

Prerequisite
1. Orientation and mobility skills (locating restroom and sink)
2. Visual and tactual discrimination (understanding and using terms *hot, cold, wet, dry, soap,* and *towel*)
3. Gross and fine motor control (grasping and turning faucet, handling soap and towel, rubbing and rinsing)

Task sequence
1. Leaves seat
2. Locates restroom unaided
3. Locates sink facing faucet handles
4. Explores sink, locating hot and cold water faucets, soap, and towel
5. Turns on water
6. Adjusts water temperature
7. Wets hands
8. Locates soap in dish
9. Grasps soap
10. Lathers hands
11. Returns soap to dish
12. Rubs each hand well
13. Rinses soap from each hand
14. Shuts off water
15. Locates towel
16. Dries hands
17. Returns towel to rack
18. Locates seat in class unaided

Figure 2.   Sample task analysis for washing hands.

tunities for gaining valuable information on personal appearance and hygiene. When teaching developmental skills, teachers should capitalize on residual hearing, vision, and touch. They should work coactively with each student, especially if directional cues are to be used, and try to fade out tangible reinforcers and prompts as early as possible. Since some students may also have motor problems, materials should be selected that are easier to use, such as velcro, oversized fasteners, and clothes one to two sizes larger than what is usually worn. Generally, unfastening and undressing are learned before fastening and dressing. Reverse chaining procedures (in which the last step is done first and the student progresses backward to the first step) may prove helpful with these activities.

Skills should be taught in places where they are most likely to occur (e.g. bathroom, kitchen, bedroom) and at times when they are most likely to be needed. In this way, transference and generalization may be easier to learn. Verbalization or signing as much as possible during the activity is important, using simple words or gestures that students understand. Table 2 lists some examples of teaching sequences and strategies in daily living skill instruction.

Table 2.   Examples of daily living skills and teaching strategies for severely handicapped students with sensory problems

Skill	Learning sequence
Using a spoon (Snell, 1978):	
Select easily manipulated spoon; work coactively with the student; provide manual assistance where necessary; carefully check for bite and gag reflexes; link activity to a communication system; modify sequence to allow for entry-level skills.	1. Tactual or visual identification of spoon 2. Gives word, gesture, or sign for spoon 3. Reaches and grasps spoon 5. Places spoon in bowl 6. Scoops food onto spoon 7. Lifts spoon 8. Raises spoon to mouth 9. Opens mouth and inserts spoon 10. Receives food and closes lips 11. Chews food 12. Swallows food 13. Returns spoon to bowl
Pouring liquids (visually handicapped):	
Work coactively; use containers that are easy to handle; listen for auditory cues and changing weight of cup to indicate task is nearing completion; check prerequisite skills of gross and fine motor control.	1. Tactually explores cup and pitcher 2. Grips cup firmly 3. Raises cup to spout of pitcher 4. Extends index finger of hand holding cup 1 to 2 inches inside lid of cup 5. Pours liquid until it reaches position of finger (or other desired amount) 6. Returns pitcher
Distinguishing clothing (visually handicapped; Suterko, 1973):	
Assess gross and fine motor control and tactual discrimination skills.	1. Explores different fabrics (wool, silk, corduroy, etc.) 2. Explores styles (collars, length of sleeves, neckline, etc.) 3. Explores ornamentation (types of buttons, belts, pockets, etc.) 4. Explores placement of labels or stitches inside clothing to determine garments that are worn together 5. Explores consistency or weave of fabric (thickness and weight of material)

School Readiness Training

Handicapped preschoolers must have as many positive experiences as possible, as early as possible. When very young, they should be held often and made to feel accepted by the other members of the family. Brothers, sisters, neighbors, and friends should be urged to interact with the child. Parents should converse with the child at every opportunity, and encourage him or her to imitate purposeful activity. As the child moves more and more, he or she learns to coordinate and control the body, thus forming a clearer notion of the physical self. This developmental milestone is particularly important for later growth. Appropriate behavior, no matter how insignificant it may seem, should be reinforced consistently. In the formative years, the so-called "golden years of growth and development," sensory stimulation is especially crucial.

Visual Stimulation   The ability to see involves not only the anatomical and physiological intactness of the visual mechanism, but also the learning opportunities and visual stimulation provided. With practice, children'learn to use their vision—to fixate, to track moving objects, to discriminate detail, and, ultimately, to give meaning to the things that are seen. For the multihandicapped, the importance of this occurrence cannot be overemphasized. Vision stimulation programs should form an integral part of the curriculum, and this is true for the other senses as well. Children and adults should be encouraged to look at objects as they tactually examine them or listen for a characteristic sound (Donlon & Burton, 1976). Some children must wear eyeglasses or contact lenses for optimal functioning, and this undoubtedly requires an adjustment period. These aids must be worn and each student rewarded accordingly, as behavioral signs of reluctance or frustration may appear. Table 3 below lists some visual stimulation activities that may prove helpful.

Auditory Stimulation   A number of severely handicapped individuals have hearing difficulties. Most of them will have residual hearing that must be developed. The use of auditory training procedures, together with hearing aids, generally provide significant help. For some, gestures and signs can be used to supplement oral communication. Around the house, auditory training should begin with simple, functional skills— awareness of sounds and identifying everyday environmental sounds. Social interaction with siblings and neighborhood children should be encouraged. If a child is in a residential setting, good language models must be present. As with eyeglasses, hearing aids must be worn consistently and periodically checked by parents, child care workers, or ward staff.

Tactile Stimulation   Touch sensitivity is particularly important for the blind person. This is true in most areas of developmental skill acquisition—self-help, cognition, mobility, socialization and so forth. Tactual exploration requires a systematic movement of the hands and fingers over parts of an object that must be then reconstructed into a meaningful

Table 3. Examples of activities for a sensory stimulation program

Sense stimulated	Suggested activities
Vision	1. Have student walk along or trace taped patterns of the floor 2. Have student track moving objects of differing sizes and colors 3. Have student move through obstacle courses of increasing difficulty 4. Using a mirror, identify body parts, and initiate body movement 5. Sort and match brightly colored objects or designs with varying degrees of contrast 6. Hold favorite objects within reach and encourage movement and grasping for them
Hearing	1. Tap rhythms and solicit imitation of sounds 2. Place ring on a stick in response to specific sounds (with severe motor involvement, student can blink eyes) 3. Encourage manipulation of objects that elicit pleasurable sounds (bell, musical toys, etc.) 4. Hide toy or noisemaker which continues to emit sounds. Have students search for the object 5. Musical games (Simon Says, musical chairs, etc.) 6. Imitate child's vocalizations and see if child imitates you
Touch	1. Sort and match common textures (fabric, sandpaper, etc.) 2. Rub child with textures that feel pleasant; later, use this approach to teach naming of body parts 3. Have students feel objects of different temperatures (warm water, ice cubes, etc.) 4. Encourage students to feel the faces of parents and explore their own bodies (Donlon & Burton, 1976). Attach verbal or nonverbal labels to the activities 5. Distinguish shapes tactually with form-boards or simple puzzles 6. Let the student experience the terrain barefooted
Smell	1. Encourage experiencing different smells around the home 2. Expose child to characteristic smells 3. Provide community experiences. Smells of the supermarket, shoe store, and restaurants are important sources of discrimination learning opportunities
Taste	1. Experiment with various foods 2. Pair pleasant tastes with jobs well done 3. Associate pleasant tastes with their referents. Either vocalize or sign their names

whole. Systematic strategies, such as organizing the tactual field into four quadrants and searching in a clockwise fashion or envisioning the tactual field as a clockface with objects at hourly designation points, helps to improve tactual localization skills. Self-initiated tactual exploration should be encouraged, especially in conjunction with the senses of vision, hearing, smell, and taste. These experiences should be linked to real-life situations and objects that are likely to be encountered, rather than models or artificial objects.

Tactual training may take a great deal of repetition, particularly at the onset of instruction. Using soft or pleasant textures in the beginning often has strong motivational value for the student.

Role of the Family

The introduction of a severely handicapped child into a family constellation often adds stresses to family integration. When the severity of the handicap(s) increases and is coupled with inadequate support services, these stresses become even more significant, especially when parents choose to keep a child at home. Coping abilities will also be determined by the quality of the family relationships prior to the birth of the handicapped child. Farber (1957) has shown that family integration is largely dependent on minimizing role tension as family members interact with each other. For these reasons, it is important that families have access to counseling help not so much at this stage, but when first learning about their child's problems.

In order to be knowledgeable of effective child-rearing practices, parents need specific answers to the common, everyday concerns of dealing with potential problems that arise from limited sensory acuity. Those who work with parents should be able to supply the following information (Patterson, 1956):

1. services and program availability in the community, or in the closest major metropolitan area.
2. easy-to-understand terminology that will enable parents to grasp more clearly the nature and scope of the problem.
3. practical suggestions of things they can do at home, rather than blaming them, talking down to them, or putting them on the defensive.
4. that a commitment of action is needed from both parents. Too often the mother must bear an awesome responsibility alone.

Parents should also remember that any hearing or vision assessment represents a single determination at any one point in time. The younger a child, the less valid the diagnostic data, and the greater the chance of finding wide fluctuations from one examination to another. When the child has additional disabilities, these problems are magnified, so that accurate diagnoses are most difficult. Prognoses are even more tenuous, and diagnosticians are often cautious about making predictions and promises that are based on test instruments with limited reliability and validity. On the other hand, parents need to know the nature of these handicapping conditions as early as possible — what they mean, how they may affect future planning, and that their child should be accepted as he or she is.

In addition to acceptance, parents can react in other ways to the knowledge that their child is multiply handicapped. They may deny that there is a problem, reject the child, blame themselves, feel guilty, ashamed, depressed, or express a combination of these feelings and reactions. Some parents overprotect their child, and inadvertently remove the very sources of environmental stimulation so vital for a person with a sensory loss.

For many people, there is a mystique about blindness that identifies it as the worst fate that can befall a human being. Because people are so heavily visually oriented, it is difficult for some to accept the idea that avenues exist that can compensate for a visual loss. Like the general public, parents need to replace the common misconceptions of blind people as dependent, poorly adjusted, and less capable with more positive feelings and descriptions.

Deafness, too, brings with it a set of unique concerns. Some parents of deaf preschoolers are pressured into expecting unrealistic verbal competence from their children, which leads to emotional stress and family interaction difficulties. Other parents equate normalcy with speaking and, because of this, have trouble in accepting their child (Mindel & Vernon, 1971; Moores, 1978). This feeling also interferes with the parents' ability to cope with the problem and help their child adjust to the realities of his or her hearing impairment. As with other handicapping conditions, parents of deaf children must be careful not to compare their child to normal siblings, nor to internalize the negative stereotypes that have evolved over many years.

In any parent training program, it is advisable to include normal siblings of handicapped children. They may resent the excess attention paid to their brother or sister. They may respond with feelings of guilt, fear (of contracting or passing on a disability), shame, or embarrassment. Many siblings, on the other hand, do react most positively and are valuable resources at home.

Parents must be aggressive advocates for their children. P.L. 94-142 requires nondiscriminatory services in the least restrictive environment possible, and parents should be knowledgable about the guarantees of this legislation. Parent groups with strong lobbying efforts can have significant impact on improving services for all the handicapped — recent history has borne this out. Today, parents have more opportunities than ever before to be involved with home and school-based training programs. It is crucial that they capitalize on this chance and take an active advocacy role in the school and in the community.

The proper use of the hearing aid by the child has long been a problem for teachers, audiologists, and other service providers. Parents (childcare workers, ward staff) can play an important role in this endeavor by checking the following potential problem areas (Downs, 1971):

1. *proper amplification.* Place a mark at the appropriate control setting. Parents should have a second earmold made for them so that they can periodically monitor the quality of the amplified sounds.

2. *battery operation.* Batteries must be inserted properly and be free from corrosion. When the aid is not in use, batteries should be removed, and extra ones should be kept on hand at all times.

3. *transmitter.* The transmitter should be worn with the receiver facing out, without layers of clothing covering it. The aid must be kept dry, cleaned regularly with a damp cloth, and should not be exposed to high temperatures or radiation.

4. *receiver.* Avoid severe, jarring blows when the aid is worn. Keep a spare receiver on hand if possible.

5. *cords.* When removing the cord from the transmitter, always grasp it by the plug connector. Never put anything through the cord. Keep cord prongs clean (use a damp cloth dipped in baking soda) and have spare cords available. Malfunctioning cords often result in a crackling sound when the aid is worn. Anchoring the cord to the back of the shirt collar may be helpful in situations in which the cord blocks hand movement.

6. *earmolds.* They should be washed regularly (with soap and warm water) and dried carefully by blowing moisture out of the canal. Dirt and wax can be removed using a pipe cleaner or a toothpick wrapped in cotton. Check regularly for any squealing noises which sometimes indicate improper sealing. This may necessitate a fitting with a new earmold.

SPECIAL ADAPTATIONS ON THE JOB

Career Education

This is a concept used to describe the educational, psychosocial, and vocational needs that an individual has in preparing for the world of work (Flexor & Martin, 1978). This involves not only the specific skills of a certain job, but also work habits and attitudes, social skills, physical and mental stamina, and recreation and leisure activities. Today, career education programs for the multihandicapped are for the most part located in state vocational rehabilitation agencies or commissions for the blind, rehabilitation and independent living centers, and some schools.

A great many multihandicapped people require some type of sheltered environment in order to reach their potential as workers. Extended employment workshops pay workers who are unable to function in the competitive marketplace. Other workers may be placed in training and evaluation settings (transitional workshops) in preparation for competitive employment. Work-activity centers are geared for the more severely and multiply handicapped who cannot do well in extended settings, and whose production capabilities are quite low (Fishler, 1976).

Sheltered workshops have increased in number in recent years, but many multiply handicapped people do not yet have access to individualized vocational rehabilitation programs (Rusalem, 1972). Noteworthy exceptions are the Helen Keller National Center for Deaf-Blind Youths and Adults and the Industrial Home for the Blind, both in New York.

Factors that may account for the relatively few career education programs for the severely handicapped include: (1) public lack of knowledge of need as well as limited contact with this group, (2) the relative isolation of the blind, (3) misplacement of these individuals in nonwork-oriented programs, and (4) the public's negative stereotypes of the blind and lowered expectations of their vocational potential. Because of recent federal legislation and funding priorities, career programs for the severely handicapped have increased, but much is yet to be done.

A final factor that merits attention is the level of professional expertise available. Vocational rehabilitation workers must be fully aware of how blindness and deafness interact with other disabilities and how this interaction affects vocational potential. Equally important, counselors must have the opportunity to seek out receptive employers and become aware of community resources for job development and placement. Too often, disincentives such as the threat of increased levels of meaningless paperwork for potential employers serve as significant deterrents to appropriate job development and placement. A much closer cooperation between teachers and counselors is needed, because career education is a key concept to be shared by both disciplines.

Vocational Training

Perhaps one of the most important findings in the research literature on vocational training is the statement by Gold (1978) that the level of handicapping condition or the presence of additional disabilities is a poor indicator of a person's ability to perform complex tasks. The oversimplicity of tasks offered at many workshops employing the handicapped are due as much to low expectation levels by the professional staff and to the inability of the procurement staff to get complex contracts as to industry's disdain of sheltered workshops (Flexor & Martin, 1978).

Rather than looking at specific training skills which vary from job to job, Gold (1978) has developed the following guidelines for determining strategies for improving vocational opportunities:

1. Skills must have both current and future usefulness.
2. Vocational skills must be those that the business community value.
3. The training program must reflect community resources and needs.
4. The outcomes of the training programs must be clearly delineated; tasks ultimately must be performed in the environment in which the activity normally takes place.

Some investigators feel that a core of prevocational skills are essential prerequisites for success on any job. These include self-help, socialization, and communication skills. Bellamy (1976), however, cautions that although these skills may be valuable, they are not necessarily essential to ensure vocational success as measured by the level of remuneration. This approach emphasizes development not of generic skills, but of those which have direct applicability to specific job requirements. Although this issue certainly merits further study, there seems to be a growing feeling that training must be seen as a means of acquiring skills that have payoff value in the environment in which jobs are sought.

APPENDIX A / Annotated List of Commercially Available Curricula

Project vision-up (N. Croft and L. Robinson, Worldwide Achievements Corporation, Idaho Falls, Idaho, 83401, 1976).

Six curriculum areas (physical development, fine motor, self-help, social-personal skills, and language development) are arranged according to age norms from birth to 6 years. Items and activities in each area are based on the work of Piaget, Gesell, Dunn, Uzgiris and Hunt, and others.

An initial assessment questionnaire provides a developmental profile. From this data, a number of program (activity) cards are selected for use in each area. As instruction proceeds, change data is collected and performances are evaluated. Strong emphasis is placed on auditory, tactile, and kinesthetic stimulation, and reverse chaining is commonly employed. A strength of this program lies in its organization of skills into small, behavioral increments, thus making it useful for visually handicapped students functioning at lower developmental levels.

A standardization of the questionnaire should be done with various groups of handicapped students to get more valid and reliable developmental ages, especially since items have been selected from a wide variety of existing test instruments. The language section probably requires the most substantial modification of any area a teacher may use.

Autistic and severely handicapped in the classroom: Assessment, behavior management, and communication training (D. Krug, J. Rosenblum,

P. Almond, and J. Arrick, ASIEP Education Company, Portland, Oregon, 1980).

This is a communication-centered approach for severely and profoundly developmentally delayed students. Based on the signed-speech model of Schafer et al. (1977), the emphasis is on total communication using principles of behavior modification. Specific guidelines and teaching activities are delineated for facilitating vocalization, signing, and prerequisite behaviors (motor imitation, compliance with commands, etc.).

Strengths of this approach lie in its stress on precise data collection as a basis for decision making, suggestions for behavior management in the classroom, and a well-researched chapter on the use of other assessment instruments for the severely handicapped. This model has direct applicability for many multiply handicapped students, especially the deaf and blind.

The Portage guide to early education (D. Shearer et al., Cooperative Educational Service Agency No. 12, Portage, Wisconsin 1972).

This is a useful program for preschoolers and those who function in the mental age range of 0–5. It can be easily administered by parents, teachers, aides, nurses, etc., in most environments. Behavioral areas include cognition, self-help, motor, language, and socialization.

Assessment information is determined by an electric, sequentially ordered checklist based on items from a wide variety of other tests (e.g., Alpern-Boll, Gesell, Vineland, etc.) As a result of the checklist administration, behaviors and skills to be developed are targeted as curriculum goals. A card file is then employed. These cards contain teaching suggestions, materials to be used, and acceptable performance levels (which will necessitate adjustments).

For this program to be successful, there should be close cooperation between parents and teacher. As with most other guides, some items must be modified for the deaf and/or totally blind student.

Building blocks for developing basic language (Language Curriculum for the Deaf Multihandicapped, B. Peterson and S. Schoenmann, Dormac Inc., Beaverton, Oregon, 1977).

The Building Blocks Program was designed at the Deaf Multihandicapped Unit of the California School for the Deaf. It is a synthesis of the color coded Fitzgerald Key used with the deaf, and the Apple Tree sentence structure approach used at this school.

The curriculum is designed to be useful with many different subgroups of hearing-impaired students, and individualization is encouraged. For example, vocabulary building is left to the discretion of the teacher, quantitatively as well as setting criteria for progression of the next highest language level. Four levels of language comprehension are included, from developing receptive skills through spontaneous use of language concepts. Excellent teaching suggestions and activities are offered.

For many teachers, this guide may be extremely worthwhile, especially when used in conjunction with an appropriate and comprehensive language assessment tool. One potential problem with using the Fitzgerald Key structured speech format is the development of abrupt, mechanical speech patterns that lack fluency, and this will call for refinement at a later time.

Joy of learning—Creative individualization for deaf multihandicapped children (P. Eaton and L. Eiring, Dormac, Inc., 1976).

Joy of Learning is an individualized approach to promote preacademic and academic skills. It is largely based on a learning center format of presenting skills in order of increasing complexity. Easy to follow pictures are presented to illustrate skills as well as activity implementation. Included are a sample record-keeping checklist, teaching material suggestions, and variations for modifying activities.

This guide appears helpful for parents, aides, and teachers. It should, however, be articulated with an on-going assessment system. This program is very flexible, emphasizing the individuality of each student and the need to make program modifications accordingly.

The teaching research curriculum for moderately and severely handicapped (H. Fredericks et al., Charles C Thomas, Springfield, Ill., 1976).

The Teaching Research Curriculum has been used with a wide variety of severely handicapped children (trainable mentally retarded, deaf-blind, preschoolers, etc.). Developmental areas include gross and fine motor skills, receptive and expressive language, self-help skills, cognitive skills, reading, and writing. Each area is further subdivided into skills and phases. For example, the area of self-help may include the skill of feeding and the phase of spoon utilization. Strengths of this behavioral approach include (1) its emphasis on individualizing objectives, and (2) requiring precise and continual data collection and evaluation that serve to modify on-going instruction. Consistent use of the behavioral principles of shaping, chaining, and branching are urged.

As with most curricula, task analysis of behaviors can result in many alternative, but equally effective steps, i.e., there are a number of different and acceptable ways to break down the same behavior.

Users of this curriculum must carefully weigh how behavioral repertoires require instructional modification when vision, hearing, orthopedic, verbal, and other abilities are compromised. Better picture contrast in the language section is helpful, and modifications of some tasks are also required for those with no useful vision.

The John Tracy Clinic Correspondence Learning Program for Parents of Preschool Deaf-Blind Children (V. Thielman and S. Meyer, John Tracy Clinic, Los Angeles, California, 1973).

This developmental guide for parents of deaf-blind preschoolers is composed of two separate units, *You and Your Child*, and *Communication*, which is mailed to parents. As periodic assignments are completed, training guidelines are sent in the developmental areas of gross and fine motor skills, eating, toilet training, personal hygiene, etc. Although many skills are targeted, this model can be best characterized as a communication-centered approach.

Strengths of the program include: (1) multisensory training and stimulation of residual vision and hearing, (2) availability of resources for parents (publications, toys, financial assistance, etc.), and (3) an easy-to-follow guide for signing, important in establishing a language base for deaf-blind children.

Correspondence courses, however, do have limitations. Some parents require closer contact and structure to implement such a program. Others may have trouble with terminology, scheduling, and self-discipline to complete the assigned tasks. Overall, the program could be strengthened by helping parents observe and collect data on their child in a more precise way.

Curriculum for Daily Living (Perkins School for the Blind, Department for Deaf-Blind Children, Watertown, Massachusetts, 1978).

This guide is intended for use with hearing impaired students with severe visual impairments. Modifications are required for totally blind individuals. Curriculum areas include: personal body care and self-help skills, social habits and manners, home assistance and group living, leisure and recreation, and moving about in the near environment. The authors indicate that the program can be implemented by teachers, houseparents, aides, and others who are engaged in daily living skill training.

As a general resource, this manual offers a diverse compilation of objectives, activities, and teaching suggestions. A companion manual would have been helpful, especially for parents and aides, to (1) task analyze skills further and (2) develop a record-keeping system for charting performance in each curriculum area. It would also have been helpful if the program had stated at the outset a clear-cut rationale for selecting these particular skills, as well as prerequisite behaviors needed to perform these skills adequately.

Guide to Early Developmental Training (Wabash Center for the Mentally Retarded, Lafayette, Indiana, 1972).

The Guide to Early Developmental Training is geared toward students in the developmental age range of early infancy through 6 years of age. Content areas are: motor, cognitive, language, self-care, basic mathematical skills. All areas contain a developmental checklist with assessment items sequenced in order of increasing difficulty. Each item is indexed to suggested teaching activities which in turn require periodic evaluation.

For the teacher of the visually or auditorially handicapped, this guide is especially useful for sensory stimulation exercises, as well as informal assessment of visual and auditory efficiency. The reader is directed to the sections on attending, visual pursuit and tracking, eye-hand coordination, imitation, and coordination of visual and auditory abilities.

The strength of this guide lies in its well-organized sequencing of teaching activities that are clearly written and easily adaptable for specific needs. For many students, task-analyzed formats undoubtedly require further modifications. Although geared for the mentally retarded, this program can be used with virtually all exceptional students who function at a preschool level.

A Comprehensive Skills Program for the Handicapped: Developing Social Acceptability (M. Moore, Walker Educational Book Corporation, New York, 1979).

One of a series of eight manuscripts for the Project Partnership Training Program, this volume stresses the development of self-help and socialization skills. The thrust of the program is making behaviors of the handicapped more socially acceptable to family, friends, teachers, and strangers. Behavioral assessment is done through a checklist of skills, followed by development of a series of goals and objectives by the teacher or parent. Strong emphasis is placed on data collection and charting performances. Pictures and symbols are used for nonreaders and those functioning at lower developmental ages.

This is a relatively simple guide that is clearly written. For visually handicapped students, drawings will require some improvement (simplification and higher contrast), and directions may need to be presented in large print, braille, or verbally. Overall, parts of this program may be very helpful, especially the assessment checklists and sequencing of skills.

Other Language Programs

(a) American Sign Language (Ameslan or ASL) and Signing Exact English. These are two manual communication systems that are used by some deaf and deaf-blind students. Signing Exact English follows the same syntax as the English language (i.e., word-for-word equivalency), while ASL is concept-based (one sign may have many meanings, and recognition is dependent on contextual clues). Hearing-impaired students with neurological orthopedic problems may be adept at understanding a manual system, but may have considerable difficulty in producing the signs. Teachers should also explore the feasibility of students using both speech and signing simultaneously (i.e., total communication, Rochester method, cued speech, etc.)

No definitive evidence exists to clearly substantiate the notion that total communication promotes the development of speech at a later time. Kopchich and Lloyd (1976), however, have reported that total communication may hold much promise for students who have good receptive skills, but poor expressive skills, and those who show minimal responses to oral approaches.

(b) The Language Acquisition Program developed by Kent (1974) for nonverbal, severely retarded children includes a signing component for those children who are also deaf. This program is composed of preverbal, verbal-receptive, and verbal-expressive stages. Training during the pre-verbal stage stresses attending skills and simple motor imitation. This is followed by initiation of receptive skills, and the refinement of motor responses. The verbal-expressive stage emphasizes verbal imitation in gradually escalating complexity. Behavior management techniques are used throughout this structured program.

(c) Functional Speech and Language Training for the Severely Handicapped (Guess, Sailor, & Baer, 1976) is a learning-theory-based approach used with a number of different subgroups of multi-handicapped individuals. Waldo et al. (1978a, 1978b) have reported success using this program with a signing format, with signs and some speech, and with communication boards. A corresponding scoring system has been developed for each communication mode.

The core of the program serves to emphasize functional speech coupled with the occurrence of natural reinforcers. Expressive skills are taught prior to receptive skills (i.e., speech training or labeling precedes object identification), and operant techniques are employed throughout the program. An essential entry level behavior is the ability to imitate. This approach can be used by parents, communication specialists, and teachers.

APPENDIX B / Resources for Further Information

For additional information, the reader is directed to the following resources:

Alexander Graham Bell Association for the Deaf, 3417 Volta Place, N.W., Washington, D.C., 20007. Information resource for teachers, parents, and others interested in the education of the hearing impaired. Emphasizes oral communication. Publishes *Volta Review.*

American Foundation for the Blind, 15 West 16th Street, New York, 10011. Professional publications and conferences, films, consultation resource, aids and appliances. Publishes *Journal of Visual Impairment and Blindness.*

American Printing House for the Blind, 1839 Frankfort Avenue, Louisville, Kentucky, 40206. Educational materials for students and teachers, publications in print, braille, and recorded forms.

Conference of Executives of American Schools for the Deaf, 5034 Wisconsin Ave., N.W., Washington, D.C., 20016. Organization of administrators of schools for the deaf in the U.S. and Canada. *Publishes American Annals of the Deaf.* Promotes the welfare of the hearing impaired.

Council for Exceptional Children, 1970 Association Drive, Reston, Va., 22091. Broad-based organization to help all the handicapped and has separate divisions for the visually handicapped and hearing impaired. Publishes professional materials, including *Exceptional Children* and *Teaching Exceptional Children.*

Gallaudet College, Seventh and Florida Avenue, N.E., Washington, D.C., 20002. Provides community services, professional publications, and educational materials about the hearing impaired and deaf-blind. Offers undergraduate and graduate programs for deaf students.

Hadley School for the Blind, 700 Elm Street, Winnetka, Illinois, 60093. Offers correspondence courses for and about deaf-blind students, as well as the visually handicapped.

Helen Keller National Center for Deaf-Blind Youth and Adults, Comprehensive assessment and evaluation services and consultative rehabilitation services for the deaf-blind.

International Association of Parents of the Deaf, 814 Thayer Avenue, Silver Spring, Maryland. Parent section of the Convention of American Instructors of the Deaf. An advocacy organization composed of parents of deaf children as well as others organized to improve programs and services for the deaf.

John Tracy Clinic, 806 W. Adams Blvd., Los Angeles, California, 90007. Provides correspondence courses for parents of deaf-blind children and programs for the hearing impaired.

Library of Congress, Division for the Blind and Physically Handicapped, Washington, D.C., 20542. Provides talking book machines and records, braille materials, and tape recordings, often through local and regional libraries.

National Association for Retarded Citizens, 2709 Avenue E East, Arlington, Texas, 76011. An advocacy organization for the mentally retarded.

National Association of the Deaf, 814 Thayer Ave., Silver Spring, Maryland, 20910. Information resource and advocate for deaf adults and parents of deaf children. Provides professional and nonprofessional materials.

National Center on Law and Deafness, Florida and Seventh Avenues, N.E., Washington, D.C., 20002. An advocacy organization, it supplies information on current and pending litigation concerning the needs of the deaf.

National Society for the Prevention of Blindness, 79 Madison Avenue, New York, 10016. Information on eye care, professional publications, and prevention of eye problems.

The Association for the Severely Handicapped, 1600 N. Armory Way, Garden View Suite, Seattle, Washington, 98119. Professional organization for teachers, parents, researchers, and others interested in working with the severely and profoundly handicapped.

Teaching Research Infant and Child Center, Monmouth, Oregon, 97361. Provides educational services for severely handicapped, hearing-impaired children, including in-service training for those who work with these individuals.

United Cerebral Palsy Association, 66 E. 34th St., New York, 10016. Provides publications, information dissemination, conferences, and workshops to aid those with cerebral palsy.

REFERENCES

Baker, B., & Heifetz, L. The read project: Teaching manuals for parents of retarded children. In T. D. Tjossem (Ed.), *Intervention strategies for high risk infants and young children*. Baltimore: University Park Press, 1976.

Bellamy, G., & Snyder, S. The trainee performance sample: Toward the prediction of habilitation costs for severely handicapped adults. In G. Bellamy (Ed.), *Habilitation of severely and profoundly retarded adults*. Eugene, Ore.: Rehabilitation Research and Training Center in Mental Retardation, University of Oregon, 1976.

Bricker, N., & Bricker, D. Development of vocabulary in severely retarded children. *American Journal of Mental Deficiency*, 1970, *74*, 599–607.

Brown, L., Nietupski, J., & Hamre-Nietupski, S. The criterion of ultimate functioning and public school services for severely handicapped students. In M. Thomas (Ed.), *Hey, don't forget about me: Education's investment in the severely, profoundly, and multiply handicapped*. Reston, Virginia: Council for Exceptional Children, 1976.

Burke, J. *Mobility for deaf-blind.* Paper presented at the joint conference of the South Regional Center for Deaf-Blind Children and the Helen Keller National Center for Deaf-Blind Youths and Adults, 1976.

Craig, W., & Craig, H. (Eds.) Directory of services for the deaf. *American Annals of the Deaf,* 1975, 120.

Croft, N., & Robinson, L. *Project vision-up.* Boise, Idaho: Educational Products Training Foundation, 1976.

Donlon, E., & Burton, L. *The severely and profoundly handicapped: A practical approach to teaching.* New York: Grune & Stratton, 1976.

Downs, M. Maintaining children's hearing aids—the role of the parents. *Maico Audiological Library Series,* 10, Report 1, 1971.

Eaton, P., & Eiring, L. *Joy of learning—creative individualization for deaf multi-handicapped children.* Beaverton, Ore.: Dormac, 1976.

Eisenberg, R. Auditory competence in early life. Baltimore, Md: University Park Press, 1976.

Farber, B. An index of marital integration. *Sociometry,* 1957, *20,* 117–134.

Ficociello, C. Visual stimulation for low functioning deaf-blind rubella children. *Teaching Exceptional Children,* 1976, *8,* 128–130.

Fishler, A. *Development of work programs for the multihandicapped.* New York: Professional Services Program Department, United Cerebral Palsy Association, 1976.

Flexor, R., & Martin, A. Sheltered workshops and vocational training settings. In M. Snell (Ed.), *Systematic instruction of the moderately and severely handicapped.* Columbus, Oh.: Charles E. Merrill, 1978.

Franklin, B. Audiological assessment of the deaf-blind and multihandicapped child. In *Proceedings, Basic assessment and intervention techniques for deaf-blind and multihandicapped children.* Sacramento, Calif.: California State Department of Education, 1977.

Fredericks, H., et al. *The teaching research curriculum for moderately and severely handicapped.* Springfield, Ill.: Charles C Thomas, 1976.

Gold, M. Issues in prevocational training, In M. Snell (Ed.), *Systematic instruction of the moderately and severely handicapped.* Columbus, Ohio: Charles E. Merrill, 1978.

Guess, D., Sailor, W., & Baer, D. *Functional speech and language training. Part 1: Persons and things.* Lawrence, Kansas: H & H Enterprises, 1976.

Haring, N., & Bricker, D. Overview of comprehensive services for the severely/profoundly handicapped. In N. Haring & L. Brown (Eds.), *Teaching the severely handicapped,* Vol. 1. New York: Grune & Stratton, 1976.

Heward, W., & Orlansky, M. *Exceptional children.* Columbus, Ohio: Charles E. Merrill Publishing Co., 1980.

Hobbs, N. *The futures of children.* San Francisco: Josey-Bass, 1975.

Kaplan, R. *Classroom manual for evaluating and developing perceptual motor skills.* Houston, Texas: University of Houston College of Optometry, 1976.

Karnes, M., Wollersheim, J., Stoneburner, R., Hofgins, A., & Teska, J. An evaluation of two preschool programs for disadvantaged children: A traditional and a highly structured experimental preschool. *Exceptional Children,* 1968, *34,* 667–676.

Kent, L. *Language acquisition program for the severely retarded.* Champaign, Illinois: Research Press, 1974.

Kopchick, G., & Lloyd, L. Total communication programming for the severely impaired: A 24 hour approach. In L. Lloyd (Ed.), *Communication assessment and intervention strategies.* Baltimore: University Park Press, 1976.

Krug, D., Rosenblum, J., Almond, P., & Arrick, J. *Autistic and severely handicapped in the classroom: Assessment, behavior management, and communication training.* Portland, Ore.: ASIEP Education Company, 1980.

Langley, B., & Dubose, R. Functional vision screening for severely handicapped children. *New Outlook for the Blind*, 1976, *70*, 346–350.

Lowenfeld, B. Psychological considerations. In B. Lowenfeld (Ed.), *The visually handicapped child in school.* New York: John Day, 1973.

Mangold, S. *Mangold program of tactile perception and braille letter recognition.* Castro Valley, California: Exceptional Teaching Aids, 1977.

Maron, S. Preparing teachers of the severely handicapped: Issues and training needs. *Interact*, 1979, Nov./Dec., 1–3.

Mindell, E. & Vernon M. *They grow in silence.* Silver Spring, Md.: National Association of the Deaf, 1971.

Moore, M. *Developing social acceptability: Book 4.* New York: Walker Educational Book Corporation, 1979.

Moores, D. *Educating the deaf: Psychology, principles, and practices.* Boston, Mass.: Houghton Mifflin, 1978.

Northcott, W. *Curriculum guide for hearing impaired children 0–3.* Minneapolis, Minn.: State Dept. of Education, 1972.

Patterson, L. Some pointers for professionals. *Children*, 1956, *3*, 13–17.

Perkins School for the Blind, Department for Deaf-Blind Children. *Curriculum for daily living.* Watertown, Mass.: Perkins School for the Blind, 1978.

Peterson, B., & Schoenmann, S. *Building blocks for developing basic language (language curriculum for the deaf multihandicapped).* Beaverton, Ore.: Dormac, Inc., 1977.

Pollack, D. *Educational audiology for the limited hearing child.* Springfield, Ill.: Charles C. Thomas, 1970.

Pollack, D. Acoupedics: A unisensory approach to auditory training. *Volta Review*, 1964, *66*, 400–409.

Ries, P. Further studies in achievement testing, hearing impaired students, Spring, 1971. *Annual survey of hearing impaired children and youth.* Gallaudet College Office of Demographic Studies, Wash. D.C. 1973.

Rusalem, H. *Coping with the unseen environment.* New York: Teachers College Press, 1972.

Ryan, T., Johnson, J., & Lynch, V. So you want to write objectives (or have to). In N. Haring (Ed.), *The experimental education training program for personnel serving the severely handicapped*, Vol. 1. Seattle: University of Washington, 1977.

Sailor, W., Guess, D., Goetz, L., Schuler, A., Utley, B., & Baldwin, M. Language and severely handicapped persons—deciding what to teach to whom. In W. Sailor, B. Wilcox, & L. Brown (Eds.), *Methods of instruction for severely handicapped students.* Baltimore: Paul H. Brookes Publishers, 1980a.

Sailor, W., Goetz, L., Urley, B., Gee, K., Baldwin, M., & Sweetow, R. *Auditory assessment and programming manual for severely handicapped and deaf/blind students.* Unpublished manuscript, Bay Area Severely Handicapped Deaf/Blind Project, San Francisco, Cal. 1980b.

Schaeffer, B., Kollinzas, G., Musil, A., & McDowell, P. Spontaneous language for autistic children through signed speech. *Sign Language* Studies, 1977, *17*, 287–328.

Shearer, D., Billingsley, J., Frohman, A., Hilliard, J., Johnson, F., & Shearer, M. *The Portage guide to early education.* Portage, Wisc.: Cooperative Educational. Service Agency, 1972.

Simmons, F., Automated screening test for newborns: The crib-o-gram. In B. Jaffee (Ed.), *Hearing loss in children.* Baltimore: University Park Press, 1977.

Snell, M. Classroom management and instructional planning. In M. Snell (Ed.), *Systematic instruction for the moderately and severely handicapped.* Columbus, Ohio: Charles E. Merrill, 1978.

Suterko, S. Life adjustment. In B. Lowenfeld (Ed.), *The visually handicapped child in school.* New York: John Day, 1973.

Thielman, V., & Meyer, S. *The John Tracy Clinic correspondence learning program for parents of preschool deaf-blind children.* Los Angeles, Calif.: John Tracy Clinic, 1973.

Van Etten, G., Arkell, C., & Van Etten, C. *The severely and profoundly handicapped.* St. Louis: C. V. Mosby, 1980.

Von Bruns-Connolly, S., & Shane, H. Communication boards: help for the child unable to talk. *Exceptional Parent,* 1978, *8,* 19–22.

Wabash Center for the Mentally Retarded. *Guide to early developmental training.* Lafayette, Ind., 1972.

Waldo, L., Hirsch, M., & Marshall, A. *Functional communication board training for the severely handicapped.* Handicapped Media Services and Captioned Films Program, Bureau of Education for the Handicapped (#446AH70146), 1978a.

Waldo, L., Hirsch, M., & Marshall, A. *Functional sign training for the severely multihandicapped.* Handicapped Media Services and Captioned Films Programs, Bureau of Education for the Handicapped (#446AH70146), 1978b.

White, O. Adaptive performance objectives—form versus function. In W. Sailor, B. Wilcox, & L. Brown (Eds.), *Methods of instruction for severely handicapped students.* Baltimore: Paul H. Brookes Publishers, 1980.

Williams, W., Brown, L., & Certo, N. *Components of instructional programs for severely handicapped students.* Paper presented at the Conference on Education of Severely and Profoundly Retarded Students, New Orleans, La., April 1975.

Williams, W., Brown, L., & Certo, N. Components of instructional programs for severely handicapped students. In L. Brown, T. Crowner, W. Williams, & R. York (Eds.), *Madison's alternative for zero exclusion: A book of readings,* Vol. 5, Madison Wisconsin: Madison Public Schools, 1975.

Wolf, J. Multiple disabilities—an old problem with a new challenge. *The New Outlook for the Blind,* 1965, *59,* 265–271.

Chapter 10

Changing Patterns in Residential Services

Wellington L. Mock

There have been dramatic philosophical and programmatic changes during the past two decades in provision of services for all handicapped. One of the major issues during this time (as described in Chapter 1) has been the segregation of handicapped persons into large, isolated institutions. The philosophies (and legal mandates) of *normalization* and choosing the *least restrictive alternative* have brought about sweeping changes in these institutions—in their populations, their programs, and their role in community-based service provision. The merits of deinstitutionalization may still be argued among some professionals and parents, but its legal necessity is becoming increasingly clear. Both in its application to institutions and to specific cases of a handicapped individual needing services, the principle of the least restrictive alternative is becoming a dominant force in the battle between community services and institutional care (Soskin, 1977).

Clarification of Terminology

The terms *deinstitutionalization*, *normalization*, and *least restrictive alternative* are often used synonymously, both in the existing literature and in actual practice. Such use has resulted in much misconception and misunderstanding. Although it is obvious that the terms are closely related, they are not interchangeable. Normalization was defined by Wolfensberger (1972) as: "Utilization of means which are as culturally normative as possible, in order to establish and/or maintain personal behaviors and characteristics which are as culturally normative as possible" (p. 28). A definition of deinstitutionalization was given by Kelly and Vergason (1978): "A practice arising from the principles of normalization and least restrictive environment, in which retarded and emotionally disturbed individuals are moved out of institutions into community alternative living arrangements" (p. 40). Least restrictive environment (or alternative) was explained as "a concept expressed by the courts in the 1970's, in essence saying that disabled persons should be educated or served in the best possible environment for each individual, and if an individual can function with less structure or restraint, he or she should have that opportunity" (Kelly & Veragson, pp. 83–84). It should be obvious from the above definitions that they are not synonymous. Normalization is a generic, more comprehensive term; least restrictive environment and deinstitutionalization are components of the principle of normalization.

Implementation of a Double Blind   Court rulings have established that each handicapped person "should be cared for in the setting which would be the most appropriate to his needs as well as the least restrictive of his liberty" (Soskin, 1977, p. 31). Differing interpretations of these court rulings, as well as differing interpretations of the meanings of the terms normalization and least restrictive alternative, have placed administrators and staff of institutions in a double bind.

> A...double bind...faces the institutional superintendent. He is told to improve the quality of services in his institution. At the same time, he is told to economize because additional funds should go to other community-type residential facilities. He is told that his plant is not normalizing, and he should normalize his plant, but is told to spend no further money on capital improvements. He is told to reduce the population of his insitution, but is told to reduce the waiting list. He is challenged to increase his professional staff to meet ACMFR ratios. At the same time, he is told to phase out his institution. Having to recruit highly qualified professionals by saying, "Hey baby, this is like a one-year job because next year the institution will be phased out." We emphasize the need to recruit top level administrators, yet we tell them they are likely soon to become sacrificial lambs on the altars of new litigation. Even parents who are usually benign and understanding human beings, on the one hand, clamor for the elimination of institutions and, on the other hand say, "Don't put my child on the streets, I want him to remain in the institution where his future is secure and safe." These are the kinds of conflicting demands placed on institutional administrators today. (Roos, 1975, in Edelson, 1979, p. 2)

Right Ends, Wrong Means   Normalization has been described as a "conceptual disaster" because implementation usually ends up with the right ends but the wrong means. Although considerable consensus can be attained in determining the general goals of normalization, much confusion and misunderstanding surrounds the means to this end. It is erroneously and very naively assumed that normative means are always best for developing normative ends.

The definition for normalization states that means and ends for its implementation should be as normative "as possible." It does not state that means and ends must also be normative, just as normative "as possible." The means and the ends should be relative to an individual's functioning level. As Aanes and Haagenson (1978) stated, "the congruence between normalization as both means and ends becomes greater as the functioning level of the individual becomes higher" (p. 55). In other words, the more "normal" the person's functioning level is, the more normative the procedures can be. Thus, for the profoundly, multihandicapped individuals, the means must be very specialized and esoteric—that is, abnormal; while for mildly retarded, nonphysically handicapped individuals the means can be less specialized and esoteric—this is, more normal. Throne, in a 1975 article, described the handicapped as having slower developmental rates, but wrote that "the developmental rates may be speeded up through conditions that are extraordinary. . . . Normative procedures, implying ordinary conditions, will perpetuate maintenance of the developmental rates . . . [and thus] stabilize the retarded in their retarded state, instead of make them more normal" (p. 23).

Atypical means are commonly used in the areas of special education and rehabilitation to achieve the goals of normal behaviors, occupations and educational levels. In one example of such usage, Roos pointed out that:

> The use of aversive conditioning, particularly punishment, has been especially critized as a dehumanizing practice. However . . . There is now considerable evidence that judicious application of aversive conditioning can be dramatically successful in suppressing long-standing highly incapacitating behaviors. . . . In short, while deviating from the principle of normalization in its procedures, aversive conditioning has been successful in yielding more normative behavior. (1972, p. 146)

Normative ends, the goal of normalization, can justify nonnormative means if judiciously applied. In summation, perhaps Aanes and Haagenson said it best: "There can be no quarrel with normalization as the only goal; however, to make all the means to the goal normal may indeed result in a dead end street" (1978, p. 56).

Normalization within the Institution   Akin to the previously cited problems is the conceptual framework for determining the least restrictive environment. In theory this determination arises from the handicapped individual's functioning level; the least restrictive environment is that living environment and training program most appropriate to the individual being served. Individualized determinations must be made as to whether institutional residence is the least restrictive habilitation setting appropriate for optimum progress. One must realize that normalization and least restrictive environment can exist within an institution. Wyatt, interviewed by Thomas (1979), was asked: "Are you saying that an institutional environment might be the least restrictive environment for certain individuals?" (p. 192). His response was:

> Yes, I think, in all fairness, we see individuals who have been in institutions where they have had good medical care, a social program, an instructional program, and a number of other opportunities that, once they were removed from that institution, disappeared. We sometimes find them sitting in nursing homes with little or no social interaction and little opportunity for the kind of instruction that would be most beneficial for them. Under those conditions, even though the nursing home is closer to where their parents live, it really represents much more of a restrictive environment than the institutional setting might have. Obviously there are institutions with little to offer. Justifiably, there has been a strong reaction against institutions that have not provided adequate service for their residents. However, that does not mean that the institution should be discounted as an alternative. It still has a place in the whole concept of the least restrictive environment. (Thomas, 1979, pp. 192–193)

Failure to truly conceptualize and practice the principle of the least restrictive environment as it was intended is to potentially doom a person to a more restricted environment. If this happens, the intent has been negated to the detriment of the individual being served. Least restrictive environment is not an absolute of most and least; it has a relative standing on a continuum of infinite possibilities, is based on a person's optimal needs at that point in time, and is subject to change.

ELIMINATION OF INSTITUTIONS

The term *deinstitutionalization* came into general usage with the advent of normalization and as a response to the horrible conditions that existed in many large, public institutions for the retarded. The term in itself does not indicate whether institutions are to be completely closed or merely decreased in size, but need for their continued existence has been strongly attacked over the past 15 years under the broad application of the term.

Two contrasting positions are taken by professionals concerned with appropriate provision of services to the severely, profoundly, and multiply handicapped. Some leaders in this field say that the changes that have taken place in institutions over the past decade are not enough and call for nothing less than elimination of all institutions for the mentally retarded (Blatt, Ozolins, & McNally, 1979). The Association for the Severely Handicapped (formerly The American Association for the Education of the Severely/Profoundly Handicapped) passed a resolution at its 1979 national convention, calling for just such action:

> To realize the goals and objectives of The Association for the Severely Handicapped, the following resolution is adopted: In order to develop, learn,

grow and live as fully as possible, persons with handicapping conditions require access to services which allow for longitudinal, comprehensive, systematic and chronological age appropriate interactions with persons without identified handicaps. Such interactions must occur in domestic living, educational, vocational and recreational/leisure environments. Specifically, handicapped individuals should: 1) participate in family-like and/or normalized community based domestic living environments; 2) receive educational services in chronological age appropriate regular educational environments; 3) receive training in and access to a wide variety of vocational environments and opportunities, regardless of functioning level; and 4) participate in a wide range of normalized recreational/leisure environments and activities that involve persons without identified handicaps. The Association for the Severely Handicapped believes that the above conditions must be met in order to provide quality service and that these conditions can only be met by community-based services. Therefore, The Association for the Severely Handicapped resolves that it will work toward the rapid termination of living environments and educational/vocational/recreational services that segregate, regiment and isolate persons from the individualized attention and sustained normalized community interactions necessary for maximal growth, development and the enjoyment of life.

Perhaps no voice has been more pervasive, nor more persuasive, on the theme of institutional reform or elimination than that of Blatt. Although he has written many articles and other publications, there are two for which he may well be most remembered. In 1966, he and Kaplan produced the photographic essay *Christmas in Purgatory*, (quoted in Chapter 1) which poignantly documented the status of the mentally retarded in institutions and clearly argued for reform and improvement. The effect of this publication was so profound that even the most staunch supporters of institutions for the mentally handicapped had perforce to question their very existence. Thirteen years later, Blatt et al. (1979) published *The Family Papers: A Return to Purgatory*. The authors basically stated that the institution must cease to exist — that institutions cannot be improved:

> As you will see, everything has changed during the last decade. As you will see, nothing has changed. (p. 4)

> A decade or so ago, we went to five state institutions for the mentally retarded...we found little to give us hope but we were reluctant to admit that the concept of "institution" is hopeless. Today, we find much to give us hope, but we are now unable to see a way to save the institutions....We must evacuate the institutions for the mentally retarded. (p. 143)

Blatt states that all institutions should be eliminated because institutions by their very nature are not amenable to change and improvement. Proponents of a less radical view maintain that the institution is the only realistic economic, political, and programmatic alternative for providing services to those individuals who have severe behavior problems and for those who are severely, profoundly, and multiply handicapped. These contrasting views represent a major dichotomy of beliefs, one which will continue to be argued in the newspapers and journals, in the courts and in the communities. The following news item, from the *Washington Post* of August 21, 1978, illustrates such community divisiveness:

> It is a contest [whether or not to build a proposed MR institution in Maryland] between two different philosophies about the direction care for the mentally retarded should take. On one side...members of the Charles County Association for Retarded Citizens and directors of the state's Mental Retardation Administration believe that institutions must be built to care for the most severely handicapped persons in the community. Institutions, they say, must be only one part of a wide range of services the state provides to the handicapped, but they are necessary for practical and financial reasons. In contrast, the Calvert and St. Mary's Counties Associations for Retarded Citizens, the state Association for Retarded Citizens, and other advocates argue that institutions for the retarded, in any form, are outdated, improper, and possibly even unconstitutional. (Diehl, 1978)

Associations for retarded citizens across the country, individual parents of the retarded, and professionals in the area of retardation, all desiring the same ultimate goals for the handicapped, are as bitterly divided on this question as are the citizens of Maryland.

An article by Throne ("Deinstitutionalization: Too Wide a Swath," 1979) made some excellent points in regard to the conceptual, scientific, and moral problems of deinstitutionalization. Throne pointed out that society has many institutions—group homes, foster homes, and normal households. If this is true: "The issue is not one of institutionalization versus deinstitutionalization or noninstitutionalization. . . . The issue is what kinds of institutions best serve everyone, retarded and non retarded" (p. 171). Throne further stated that although proponents of deinstitutionalization are clearly against large public institutions, they do not agree on what should replace the large institution.

Concomitant to the principles of normalization, deinstitutionalization and least restrictive alternative is the belief that movement from the institution to the community results in more appropriate services in a more normal environment. This is not always true. Many leaders in the field of mental retardation feel that the institution is the most logical environment for provision of appropriate services to severely and profoundly retarded and multihandicapped individuals in our society. It is asserted by many that this population cannot benefit from community alternatives to institutional placement. Those arguing for institutionalization generally hold the view that:

> There are certain classes of mentally retarded persons who are not capable of benefiting from habilitative treatment; there are reliable procedures for determining whether or not a particular mentally retarded person can benefit from treatment; and institutions are needed for those mentally retarded persons who cannot be habilitated. (NCHL Legal Staff, 1980, p. 73)

The issue of deinstitutionalization is still being fought in the courts. Not only are there currently active cases in this area, but there are also cases in continued noncompliance with earlier court orders for reduction of populations, provision of suitable community living arrangements, development of individual training plans and, in some cases, eventual closing of certain institutions (*Halderman v. Pennhurst State School and Hospital*, 1977, 1978; *Wyatt v. Stickney*, 1971, 1972; *Gary W. v. Louisiana*, 1976, 1978). It is safe to say that the institution of two decades ago no longer exists; however, it is evident that even the most benevolent of custodial care does not meet the criterion of the least restrictive alternative for many institutionalized residents. There are exciting possibilities for changing the traditional role of the institution—for development of philosophies and programs that will in truth raise the functional level of all residents, for provision of services to the community rather than withdrawal from contact with it, and for transformation into a site for practicum experiences for staff who work in community residential programs. Whether such changes can be made quickly enough and extensively enough to reverse the current drive toward total elimination of institutions for the retarded remains to be seen.

EFFECTS OF INSTITUTIONALIZATION

Based on the results of research that has been done, it is impossible to determine the effects of institutionalization. The condition of being institutionalized is too broad and varied an experience to be considered comprehensively. As Butterfield and Zigler (1965) stated, "Anyone who treats institutionalization as a homogeneous entity must assume that certain critical social interactions are constant from institution to institution" (p. 48). In another study, Balla, Butterfield and Zigler (1974) concluded: "The condition of institutionalization, like socioeconomic status and birth order, does not constitute a homogeneous psychological variable, but at best refers to the demographic status of the child" (1974, p. 531).

Whatever the experience of being institutionalized, it is comprised of many variables lacking internal and external consistency. It therefore becomes necessary to look at individual practices and effects of these practices, rather than at institutionalization per se. One must not only study the effects of different practices within institutions, but also consider the differences among institutions. There are many studies that compare institutional residents with noninstitutionalized persons in regard to a particular variable. However, very few have been carried out that compare institutions. Obviously, without more cross-institutional studies, it is erroneous to assume that institutional effects are the same in all institutions. Consider the following description of two institutions.

In institution A, every effort was made to provide a noninstitutional, i.e., homelike, environment. School classes, residential units at the younger age levels, and frequent social events are all coeducational. Meals are prepared in the living units where the children eat in small groups. Emphasis is placed upon individual responsibility rather than upon external control by the staff. No buildings are locked; and all children who are ambulatory freely move about the grounds to school, work, and recreational activities. Isolation is rarely used for punishment. Essentially no security force is employed. There are a large number of small residential units and a number of factors are considered before assigning a child to a unit, e.g. age, sex, intellectual level, the child's attitude toward the caretakers and the other children residing in the unit, and their attitude toward him. In institution B, little effort is made to provide a homelike environment for the children. School classes, all residential units, movies, and most other social events are segregated by sex. Meals are prepared and children eat in a large central dining room with virtually no individual supervision. Emphasis is upon external control of the children by the staff rather than upon inculcating individual responsibility. All buildings are locked, and no child moves about the grounds unattended by an employee. Isolation is frequently used as a punishment. A large staff of security officers patrols the grounds regularly. Residential units are all of the large, dormitory type, and no effort is made to group children except by the gross criteria of sex, age, and general intellectual level. (Butterfield & Zigler, 1965, p. 49)

The study carried out in the above two settings demonstrated that these different institutional practices produce significantly different results on a simple motivational-type task. Further, a global assessment of the two institutions certainly suggested that one institution was more depriving than the other. However, it is far from clear what specific aspects of the social and psychological environments produced the differences found in this study. Obviously, different institutional practices produce different effects. Whatever it means to be institutionalized in one institution is different from what it means to be institutionalized in another. Because there are still too few community alternatives to institutionalization for the profoundly and multiply handicapped, the study of the effects of institutionalization is especially important at this time. Such research should be done with the positive aim of finding how to improve institutional settings and practices. Perhaps it is not a question of whether to completely eliminate institutions, but a question of how to improve the existing services.

RESEARCH FINDINGS

Until recently, most of the literature and research on the effects of institutionalization has emphasized its negative results. Balla et al. (1974) listed, from their review of literature and research studies conducted between 1954 and 1959, several negative effects of institutionalization:

1. Loss of personal possessions;
2. Group treatment, rather than individualized training;
3. Emphasis on maintenance of order;
4. Depersonalization;
5. Conformity to routine;
6. Obedience to the instruction of aides;
7. Minimization of conflict with peers as chief goals of socialization, with adverse consequences;
8. Lower quality of language development;
9. Lower quality of abstraction on vocabulary tests;
10. Residents' inability to conceptualize an affective continuum;
11. Less ability, as a group, to learn discrimination tasks and learning sets. (p. 531)

Findings of several studies and articles reporting such negative effects are briefly described below.

Passivity and Submissiveness

DeVellis (1977) used results of studies of animal behaviors to theoretically explain the passivity, submissiveness, and learning problems that many institutionalized mentally retarded individuals have. DeVellis theorized that such problems are manifestations of helplessness that are learned (somewhat inadvertently) and fostered by living in the institutional milieu. He described three possible ways in which the institution may foster helplessness and subsequently passivity, submissiveness, and learning difficulties.

1. "Staff members may punish noncontingently for their own convenience without being aware of the consequences of their acts" (1977, p. 12). The author gave an example of a nonambulatory resident whom the aides left near the bathroom, away from the group, for their own convenience. The end result of this practice is noncontingent time-out.
2. Noncontingent punishment might also come from a resident's peers. The example given is that of a severely impaired, active resident who through lack of motor control hits another resident who is unable to protect himself. This is very possible in the overcrowded conditions still existing in some institutions.
3. Spontaneous onset of violent seizures may result in a fall and consequent injuries as well as social rejection. The inability to control the onset as well as the consequences of the seizures instills helplessness. As institutions move toward serving lower-functioning individuals, the potential for such circumstances as these is even more enhanced.

Differences Caused by Etiology

Yando and Zigler (1971) studied three groups of individuals — the normal, those with organic mental retardation, and the familial mentally retarded

—in and outside institutions. Their purpose was to determine the effects of institutionalization and the etiology of retardation on degree of outer directedness (degree of dependence). Yando and Zigler (1971) found that, compared with children with normal IQ, the institutionalized made more noncued than cued errors on the discrimination learning tasks, possibly indicating their distrust of the experimenter. These children may have felt that the adults were trying to fool them and were therefore suspicious and wary, which could be a consequence of their institutionalization. However, in their discussion of this finding, the experimenters pointed out the following:

> It is, therefore, of some interest to note that, of the 48 institutionalized normal children, 20 had at least one parent who had been diagnosed as mentally ill, 17 had come from broken homes, and 16 had been classified as neglected. (p. 286)

In other words, it seems that not institutionalization per se, but rather preinstitutional social deprivation explains the results of this study. Other results demonstrated that organically mentally retarded noninstitutional individuals were more outerdirected (less independent) than their institutionalized counterparts. However, it was found that institutionalized familial mentally retarded individuals were more outerdirected than their noninstitutionalized counterparts. These paradoxical results indicated that perhaps the etiology of mental retardation and not institutionalization per se caused the different results. Yando and Zigler, in concluding their study, made two observations pointing out the tenuous nature of the results.

> Comparing studies involving different institutions as well as interpreting the institutional effects discovered in the present study demands considerable caution. Considerable evidence has now been presented indicating that the effects of institutionalization on a child vary both as a function of the particular nature of the institution and the particular pre-institutional history of the child. (p. 287)

Environmental Effects on IQ

An older study (Crissey, 1937) compared congregate home environments and institutional environments as to their effects on IQ over time. It was found that the average IQ increased in the homes and decreased in the institutional setting. Crissey's conclusions included the statement that "children develop as the environment demands development" (p. 220). Therefore, the institutional environment does not demand development and as such must be seen as a more negative environment.

Responsiveness to Social Environment

Zigler and Balla (1972) studied handicapped, institutionalized children and noninstitutionalized normal children (matched on sex and mental age) on their responsiveness to social reinforcement. Basically, they found that the institutionalized children were more socially deprived than the noninstitutionalized children. "Thus, the institutionalized retarded child seems to be severely deficient in the development of the reliance upon internal resources which determines much of his effectiveness in the adult world" (p. 71). This study vividly illustrated the problems encountered in trying to determine the effects of institutionalization. Although institutionalized mentally retarded children were all socially deprived, the most affected were with children who had experienced great social deprivation prior to institutionalization and the least affected were those children who were visited in the institution or who went home regularly for vacations. As a whole, this study indicates that institutions are still socially depriving. However, extreme caution must be exercised in generalizing these results beyond the parameter of the setting studied (i.e., to all mentally retarded children in that institution and to normal children in the surrounding middle-class neighborhood).

Negative Reaction Tendencies

Balla, McCarthy, and Zigler (1971) studied the correlates of negative reaction tendencies (i.e., wariness) of institutionalized retarded individuals. The assumption one must make in approaching this study is that wariness and suspicion are common among institutionalized retarded individuals. The findings concluded:

1. Mental age is not related to wariness.
2. Pre-institutional social deprivation is not a "dramatic component" of wariness.
3. Those institutionalized at a younger age were less wary compared to the older individuals included in this study. However, the authors pointed out that this institution made a conscious effort to promote positive reaction tendencies. One aspect of this programming was the encouragement of visitation with and by residents.
4. Maintaining contact with the outside world and wariness had different relationships depending on mental age. For the lower mental age residents, those making frequent outside contacts were less wary. For the middle mental age group, no relationship existed. For the highest mental age group, the more frequent the outside contacts, the more wary the individuals.

Considering the above, it can be said that the institutional environment does foster wariness but that the degree of wariness seems to be controlled by other variables operating apart from the institution.

Effects on Verbal Development

Lyle (1959) carried out a study to determine the effect of the institutional environment on the verbal development of retarded children. Matched subjects were studied and compared in three settings: an institution, a day school, and a home. This study provided definite evidence that the effect on verbal intelligence of institutional placement is very negative as shown in the following results.

1. There were no significant differences in nonverbal intelligence when the three groups were compared.
2. The children in the day school scored significantly higher in verbal intelligence when compared to the children in the institution.
3. Although significant differences in verbal intelligence were noted between Down's and non-Down's syndrome children in the institution, no significant differences were noted between the two in the day school.
4. Long institutional residence appeared to retard verbal much more than nonverbal intelligence.

Need for Social Reinforcement

Zigler (1963) studied rigidity and social reinforcement effects in normal and retarded children, both institutionalized and noninstitutionalized. Zigler found that institutionalized children of normal and retarded intelligence were equally perseverative. Additionally, he found that the excessive need for social reinforcement (an indication of social deprivation) was not consistently related to the length of institutionalization; longer lengths of institutionalization did not necessarily create greater social deprivation. Finally, institutionalized children, normal and retarded, tended to persist in a task longer than their noninstitutionalized peers. Persistence, and not speed, was rewarded in the institution, and both speed and persistence were rewarded outside the institution. Globally, this study suggested that social deprivation seemed more a result of institutional placement than of cognitive rigidity.

Effects of Social Climate

Earlier in this chapter, descriptions of Institution A and Institution B were given. These descriptions came from studies done by Butterfield and Zigler (1965) in which students from two residential schools were compared on their relative need for social reinforcement. It was hypothesized, based on the descriptions, that there was a significant difference between two matched groups (from Institution A and Institution B) on the effectiveness of social reinforcement. The results of the studies, "clearly indicate that differing social climates result in different performance on a simple motivational type task" (p. 55). The authors further stated,

Such a conclusion is consistent with the view that the more social deprivation experienced by the child, the greater will be his motivation for social interaction and support. A global assessment of the two institutions certainly
suggested that one institution was more depriving than the other. (p. 55)

The researchers pointed out that determining what aspects or aspects of
the social climate explained the differences found.

IMPLICATIONS OF RESEARCH FINDINGS

It should be noted that all the preceding studies were completed approximately 10 years ago, prior to the implementation of normalization and
the advent of smaller, community-based institutions. To some extent that
explains the overall conclusion indicated by the aforementioned studies—that institutional effects are predominately negative. As Balla et al.
stated, "There is little question that prior to the advent of the small community-based institution, the prevalent position was that institutions had
negative effects" (1974, p. 530). Within the last 10 years the trend toward
normalization was, and still is, designed to depopulate institutions and
promote community-based (more normal) services. Also, this trend has
resulted in attempts to make the institutional environments more homelike. These reasons, to some extent, explain why the number of studies
and literature on the negative effects of the institutional environment are
not as prevalent as before. However, it should be noted that while the
quantity of studies and literature has declined, the need for appropriately
designed research remains.

In attempting to determine what variables do create the effects of institutionalization, bad or good, caution must be exercised in not relying
on measuring gross characteristics. Balla et al. emphasized: "workers must
go beyond such gross characteristics as the size of institutions and begin
delineating the particular social-psychological characteristics and practices of institutions which determine the behavior and development of
the residents" (p. 537). These authors further stated that "it would appear
that any argument relating institution size, cost, housing system, or patient
to staff ratio to institutionalized children's behavior may be too simplis-
tic" (p. 543). As Throne (1979) emphasized, the move to close or decrease
the size of institutions in the name of deinstitutionalization has yet to be
supported by efficacy studies.

Many of the above studies have compared noninstitutionalized normal individuals with institutionalized retarded individuals in an effort to
gain insight into the phenomenon of retardation and allow more effective diagnosis and intervention. Some studies that compared these groups
found no significant differences. However, Baumeister (1967) very explicitly noted the problems encountered in studies that compare normal

persons with the retarded and indicated that extreme caution should be exercised in overgeneralizing results of all such studies. "It is clear that in some instances in which retardates have been found to perform as well as normals, limitations in the task (e.g., low range of possible performance) may have precluded the discovery of differences. Furthermore, the groups may perform equally well, but for entirely different reasons" (p. 869). Many other studies of this nature have shown that normal individuals are superior to the retarded. Again, in these studies, the very different performance of the normal and the retarded may be for different reasons. The researcher may assume that IQ is the reason for the differential performance but, as it turns out, that is not a safe assumption. As Baumeister stated: "In short, one would have to be assured that observed differences in performance are directly related to differences in intellectual ability per se rather than to sensory, motor, motivational, or other differences when these factors are not expressly included in the definitions of the groups" (pp. 869-870).

In relating this to the subject of the effects of institutionalization, obviously another variable has been introduced: institutionalization. How much of the demonstrated difference or similarity is related to institutional living versus living outside an institution? What are the social and psychological characteristics and practices in institutions that determine residents' behavior and development? What creates the effects, both positive and negative, of institutional living?

Variables Affecting Program Quality   Cleland (1965) wrote of the historical and contemporary concern about reducing resident population in institutions. The assumption, made then and commonly held now, has been that for institutions "bigness is badness." In the 15 years that have elapsed since the printing of Cleland's article, the general trend has been to decrease the size of institutions. However, Cleland made the point that "while size may be one determinant of quality, it could be far less important than popular opinion might suggest. Size represents an elastic concept that may obscure a host of more relevant variables serving to influence institutional program quality" (p. 426). "Relevant variables" that could have impact on the effectivensss of institutions include: (1) the rate of resident and staff growth, (2) technical and social change in the institution, (3) quality and stability of the work force, (4) staff productivity, (5) location, (6) leadership continuity and sophistication, and (7) relative safety of the work setting.

The arguments against institutionalization or the gross characteristics of institutionalization are clearly inadequate to explain the effects of such an environment on the residents' care and development. Until research can establish the relative importance of the variables described by Cleland and by others exploring this area, it is inappropriate to say that the variable "bigness" always equates with "badness."

One Relevant Variable: An Example   Cleland (1965) described the educational level of the attendants and aides who comprise the majority of staff in any institution as usually below that of the average American worker. He used this education-level variable as an example of one that has potential for direct impact on institutional effectiveness. This educational deficiency, he stated, "can seriously impair the communication process, can defeat the principle of delegation, and perhaps more seriously, greatly assist in the production of value conflicts and treatment orientation discrepancies between professional and sub-professional staff" (p. 429). Cleland's description is still true, 15 years later. In the institution in which this author works, there is a vast discrepancy in the relative educational levels of the aides and the professional staff. Functional illiteracy is a major problem for many nonprofessional employees. As Cleland described, communication is difficult, at best, between professional and nonprofessional staff. Many aides and developmental technicians may question the need for daily baths, brushing teeth after meals, and other personal hygiene practices required for residents, because the aides themselves may not take daily baths or participate in regular oral and personal hygiene. One wonders how enthusiastic and dedicated aides can be in carrying out personal hygiene practices that they feel are useless.

A study done by Butterfield, Barnett, and Bensberg (1968) comparing attendant attitudes in different institutions reinforces a point in Cleland's article: different attendant attitudes produce different effects. This study dealt with a comparison of attendant attitudes in separate institutions. It was hypothesized that characteristic attendant attitudes could be differentiated between institutions. Results of the study demonstrated that this was true. Additionally, it was found that each institution had characteristic profiles of attendant attitudes. Potentially, attendant attitudes toward residents can greatly contribute, either positively or negatively, toward resident progress and care in a particular institution.

THE CHANGING INSTITUTION

Institutional environments are now greatly different from the one exposed by Blatt and Kaplan (1966) in *Christmas in Purgatory*, although not all of them were, even then, the "snake pits" so vividly and poignantly portrayed in that pictorial essay. Dramatic changes are taking place across the country.

Growth of community-based residential programs has brought about a reduction in the number of institutionalized persons and a drastic change in the characteristics of the population remaining in institutions. Steady progress toward normalization of the environment for those persons is shown in many areas—renovation of physical facilities, development of individual habilitation plans for the residents, elimination of rules governing social contact between the sexes, and establishment of educational and vocational training programs.

Changes in a Representative Institution

Changes that have taken place in Arlington Developmental Center, one of Tennessee's three state-supported facilities for the mentally retarded, are representative of developments in institutions for the retarded in other states. As in many other institutions, the characteristics of this center's population have changed drastically in the last few years. There has been vigorous growth of community-based residential programs in this area of the state, and approximately 25% of the Center's former residents are now in these programs. Most of the individuals who went into these community-based programs were higher-functioning residents without behavior problems. The average functioning level of the remaining residents has therefore dropped sharply. A comparable lowering of the function level of the institutional population is occurring across the country. This has created a paradoxical and difficult problem for institutions — how to develop more normal facilities, programming, and placement while serving far less normal residents than in former years.

Movement toward Normalization

In the Arlington Developmental Center, as in other facilities and programs for the severely and multiply handicapped, there has been a dramatic philosophical change toward the concept of normalization. Orientation of programs is now toward a time-limited, transitional stay for residents, as opposed to the former assumption that institutional placement was permanent. Earlier, most institutions offered, at best, benevolent custodial care, usually predicated strictly on a medically oriented model of service provision. Now there is a change toward the developmental model and its objectives of habilitation and training.

All residents in the Arlington Developmental Center have deinstitutionalization plans that specify the kinds of training and services needed to reach that goal. The Individual Habilitation Plan (IHP) designed for each resident not only states what his or her deficiencies are, but additionally identifies the training to take place, who is to provide it, and the approximate time expectancy for goal achievement. Where possible, institutional residents are placed in community-based training centers to encourage their integration into the community outside the institution. Vocational training is gaining impetus as a viable program for residents. Areas for this training are being redesigned or newly constructed to provide appropriate training programs. Classrooms for school-aged residents provide suitable environments for implementation of Individual Education Programs (IEPs). Additionally, there is increased emphasis on provision of recreational and leisure-time activities, field trips, shopping trips, and so on.

Steps have been taken at Arlington Developmental Center to normalize the physical environment in which residents must live. There is a definite move in new construction away from the dormitorylike facility to a more cottagelike structure that provides a bedroom, with ample closet space and furnishings, for two residents. Additionally, kitchen, dining room, living room, den, and bathroom facilities are slowly replacing the dayroom and communal bathroom facilities in older institutions. Where older structures are being retained, renovation is taking place to allow for more privacy and a greater semblance of normal household living. In living areas such as the bedroom, partitions are being added so that there are 4 residents instead of 18 in each bedroom. Each resident is provided with a bed, wardrobe or chest, and any personal furnishings that he or she desires. Curtains and colorful bedspreads add a cheery note. The dayroom, a common living area, now has television, radios, pictures, lamps, and tables, and other household items. The way in which the residents are dressed is in dramatic contrast to the drab institutional garb, or the nudity, seen in earlier years in many state institutions.

Interaction with the Community

An important change in institutional orientation has been in the area of service provision to the community. Such service provision involves far more than the contact required for placement of deinstitutionalized residents into community-based homes. Over the last few years such interaction with the outside community has become the rule rather than the exception. This desirable change has been particularly evident at Arlington Developmental Center. Programs have been established that explicitly provide for community interaction. The Foster Grandparent Program provides a parent or trainer surrogate for many residents throughout the day during the week. This program allows older citizens from the community to become involved on a humanistic level with residents. A volunteer services coordinator publicizes and promotes the use of community volunteers in providing numerous services directly and indirectly to the center's residents. The Human Rights Committee, made up of professionals and citizens outside the center, was established to review both programs dealing with the residents' human rights and those proposals for research that utilize residents. The Admissions Review Board is made up of outside, interested citizens whose function is to make the final decision on all admissions, set a time limit on each admission, and review all requests for continued residency. There are many other less formal activities carried out that also involve meaningful interaction with the community.

At the Arlington Developmental Center, the Office of Community Services provides services directly and indirectly to the community. Currently this section provides: (1) outreach social services for over 500 individuals, (2) family training services for over 50 families, (3) a consultant in speech and language, (4) a foster care program for 20 individuals, (5) two group homes for 16 juvenile offenders, and (6) coordination of diagnosis and evaluation services. Furthermore, this section funds, indirectly and to varying degrees, 23 community-based programs for the retarded in this area of Tennessee. For these agencies, the Office of Community Services provides consultive, monitoring, and other supportive services. In many states, institutions are administered separately and apart from community-based services; in Tennessee there is a deliberate effort made to fund and support community-based services through the institution.

In summation, institutions for the retarded, such as Arlington Developmental Center, have made steady progress toward creating a more normal environment and toward training the residents for transition to community-based programs. Deliberate attempts are being made to interact with and become a part of the community — a task made more difficult because of the traditional physical isolation of most large state institutions. Institutions have demonstrated that their residents can indeed progress toward more normative ends.

RESIDENTIAL MODELS FOR DEINSTITUTIONALIZATION

Movement of the handicapped from the institution to the community will not of itself result in more appropriate, more comprehensive services in a more normal environment. Automatic improvement by virtue of movement to a smaller facility is a fallacy.

"Some critics of deinstitutionalization are concerned about the availability and appropriateness of services provided the mentally retarded in the community, as well as the provisions which must be made to insure their physical safety and freedom from harm. Already, there is evidence accumulating that deinstitutionalization is not yielding the expected improvements for many retarded persons" (Vitello, 1977, p. 40). Follow-up studies on deinstitutionalized persons in community-based residential facilities have shown that the quality of services provided varies greatly. The problem was succinctly stated by Gold (1972): "Where you live is not normalization. Normalization is not defined by where you live but how you live" (reprinted in Gold, 1980, p. 108).

Appropriateness of Community Residential Services

When the determination is made to move an institutional resident to the community, an implied decision has been made about the rights of that individual. That decision is that his or her rights are best served by movement to the community. Failure to consciously evaluate a particular person's ability to move into community placement is perhaps to deny him or her the right of being served and trained in the most optimum setting. It cannot be assumed that community placement will in every case be better than the institution. As Polivka, Marvin, Brown, and Polivka concluded in their 1979 study of resident progress and service provision:

> The identified discrepancy between those services needed and those provided is disturbing. Almost one half of the services received were not identified as needed in the individual habilitation plans, while 16% of the services identified as needed were not provided. The latter discrepancy seems to be greatest for services more essential to the implementation of the developmental model. (p. 229)

Authors of two studies of community alternatives for the retarded in California (Bjaanes & Butler, 1974; Edgerton, 1975) reported that many facilities were no better and were sometimes worse than institutions. As Edgerton concluded:

> The quality of life in the alternative care facilities we have studied is highly variable, with evidence here and there of exciting progress toward the goal of normalization. For most mentally retarded people in this system, however, the little institutions where they now reside appear to be no better than the large ones from which they came, and some are manifestly worse. (p. 131)

Institutional population trends, especially recidivism rates, suggest that community-based services are lacking in quality as well as quantity. "Although releases have increased considerably, readmissions have increased even more rapidly. It is suggested that the pressure for emptying institutions has been allowed to outstrip the pressure for creating adequate normalizing alternatives" (Conroy, 1977, p. 44). The community has in some cases become an environment with far greater loneliness and restriction for residents than that of the institution. Although it is foolish to say that adequate community alternatives do not have greater potential for nomalization than do institutions, if they do not provide appropriate services, placement therein is unjustifiable.

Problems in Provision of Services

O'Connor and Sitkei (1975) rank-ordered the most serious problems in initiating and maintaining residential programs, as indicated in findings of a nationwide study:

1. inadequate funds;
2. difficulty in finding qualified staff;
3. developing individualized client programs;
4. lack of community support services;
5. certification and/or licensure;
6. attitude of community toward residents;

7. staff training and development;
8. reducing parental fears;
9. difficulty of maintaining staff;
10. zoning restrictions;
11. meeting fire regulations; and
12. meeting building safety standards. (p. 36)

As one would expect, the primary obstacle to provision of appropriate services is funding. Almost all community residential facilities are dependent upon a variety of funding sources: "This means federal, state and local tax support, and very often private contributions. . . . It becomes almost a night-marish type of thing, an administrative headache, to locate; to understand the rules and regulations; to obtain funds through grant requests, purchase arrangements, or contracts; and then to be held legally accountable for the use of those funds when they are funneled from so many different sources into one service system" (Popp, 1978, p. 36). These funding sources not only provide funds, but also consult and monitor the programs—often with conflicting guidelines. When services receive funds under such circumstances, clear lines of responsibility and authority no longer exist. As the Comptroller General of the United States stated in a Report to Congress (January 7, 1977):

> When persons are patients or residents in public institutions, responsibility for their care is usually evident. . . . When mentally disabled persons are released from institutions, however, responsibility for their care and support frequently becomes diffused among several agencies and levels of government. (p. 23 & 24)

Many of the practical problems of adequately, appropriately, and effectively integrating the mentally handicapped into the community arise from such a situation.

Community Problems

Much money, time, and effort has been expended in initiating, promoting, and funding appropriate community-based services for the retarded, but little has been done to systematically and consistently inform the public—and parents—of the characteristics of the services, the staff providing the services, and the service recipients themselves. Several of the problems in service provision listed by O'Connor and Sitkei can be caused by failure to carry out a public relations program.

   Community prejudice and parental fears may do more to thwart the successful movement of retarded individuals from the institution to the community than any other factors. Two of the problems that arise consistently involve community acceptance of group homes and parental inhibitions about allowing children (whether at home or institutionalized) to move into the community. Although handicapped persons are accepted in some neighborhoods without much opposition, persons in other neighborhoods are protesting vehemently. Kastner, Reppucci, and Pezzoli (1979) initiated a study of reasons for the discrepancy between surveys reporting positive attitudes toward the mentally retarded and those demonstrating evidence of discrimination in employment, education, and housing against those so labeled. Families living in a neighborhood in which houses suitable for group homes were for sale were asked to complete a questionnaire. Those families living next door to such houses were considered the experimental group, and families living farther away served as the control group. The questionnaire used for both groups contained questions designed to elicit attitudinal responses. Examples are listed below.

> #19. Mentally retarded persons living in this neighborhood would tend to lower the value of property.
>
> #23. Community residencies should be outside of town limits to help protect them from the dangers of in-town living.
>
> #33. Efforts to take mentally retarded out of the institution for community placement and help them become more independent are really pressing them to do more than they are capable of doing. (p. 143)

Overall, the results were positive toward the retarded, but those living next door to the potential group home gave less favorable responses. Generally, it was found that people felt the handicapped should have the same rights as other people — as long as they would not be moving in next door. The conclusion drawn from this study was that generally people want to respond with positive attitudes toward the retarded, but when it impacts them personally they are unsure and less positive. Negative attitudes toward having handicapped neighbors arise not only from fears that property values will decrease, but also from the perception by society of the retarded as being deviant or menacing. This false perception is still widely held. Kastner et al. suggested that there be an effort to:

> Encourage public education and facilitate community integration to move actual sentiments more in line with survey responses...by promoting...as much public exposure as possible, both through information modes...and through increased contact among mentally retarded people and their neighbors in the community. (1979, p. 143)

A similar paradox in regard to attitudes toward normalization for the retarded is exhibited by their own parents. Parents of retarded children are generally positive toward normalization activities (e.g., moving out of the home or institution into the community) until it concerns their own child. Then they are more reserved and sometimes negative. Many parents are resisting the trend toward deinstitutionalization. In referring to parental fears, Perske (1980) stated:

> Not so very long ago, we as professionals convinced parents to leave their handicapped children in our institutions, and we told them to go on living

their lives as if they had no such relative. Many parents went through sheer agony before accepting such advice. Now—with the shift—some will agonize again. (p. 1)

The intent and philosophy of normalization has been explicitly reflected in law. The Intermediate Care Facility-Mentally Retarded (ICF-MR) program of Title XIX of the Social Security Act, the Education of all Handicapped Children Act (P.L. 94-142), and Section 504 of the Vocational Rehabilitation Act (P.L. 93-112) mandate services and extra resources to accomodate, serve, and train handicapped individuals to a level that will allow them to enjoy, to the greatest extent, the same rights and privileges as the nonhandicapped. Most of the aforementioned laws have due process provisions built in that allow for parental participation in the placement process and in the development of individual service plans for their children. Ferrara (1979) researched the attitudes of parents of mentally handicapped children toward normalization activities. The questionnaire developed by Ferrara elicited responses from parents in regard to normalization activities for the retarded and for their retarded child in particular. The results of this study demonstrated that although parents support and accept the concept of normalization for retarded in general, its application to their own children is not endorsed. Therefore, to the extent that this is true in a particular town or geographical area, facilities might be built, staff hired, and programs designed, only to have no clients to take advantage of them.

Obviously, there are more facets of the community's attitudes that need to be studied and dealt with; however, an examination of only these two (neighborhood and parental attitudes) indicates that much work is yet to be done if normalization is to be fully realized. It is obvious that although society is quite willing to embrace the concept of normalization in general, individuals are much more reluctant to do so if it affects them specifically.

PROGRESS IN PROVISION OF SERVICES

Recent studies have shown that deinstitutionalization of the mentally retarded has produced beneficial effects. Community-based services have in many instances created more self-reliant, less dependent individuals with the potential of becoming contributing members of society. Other studies have shown that the quality of community placement services varies. O'Connor (1976) studied more than 100 community facilities for the deinstitutionalized and was generally optimistic about her findings. However, she cautioned her readers.

The philosophy that anything is better than an institutional placement must be seriously questioned, at least on a short-term basis. With sufficient planning, appropriate program implementation, and careful monitoring, community placement can provide excellent opportunities for our handicapped citizens. Without these precautions, hundreds even thousands of individuals could end up in mini institutions without public attention and resources now available in public institutions. (p. 68)

Recent Studies of Community Services

Two studies of the perspectives and experiences of retarded individuals in community residential programs give a comprehensive picture of such services as they currently exist, describing both the successes and the problems of such programs. The O'Connor study was a nationwide study with 9,339 subjects, 53% of which had been previously institutionalized. Another well-done but more localized study was that of Gollay, Freedman, Wyngaarden, and Kurtz (1978), who investigated the progress of 440 previously institutionalized individuals.

Demographic characteristics of the populations studied indicated that very few were profoundly retarded, but that a significant number had additional handicaps. Areas investigated in both studies included those of day placement (e.g., competitive employment, sheltered employment, and various training programs) and participation in leisure activities. Many families of individuals involved in these studies felt that too few opportunities for participation in leisure activities were available in the community (Gollay et al., p. 85).

In addition to basic day and residential services, supportive services are very crucial to optimum development of the retarded in community placements. Overall conclusions of the two studies compared showed that most of the residents needing services were receiving them. O'Connor reported, "Ninety percent of the residents lived in facilities reporting a need for one or more of the 15 types of community services; nearly one-half were living in facilities in need of four or more services" (1976, p. 67). The areas of vocational services, social and recreational services, transportation services, community services, referrals to identify and obtain needed services, and financial assistance represented the greatest unmet needs. The Gollay study stated that "over one-quarter of the families felt that obtaining adequate support services for the retarded person posed at least somewhat of a problem for them. Perhaps this indicates that even when services were used they may not have been adequate or may have required considerable effort to obtain" (pp. 111 & 112). Support services are often extremely difficult to obtain and are often inadequate. The very existence of retarded individuals in the community depends in large measure on the availability and adequacy of support services. Provision of such services is especially imperative for the severely and profoundly handicapped.

Difficulty of finding qualified residential staff was listed by O'Connor and Sitkeli (1975) as the second most serious problem in provision of appropriate services. The necessity of having trained staff is emphasized by the Gollay report on the location of needed training programs. In the areas of personal maintenance, domestic living, use of community resources, and behavior management the family or residential staff did most of the training. The only area in which the greater part of training was done in the day program was that of education and employment. Gollay noted that for over 40% of the individuals studied, the family acted as case managers and "on the average, one-fifth of the services and over half the training received by mentally retarded persons were provided by families. In fact, over two-thirds of the study group members were trained by their families in personal maintenance, domestic living, and community use skills" (1978, p. 125). In 9 of the 24 training areas, there was a clear indication that more training should be provided. These areas include speech and language, education, employment, money management, and training from community resources. Although most training needs were met, much of the training was coming from the family rather than from outside individuals and agencies. This seems to suggest that having a family willing to act as an advocate and trainer to some extent enhances the handicapped person's potential for successful community placement. It also emphasizes the necessity for development by institutions of extensive and appropriate training programs to be implemented prior to community placement. Such preplacement training programs should be addressed to the development of skills needed for success not only in the type of residential placement proposed for the individual, but also for the specific facility and neighborhood in which he or she will reside.

Problems encountered in the community by the retarded and their families were identified by the Gollay study. Problem areas included (1) employment (i.e., finding and keeping a job), (2) social behavior (e.g., family relationships, social relationships, loneliness, behavior such as social unacceptableness, and self-confidence), and (3) skill and service needs (e.g., medical problems, self-care, managing money, and getting help from community agencies). Although the problems of the handicapped were not qualitatively different from those of the normal population, the Gollay study showed quantitatively that there were more of them. This has implications as to the inability of the community to assimilate retarded individuals, especially the severely handicapped. Gollay also noted discrepancies between what families of handicapped individuals perceive to be problems and what the retarded themselves see as problems. The areas of job finding, family relationships, loneliness, self-confidence, and managing money had very large discrepancies. Typically, the handicapped person perceives problems to be more serious than does the family, which suggests that whether or not the actual extent of the problem is as great as perceived by the retarded person, the fact that it is so perceived increases its importance, especially as to how well the handicapped person will be able to adjust to or cope with its consequences (Gollay et al., 1978).

Absence of Community Services

The studies show that many individuals, who have been previously institutionalized or unserved in the community, can be and should be provided with services in a community setting. Authors of most studies are generally positive in concluding that not only can the retarded be served in the community, but that they are being served reasonably well. However, three areas of caution are indicated. First, for a number of reasons community services are not adequate either quantitatively or qualitatively to meet the needs of all retarded individuals. Secondly, by far the majority of individuals served are in the moderate range of retardation or above. Some severely retarded are served, but very few profoundly retarded individuals are found in community-based residential settings. Although society has come a long way in the provision of community programs for the less retarded, planning for provision of optimum services for the severely, profoundly, and multiply handicapped within the community is lacking. A nationwide study on community residences for the handicapped (Baker, Seltzer, & Seltzer, 1977) showed that 74% of the residents in the 381 programs studied were mildly or moderately retarded, 12% were severely retarded, and only a small percentage was multihandicapped. Fourteen percent were either not retarded or the diagnosis was unclear. In contrast to these percentages are the following institutional population characteristics from a study done by Albridge (1980) in Arlington Developmental Center (programs of which were described earlier): One percent of the residents was classified as borderline retarded, 6% as mild, 5% as moderate, 13% as severe, and 74% as profoundly retarded. Additionally it was found that 23% had a psychiatric impairment; 68% had perceptual or expressive disorders or both; and 77% had various motor disfunctions, predominantly classified as moderate or severe. All of the residents had sensory impairments, with 56% having both visual and auditory impairments. These percentages are generally representative of institutional populations today.

Two reasons for the general exclusion of this population from community residential programs are quite obvious. The major problem in the provision of any type of services to the handicapped is funding. Cost of appropriate provision of services to the severely and profoundly handicapped is much higher because of the multiplicity of their needs and the high staff-to-resident ratio required to meet these needs. A second serious concern is the finding, training, and retraining staff who can work effectively with these low-functioning individuals. A less obvious but very serious reason for failure to deinstitutionalize the severely and profoundly handicapped lies in the generally held assumption that these individuals are incapable of fulfilling any community role. In contrast to this commonly accepted stereotype, the "try another way" philosophy of Marc Gold (1980) emphasizes that:

> any individual, given prerequisites, powerful training procedures, and time, can be brought to criterion on any piece of learning. No one is thought to be incapable of learning. This does not deny that all individuals have limits, some more than others, but it does promote a recognition of the impossibility of evaluating limits in the absence of powerful training. (p. 149)

Gold's belief, borne out by results of his research, is that the discrepancy between trainer expectations and the actual performance abilities of the retarded has been one of the greatest deterrents to the provision of appropriate training. Success of the few community-based programs for the severely and multiply handicapped has shown that this population *can* be appropriately served in the community. Such services may be provided in various types of community settings. There is no one model for optimum service provision.

TYPES OF COMMUNITY RESIDENCES

Residential models for community service provision to the less retarded were described in the Baker et al. study mentioned above. A brief description of these various options may aid the reader investigating possibilities for community programs. This 1977 study (hereinafter referred to as the Baker study) was one of great magnitude. Its authors undertook the difficult task of examining residential models for retarded citizens throughout the United States. They mailed 1,140 questionnaires to identified community facilities; of the returned questionnaires, 381 were useful for statistical purposes. Almost 75% of these 381 facilities had been established since 1968. The residential models were found to be in fairly equal proportions in communities of all sizes, from villages with a population of less than 500 to cities of more than 100,000 persons. The average age of the retarded individuals living in these community residences was 35, and the sexes were evenly divided.

Individuals who were higher in intellectual functioning were more likely to be found in residential settings that were smaller, while lower-functioning individuals were likely to be found in larger congregate settings. Previous to their current community residential placement; 48% had been in institutions; 28% lived with their families; 13% came from other community placements; 9% came from hospitals; and 2% came from the regular community. In looking at the day placement of these individuals, it was found that 16% were involved in competitive employment; 43% were in sheltered workshops; 13% were in day activity centers; 10% worked at the community residence; and 18% had no day placement. Community residential facilities were classified in the Baker study as follows:

Small group homes (10 or fewer residents)
Larger group homes
    Medium group homes (11 to 20 residents)
    Large group homes (21 to 40 residents)
    Mini-institutions (41 to 80 residents)
    Mixed group homes (various handicapping conditions)
Protected settings
    Group homes for older adults
    Foster family care
    Sheltered villages
Training programs
    Community preparation programs
    Workshop-dormitories
Miscellaneous
    Semi-independent apartments
    Comprehensive systems

Small Group Homes   As reported in the Baker study, these group homes, housing from 6 to 10 residents, represented the greatest number (approximately one-third) of community residences studied. These homes were usually located in residential neighborhoods, in older houses, within a reasonable distance of public transportation. Work, shopping, and recreation were reasonably convenient. There is now some movement away from the older houses, as new replacement group homes are being built with the aid of federal Housing and Urban Development (HUD) funds.

Of the residents of the homes, 55% had come from institutions, 13% were classified as severely retarded, 48% as moderately retarded, and 35% as mildly retarded. The remaining 4% were nonretarded, but were otherwise handicapped. The mean age of the individuals was 29 years.

In these small group homes, the ratio of staff to resident was two or three to one. The Baker study reported a relatively large amount of resident autonomy and responsibility for household tasks. In this author's experience, it has been found that the degree of resident responsibility can vary widely depending on the commitment and competence of the staff of the group home.

The appropriateness of small group homes for all retarded is questionable. These homes, in some areas, have tended to become terminal rather than transitional placements, principally because of the lack of adequate funds to develop other alternative living arrangements. Most movement from the homes is to an equally or more restrictive residential setting.

Large Group Homes   There are, according to the Baker study, several potential advantages to larger group homes. These revolve around the greater income generated by the greater number of residents.

1. The greater number of staff members could allow for more well-differentiated roles and some specialized functioning. Also, duty shifts could result in better staff morale than in programs where houseparents live in and assume more all-inclusive responsibility. The net result may be better resident training.
2. The larger number of residents could allow for subgrouping according to individual needs, and specific programs could be developed for given subgroups. For instance, the "need" of one resident in a small group home of eight for sex education, a special workshop, or a pool table might remain unmet, while a similar need of four residents in a large group home of 32 could inspire development of a special program.
3. The larger facilities could be less expensive per resident to operate. (pp. 59–60)

It has always been felt, as mentioned earlier in this chapter, that bigness is badness. However, this has not been supported by research. If the normalization definition is conceptualized as means and ends "as close as possible", then larger group homes must be considered as viable residential facilities.

There are disadvantages to large, or even medium-sized, group homes. Staff and staffing patterns in these resemble those of an institution. Large group homes are less likely to be integrated into neighborhoods, and for this reason some would say that they represent a return to institutionalization and thus run counter to the current push for normalization.

In referring to larger group homes, the Baker study stated "the larger group home models have not always arisen from a careful assessment of the needs of a given group of potential residents" (p. 59). Possibly this would be true no matter what community-based service is being contemplated or implemented. This nation's community residential services for the retarded are not generally established according to research-based planning and needs studies. The primary bases for instituting residential programs are usually political and economic rather than based on individual service needs. As the Baker study added:

> More often a [residential] model is selected on the basis of such factors as the availability of a facility, the bias of the sponsoring group, zoning restrictions, or the guidelines of a state bureaucracy. Consequently, the variability existing in the programs of different models of group homes is largely unplanned. (p. 59)

The Baker study found that larger group homes were usually located in larger cities and were generally very large, older houses with as many as 30 rooms. As with medium-sized group homes, there were typically two sets of live-in houseparents, plus only six additional day staff members. In fact, "The numbers of day staff, professional staff, and live-in staff per resident were each significantly lower in large group homes than in all the other community residences combined" (p. 68). This seems puzzling because, as a group, the residents in large group homes tended to be more severely retarded than in small and medium-sized group homes.

The authors of the Baker study found that generally these group homes had many of the negative aspects of institutional placement, and felt that, overall, the individuals operating the large group homes were less concerned with normalization than were the operators of small and medium-sized group homes. There was one exception to this pattern.

> One former apartment house with 31 residents has only two residents in each five-room apartment, thus providing spacious living quarters and minimal direct supervision. Individual and small group activities are encouraged in an atmosphere of reasonable autonomy; telephones are in the resident's names, residents have keys to their own apartments, they may entertain non-residents of the opposite sex between 6 A.M. and 2 A.M., alcohol is permitted, and there is no curfew. (p. 68)

Mini-institutions

Although the relevance of considering any institution as a community residential facility can be questioned, the Baker study did include the mini-institutional model. The mini-institution is a restricted environment compared with other group home models, but is much less restricted when compared with some large, public institutions. The five mini-institutions included in the Baker study had an average of 58 residents (a range from 41 to 80), who were housed in ex-hospitals or in new structures. Although a great deal of variability was found in these five facilities, the following things were found in common:

> [There were] relatively few staff members per resident, limited organized involvement with the outside community, and considerably restrictive rules and policies. Indeed, mini-institutions ranked lowest of any model on these variables. . . . And while all facilities reported some involvement of outside professionals, these were primarily medical personnel. Indeed, most strikingly missing in these staffing patterns were trained staff members to educate the residents in community living or vocational areas. (p. 69)

This, when contrasted with the descriptions of the aforementioned group homes, seems to depict a rather dismal, custodial, institutional model with very little to recommend it as an alternative to larger, public institutions. However, the authors pointed out that quality of daily life was much better than that of many large institutions. In the five facilities studied, there were only two or three residents per bedroom and the residents had their own television sets, record players, and radios. One facility had a fireplace that was extensively used during the winter and others had gardens, bicycles, and crafts and provided shopping trips into the community. In summary, the Baker study stated: "The mini-institution, like any other program, looks better or worse, depending on what aspect of it one looks at and the comparative standard" (p. 72).

In the residential models reviewed so far, group home size seemed to have no relation to the sex, age, or intellectual level of its residents. (In this author's experience, mini-institutions serve proportionally much lower functioning individuals who in addition have other handicaps.) The Baker study reported, however, that the larger the group residential facility, the smaller was the number of professional and direct service staff; fewer residents were involved in daily chores, and fewer were involved in work training programs.

This would seem to suggest that larger grouping in community residential facilities results in fewer normalizing experiences. However, normalization results not so much from the size of the facility or the number of residents, but rather from the quality, the commitment, and the competence of the staff, as well as their philosophical stance. As the Baker study emphasized:

> In considering these relationships to size, we should first note that a larger facility need not, per se, be more custodial. There is a shared feeling among those promoting the normalization philosophy that smaller facilities are better so it stands to reason that these persons would have become more involved in developing smaller facilities. It may well be that if these same administrators and staff members were transferred to a larger facility, they would or could make it much less custodial. This is to say that correlation does not imply causation—the correlation with size may not reflect fixed consequences of house size as much as it reflects the actions of those who develop small or large facilities. (p. 73)

It is not so much the setting or size of the residential program, but the quality of the program that determines how beneficial it is. This quality is demonstrated by the commitment and competency of the staff. Life in any residential model considered can be highly negative or can be beneficial. There is probably no residential service model that is negative or positive in and of itself; however, some models may have the potential to produce greater negative or positive effects.

Mixed Group Homes   Residents of the mixed group homes described in the Baker study included "both mentally retarded individuals and former mental hospital patients, persons with problems of alcoholism, and/or adult ex-offenders" (p. 75). Usually, retarded residents of these homes were in the minority. Although, as the Baker study pointed out, there is virtually no research on the effects of this mixed arrangement, it is *not* a generally accepted practice to combine individuals with different handicapping conditions. Clearly, the history of the retarded is replete with arguments against combining the mentally ill and the mentally retarded. The principal reason has always been that mental illness requires a medical model to cure, while retardation cannot be cured per se and therefore requires an educational model with emphasis on training. Wolfensberger (1972) argued against combining the retarded with other perceived deviant members of society because the public is likely to mistakenly associate deviant behaviors of other handicapping conditions with retardation.

Residence in these homes was very transitional, as one would expect, with the average stay being just over 6 months. The homes were more therapeutic than training oriented, requiring that the retarded individual be relatively high functioning in order to profit from the experience. Even more apparent than the therapeutic function of the homes, however, was that they were viewed as primarily room-and-board facilities. As such, their use for the wider retarded population, especially the lower functioning, is highly questionable.

Protected Settings   In the Baker study, group homes for the older retarded, foster homes, and the grouped sheltered village were under the heading of protected settings because, despite great differences, "themes of 'separation and protection' bind these models together in important ways" (p. 82). The reader is again reminded that it is not so much the setting, but the philosophical belief and the commitment of a competent staff that set apart good and bad programs.

Most group homes for older adults were located in towns of 30,000 people or less and most did not have public transportation available. When these facilities were compared with the previously mentioned group homes, there were some stark differences. These facilities had been in existence an average of 10 years, longer than most group homes. The operators generally were also the owners of the group home, and additional staff was very minimal. The average age of the residents was 59 years of age. Only 24% of these residents had been institutionalized, while 19% had come from hospitals, and 17% had come from other community residential programs. Twenty-nine percent of the residents in these homes were not retarded and nearly two-thirds of these residents were female. Compared with all other models included in the Baker study, the residents of the group homes for older individuals were higher functioning (pp. 86–87).

These group homes, in contrast to other group homes, did not have a training program. Only 7% of the residents had any kind of a day placement and all residents were unlikely to be involved in any kind of in-house responsibilities. With no exception, these group homes provided 24-hour supervision. Institution-like restrictions were placed on the residents. This seems strange in light of the fact that most residents were quite capable and generally higher functioning than other, younger residents in other group home settings.

Even though these homes were considered permanent (versus transitional) placements, the turnover rate in those studied was 32%. It was found that 14% became ill and went to medical facilities, 15% went to other community residences, 15% went to institutions and 7.4% went on to independent living (p. 91).

In summation, the Baker study found that although these homes for older individuals were better in some ways than institutions, they were worse in other ways. For instance, in one home women had no opportunity for outside contacts, especially not with men. Additionally, there was no opportunity for useful or remunerative work. This author agrees with many of the conclusions of the Baker study in regard to these settings. Clearly the potential of older retarded individuals is underestimated and underutilized. Geriatric facilities are needed in most communities, but the total lack of training for responsibility and freedom for residents in such facilities is untenable. Segregation of the residents by age and sex must also be questioned. It is obvious that the operators of group homes for older individuals need training, supervision and monitoring.

The fact that the Baker study classified foster family care as "protected settings" hints at the type of services found. As one would assume, most foster family care was housed in private residences. There were four to five residents in each home; 26% of these residents were severely retarded. As in the case of group homes for older individuals, the Baker study showed that foster care families were basically ignorant of training methods and were overprotective of those in their care. It was found that foster family care "fell short on two fundamental components of normalization: having productive daytime activities and allowing residents to participate in the management of their physical environment" (pp. 97 & 99). This lack of programming dooms a potentially good situation to be at best nothing more than good benevolent care and as such to be clearly unacceptable.

Not all foster care programs are as barren in their aspects as were those reported by the Baker study. For example, an exemplary, very vigorous program of foster care has been initiated in western Tennessee and implemented over the last 3 years. Its success is predicated on the premise of "developmental" foster care. Potential foster parents are carefully screened, trained, and monitored often to ensure that training is taking place.

Sheltered Villages   Of all the noninstitutional residential models to be discussed, sheltered villages seem to run most counter to the philosophy of normalization and are reminiscent of the thrust that eventually resulted in the establishment of large, public institutions for the retarded in the late 1800s. Yet the Baker study stated: "Sheltered Villages raise a host of issues and confront some of our most easily held assumptions" (p. 109).

The nine sheltered villages included in the Baker study were located in predominately rural areas of seven states. The median site had 40 acres while the smallest was 9 acres and the largest over 500 acres. Most villages had a central administrative building or buildings, a number of residential houses, and some workshop facilities. The villages had an average of 39 residents (from 12 to 89) with an average resident age of 30. Seven of the nine villages were coeducational. Most of the residents had previously lived with families prior to coming to the village. This residential model had the lowest functioning level of all those studied. This model also was the best staffed, with more full-time staff. Most of the staff was live-in; its commitment was not only to the retarded, but also to the sheltered village as a way of life.

The turnover rate in the sheltered village was the lowest of all residential models studied, the village being considered a permanent home. Of the nine villages, the amount of work and village responsibilities assumed by the residents varied widely. Contact with and integration into the local community by definition was limited, but also varied considerably.

There are many issues as to the relevance and viability of sheltered villages; however, the issue of segregation is perhaps most often raised. The marginal success and acceptance of some community-based programs for the retarded is often the result of nonacceptance by the community. The public basically fears and is reluctant to accept what it does not know and understand; segregation of the retarded into villages might appear to exacerbate the problem. As the Baker study stated:

> Whether the "safe" sheltered village serves as a first step toward broader acceptance of the retarded by the community or, conversely, further strengthens attitudes of segregation, remains unclear. The latter, however, would seem more likely. (p. 131)

Some good arguments can be formulated in support of sheltered villages. As alternatives to traditional large public institutional placement for the severely, profoundly, and multiply handicapped, they may be quite desirable. If communes are considered viable and "normal," then sheltered villages may certainly be. Several recently initiated villages have proved successful in providing well-paying jobs for the residents and in initiating much interaction with the immediate community and the surrounding territory.

Training Programs The Baker study described three transitional models in various settings which were designed to prepare retarded individuals for community living. One transitional training program for young retarded adults was located on the grounds of the institution in facilities that were formerly employee living quarters. These facilities had 20 bedrooms, two bathrooms, a reception area, and a basement. There was no dining room or kitchen, which obviously need to be included as training areas. The authors of the Baker study found such paradoxes as these not only in the physical facilities, but also in regard to the grounds, the daily routine, and the program. The staff included a physician, LPNs, houseparents, social workers, a director, a psychologist, counselors, and student interns. Additionally, the staff had access, on a consultant basis, to other professionals as needed.

The residents of both sexes, were not, for the most part, severely and profoundly retarded, multihandicapped, nonambulatory, or emotionally disturbed. The program of the transitional training facility was quite varied:

> Cooking, shopping, money budgeting, and time skills along with reading, writing, arithmetic, and current events are taught at night school in the adult education department of the state school. A special course, Community Living and the Law, was added to the adult education curriculum to teach the residents about their human rights. Housemothers instruct residents in such areas as housekeeping, laundry, mealtime skills, and shopping. Work skills are taught only in the workshop. (p. 141)

Such a program, coupled with the fact that the staff directly connected with this transitional training program spent 50% of its time in the community facilitating the transition from the institution, spoke well for the viability of this program. The suggestion was made by the authors of the Baker study that, in addition to screening potential participants in this program for IQ and functional skill levels, more emphasis should be placed on emotional stability and ability to cope with the loneliness that sometimes characterizes community placement.

Of the 16 workshop dormitories reviewed in the Baker study, over half were located in towns of 30,000 people or more. The Baker study found that:

> Typically, the workshops have been operating prior to the opening of the dormitories, which, in general, provide a home for only a small proportion of the workshop's clientele. Residents remain in workshop-dormitories for an average of only one and a half years before moving on to other models of community residential facilities and it is hoped, more challenging jobs. (p. 149)

Of the individuals served in this type program, 36% were mildly retarded, 45% were moderately retarded, and 12% were severely retarded. Most of the remaining 7% were assumed not to be retarded. Programmatically, more than any other residential model found in the Baker study, the workshop dormitory program had 81% of its residents in vocational training programs or sheltered workshops" (p. 150). The remainder was composed of either new residents not yet placed in a day program, those in a day activity center, or those involved in competitive employment. This residential model ranked second in the amount of house maintenance responsibility expected and assumed by residents. However, these programs "are geared not as much toward training for independent living as toward providing a place for people to live, and learn, while attending a work program" (p. 150).

In summation, there is much about this residential model to warrant serious consideration; however, as noted by the Baker study review of the one program, it can have serious shortcomings. To quote the Baker study, "If staff members from both spheres (residential and work) fail to work together to set goals and carry out programs for residents, the true potential of this model will not be realized" (p. 152).

A coordinated program providing similar services to that of the workshop dormitory can be found in many states. Most of the private, nonprofit boards contracted with by State Departments of Mental Health and Mental Retardation to provide residential services also provide adult activity center programs, extended employment (workshop) programs, or both. In these agencies there is generally an explicit attempt made to coordinate the day and residential programs to complement and enhance the retarded individual's training experiences. As the proportion of severely retarded individuals gradually increases in the community, community-based services assume greater relevance.

Comprehensive Systems   As the name implies, comprehensive systems of community residential accommodations try to provide for all retarded individuals' residential needs. As such, each of the six comprehensive systems reviewed in the Baker study served the severely retarded as well as the moderately and mildly retarded. The six comprehensive systems reviewed in the Baker study had many things in common. Residential models usually included group homes and semi-independent apartments. These were large operations; the number of individuals served ranged from 33 to 450. All six systems studied placed marked emphasis on vocational training and employment, and there was an explicit commitment to moving individuals continuously toward more independent residential settings.

One of the two comprehensive systems described in the Baker study served not only retarded individuals but the emotionally disturbed as well. Although this is not common in many community programs, in this one there was a deliberate attempt to mix handicapping conditions so that the individuals "teach each other" (p. 188). Most of the comprehensive systems studied not only accepted severe to mild retardation, but individuals who were multihandicapped as well. It seems that this model of community residential services has the greatest potential to serve lower-functioning multihandicapped individuals when compared with the other residential models described. Such a system provides a variety of alternative settings and services with less operational overhead than is the case with some alternative models.

GUIDELINES FOR ESTABLISHING RESIDENTIAL SERVICES

Few community-based residential facilities are designed to accommodate multihandicapped, nonambulatory, frail persons whose primary needs are medical treatment and supervision. Indeed, such programs have only occasionally included the severely retarded. However, it is not the physical facility, grouping, or setting that controls the quality and viability of a particular program. The success of any residential program is determined not by the type of resident or the size of the facility, but by the competence of the staff and its commitment to the achievement by each resident of a more normal, more independent level of functioning. It is therefore quite appropriate to examine currently successful programs for the less handicapped for characteristics that may suggest some general guidelines and considerations for the establishment of appropriate residential facilities for the more retarded as well as for the less handicapped. Although the nature of most community-based residential services has primarily been determined by economic, political, and litigative reasons, such a primary motivating factor for establishment of such services is not necessarily a deterrent to their success. Ideally, however, "every region must make a thorough assessment of the present and future needs of retarded persons within that region and then provide a network of different residential models" (Baker et al., p. 179). Future provision or expansion of residential services must be based on such an assessment.

Target Population

Many times fund-raising drives have provided special programs, and only after their establishment has it been discovered that there was not so great a need of such programs as had been assumed. In other instances, the need has been transitory and has not continued to exist to the extent anticipated. It is suggested that program planners identify (by name and location) those individuals currently in need of residential services and those who will need such services at points in the future. Answers must be found to such questions as the following: How many individuals need what kind of a residential setting and for how long? How many are currently receiving appropriate, and inappropriate, residential services? Are there private agencies currently providing these services? If so, would it be best to use public funds to allow these agencies to expand their services? What additional parts of a continuum of residential alternatives need to be established? How soon do these services need to be in operation?

In planning for services for the more retarded, one should not make the mistake of considering a group of individuals with IQs of 30 or below a homogeneous one. Some of these people can become quite independent, while others remain totally dependent. Some are ambulatory; others are completely helpless. The assessment of community needs must determine not only the number of individuals to be served, but also the specific needs of each. Another decision to be made is whether to serve the individual who is less retarded but severely physically or multiply handicapped. Will services be provided for the developmentally disabled, the autistic, the emotionally disturbed and retarded, the retarded delinquent? What are the age parameters for service provision? If all ages, from birth to death, are to be served, obviously a greater number of residential alternatives and ancillary services from various agencies need to be involved.

There are other areas that must be explored when proposing to develop a relevant continuum of residential services. One important one is the proposed location of such facilities.

Location

When considering community reaction to residential placement for the severely and profoundly handicapped population, one must be aware that although a few severely retarded individuals may have been placed in the community, the profoundly retarded have been and still are generally nonvisible to the public. People in the community generally expect the profoundly handicapped to be out of sight and mind, either in an institution or in the back bedroom of the family home. Baker, Seltzer, and Seltzer (1977) reported in their study of 381 residential facilities that 35%, including some for high-functioning handicapped individuals, received some community resistance to their inception. The authors further stated, "we do not know of a single neighborhood in which the citizens met and decided it was in their best interests to have a community residence within their town boundaries" (p. 215). It can generally be expected that the interests of the community are in opposition to the interests of the handicapped population. Obviously, meaningful integration into a community, especially for the severely and multiply handicapped population, requires an extensive program of public education and public relations prior to implementation of any residential program.

Another locational concern that is especially important for this population is the proximity to the residential center of day training services and supportive and ancillary services. This group is in constant, grave need of physical therapy, occupational therapy, speech and language therapy, educational therapy, and medical, dental, and nursing care. Are such services to be provided in-house or to be procured from outside agencies? Questions such as these must be addressed.

Another problem in locating residential facilities is the legal one of local zoning regulations. In many communities, zoning statutes have impeded the establishment of community-based services for the handicapped (*Amicus*, 1978). Two types of zoning ordinances cause problems: the "single family dwelling ordinance," which in many instances defines "family" as "a housekeeping unit related by blood, marriage, or adoption" (*Amicus*, 1978, p. 31) and the exclusionary ordinance that often lists the "feebleminded" among those categorical groups specifically banned from certain community areas. Such ordinances have been successfully challenged through litigation. In other instances, state legislation that allows community residential facilities to be placed in desirable areas has prevented local governments from passing ordinances designed to exclude such facilities. Such preemptive state laws have been passed or are pending in nearly half the states.

Financial and Administrative Considerations

Funding is obviously the most important factor to consider in developing a needed continuum of residential services. Theoretically and philosophically, development of programs to meet needs is more important than money considerations, but the reality is that there will be *no* services if a stable funding and administrative base is not available. As was stated in the Baker et al. study (1977):

> Perhaps the very first decision to be made in beginning either a single community residence or a comprehensive system concerns its sponsorship. Sponsorship refers to an agency or body of people that serves as the administrative and/or financial overlay of a community residence. Patterns of sponsorship vary. The administrative leadership may or may not be separate from the sources of support, which may come from public or private monies, and monies may be allocated on a program or per-person basis. The method of sponsorship affects both the nature of the program developed and the type of residents admitted to a particular community residence. Also, it is the most important factor in determining how a community residence becomes associated with the political and social structure of a particular state or region. (p. 210)

Generally there are three funding and sponsorship patterns that have evolved in implementing community-based residential services: (1) private funding and sponsorship; (2) public funding and sponsorship; and (3) public funding and private sponsorship. Tennessee provides an example of the third pattern; community residential programs in the state are privately sponsored but financed with public funds. Its residential services are provided through contracts with private, nonprofit corporations. State funding amounts go from 49% to 72% of the total cost; Supplemental Security Income (SSI) payments and local tax support and private contributions supply the remainder of the cost.

Different types of funding and sponsorship patterns result in different strengths and weaknesses. The advantages and disadvantages of public and private funding and sponsorship should be thoroughly investigated in order to determine what pattern of support and program management is best suited to the individuals to be served and to the community.

Finally one must take into consideration the availability of funds from different sources in the future. One is ill-advised to depend on federal monies as a stable funding base. Federal money is categorically earmarked, is usually time limited, and is very dependent on the state of the economy for availability. However, for the creative grant writer, it is a source of initial operating funds. Of course, when time-limited federal grant dollars dwindle, other funds, typically state or local, must be procured. Otherwise, as has happened too many times, programs decline and disappear because of a lack of funds.

The Community

Serious consideration needs to be given to the philosophies and attitudes of the community in regard to the severely handicapped. How does the community perceive the profoundly defective individual?

> Deinstitutionalization is rooted in a value system which recognizes that mentally retarded persons belong in the community rather than total institutions. This value system has been articulated strongly and eloquently by advocates for the mentally retarded. As a result of this advocacy, there is presently momentum for rapid change in the nature of delivery systems for retarded individuals. (Vitello, 1977, p. 40)

There is a need to determine the collective attitude of the community before attempting to initiate a continuum of residential services for the severely and multiply handicapped. Does the community really accept the philosophy of deinstitutionalization? Generally held attitudes and views must be taken into account in anticipation of provision of services.

The way in which the community perceives the handicapped individual obviously determines the degree to which the principles of normalization and the least restrictive environment are accepted. Perception of the profoundly handicapped person as "human" or a "human vegetable," as having innate worth or being worthless, affects the pragmatic decisions made by the community. Should all these individuals be stored away in large institutions with, at best, benevolent custodial care, or should they be treated and trained in smaller, multidisciplinary facilities? What proportion of this population is the community willing to serve? Is it committed to provision of full services to these individuals or to providing anything at all? Is the provision of support and services to the handicapped considered the responsibility of the family alone, rather than one to be shared by the community? How much is the community willing to spend for no tangible return for the dollars expended (i.e., what is the relevant price for humanness)? To not consider these issues is to severely limit the effectiveness of any provision of services, perhaps even to ensure that the project ultimately fails.

SUMMARY

Although institutional environments and training programs today are greatly improved compared with those of 15 or even 10 years ago, there is still too little being done in provision of services that will maximize resident progress. What role the large institution ultimately plays in the normalization of services to the severely, profoundly, and multiply handicapped can not be determined at this time. There are knowledgable and influential leaders who call for its abolishment. Others equally outstanding view the institution as an essential component of the continuum of residential services to the handicapped. What its function will be in this continuum depends on a number of variables. These include community acceptance of the normalization philosophy, the number and quality of community services provided, and the attitudes, abilities, and commitment of the institutional staff. The institution may be allowed to exist only as a provider of life-sustaining care to "human vegetables." On the other hand, it has the potential to become a dynamic partner with the community in a collaborative drive toward full application of the normalization principle to all handicapped persons. The phrase "a part of, not apart from" is as appropriate for institution and community interaction as for the interface of special and regular education.

REFERENCES

Aanes, D., & Haagenson, L. Normalization: Attention to a conceptual disaster. *Mental Retardation*, 1978, *16*, 55–56.

Albridge, U. J. *Profile of resident population in Tennessee: Developmental centers as of June 30, 1980*. Nashville: Tennessee Department of Mental Health and Mental Retardation, October 1980.

Amicus. Disabled citizens in the community: Zoning obstacles and legal remedies. 1978, *3*, 30–34.

Baker, B. L., Seltzer, G. B., & Seltzer, M. M. *As close as possible: Community residences for retarded adults*. Boston: Little, Brown & Co., 1977.

Balla, D. A., Butterfield, E. C., & Zigler, E. Effects of institutionalization on retarded children: A longitudinal cross-institutional investigation. *American Journal on Mental Deficiency*, 1974, *78*, 530–549.

Balla, D. A., McCarthy, E., & Zigler, E. Some correlates of negative reaction tendencies in institutionalized retarded children. *Journal of Psychology*, 1971, *79*, 77–84.

Baumeister, A. Problems in comparative studies of mental retardates and normals. *American Journal on Mental Deficiency*, 1967, *71*, 869–875.

Begab, M. J., & Richardson, S. A. (Eds.). *The mentally retarded and society: A social science perspective*. Baltimore: University Park Press, 1975.

Bjaanes, A. T., & Butler, E. W. Environmental variation in community care facilities for mentally retarded persons. *American Journal of Mental Deficiency*, 1974, *78*, 429–439.

Blatt, B., & Kaplan, F. *Christmas in purgatory: A photographic essay on mental retardation*. Boston: Allyn & Bacon, 1966.

Blatt, B., Ozolins, A., & McNally, J. *The family papers: A return to purgatory.* New York: Longman, 1979.

Butterfield, E. C., Barnett, C. D., & Bensberg, G. J. A measure of attitudes which differentiate attendants from separate institutions. *American Journal of Mental Deficiency*, 1968, *72*, 890–899.

Butterfield, E. C., & Zigler, E. The influence of differing social climates on the effectiveness of social reinforcement in the mentally retarded. *American Journal of Mental Deficiency*, 1965, *70*, 48–56.

Cleland, C. C. Evidence on the relationship between size and institutional effectiveness: A review and analysis. *American Journal of Mental Deficiency*, 1965, *70*, 423–431.

Comptroller General of the United States. *Report to the Congress: Returning the mentally disabled to the community: Government needs to do more.* Washington: Department of Health, Education & Welfare, January, 1977.

Conroy, J. W. Trends in deinstitutionalization of the mentally retarded. *Mental Retardation*, 1977, *15*, 44–46.

Crissey, O. L. The mental development of children of the same IQ in differing institutional environments. *Child Development*, 1937, *8*, 217–220.

Diehl, J. Proposed facility for the retarded stirs Maryland dispute. *Washington Post*, August 21, 1978.

DeVellis, R. F. Learned helplessness in institutions. *Mental Retardation*, 1977, *1*, 10–13.

Edelson, D. *Deinstitutionalization: Avoiding disaster. An occasional paper.* National Association of Superintendents of Public Residential Facilities, 1979.

Edgerton, R. B. Issues relating to the quality of life among mentally retarded persons. In M. J. Begab & S. A. Richardson (Eds.), *The Mentally Retarded and Society: A Social Science Perspective.* Baltimore: University Park Press, 1975.

Ferrara, D. M. Attitudes of parents of mentally retarded children toward normalization activities. *American Journal of Mental Deficiency*, 1979, *84*, 145–151.

Gold, M. W. *Marc Gold: "Did I say that?".* Champaign, Ill.: Research Press, 1980.

Gollay, E., Freedman, R., Wyngaarden, M., & Kurtz, N. R. *Coming back: The community experiences of deinstitutionalized mentally retarded people.* Cambridge, Mass., Abt Books, 1978.

Kastner, L. S., Reppucci, N. D., & Pezzoli, J. J. Assessing community attitudes toward mentally retarded persons. *American Journal of Mental Deficiency*, 1979, *84*, 137–144.

Kelly, L. J., & Vergason, G. A. *Dictionary of special education and rehabilitation.* Denver: Love Publishing Co., 1978.

Lyle, J. G. The effect of an institution environment upon the verbal development of imbecile children. *Journal of Mental Deficiency Research*, 1959, *3*, 122–128.

NCLH Legal Staff. Challenging the experts for—The right to habilitation in the community. *Amicus*, 1980, *5*, 73–81.

O'Connor, G. *Home is a good place: A national perspective of community residential facilities for developmentally disabled persons.* Washington, D.C.: American Association on Mental Deficiency, 1976.

O'Connor, G., & Sitkei, E. Study of a new frontier in community services. *Mental Retardation*, 1975, *13*, 35–39.

Perske, R. National perspective. *Transition*, 1980, *7*, 1 & 8.

Polivka, C. H., Marvin, W. E., Brown, J., & Polivka, L. J. Selected characteristics, services and movement of group home residents. *Mental Retardation*, 1979, *17*, 227–230.

Popp, D. A conversation with Dennis Popp: How an administrator views residential service needs. *Amicus*, 1978, *3*, 35–37.

Roos, P. Reconciling behavior modification procedures with the normalization principle. In W. Wolfensberger, *The principle of normalization in human services*. Toronto: National Institute on Mental Retardation, 1972.

Soskin, R. M. The least restrictive alternative: In principle and in application. *Amicus*, 1977, *2*, 28–32.

Thomas, M. A. Adapt the program to fit the needs: A conversation with Kenneth E. Wyatt about the least restrictive environment for mentally retarded students. *Education and Training of the Mentally Retarded*, 1979, *14*, 191–197.

Throne, J. M. Normalization through the normalization principle: Right ends, wrong means. *Mental Retardation*, 1975, *13*, 23–25.

Throne, J. M. Deinstitutionalization: Too wide a swath. *Mental Retardation*, 1979, *17*, 171–175.

Vitello, S. J. Beyond deinstitutionalization: What's happening to the people? *Amicus*, 1977, *2*, 40–44.

Wolfensberger, W. *The principle of normalization in human services*. Toronto: National Institute on Mental Retardation, 1972.

Yando, R., & Zigler, E. Outerdirectedness in the problem-solving of institutionalized and noninstitutionalized normal and retarded children. *Developmental Psychology*, 1971, *4*, 277–288.

Zigler, E. Rigidity and social reinforcement effects in the performance of institutionalized and noninstitutionalized normal and retarded children. *Journal of Personality*, 1963, *31*, 258–269.

Zigler, E., & Balla, D. Developmental course of responsiveness to social reinforcement in normal children and institutionalized retarded children. *Developmental Psychology*, 1972, *6*, 66–73.

Index